The River, the Plain, and t

On July 19, 1048, the Yellow River breached its banks, drastically changing its course across the Hebei Plain and turning it into a delta where the river sought a path out to the ocean. This dramatic shift of forces in the natural world resulted from political deliberation and hydraulic engineering of the imperial state of the Northern Song Dynasty. It created 80 years of social suffering, economic downturn, political upheaval, and environmental changes, which reshaped medieval North China Plain and challenged the state. Ling Zhang deftly applies textual analysis, theoretical provocation, and modern scientific data in her gripping analysis of how these momentous events altered China's physical and political landscapes and how its human communities adapted and survived. In so doing, she opens up an exciting new field of research by wedding environmental, political, economic, and social history in her examination of one of North China's most significant environmental changes.

Ling Zhang is Assistant Professor of History at Boston College.

Studies in Environment and History

Editors

J. R. McNeill *Georgetown University*
Edmund P. Russell *University of Kansas*

Editors Emeritus

Alfred W. Crosby *University of Texas at Austin*
Donald Worster *University of Kansas*

Other Books in the Series

Andy Bruno   *The Nature of Soviet Power: An Arctic Environmental History*
Erik Loomis   *Empire of Timber: Labor Unions and the Pacific Northwest Forests*
David A. Bello   *Across Forest, Steppe, and Mountain: Environment, Identity, and Empire in Qing China's Borderlands*
Peter Thorsheim   *Waste into Weapons: Recycling in Britain During the Second World War*
Kieko Matteson   *Forests in Revolutionary France: Conservation, Community, and Conflict, 1669–1848*
George Colpitts   *Pemmican Empire: Food, Trade, and the Last Bison Hunts in the North American Plains, 1780–1882*
Micah Muscolino   *The Ecology of War in China: Henan Province, the Yellow River, and Beyond, 1938–1950*
John Brooke   *Climate Change and the Course of Global History: A Rough Journey*
Emmanuel Kreike   *Environmental Infrastructure in African History: Examining the Myth of Natural Resource Management*
Paul Josephson, Nicolai Dronin, Ruben Mnatsakanian, Aleh Cherp, Dmitry Efremenko, and Vladislav Larin   *An Environmental History of Russia*
Gregory T. Cushman   *Guano and the Opening of the Pacific World: A Global Ecological History*
Sam White   *Climate of Rebellion in the Early Modern Ottoman Empire*
Alan Mikhail   *Nature and Empire in Ottoman Egypt: An Environmental History*
Edmund Russell   *Evolutionary History: Uniting History and Biology to Understand Life on Earth*
Richard W. Judd   *The Untilled Garden: Natural History and the Spirit of Conservation in America, 1740–1840*
James L. A. Webb, Jr.   *Humanity's Burden: A Global History of Malaria*
Frank Uekoetter   *The Green and the Brown: A History of Conservation in Nazi Germany*
Myrna I. Santiago   *The Ecology of Oil: Environment, Labor, and the Mexican Revolution, 1900–1938*
Matthew D. Evenden   *Fish versus Power: An Environmental History of the Fraser River*
Nancy J. Jacobs   *Environment, Power, and Injustice: A South African History*
Adam Rome   *The Bulldozer in the Countryside: Suburban Sprawl and the Rise of American Environmentalism*

Judith Shapiro   *Mao's War Against Nature: Politics and the Environment in Revolutionary China*

Edmund Russell   *War and Nature: Fighting Humans and Insects with Chemicals from World War I to Silent Spring*

Andrew Isenberg   *The Destruction of the Bison: An Environmental History*

Thomas Dunlap   *Nature and the English Diaspora*

Robert B. Marks   *Tigers, Rice, Silk, and Silt: Environment and Economy in Late Imperial South China*

Mark Elvin and Tsui'jung Liu   *Sediments of Time: Environment and Society in Chinese History*

Richard H. Grove   *Green Imperialism: Colonial Expansion, Tropical Island Edens and the Origins of Environmentalism, 1600–1860*

Elinor G. K. Melville   *A Plague of Sheep: Environmental Consequences of the Conquest of Mexico*

J. R. McNeill   *The Mountains of the Mediterranean World: An Environmental History*

Theodore Steinberg   *Nature Incorporated: Industrialization and the Waters of New England*

Timothy Silver   *A New Face on the Countryside: Indians, Colonists, and Slaves in the South Atlantic Forests, 1500–1800*

Michael Williams   *Americans and Their Forests: A Historical Geography*

Donald Worster   *The Ends of the Earth: Perspectives on Modern Environmental History*

Samuel P. Hays   *Beauty, Health, and Permanence: Environmental Politics in the United States, 1955–1985*

Warren Dean   *Brazil and the Struggle for Rubber: A Study in Environmental History*

Robert Harms   *Games Against Nature: An Eco-Cultural History of the Nunu of Equatorial Africa*

Arthur F. McEvoy   *The Fisherman's Problem: Ecology and Law in the California Fisheries, 1850–1980*

Alfred W. Crosby   *Ecological Imperialism: The Biological Expansion of Europe, 900–1900, Second Edition*

Kenneth F. Kiple   *The Caribbean Slave: A Biological History*

Donald Worster   *Nature's Economy: A History of Ecological Ideas, Second Edition*

The River, the Plain, and the State

An Environmental Drama in Northern Song China,
1048–1128

LING ZHANG
Boston College

CAMBRIDGE
UNIVERSITY PRESS

CAMBRIDGE
UNIVERSITY PRESS

University Printing House, Cambridge CB2 8BS, United Kingdom

One Liberty Plaza, 20th Floor, New York, NY 10006, USA

477 Williamstown Road, Port Melbourne, VIC 3207, Australia

314-321, 3rd Floor, Plot 3, Splendor Forum, Jasola District Centre, New Delhi - 110025, India

79 Anson Road, #06-04/06, Singapore 079906

Cambridge University Press is part of the University of Cambridge.

It furthers the University's mission by disseminating knowledge in the pursuit of education, learning and research at the highest international levels of excellence.

www.cambridge.org
Information on this title: www.cambridge.org/9781316609699

© Ling Zhang 2016

First published 2016
First paperback edition 2019

A catalogue record for this publication is available from the British Library

ISBN 978-1-107-15598-5 Hardback
ISBN 978-1-316-60969-9 Paperback

Cambridge University Press has no responsibility for the persistence or accuracy of URLs for external or third-party internet websites referred to in this publication, and does not guarantee that any content on such websites is, or will remain, accurate or appropriate.

For my parents, Qiqi, and David

Contents

ix

Illustrations

Tables

Acknowledgments

In summer 2008, I finished my doctoral dissertation at Cambridge, which was an economic history of north China during the Northern Song Dynasty. A small section of the dissertation deals with the Yellow River's floods. Because of that, I was offered a fellowship at Harvard in fall 2009, which enabled me to move across continents to pursue an "environmental history" of medieval China. Yet, having read only Donald Worster's *Dust Bowl* and Mark Elvin's *Sediments of Time* and *The Retreat of the Elephants*, I saw "environmental history" as a rather foreign concept and debated its legitimacy as a self-defined sub-discipline of history. I viewed the title of "environmental historian" as a heavy hat people placed on my head rather than a self-identity deriving from proper scholarly training.

Confused yet intrigued by the murky path laid in front of me, I have since begun a journey of soul searching, identity building, and intellectual self-reinvention. While this journey has been full of frustration – not knowing what to do or whether I'm doing it right – and loneliness – being at the margins of many established scholarly fields – it has also liberated me from various constraints and allowed me to venture into a splendid intellectual universe. Like a hungry child, I have tried to devour whatever seemed tasty and nutritious, be it history or social science or natural science, theoretical or empirical, and about medieval China or about the modern West in the twenty-first century.

The present book is the outcome of this six-year journey. It is a modest experiment that seeks to capture how things entangle to constitute a messy, wild, blossoming world – a process similar to my formation of a new identity through wonderful encounters with different people and ideas. It is a peculiar telling of history that embodies my current philosophical positions, political pursuits, and intellectual desires. This book is not simply a study of a remote history; it is a documentation of the growth of my personhood.

This book and this wonderful journey would never have become possible without the support from many individuals and research institutes. My longtime mentor Wang Xiaofu at Peking University has never stopped inspiring me with this powerful line: "Ling, one must first have dreams." St John's College, Asian Studies, and the Needham Research Institute at the University of Cambridge paved a solid foundation for my training in Sinology and my interests in economic history and the history of science and technology. My loving doctor-parents Joseph and Hiroko McDermott watched every moment of my growth. They patiently taught me how to think, what makes an argument, and why some ideas are more meaningful than others. Taking the role as my first teacher for academic English, Joe painstakingly corrected my grammatical errors, which were nearly in every sentence I composed. For all the headaches and grey hair he got from my writing, I offer my sincere apology and deep appreciation.

A fellowship at the Harvard University Center for the Environment opened this medieval historian of China to the worlds of environmental science, marine biology, earth science, and zoology, all of which were completely alien to me. I thank my mentors Peter Bol and Daniel Schrag and my colleagues James Clem and many others for two eye-opening years. The post-doctoral fellowship in the Program of Agrarian Studies at Yale University drew me toward the world of social science, where I was intensely exposed to anthropology, political science, and various stripes of social theory. I thank my mentors James Scott, Kalyanakrishnan Sivaramakrishnan, and Peter Perdue and my fellow scholars in the program for a life-changing year. I have become quite a different person in terms of what I care about and how I think. During the past few years, the Fairbank Center for Chinese Studies at Harvard University has not only provided me much needed office space but also sponsored me to organize several seminars and conferences. These events drew together scholars from various fields, offering me rare opportunities to learn from different kinds of scholarship. For their administrative and intellectual support, I thank the Center's directors William Kirby, Mark Elliott, and Michael Szonyi, as well as Lydia Chen, Jennifer Rudolph, and many other colleagues. I am grateful to the Chiang Ching-kuo Foundation for International Scholarly Exchange, which generously funded a year of teaching leave, allowing me to focus on the writing of the book. My home institution, Boston College, has provided a friendly work environment and supported many of my research activities. My warmest thanks to my caring colleagues both in the History Department and in other departments.

During the past six years, countless colleagues and friends read parts of this book or heard me talk about some part of it. They invited me to their conferences or participated in activities I organized. They shared with me lengthy conversations or exchanged brief but insightful opinions. As I went through difficulties and doubts, many lent comfort and encouragement. For their advice, assistance, support, and friendship, my gratitude goes to Alan Mikhail, Arupjyoti Saikia, Bin Wong, Caroline Baltzer, Chris Neilsen, Dana Sajdi, Dario Gaggio, Deborah Levenson-Estrada, Deng Xiaonan, Devin Pendas, Donald Worster, Emily Yeh, Eugene Wang, Felix Wemheuer, Franziska Seraphim, Gunnel Cederlöf, Han Maoli, Han Zhaoqing, He Xiaoqing, Heping Liu, Hilde de Weerdt, Ian Miller, Ian J. Miller, Iftekhar Iqbal, Jinping Wang, John Lee, Judith Shapiro, Julian Bourg, Kenneth Pomeranz, Kevin Kenny, Kevin O'Neill, Lincoln Tsui, Ma Junya, Marilynn Johnson, Micah Muscolino, Michael Puett, Mike McGovern, Nancy Langston, Noah Snyder, Paul Sabin, Paul Smith, Prasannan Parthasarathi, Qian Ying, Ralph Litzinger, Rebecca Nedostup, Robert Hymes, Robert Marks, Robin Fleming, Roseann Cohen, Ruth Mostern, Sakura Christmas, Sabine Dabringhaus, Sarah Ross, Scott Moore, Shi Lihong, Shirley Ye, Stephen Ford, Tim Wright, Tineke D'Haeseleer, T. R. Kidder, Victor Seow, Virginia Reinburg, Wang Ao, Wang Jiange, Wen Xin, Xia Mingfang, Yajun Mo, Yang Rui, Ying Jia Tan, Zhang Ping, and Zuo Ya. Some of these people (and many others who are not mentioned here) may have forgotten their brief encounters with me, but I cherish their profound influences.

I thank Edmund Russell and John McNeill for taking a real interest in my work and waiting patiently for me to complete the manuscript. I am grateful to two anonymous readers who treated my manuscript with care and support and peppered it with thoughtful critiques. I thank my wonderful editors Deborah Gershenowitz, Amanda George, Arindam Bose, and Cynthia Col who deserve every credit for making this book beautiful. Any error that remains belongs to me.

My wonderful friends and colleagues Corey Byrnes, Cynthia Lynn Lyerly, David Bello, Kathryn Edgerton-Tarpley, James Scott, Peter Perdue, Priya Lal, Robert Marks, and Ruth Mostern read parts or the whole of the final manuscript. I am deeply indebted to them. My dearest Eleanor Goodman – my favorite poet in the world – polished every single sentence and corrected every mistaken punctuation mark in the book.

My love goes to my trusting parents and supporting sister. Sometimes even I wonder how they can so wholeheartedly believe in me and trust what I do. Nothing I do compares to what they have given me. My thanks to Chuck and Kitty for putting up with me when I spent most of the Christmas holidays writing. And David. Oh, David. This book is made of the strawberry smoothies you prepared every morning, of the literature and poems you whispered at nighttime, and of the moments when we debated uses of a word or implications of a concept. With all the joy, excitement, challenges, and adventures that we have shared, for all my silliness, stubbornness, and even tears that you have endured, I read this book as my not-terribly-romantic love letter to you.

Abbreviations

GSJ	*Gongshi ji*
MXBT	*Mengxi bitan*
OYXQJ	*Ouyang Xiu quanji*
QSW	*Quan Songwen*
SHY	*Song huiyao jigao*
SHYBB	*Song huiyao jigao bubian*
SMCZY	*Song mingchen zouyi*
SS	*Song shi*
SSWJ	*Songshan wenji*
XCB	*Xu Zizhitongjian changbian*
XCBSB	*Xu Zizhitongjian changbian shibu*
XSBGZY	*Xiaosu Baogong zouyi*

Prologue

1048: The Opening of an Environmental Drama

The Sixth Day of the Sixth Month,
"People Were Flushed Away Like Fish and Turtles"

On the sixth day of the sixth lunar month in the eighth year of the reign of Emperor Renzong 仁宗 (1010–1063), the "Festive Era" (July 19, 1048 of the Common Era), China's second largest river, the Yellow River 黄河, breached its northern bank at a site called Shanghu 商胡. From this location in modern northern Henan 河南 Province, the river tore apart over 700 meters of its banks. Its torrents burst through the rupture and surged northward into the Hebei 河北 Plain. Over the next few days, the river gouged the earth to open up a channel for a new "northern flow" and made its torturous way nearly 700 kilometers toward the vicinity of the present Tianjin 天津, where it eventually exited into the Bohai 渤海 Gulf. With this incident, the river's lower reaches turned counterclockwise by 30 degrees, bringing its river mouth northward by one latitude degree to 39° north. This drastic shift of the river terminated an eastern course that the river had taken between southern Hebei and northern Shandong 山東 for the previous millennium. For the first time since the second century BCE, the river crashed into the heart of the Hebei Plain, turning it into a delta where the river's lower reaches sought a path out to the ocean.

Caught completely unawares, people in Hebei were drowned or carried away by the water, "dispersing like fish" or "turning into food for fish and turtles," as some contemporary officials and poets described it.[1]

---

[1] Liu Chang, "Yonggu [Verses on antiquity]" (No. 8) and "Kuyu [Suffering the rain]," *GSJ*, 4: 6b, pp. 1095-1430 and 4: 12b, pp. 1095-1433.

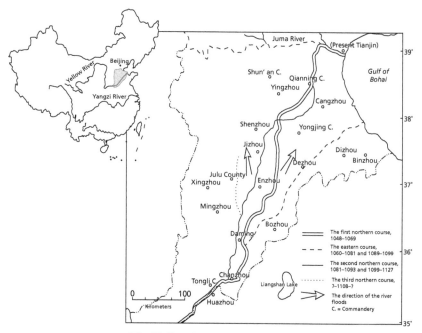

ILLUSTRATION 1. The Yellow River's Courses in Hebei: 1048–1128

Indeed, how could anyone have anticipated this violent arrival of the river? In the middle of the Northern Song Dynasty 北宋 (960–1127), Hebei, like other regions in the empire, had enjoyed a decades-long peace and a steady growth in terms of both population and economy. To Hebei people, their homeland had had no deep connection with the Yellow River for nearly a thousand years; their daily lives had nothing to do with the remote river. The river existed only in the classics and literature for those who read books or in legends and folklore that people passed on orally.

The sudden encounter between the river and the northern land brought an end to the peace and prosperity. The flood destroyed enormous numbers of buildings and villages and submerged field after field of crops. Its immediate attack, its aftermath, and the ensuing famine killed and displaced at least one million people, more than 20 percent of Hebei's entire population. Refugees were forced to leave their homes in search of a dry, safe place to live, and the most basic supplies. In a literary, somewhat exaggerated fashion, contemporaries of the eleventh century lamented that "In a distance over a thousand *li* 里 (lit. about 500 kilometers), the roads are full of corpses of dead men."[2] "Eight or nine households out of ten have migrated out of Hebei."[3] This was the first time since 1005, when war ended and peace returned to Hebei, that this land suffered such a dramatic loss of population.

From the autumn of 1048 through 1049, the standing waters of the Yellow River ruined three seasons of crops. Continuous harvest failures drove starving people to horrifying extremes. As statesman Sima Guang 司馬光 (1019–1086) later recalled, "fathers and sons ate each other."[4] The Song's imperial court ordered its regional and local governments to open up granaries to relieve Hebei's starvation. Yet, government officials were not trained for this kind of emergency. Unsure how to cope with the large numbers of refugees, they gathered the refugees into small urban slums, where they set up stoves to cook and feed the refugees collectively. As large crowds congregated, hardship, malnourishment, and poor hygiene led to the outbreak of infectious diseases. Death tolls mounted even higher. As the prefect of Qingzhou 青州 Fu Bi 富弼 (1004–1083) saw it, the government measures to supply relief were "in the name of saving people, but in fact killed them."[5]

Soon, civilian granaries were exhausted by the refugees. The government began to draft male refugees into armies and provide them with military rations, as a way to reduce the refugee population.[6] But even military granaries were overburdened and soon became short on supplies. Some men became outlaws, raiding towns and cities to obtain food. Those who were more vulnerable or physically weak, like children, the elderly, and women, turned to begging on street, sometimes selling themselves in exchange for food. Running out of resources as well as relief strategies, the Song government had to permit such trades of human labor and encouraged wealthy, powerful families to "adopt" refugees as servants.[7]

Hebei's disasters and sufferings crossed regional boundaries. The effects rippled south, dragging the entire eastern part of north China into hardship. From 1048 to the early 1050s, the central government

[2] Fu Bi, "Dingzhou Yuegutang xu [Prose on the Hall of Yuegu in Dingzhou]," *Dingzhou zhi*, 21: 26a–b, pp. 1823–1824.
[3] Ouyang Xiu, "Lun xiuhe diyizhuang [The first memorial on repairing the Yellow River]," *OYXQJ*, 108: 5b–7b.
[4] *XCB*, 3: 125.
[5] *XCB*, 166: 3985.
[6] *XCB*, 164: 3957 and 166: 3985.
[7] *XCB*, 165: 3974–3975.

continued to ship bulk grain from southern regions, such as the Huai River 淮河 valley and the lower Yangtze River 長江 valley.[8] However useful this interregional transport of goods was in terms of alleviating the suffering in the north, its efficacy was significantly weakened when the lower Yangtze and Huai valleys experienced drought and harvest failures in the early 1050s. Farmers there suffered food shortages, becoming less capable of meeting the central government's demands and contributing to the welfare of Hebei.[9] As various environmental and socio-economic problems mushroomed across the empire, the imperial state of the Song sank into a fiscal and governing crisis.

"The Yellow River's floods have always done damage since ancient times, but never to an extent like this!" cried Jia Changchao 賈昌朝 (997–1065), the former Grand Councilor to the emperor and now the prefect of Daming 大名, the most significant and prosperous district in southern Hebei whose territory was now penetrated by the river.[10] Jia was right. Indeed, the river had rarely caused flooding disasters of this intensity and magnitude in its previous history – none since the first century CE. What Jia did not know, however, is that the worst was yet to come. What happened in the summer of 1048 was not a single incident, but rather a harbinger of the difficult time ahead.

An Environmental Drama

The Yellow River's shift into the Hebei Plain was a clash between two marginally connected environmental entities and their consequential convergence into a giant Yellow River–Hebei environmental complex. This violent encounter inaugurated an environmental drama that lasted over the next eighty years, during which the river occupied the land and flooded nearly every other year. With multiple episodes of flooding, the river's 700-kilometer-long meandering flow created three other courses that stretched in different directions inside Hebei. More and more areas were attacked by the torrents or submerged in the river's stagnant water. Crops were washed away or rotted in the fields. As agriculture continued to decline, various kinds of hardship continued to escalate. Some hungry refugees turned violent; raids and riots exploded in both rural and urban

[8] *XCB*, 165: 3968. Also Han Qi, "The epitaph of Han Gongyan," *QSW*, 856: 73.
[9] *XCB*, 171: 4119. Ouyang Xiu, "Zailun shuizai zhuang [The second discussion on the flood]," *QSW*, 687: 244.
[10] *XCB*, 165: 3976–3978.

areas. To survive, the remaining population resorted to a variety of local solutions. Some destroyed government dykes or built private dykes to defend themselves from the waters; some gave up farming and adapted to other kinds of livelihood, including fishing and salt production. At the turn of the twelfth century, Hebei was a desolate land stricken with suffering people, turbulent waters, wild weeds, and numerous patches of yellow sand.

The environmental drama came to an end in 1128, as the Yellow River shifted out Hebei, turning clockwise by 90 degrees to head toward south China. After that time, the river never again entered Hebei. Despite its departure, however, the dramatic episodes between 1048 and 1128 caused tremendous environmental trauma that continued to haunt the land and water of Hebei throughout the second millennium. Consequences of the river's eighty-year occupation of Hebei – a disordered water system, the deterioration of soil due to salinization and sandification, and the exhaustion of forests and other vegetative materials – have continued to shape the region's environmental conditions and socioeconomic challenges up to today.

This environmental entwinement of the Yellow River and the Hebei Plain and the resulting socio-economic problems were not merely regional issues. They trapped the imperial state of the Northern Song in often unsuccessful policies of environmental management and exhausted the state politically, financially, and mentally. With an eye to improving its geopolitical and environmental circumstances, the state employed political rationales and technological means to push the river to shift northward in 1048. However, facing the overwhelming Yellow River–Hebei environmental complex after 1048, the state became increasingly anxious about the prospect that the devastation of Hebei, the empire's key frontier region, would elicit an invasion by its nomadic enemy in the north. Equally disconcerting was that the Yellow River continued to undermine the state's domestic environmental, political, and social stability. Troubled by both external and internal concerns, the state formed contradicting hydraulic policies and practices, which competed for resources and political capital, and were thereby mutually defeating. These concerns also divided the ruling members of the state. Emperors, their imperial courts and senior statesmen, and various levels of institutions in Hebei split into multiple politico-hydraulic factions. The lack of consensus in state policies and of persistence in executing the policies led the government to switch frequently between polarized approaches in handling the environmental challenges.

Paradoxically, the more the state engaged in regulating the Yellow River–Hebei environmental complex, the less return it gained, and the deeper it sank into a costly dilemma. The worsening environmental conditions brought down the social and economic conditions in north China. Hence, along with managing the hydraulic works, the state had to sustain its military forces in Hebei to safeguard this region's strategic significance; it also had to rescue Hebei's civilian society and economy from a complete collapse. It had no choice but to endlessly funnel a significant portion of state finances into Hebei, mobilize the transportation of enormous resources from south China to Hebei, subject itself to speculative activities and exploitation by private merchants, draft large numbers of laborers from all over north China to fulfill the military and hydraulic services in Hebei, and even fell trees and bushes throughout north China in order to supply construction materials for Hebei's hydraulic works.

The imperial state and its empire were trapped in a "hydraulic mode of consumption" – a key concept to be developed throughout the second half of the book – that extracted political capital, labor, and other resources and channeled them toward the bottomless black hole of the Yellow River–Hebei environmental complex. During this interregional exchange and distribution of resources, the disaster-ridden land of Hebei failed to serve the empire as a self-sufficient, stable, and obedient periphery that the state endeavored to make it. Instead, it became a *de facto* center of the empire, the "root of All-Under-Heaven (*tianxia zhi genben* 天下之根本)," where resources flowed in to be consumed, rather than the reverse. The state's decades-long efforts to achieve imperial centralization by militarizing Hebei and marginalizing it socio-economically as well as environmentally only led to an inverse core-periphery structure in terms of wealth distribution and resource consumption. Seen from an environmental perspective, the Yellow River–Hebei complex established its own environmental regime: it wielded power to intervene in human politics, affect human lives, and organize wealth that the human society produced. Along the way, it incorporated the Song state into a vast environmental world, demanded its services, and shaped many ways in which the state ran its political, financial, and environmental life.

This book documents this eighty-year environmental drama. Using the 1048 flooding catastrophe as an anchor, the book investigates how three major environmental entities – the Yellow River, the Hebei Plain (the land and its people), and the Northern Song state – had developed a deeply entangled history over a span of centuries and eventually created a unique, delta-like physical landscape in north China in 1048. There, these historical actors continued to interact with each other and produce a variety of environmental, political, and socio-economic tensions between 1048 and 1128. Some of the historical implications of this environmental drama even lasted through the second millennium. This book investigates but does not dwell on various dialectical relationships, such as how the state wrestled with a region and the physical environment or how a regional population negotiated with environmental disasters. Instead, it explores complex relationships in which, for instance, the state's wrestling with a region was complicated or destabilized by its attempts to tame the river and by the river's unpredictable reactions, or how the negotiation between a regional society and environmental disasters were not only mediated, appropriated, and destabilized by the imperial state's changing policies but also affected the execution and results of such policies. In this sense, the book explores the constantly evolving, open-ending "trialectic" complexity among the river, the plain, the state, and other small-scale, subordinate entities.[11] It demonstrates how a multiplicity of actors like water, silt, trees, earth, different state institutions, communities, and individuals interacted, through supplying possibilities or asserting constraints to each other, to make a certain history happen.[12] The history told in this book is simultaneously an environmental history of politics and a human

[11] The concept "trialectics" originates from studies on space and spatiality. Marxist philosopher and sociologist Henri Lefebvre critiqued binarism-rooted dialectic thinking by conceptualizing space and spatiality as the complexity of three types of space (perceived, conceived, and lived). Postmodernist geographer Edward W. Soja (1996: 60–82) developed the concept of trialectics to highlight the instability and blurred boundaries of these spaces and conceptualize a "Thirdspace" that not only encompasses all spaces but also is "radically open to additional otherness, to a continuing expansion of spatial knowledge." Although Lefebvre and Soja elaborated the concept specifically to understand space and spatiality, trialectic thinking carries broad theoretical implications. It challenges conventional binary epistemologies (e.g., reality and representation, natural and cultural, subject and object); it destabilizes dialectical modes of understanding of any relationship or historical process as a predictable, orderly progression toward a teleological synthesis. "Thirding" pays attention to otherness to capture the uncertainty, destruction, and complexity in a relationship or process. Not focusing on its "logico-epistemological" aspect of the concept as Lefebvre did but attending to the ontological trialectic as Soja theorized (Soja, 1996: 62 and 70), I use the concept to denote simultaneous material existence, continuous reciprocations, and various interactions among a multitude of environmental entities in an open-ending process that makes and remakes a flourishing, unruly, and unpredictable environmental world.

[12] As Soja (1996: 61) insightfully maintained, in the trialectic, "The 'third' term – and Thirdspace as a concept – is not satisfied in and of itself. The critique is not meant to stop at three, to construct a holy trinity, but to build further, to move on, to continuously expand the production of knowledge beyond what is known."

society, and a political, social, and economic history of various environmental entities in a chaotic environmental world.

The book asks two questions. First, how had these environmental entities evolved over a long time to encounter each other and how had their interactions increased over several centuries to eventually lead to the outbreak of the environmental drama? This question points to the long-term pre-history of the 1048 event. Second, how were these actors affected by the 1048 event and how did they respond to the continuous environmental changes, as they vied with each other to occupy physical space and acquire resources? This question points to both the short-term and the long-term implications of the 1048 event.

Part I of the book, Chapters 1–4, answers the first question. Chapter 1 begins with an introduction to the Yellow River's hydrological characteristics and its historical movements within the context of millennia-long environmental changes across north China. Adjacent to the Yellow River, the geographical entity of the Hebei Plain had enjoyed economic success and military strength over many centuries. Its people had constantly pursued political autonomy and challenged the central rule of imperial states on the other side of the Yellow River. Chapter 2 presents the imperial state of the Northern Song, the newcomer to history in 960. The state's desire to consolidate into a centralized empire led to a multi-dimensional project that, in political, military, environmental, and economic terms, appropriated Hebei into a stable, obedient periphery of the empire. These state building efforts, however, faced a series of crises in the 1040s. As Chapter 3 shows, military, financial, and environmental problems continued to mount both across the empire and inside Hebei right before the Yellow River shifted its course to the north in 1048. Chapter 4 suggests that, along with peripheralizing Hebei, the state pursued Yellow River hydraulics simultaneously. Its perceptions of critical geopolitical and environmental conditions in north China led to the formation of a particular kind of politico-hydraulic discourse and policies, which designated Hebei as the land to bear the river's violent torrents. Guided by such discourse, state-sponsored hydraulic practices had over several decades manipulated the river's hydrological conditions and forced the river to turn northward. The shift of the river's course and the creation of a river's delta inside Hebei in 1048 was a product of the state's politico-hydraulic enterprise.

Part II of the book, Chapters 5–8, offers answers to the second question formulated above: how various environmental entities responded to the 1048 environmental change and continued to evolve and interact with each other. The river's crashing into Hebei drew these two environmental entities together to form a giant environmental complex. However, the creation of the Yellow River–Hebei environmental complex did not pacify the turbulent river; rather, it triggered even more environmental disasters. Chapter 5 suggests that continuous river disasters forced the state to invest enormous political, financial, material, and human resources in Hebei in order to sustain Hebei's strategic stability and the state's constantly failing hydraulic works. The struggles between humans and nature, intensified by political contestations within the government, continued to erode state power. Meanwhile, Hebei's human society suffered tremendously from both the disasters and the state's environmental management. As Chapter 6 examines, the decline of Hebei's population, in terms both of quantity and its socio-economic capacities, led both to tremendous human suffering and to the emergence of various local strategies and solutions, by which the impoverished Hebei people attempted to maintain a subsistence livelihood. The society's emphasis on subsistence went hand in hand with the overall decline of the agricultural economy. Chapter 7 shows that Hebei failed to join south China in a revolutionary growth of economy. Instead, it became a center of consumption that endlessly drew in supplies – mainly cheap goods like grain – from the state and south China. Hebei's utter dependence on the state and its consumption of external wealth dragged the imperial state down in a spiral that headed toward irremediable financial exhaustion. The final chapter turns to the earth and waters in Hebei. The eighty years of co-inhabitance and interactions between the Yellow River and Hebei's indigenous environmental entities had profound and long-term effects on this region. They continued to shape the region's environment and society in negative ways (such as soil deterioration and deforestation) throughout the second millennium.

Three Histories in Middle-Period China

This book contributes to our understanding of middle-period China by presenting three untold, deeply entwined histories.

The first is a regional history of Hebei. The book analyzes how this region was transformed from an environmentally, economically, and politically highly independent entity to a military-oriented, peripheral component of a centralized empire. This transformation culminated in the face of escalating environmental pressure, when Hebei was deliberately chosen by the imperial state to serve as a flooding ground of the

Yellow River and to become an environmental victim that would free its neighboring regions from disasters. In this era, which historians have lavishly praised for its demographic boom, cultural advancement, economic prosperity, and technological innovations – to the extent that many have even accepted the assumption that Song China entered an early modern age and headed toward a proto-capitalist economy[13] – it is Hebei who bore the tragic cost for such growth. Hebei not only lost its traditional political superiority, economic strength, and environmental solidity but was also thrown off the empire's fast-running economic train and was reduced to serving as the crossties and rails underneath it in order to promote the interests of the state and other regions. The environmental and socio-economic sacrifices made by Hebei contributed to the success stories of the empire and of other parts of China.

This regional history of Hebei addresses two issues only inadequately addressed in previous scholarship. The first is the issue of what north China was like after China's economic, social, and cultural centers moved southward into the Yangzi valley, a developmental trajectory that scholars advocating the Tang–Song transition theory have largely agreed on.[14] The second is the question of why Chinese scholarship of the past few decades has followed such trajectory to shift its attention to China's geographical south and to tell stories of growth associated with the rise of south China and the expansion of the empire.[15] Although contemporary

---

[13] Inspired by Naitō Torajirō and Miyazaki Ichisada's thesis on a multi-dimensional Tang–Song transition that facilitated China's entry into an early modern era, many scholarly works have emerged to study Song's exceptional economic development. Among English authors Mark Elvin (1973) has famously argued for the occurrence of a medieval economic revolution; Hill Gates (1996) believes the development of "petty capitalism" from the Song period. Joseph McDermott and Shiba Yoshinobu critique such optimistic views and offer a more moderate assessment of Song economy in Chaffee and Twitchett (2015: 321–436). Robert Hymes critiques the use of overgeneralized notions of "early modern" and "modern" to categorize the complex history in the Song period, in Chaffee and Twitchett (2015: 661–664).

[14] Ch'ao-ting Chi (1936) argued for the shift of key economic centers to south China. His thesis has inspired a great number of scholarly works that focus on the rise of south China. For a comprehensive survey of the Naitō thesis and the Tang–Song transition scholarship in Chinese, Japanese, and English, see Li (2010).

[15] In "a regional overview" of the Song's countryside, Golas (1980, 292) provides an impression of Hebei: "The Hebei Circuits located on the north China plain, had a high proportion of their land under cultivation (some of it in rice) and a dense population." The present book shows such impression is not based on studies of historical nuances and is incorrect.

scholars have enthusiastically responded to calls from G. William Skinner and Robert M. Hartwell to study histories from regional and macro-
regional perspectives, the existing scholarship tells us very little about
north China, where most of the political competition, economic innovation, and social development took place in the first millennium. Is this
scholarly emphasis truly about the historical insignificance of north China
or simply a reflection of modern historians' preference to study growth
and successes?[16] By telling the untold stories of death, suffering, and
degradation, this history of Hebei complicates the empire-wide political,
economic, and environmental landscape and illuminates the widening
regional disparities in middle-period China. It unveils a long-neglected,
dark side of the rosy image of growth that scholars of the Tang–Song
transition have ardently portrayed. Without considering the history of
impoverishment and deprivation in northern regions like Hebei, the stories of growth and prosperity often associated with south China should
be regarded as merely regional specificity.[17]

The second history takes place on a more macro level. The book
presents an illuminating account of the imperial history of the Northern
Song state. State building in the Song period has been studied repeatedly
from political, military, institutional, socio-economic, cultural, and technological perspectives.[18] What distinguishes this book is that it grounds
this state-building process within – rather than keeping it apart from –
the state's everyday encounters and lived experiences with environmental realities. It explores how the state's existential anxiety derived from
its environmental experiences, not only from war, politics, and financial
stress – various human issues that previous scholarship has focused on.
Such anxiety influenced every step of the state's decision-making in handling the Yellow River–Hebei environmental complex and, by extension,
the ways in which the state ran its empire and managed its everyday

[16] We must acknowledge that the south-China focus of the Tang–Song scholarship is due
partly to the relative richness of historical sources for south China. However, the present
book demonstrates that, by taking new research perspectives like an environmental
perspective, we may better utilize the limited sources in regard to north China and
produce new narratives and discourses about Chinese history in that period.
[17] This invariably invites a reassessment of the Song's position in entire Chinese history,
which has previously been overviewed by von Glahn (2003: 35–70) and Chaffee and
Twitchett (2015: 16–18).
[18] To learn about this giant scholarship, see various chapters in Chaffee and Twitchett
(2015), or a survey of the scholarship in English by North American scholars by de
Weerdt (2013: 23–53).

political and financial life. This book examines the discrepancy between the state's intentions in its environmental management and the unexpected results of its hydraulic practices. It reveals the state's inherent struggles between its desires and its limitations.[19]

Such struggles of the state evolved into two historical ironies, which form the book's arguments about this peculiar version of the Song's imperial history. The first irony occurred in the relationship between the state and hydraulics. According to Karl Wittfogel and most hydraulic historians of China who have adopted Wittfogel's productive mode of theoretical reasoning – although denouncing his reductive conclusion in terms of its empirical applicability – the more a state attended to and invested in hydraulic management, the more likely environmental conditions became sound, and the more likely the human society reliant on the hydraulics prospered, and it felt content about and thus better served the state. A hydraulically negligent state would see not only the dysfunction of hydraulic systems but also, by extension, the decline of the society and the rise of social resentment and disturbance toward the state.[20] Contradicting such Wittfogelian logic of a mutually constitutive relationship between hydraulic management and state power, this book unveils an irony that arose from the Song state's unbreakable and exhausting commitment to environmental management. Not only did the Song's increasing investments in water control not bring along environmental and social stability, but bounded by its hydraulic commitment, the state's political, strategic, and economic life became conditioned, oriented, and even overburdened by its environmental life. What happened to the Yellow River and inside Hebei determined how the state extracted and distributed labor and wealth from different parts of the empire, and how the state established institutions and negotiated with its contentious politicians and bureaucrats. Trapped in a "hydraulic mode of

---

[19] McNeill (1998: 36) correctly points out: "The Chinese imperial state was a meddlesome one, carefully looking after its own interests and, in keeping with cultural traditions, actively seeking to develop resources and rearrange nature so as to maximize tangible and taxable wealth." While exploring this point in its first four chapters, this book furthers the point to a deeper level in its remaining four chapters by questioning how the state's "carefully looking after its own interests" turned to defeating its own intentions and efforts.

[20] Wittfogel (1957). The existing scholarship of Chinese history has discredited Wittfogel's postulation of "oriental despotism" for its empirical invalidity, but they have largely accepted and followed the productive logic prescribed by his "hydraulic mode of production." My critique of such Wittfogelian thought targets on its productive logic (see Chapter 5.3).

consumption," the state saw its power being continuously worn down by its environmental commitment.[21]

The second irony is, as aforementioned, the unexpected inversion between geopolitical, socio-economic core and periphery. The Song pursued state building and power centralization by establishing a core–periphery structure within the empire. In territorial and geopolitical terms, this structure sought to strengthen a core region where the empire's political, economic, and military weight congregated and resided – this went along with a paralleling process that sought to produce an array of peripheral regions that each reinforced certain regional functions but downplayed others in order to best serve the needs of the state. As for Hebei, the state painstakingly undertook a multi-dimensional project to appropriate Hebei into a militarily oriented, economically dependent, and environmentally cooperative region. However, the intrusion of the Yellow River and the emergence of the River–Hebei environmental complex in 1048 turned this region into a land of massive social destruction, heavy military burdens, and tremendous environmental turbulence – all of these fueled the hydraulic mode of consumption, through which the state and

---

[21] We must distinguish this entrapment from Mark Elvin's (2004: 123–124 and 2006: 115) use of "technological lock-in." Elvin uses the notion to explain the "inherently unstable" manmade systems of water control in late-imperial China from a technological perspective. This notion is useful for understanding the constant failures of state-sponsored hydraulic projects in the Northern Song time; on surface, it seems to some degree to overlap the "hydraulic mode of consumption," because both notions signify a state of entrapment. But this book does not rely on "technological lock-in," partly because the book does not take technological issues as its prime research agenda. The Song's environmental and especially hydraulic technology demands careful treatment. The task is beyond the scope of this book. More importantly, "technological lock-in" derives from a theoretical assumption different from that in the present book. It postulates that at a certain stage of technological development, a particular technology becomes the dominant kind; although it remains productive and continues to generate returns to scale, it squeezes out the chance for the growth of other technologies and thus prevents any technological breakthrough. By extension, the dominant mode of production, although being productive, entails increasing opportunity costs that prevent the development of "a different, and possibly ultimately more productive, fashion." Behind this postulation is optimism in growth and belief in technology-driven production. Given this productive assumption, "technological lock-in" should be seen as a companion notion to Elvin's economic thesis, "high-level equilibrium trap." In this book, I do not share Elvin's optimism for growth, especially technological growth. Neither do I take the actuality of production as a theoretical starting point. Rather, from a consumptive approach, I suggest that whether or not Song technological innovations had reached a high-level equilibrium is highly questionable; hence, a dominant and productive technology, a decline in the marginal return, and a consequential "lock-in" might never have happened. I shall elaborate such theoretical differences more fully in future publications.

the empire had no choice but to funnel tremendous wealth and material resources into Hebei in order to sustain the region's existence. The core and the periphery swapped, against the Song's state-building intentions. Hebei became a destination of the flow of resources and the center where such resources gathered to be consumed, while the state was trapped in not a dominant, managerial but a serving role.

The imperial history told in this book is not about the growth of a strong state that subdued and incorporated both nature and a regional society. Neither is it a history of scientific and technological progress, for it does not celebrate human triumph over nature.[22] Nor does it confine its argument to a simplistic condemnation of the policies and activities of the imperial state that inflicted environmental damage and human suffering. Rather, this book observes and analyzes the state's efforts and failures in seizing power from both the society and the environmental world that the state itself inhabited as one environmental entity. This book urges readers not only to ask with James C. Scott "how certain schemes [centrally planned by the state] to improve the human condition have failed."[23] It also asks a further question – how did the state's engagement in such schemes, like environmental management and appropriation of Hebei, lead to the failure of the imperial state itself?

The third history lays the foundation to both the regional history of Hebei and the imperial history of the state – both could only take place within the environmental history of the Yellow River–Hebei environmental complex. Every shift of the river, every increase in the sedimentary cover over the land surface, and every felling of a tree did not merely provide a stage for humans and their institutions to perform, act on, and interact; they were not merely objects that were manipulated by the state and the human society. Rather, these environmental entities actively participated in creating the eighty-year environmental drama. Insomuch as these entities played roles in different versions of human histories, they inducted individual human beings, their communities, and the imperial state into a grand environmental world, in which the river hydrology, geological movements of the earth, climatic changes, and exchanges between non-organic entities and organisms laid the structure and offered possibilities for human struggles and creativity.[24]

[22] For hydraulic science and technology during the Song period, see Needham et al. (1971) and Flessel (1974).
[23] Scott (1998).
[24] This book does not utilize as conceptual frameworks some important notions in environmental studies like "nature," "anthropogenic," and "ecology," due to their peculiar

In a seminal collection of scholarship, *Ordering the World*, scholars of Song China have pondered different *Approaches to State and Society in Sung Dynasty China*.[25] They have examined how the imperial state and its prominent individuals conceived of and performed various kinds of statecraft to order the world in which they were situated. The present book critically redefines the notion, "the world": the state and the society and individual humans were deeply embedded in an "environmental

theoretical associations and implications. "Nature" is bound with its contrasting notion, "culture." This book chooses not to cling to the nature-culture binarism, because none of the entangled interactions among environmental entities the book explores can be clearly differentiated as between something natural versus something cultural. The natural and the cultural have simultaneously existed and intricately intermingled in the formation and evolution of various environmental entities as well as of their entanglements. These entities and their entanglements manifest as being geological, physical, chemical, social, political, cultural, or all at once. The particular entanglement of environmental entities that this book explores – the formation and evolution of the Yellow River–Hebei environmental complex – is both natural and cultural, both physical and social, both real and imagined, and both material and discursive at the same time. Being natural or cultural is a matter of degree in terms of phenomenon, not of kind. For the same reason, the book does not stress the notion "anthropogenic," as our question is not to distinguish between something anthropogenic and something naturally produced – that both have to interact and cooperate to make an entanglement happen is the theoretical premise of this book. Accepting McNeill's (1998: 38) assessment about China's "hyperanthropogenic landscape," I consider that asking about anthropogeniety is no longer interesting as a question or argument; the notion "anthropogenic" has lost its critical edge and is insufficient for addressing the kind of environmental entanglement at question in this book. The book equally downplays the notion "ecology," for ecological thinking keeps at its ontological core the flow and transformation of some essential matter, such as energy. It acknowledges matter's immanent connectedness and its directional enchainment through various transformations. This book does not take matter as its conceptual basis; it does not stress the flow and innate connectedness of matter in its various forms. The book makes this choice due partly to the limitation of the historical sources from middle-period China, which prohibits the construction of a satisfactory ecological discourse. Instead, the book conceptualizes various environmental entities that manifest as a river, a tree, a political institution, an individual or collective human bodies, and etc. It emphasizes the process that these entities enter an initial encounter and develop a deep evolvement – a process of the complex, contingent materialization of an entanglement. Such encounter and evolvement is participatory, relational, multidirectional, and thus chaotic. The emergence of an entanglement is not prescribed or guaranteed by any essential matter or its innate connectedness; likewise, the flux of entities does not follow ecological trajectories. Given these theoretical concerns, the book favors the notions "environment" and "environmental," as they better capture both the inclusiveness of an entanglement and preserve the contingent, relational disorderliness within that entanglement. Readers should note that "nature," "culture," and "ecology" are still used sporadically in the book for their literal meanings wherever they are at issue, although they do not supply the book's theoretical frameworks.

[25] Hymes and Schirokauer (1993).

world," in which they acted as environmental entities.[26] Their entanglement and interactions with other, non-human entities form and transform
the world. This complex environmental world compelled humans and
their institutions to experience the torrential waters and the desertifying
earth in material and tangible ways and to negotiate with the non-human
environmental entities on a daily basis. The human intentions and activities to order the world involved their painstaking, costly, and nevertheless
often failing ordering of the physical environment. Equally inevitably,
these human efforts to "order the world" were inextricably bound with
their inescapable experiences of "being ordered by" their environmental
world. The unfolding environmental drama during 1048–1128 governed
how local people pursued their farming, fishing, and salt-making livelihoods; it shaped the ways in which the state and its ruling members played
politics, managed finances, and consumed resources.

The Yellow River–Hebei environmental complex at the core of the
particular environmental world, whose formation and evolution are at
question in this book, composed its own imperial history. Its environmental powers penetrated the human society to affect the everyday life of
many Hebei people or expanded toward remote distances to enfold people or things there into its environmental processes. Such environmental

---

[26] "An environmental world" is not a descriptive expression for the natural or physical
surrounding outside and around a certain human community or institution. I coin this
notion to address a particular situation, which encompasses certain environmental entities that matter to each other, interact with each other, and form specific environmental
relationships and processes. To identify an environmental world is to determine what is
at issue in its environmental relationships. In this book, what is at issue is the formation and evolution of the Yellow River–Hebei environmental complex – the making of
a river delta in a particular swath of land. Those who organized, participated in, and
were implicated by such formation and evolution constituted the particular environmental world. Hence, an environmental world does not encompass every environmental
event and process occurring globally at the same time. A "world" is not a geographical
or spatial entirety, but a phenomenon of certain entangled relationships. My conception of "world" is congruent with Immanuel Wallerstein's interpretation of "world" in
the concept of world systems. Wallerstein (2004: 17) maintains: "[W]e are talking not
about systems, economies, empires of *the* (whole) world, but about systems, economies,
empires *that are* a world (but quite possibly, and indeed usually, not encompassing the
entire globe)." As Wallerstein insists upon multiple world systems, each of which con-
stitutes a singular world of a different nature, I recognize the coexistence and occasional
overlap of multiple environmental worlds, which are distinguished from each other based
on a given issue at hand. In this sense, the all-encompassing approach that I advocate (in
the ensuing pages) does not suggest a thorough geographical or spatial inclusiveness as
Andre Gunder Frank advocated. Frank disagreed with Wallerstein by calling for breaking down areal boundaries across the globe and insisting on the existence of one single
world system.

powers demonstrated stronger permeability than that of the state power. They broke down manmade political, social, and economic boundaries, both to disturb and regulate spatial and economic relationships within its environmental domain, and to command its subjects – humans and their institutions – to integrate, comply, and provide.

Spatially, this imperial history of the environment did not observe the orderly and stable structure of autonomous region/macroregion that G. William Skinner conceptualized for Chinese society.[27] Environmental spaces and the exchanges happening within them stretched and shrank in a far more chaotic and elastic fashion. To be shown in various chapters, multi-spatialities were in play: flooding disasters taking place at certain downstream locales found hidden causes from the Loess Plateau situated more than a thousand kilometers away; hydraulic activities to control the disasters inside Hebei not only implicated the central government in Henan but also, through the managerial role of the state, fueled the trans-regional mobilization and circulation of refugees, labor, wealth, and various kinds of material resources across the empire. Through a butterfly-effect mechanism, what occurred at minute locales were both products and producers of transregional and even empire-wide exchanges and movements. Driving these multi-spatial interactions and fluxes were not only human activities and human institutions but also the flourishing, contingent liveliness of non-human environmental entities.

Temporally, this environmental history did not ebb and flow according to the rise and fall of a dynasty, a human community, or individual life spans; rather, it followed its own timelines. In addition to the instantaneous creation or destruction of a landscape as in 1048 and 1128, as well as the decade-long surge and recession of floods and course changes of the river that led to the rapid shifts of governmental hydraulic policies,

---

[27] Skinner (1964–1965, 1977). To Skinner, river courses and their valleys that function as organizational entities to construct and sustain his stable macro-regions structure are abstract, conceptual waterbodies, which hold little material substance and show few changes to their geophysical and hydrological characteristics. Such anthropocentric assumption that static, lifeless, immaterial objects lay a foundation for vibrant, lively human activities is what environmental histories, including the present book, seek to challenge. My critique of Skinner resonates with and gives an environmental push to the critique by Richard von Glahn (1987, xx–xxi): "Although Skinner stresses the necessity of studying each region in terms of its own separate history, he and other who have borrowed his models have simply elaborated synchronic profiles of regional systems rather than attempting to study the history of regions. In part this omission results from the theory itself, since the central place concept is much more useful for describing a region at a given point in time than for explaining in history."

this environmental history unfolded through centuries of slow transformations of soil, water, and forests long before 1048 and long after 1128. Multiple temporalities interacted to bring humans, the state, and various non-human environmental entities along into the history's environmental times and cycles.

The environmental history told in *The River, the Plain, and the State* demonstrates a different way to conceptualize the history of middle-period China. It suggests new methodologies to approach not only the human history but also the more-than-human history. Previous scholarship of middle-period China has paid limited attention to the physical environment, treating it as a static platform or a collection of still objects that passively bear human activities and are subject to human appropriations and representations. The environment and environmental entities, at best, carry symbolic meanings and human interpretations. They do not seem to hold material substances that exert force on every aspect of human life and, hence, make history. When mentioning environmental events, like the shifts of the Yellow River's course in 1048 and 1128, previous historical studies have too often treated them as random incidents or "natural" disasters, which seem to have neither derived from lengthy historical processes nor borne any widespread, long-lasting implications.[28] These views toward the environment have determined the ways in which scholars use historical records. They have privileged records about human activities and deemed information about other-than-human events insignificant in their own right.

This book foregrounds environmental events and processes and regards both humans and non-humans implicated in these events and processes as environmental entities. It rejects "a compartmentalized perspective" (to borrow Andre Gunder Frank's words) toward history that brackets off non-human historical actors.[29] Instead, it calls for an

---

[28] Chinese historical geographers have studied these events from the perspective of historical geography, but they have not integrated their studies with the complexity of human political, economic, and social history. Unfortunately, these Chinese studies have been largely ignored by the scholarship in English. Despite advocating spatial and ecological awareness in studying Chinese history, scholars of previous generations like Skinner and Hartwell were not aware of the shifts of the Yellow River's course in 1048 and 1128. A most recent monograph on the Yellow River by David A. Pietz (2015) does not include these environmental events. Christian Lamouroux (1998: 545–584) provides the first study in English about the river's course shift in 1128; yet, his article focuses on the political debate on hydraulic management rather than on how these environmental events were and how environmental forces operated.

[29] Frank (1998: 358).

all-encompassing approach that respects non-human environmental entities as fellow players in the historical making of a complex, fluid environmental world. By doing so, the book seeks to push the boundaries of
historical inquiries beyond anthropocentric concerns that have dominated
studies of Tang–Song China. Methodologically, by using a great variety
of material – not only conventional textual sources like official histories
and private writings, but also archaeological materials, geographical studies, earth science, and hydrological studies – this book demonstrates that
an all-encompassing, interdisciplinary approach to the study of middle-
period China is both possible and fruitful.[30]

It is beyond question that human histories, like that of the Song state or
of the Hebei people, cannot be fully comprehended without understanding the environmental conditions in which they took place. But this book
advocates a further point: such human histories *could not be made* in the
first place without being bound up with non-human actors in a complex,
chaotic, and entangled environment world. The making of history was
never only a human affair. Let's "bring the society back in" and "bring
the state back in" to their everyday environmental life, where the river,
the plain, and the state reciprocated with each other to make a history
for China together.[31]

---

[30] Readers should be aware that due to the scarcity of historical sources for middle-period
China, in particular for north China, the range of questions and issues that the present
book may raise and address is limited and its analysis on certain issues is not systematic
or in great depth. There are many interesting and significant issues the book cannot
pursue due to such material constraints.

[31] To paraphrase the titles of two influential books: Evans et al., *Bringing the State Back
In* (1985) and Weber's *Bringing Society Back In* (2003).

PART I

PRE-1048

Prelude to the Environmental Drama

In the following four chapters, we shall approach these questions:

How had the river, the plain, and the state each evolved over a long time to encounter each other? How had their interactions gradually increased over several centuries to eventually produce the environmental drama?

I

Before the Yellow River Met the Hebei Plain

1.1 Loess, Silt, Floods, and a Thousand Years of Tranquility

This book is about the making of a Yellow River delta in the flat, low land of Hebei. The emergence of a delta landscape was an instantaneous result of the dramatic environmental change in summer 1048. But, for this event to happen and for the river to build up enough momentum to push its 700-kilometer-long flow into a different direction and to carve open the earth for a new river course, various environmental entities had to work in concert: not just the river itself, but also the land of Hebei that received the intrusion of the river's course, the imperial state that intervened in the river's movement, and many other factors. It took an extended period prior to 1048 for each of these entities to experience some environmental, geological, and political transformations and to encounter and entwine with each other. The following four chapters will examine the complex history behind the occurrence of the 1048 event. Through the interplays among the longue durée of environmental transformations, the middle term of political and social changes, and instantaneous events, the river, the plain, and the state crossed different temporalities and geographic zones to connect to each other. They together interacted to change the face of the physical landscape and the history of north China.

Our opening chapter begins with a panoramic view of the Yellow River's changing situation during the two thousand years prior to the 1048 environmental drama. This broad-brush depiction of the river's history offers two vital observations. First, the Yellow River's turning turbulent toward the eleventh century and its eventual crushing of Hebei to produce a new river delta had begun long before 1048. The long-term environmental changes in north China and the river's hydro-logical characteristics – the worsening soil erosion and consequential increase in the river's silt load – had destabilized the river's situation toward the end of the first millennium. Together, they had produced a river that was more and more prone to flooding. By the time the Northern Song Dynasty stepped onto the historical stage in 960, the environmental history of the Yellow River had sown and nourished the seeds for a catastrophic event like the one that occurred in 1048. Meanwhile, the longue durée of such environmental transformations saw a spatial disjunction. The seeds that eventually sprouted into disastrous fruits in downstream areas like the Hebei Plain were planted by the joint forces of nature and human activities more than a thousand kilometers upstream in north-western China. This extraordinary distance proved to be deceptive, as it concealed the causal relationship between environmental transformations going on in different geographic units from the spatial conception of the Chinese in medieval times and from our modern conception as well.

The second observation is not about the river's flooding issues *per se* but about the river's relationship with the Hebei Plain. For nearly one thousand years prior to 1048, the river served as the plain's southern border and did not impinge upon the plain in any remarkable way. The river and the plain had remained two marginally intersected, largely independent environmental entities. After 1128, the river shifted toward south China, and up to today it has never entered the center of the Hebei Plain again. This means, after 1128, the river and the plain restored their long-term relationship as two marginally related entities. Clearly, the environmental drama played out by the river and the plain during 1048–1128 was a rare, extraordinary episode in the entire environmental history of north China. Positioning the eighty years within the context of two millennia leads us to wonder how the change in the river–plain relationship actually took place.

This second observation demands an understanding of the long-term history of the Hebei Plain. The second half of this chapter will present Hebei as a geographically and environmentally well-defined plain. Partly thanks to the geographical division set by the Yellow River, Hebei had developed a martial tradition and a high level of political autonomy in its human society. This historical survey of Hebei will prepare us to understand the interventions of the Northern Song state from the late tenth century in Chapters 2–4. From political, socio-economic, and environmental perspectives, the state interventions peripheralized Hebei, broke down its marginal relationship between the river, and brought the two into an intricately knitted entanglement.

Loess, Silt, and Floods

The Yellow River, the sixth longest river in the modern world, originates in the Tibetan Plateau and reaches the coast in northeastern China after coursing through 5,464 kilometers. Along its route, the river has developed a drainage area of 752,000 square kilometers that covers most of the North China Plain, an area nearly the size of modern-day Turkey. A hundred thousand years ago, the river evolved from several small local streams into a full-length course similar to what we see today. Since then, its currents have continuously eroded the earth and picked up soil and rocks on its way. The water flow grinds these materials into fine silt, carries it long distances, and deposits it along its course. The silt builds up the flat ground in north China. As the river continues to run eastward toward the ocean, this land-building process spreads eastward as well, pushing the coastal line further into the ocean.

This process still continues today. Between 1855 and 1953, before the People's Republic of China was established to carry out enormous hydraulic works, the river's estuary extended 2 kilometers toward the ocean annually, creating 23.6 square kilometers of new land every year.[1] This unstoppable process over the past hundred thousand years makes the Yellow River one of the geological builders of the land of north China. It is fair for those in north China to call the Yellow River their mother river, similar to the way the Egyptians think of the Nile River and the Indians the Ganges. The Yellow River brought the land of north China, including Hebei – a northeastern part of the river's alluvial plain – into being, long before the first human being appeared to make use of its water and to cultivate the land it produced.

Ironically, as much as the Yellow River is widely acclaimed to be the cradle of China and the Chinese, it also has a notorious reputation as "China's Sorrow." This nurturing mother also shows an unpredictable face of rage and punishment. In historical times, she wielded her power and raised torrential floods again and again, devouring massive amounts of land and people. Historians have found that the river changed the course of its 700-kilometer-long lower reaches at least twenty-five times. Six of these events took place on an extraordinary scale: (1) the river shifted into southern Hebei in the seventh century BCE; (2) into southern

---

[1] Huanghe shuili weiyuanhui (1995: 58).

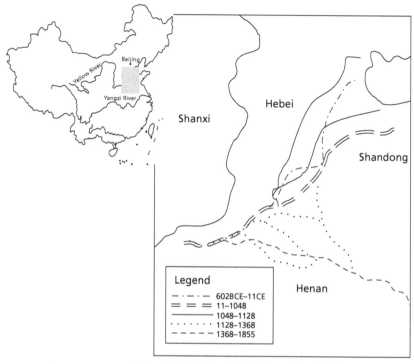

ILLUSTRATION 2. Historical Shifts of the Yellow River's Courses

Hebei again in the second century BCE; (3) out of Hebei and into northern Henan in the first century CE; (4) into central Hebei between 1048 and 1128; (5) south toward southern China in 1128; and (6) northward between Hebei and Henan-Shandong in 1855.[2]

These major shifts created multiple courses to the river's lower reaches. The separate courses infiltrated the vast space in the eastern part of the North China Plain and stretched out in different directions. Geographically, these courses were grouped into three clusters: northern courses, eastern courses, and southern courses, referring respectively to those within the Hebei Plain, those flowing through northern Henan and Shandong, and those tending toward the south to converge with the Huai River drainage area. These courses swept clockwise and anti-clockwise and moved the river estuary back and forth between latitudes 39° and 32° north. All together they have formed a vast alluvial fan of the Yellow River over 250,000 square kilometers.

[2] Huanghe shuili weiyuanhui (1982).

This enormous area is the river's floodplain, where it breached its banks along multiple courses to cause tremendous floods. Historians have identified 1,590 flooding events in the past 2,540 years.[3] No single historical period was completely free of the Yellow River's floods. From the statistics, we may observe a growing curve in the frequency of flooding events, increasing from once every thirty years before the fourth century, to once every ten years between the fourth and the mid-tenth century, to almost once every year in the Northern Song period, and to twice a year from the late thirteenth century onwards.[4] The Northern Song period from the mid-tenth century through the early twelfth century saw a height of river disasters. The environmental drama of 1048, when the river crashed into Hebei and created a cluster of northern courses, occurred right in the middle of these terrible events.

Situating our environmental drama within the long-term trend of the Yellow River's changes makes us wonder how the hands of nature and other environmental forces had collaborated, little by little, to lead the river toward its chaotic condition in the eleventh century. There were two major forces at work: unique hydrological dynamics that caused the river to be flood prone; and historical environmental degradation of the Loess Plateau in the river's middle reaches, which produced and then reinforced the river's hydrological characteristics.

In the past century, dozens of chronicles of Yellow River floods have been compiled in Chinese.[5] In nearly all of them, within the opening few

---

[3] Huanghe shuili weiyuanhui (1996: 18).

[4] Han Zhaoqing (1999: 208).

[5] A considerable number of publications on the Yellow River, both on its technological aspects and historical aspects, has been published by the Yellow River Conservancy and its associated Yellow River Hydraulics Press, and by the Water Resources Press associated with China's Ministry of Water Resources. Among Chinese historical geographers who have published extensively on historical transformations of the Yellow River, a great number are associated with two leading scholars, Shi Nianhai at Shaanxi Normal University and Tan Qixiang at Fudan University. Most of their works have been published through the university presses of these two institutes. In English, there are a few studies dedicated to the Yellow River. For example, Wang Ling and Lu Gwei-djen's volume in Neeham's *Science and Civilization in China* contains sections on hydraulic technology. Randall A. Dodgen (2001) studies the political and technological responses to river disasters in the 19th century. Jane Kate Leonard (1996) studies political reasoning and technological solutions about managing the Grand Canal and the canal's relations with the Yellow River. David Pietz (2015) provides an excellent study about the history of flood control, dam construction, and their environmental implications in twentieth-century China. Micah S. Muscolino (2015) offers a nuanced examination of the river's bank rupture in 1938 and its ecological, political, and socio-economic complications before the mid-twentieth century.

pages, the authors employ three phrases to characterize the river: "prone to siltation, prone to overflow, and prone to course shifts" (*shanyu shanjue shanxi* 善淤善決善徙). This narrative establishes a causal relationship: because the river contains high silt levels and tends toward sedimentation, it is thereby prone to overflow, breach its banks, and shift its course. This causality suggests that it is the river's own hydrological characteristics – in particular its heavy silt and rapid siltation – that have caused various river disasters. To understand where the silt came from and how it led to the exacerbation of the river's situation over a millennium before 1048, we must journey upstream to take a close look at the river's middle reaches, where soil erosion delivered a massive volume of mud, sand, and rocks into the river.

The middle reaches of the Yellow River wind through the northern edge of the Loess Plateau, the world's largest, deepest loess deposit, which is nearly the size of modern-day France. Today, this area supplies 90 percent of the silt that feeds into the Yellow River. The raw material of this silt consists of fine, loose, porous grains of loess. Given extremely low natural precipitation in this area, loess suffers from serious aridity as its porous texture interferes with the retention of moisture.[6] Environmental conditions appear even worse as we travel further north to the Ordos area, on the northern edge of the plateau. There, the landscape features extensive deserts and sandy groves, among which the Maowusu 毛烏素 and Kubuqi 庫布齊 deserts being the most famous and well studied. This area is sparsely dotted with drought-resistant grass, small lakes of high salinity, and little patches of oases. Its surface is largely covered by coarse sand.

The texture of the earth, climatic aridity, and the shortage of water all make the Loess Plateau ecologically fragile. The land has a limited capacity to support even thin vegetation and carries little environmental resilience. The vegetation cover – trees, bushes, and grass – does not readily return once gone. Trees, crops, and grazing land for livestock are all difficult to sustain. The latter two form the major human activities that have destroyed this area's natural vegetation in historical and present times. Today, a considerable part of the Loess Plateau appears completely barren year-round. Without a heavy cover of vegetation to shield the land surface, and without the roots of plants to anchor the soil, the fine,

---

[6] There are enormous studies on Chinese loess from earth science and soil studies, for example, Liu (1964) and (1985). For the Yellow River's silt specifically, see Zhao (1996).

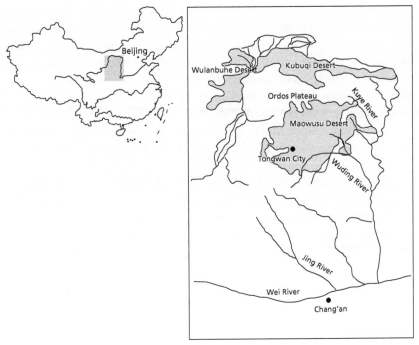

ILLUSTRATION 3. The Middle Reaches of the Yellow River

lightweight loess is exposed to the open air and can easily be carried away by wind or water.

The Yellow River courses around the Loess Plateau and the Ordos area, forming a "Great Bend." Along its journey, it picks up loess, fine sand, coarse sand, and rocky debris. It is also joined by multiple tributaries that cut through the loess, producing a distinct geomorphology of thousands of tall, earthy masses. Large or small, each of these masses presents a flat, barren top surface and steep cliff-like facets, and each is separated from its neighbors by deep gullies. For millions of years, these local rivers have gushed through the gullies and eroded away the earth, becoming even more loaded with silt than the Yellow River itself. The Wuding 無定 River's silt load, for instance, is 4.9 times that of the Yellow River's, and an even smaller tributary, the Kuye 窟野, has 6.4 times the Yellow's silt load.[7] These local rivers stretch deep into every corner of the Loess Plateau to collect silt and then discharge it into the Yellow River.

7 Huanghe shuili weiyuanhui (1995: 42–43).

By the time it finishes circling the Loess Plateau and turns eastward to its low-lying flood plain, the Yellow River has collected 1.6 billion tons of silt – the river's mean silt load per annum in the past few decades. This is seven times the amount of annual sediment discharged by the Mississippi River in the early 1980s and nineteen times the amount of sediment fed into the Colorado River at the Grand Canyon gate from 1948 to 1960.[8] In comparison with the North American "Big Muddy," the Yellow River is no doubt a "Super Muddy." Its muddy nature determines its hydrological dynamics, as silt blocks up the channel and forces the water to overflow.

Historically, the Yellow River was not always muddy, and the source of its muddy contents, the Loess Plateau, was not always a desolate, denuded land. Behind the river's rapid siltation is a long-term deterioration of the environmental conditions on the Loess Plateau. The dry, barren image of this area did not manifest in historical literature until the ninth century. It took more than two millennia for the Plateau to develop the unpleasant environmental conditions similar to what we witness today.[9]

Three thousand years ago, the Loess Plateau seems to have been rather humid.[10] The average temperature might have been 2°C higher than today. Under the cover of bushes and broad-leaf trees, animals lived comfortable lives. Tigers, elephants, and rhinoceros that appear in tropical areas today seem to have existed widely in this part of north China. Before sedentary agriculture began, the rich vegetation (both forests and grasslands) sustained in a relatively warm and humid climate and guarded the loess and held it in place. Soil erosion had not yet significantly affected the Yellow River. The river's water ran clear, and it was simply called the "River" or the "Great River" in early Chinese sources.

The mass migration of agricultural population and the colonization of the land gradually transformed this ecologically sensitive zone. Han Chinese began to settle in the region when the Qin 秦 (221–202 BCE) and Han 漢 (202 BCE–220 CE) dynasties competed with nomads for land and sought to incorporate this borderland area into their empires. The first

---

[8] Gupta (2007: 31), "Table 3.1, The Basic Characteristics of the World's Largest Rivers." The U.S. Geological Survey (online source), "Table 1. Discharge of suspended sediment to the coastal zone by 10 major river of the United States, about 1980." See Topping et al. (2000: 515–542); Morris (2012: 2, 225).

[9] There is a large body of scholarship in Chinese on historical environmental changes on the Loess Plateau. For example, Tan (1986), Shi (1981, 1985, 1988a, 1991, 2002), and Hou and Deng (2006).

[10] Shi (2002: 433–448); Shi et al. (1985: 1–74); Ho (1969); Elvin (1993: 30–33); and various sections in Elvin (2006). For a comprehensive survey of regional environmental changes, see Marks (2012).

emperor of the Qin 秦始皇 sent 300,000 men to this region to "attack the *hu* (non-Han peoples)."[11] Along with the military actions there arrived an enormous number of corvée laborers, who built and repaired the Great Wall. These men were the first wave of Han Chinese settlers to the Ordos area. During the next three centuries, continuous battles between the Han and the Huns and their struggles for the Great Bend area brought a sizable military population to the area. In 119 BCE, for instance, Emperor Wu of the Western Han 漢武帝 sent 725,000 people from the eastern part of the North China Plain to the Great Bend of the Yellow River to boost agricultural colonization.[12]

Han Chinese farmers brought a sedentary lifestyle and an agricultural economy to the area. The material provision agriculture provided in turn supported a stable growth in human reproduction. Unfortunately, the gradual increase in human inhabitants and the way they dealt with the surrounding environment led to irreversible negative environmental effects.[13] In comparison with nomadic animal husbandry, agricultural cultivation cleared the land more thoroughly; the steady population growth also required the plowing of more and more land, causing forests and grasslands to disappear. Stripped of its vegetation, the once-moist earth became dry and the porous soil began to travel. As a result, the siltation of the Yellow River accelerated and clogged the river's lower reaches. Between the mid-second century BCE and the first century CE, the river produced serious floods, and the river itself became known as the "Yellow" river.

After the first century, the environmental situation seems to have improved temporarily. The fall of strong imperial powers in northern China might have put a pause to the mass migration into the area. The return of nomads possibly drove some Han farmers out, replacing farming with a mixture of both farming and animal husbandry. It is likely that the land was given enough time for its natural vegetation to recover, leading to a reduction of soil erosion and corresponding silt in the river.

For a while, the environmental conditions on the Loess Plateau appeared favorable. In 407, Helian Bobo 賀連勃勃, a chieftain of the Huns, established the Xia 夏 Kingdom and built his capital, Tongwan Cheng (統萬城, *lit.*, City to Rule the Myriad), in middle of the Ordos. Today, this part of the Ordos is covered by sand and is known as the

---

[11] *Shiji*, 6: 252.
[12] *Han shu*, 6: 178.
[13] For environmental implications of the northward expansion of Han Chinese in the Qin-Han period, see Wang (2007: 310–332; 485–498).

Maowusu desert, but in Helian's time the land was verdant with natural streams and lush grasses. As Helian remarked, "I have traveled to many places, but none of them are as beautiful as here." Archaeological works also suggest that the earth stratum associated with that historical period consisted of dark, moist, and quite fertile soil. Helian resettled 400,000 Han Chinese slaves there to engage in agricultural production for his state.[14] It seems that for the founder of the Xia Kingdom, the northern part of the Loess Plateau was rich enough in natural resources to support all sorts of economic activities that sustained his myriad subjects as well as his military. This suggests that in the fifth century environmental conditions must have been rather benign; large-scale deserts had not yet come into being.

It is very likely that the resettlement and re-colonization of the land by farmers – introduced by Helian as well as rulers and warlords over the next several centuries who had to rely on the Loess Plateau as their production base – once again exposed this area to the same environmental destruction it experienced centuries before. The establishment of centralized empires in the Sui 隋 (598–617) and Tang 唐 (618–907) dynasties once again turned the northern Loess Plateau into the Chinese northern frontier. The old strategy of the Qin and the Han to stuff the land with Han migrants was used again. The land within the river's Great Bend was filled with state-sponsored military colonies, Han Chinese farmers, and non-Han groups that adopted a sedentary lifestyle.[15]

The revival of agriculture and the population boom challenged the environmental capacity of the Loess Plateau. By the mid-ninth century, excessive cultivation had depleted the vegetation and nutrients in the soil; temporary settlers migrated from one place to another to search for new land, leaving desolated earth in their wake. Helian Bobo's Tongwan City had been seriously eroded by sand and wind. In 822, a sandstorm could easily toss up sand dunes as high as the city walls. Several decades later, travelers who came in search of the past splendor would only find a pile of remnants in a vast stretch of yellow sand. By the end of the Tang period, soil erosion became so serious that the Yellow River's tributaries were heavily silted and blocked up. The Wuding River flooded and shifted its course many times and eventually acquired its name as the "Unsettled

---

[14] For studies about Helian Bobo's city construction and its environmental impact, see various articles in Hou and Deng (2006), and He and Wang (2010: 186–191).

[15] See various articles in Tan (1986), multi-volume *Heshan ji* by Shi (1981, 1985, 1988a, 1991, 2002).

River." The Wei 渭 River in the southern Loess Plateau ran through the suburb of the Tang capital, Chang'an 長安. It was so silted that, starting in the late eighth century, its water overflowed frequently and put the capital city in great danger.[16]

After the first century, the Yellow River was rarely reported to flood. Sadly, this eight-century-long state of tranquility, "*anliu* 安流 (lit., peaceful flow)" as Chinese historical geographers call it, was to end in the Tang period. At first, the river's middle reaches on the Loess Plateau became so unstable that the river often meandered from its mainstream. Military towns and garrisons originally considered to be "inside the river" became "outside the river," or vice versa, not because these settlements were relocated or the districts had been displaced, but because the river's course had shifted.[17] As the decades passed, the impact of soil erosion slowly extended eastward to the river's lower reaches. A few small-scale floods were observed by people living downstream in the ninth century. These minor events would develop into serious floods that took place nearly once every four years in the tenth century.

As the tenth century approached, the climate showed a drier tendency, and this played a significant role in the worsening of environmental conditions in north China. Statistics of disaster records in the tenth and eleventh centuries show that drought frequently affected the Loess Plateau.[18] This increasing aridity would have harmed vegetation, depleted the earth's moisture, and accelerated the desertification of the land. As a result, more sandy material entered the river. Reports of sandstorms (*yutu* 雨土, *lit.* earth storms) increased greatly in the eleventh century.[19] Although most of the sandstorms affected the lower Yellow River valley and were witnessed by people there, the sandy materials that produced such storms came from a place nearly a thousand kilometers away, namely the Loess Plateau.[20]

The dual impact of human activities and the climatic tendency together modified the environmental conditions in the Yellow River's middle reaches. Within this broad temporal and spatial context, the making of the environmental drama in 1048 had come about as a result of profound interregional environmental and geological exchanges.

[16] See Wang Yuanlin (2005).
[17] Chinese historical geographers have debated for decades if there was a tranquil period in the Yellow River history and why. See Tan (1986), Yao (1987), and Shi (2002).
[18] Yang (2008: 218–237). For more historical climatic data, see Zhang (2004).
[19] Zhang (1984: 825–836) and Song and Zhang (2006).
[20] Zhang (1982) and Zhang and Sun (2001: 1–7).

A Thousand Years of Tranquility

As the Loess Plateau continued to feed the river tremendous amounts of silt from a thousand kilometers upstream, the failure of the downstream flow to process and digest that silt eventually led to flooding disasters along the river's lower reaches. Today, every year the river carries 46.4 billion cubic meters of water, merely 8 percent of the 562 billion cubic meters of the Mississippi; at 1,880 cubic meters per second, the Yellow River's discharge rate is only 12 percent of the 15,500 cubic meters per second of the legendarily sluggish Mississippi.[21] Given such low water level and low velocity, the river has trouble discharging its heavy silt into the ocean; instead, it deposits silt in the riverbed or spreads it over the land of north China along its course. The flow's inability to transport silt is significantly worsened by the flat, low terrain of the North China Plain. Here, the land stands less than 50 meters above sea level and offers little gradient. Today, nearly 40 percent of the 1.6 billion tons of silt is deposited unevenly over the river's lower reaches, causing the riverbed to rise at a rate of 2–3 centimeters each year. The continuous accumulation of sediment in the past three thousand years has produced a "suspending river" on the North China Plain. This means that a substantial portion of the flow does not stay in the ground but instead stands meters above the surrounding low-lying ground – a phenomenon that historical writings recorded as early as in the second century BCE.

The higher the river body rises, the more likely it will overflow, and the more powerful its flooding will be. Beginning in the seventh century BCE, kingdoms along the river's lower reaches entered a "dyking race," meaning that they competed with each other to construct lengthy high dykes to keep out both floods and silt. Those who did not build dykes would become victims not only of the river's torrents but also of their neighbors' hydraulic infrastructure. The dyking technique, however, induced negative consequences and led to more flooding disasters. The dykes straightjacketed the river course and fixed the water and silt within a limited space. Such spatial confinement accelerated the accumulation of sediments in the riverbed and thereby the latter's elevation. As a result, the river's hydrological force pushed even harder against the dykes, and the river's water was more likely to burst through them.

The one and a half millennia prior to 1048 saw an endless wrestling between human efforts to build more dykes and the river's desire to

---

[21] Gupta (2007: 31).

run free. When the river succeeded in overcoming the dykes, the massive force of water would pour out onto the surrounding low ground and wreak havoc over a vast area. In 132 BCE, for instance, a terrible bank rupture at the site of Huzi 瓠子 led to the inundation of all of southern Hebei and northern Henan. It took Emperor Wudi of the Western Han Dynasty twenty years to come to the conclusion that the bank rupture had to be fixed at any cost. He visited the bank rupture personally and presented extravagant sacrifices to Heaven and Earth. He even composed a prose poem to express his despair over the calamity, as well as to document the tremendous human efforts under his leadership to fix the rupture. His officials, regardless of status and position, carried wood and stones to the riverside to perform flood-control work. Dealing with the aftermath of the floods took the state over twenty years; as one of its many costs, the bamboos in the state-owned forests in Henan were completely felled for use as construction material.[22]

The river's destruction seems to have become even more severe at the turn of the first millennium. Archaeological works led by T. R. Kidder have shown a remarkable earth stratum 10 meters under the present land surface, which was produced by floods and resulting sediments in that period.[23] Continuous flooding certainly contributed to the political upheaval and social instability, so it is reasonable for us to consider that river-related environmental disasters must have played a significant role in the dwindling of the Western Han Dynasty and the tragic failure of Wang Mang 王莽's short-lived Xin 新 Dynasty. The environmental conditions of the river carried immense political and socio-economic implications.

Flooding began to reduce in the first century, partly because of the improvement in environmental conditions after human activities on the Loess Plateau decreased, and partly because of innovations in hydraulic knowledge and technology. Previous historical writings have generally attribute the decrease of floods to the hydraulic works conducted by Wang Jing 王景 in the first century. Wang witnessed the overwhelming power of the Yellow River and learnt the technical limitation of fragmented dykes. To tame the violent river, he believed it necessary to observe the natural conditions of geography, to choose and design a suitable route for the river, and then to install a holistic dyke system that contained the entire river rather than only sections of it. Not much is left of Wang's hydraulic

[22] *Shi ji*, 29: 1412–1413.
[23] Kidder et al. (2012: 30–47).

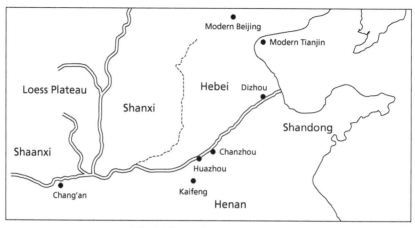

ILLUSTRATION 4. The Yellow River's Lower Reaches before 1048

legacy today, but historical literature suggests that he developed a brand new course for the river, flanking it on both sides with strong dykes that stretched over 500–600 kilometers.[24]

Wang Jing's river course remained functional for the next nine centuries, and the river's lower reaches appeared peaceful. Very few flooding events were reported in the North China Plain. We cannot judge to what extent the tranquil state of the river is attributable to Wang's hydraulic work, because there are not many extant historical sources that offer evidence. Whatever brought about a stable, gentle river, we know for certain that the first century marked a significant change in the river's relationship with the land of Hebei. Wang Jing's eastward-flowing river course divided the land of Hebei from that of Henan. The river's long-lasting geographical stability even granted these two regions their identities: Hebei eventually acquired its literal name as "the land north of the river," in contrast to Henan, "the land south of the river." From then until the tenth century, the river made very little trouble for Hebei and its people; it certainly never invaded Hebei's territory before the eleventh century.

Sadly, the tranquility that people on the North China Plain had enjoyed for nearly one thousand years gradually came to an end, as the environmental conditions in the upstream area continued to deteriorate and, very likely, Wang Jing's dykes slowly broke down. The accumulation

[24] For the debate on Wang Jing's hydraulic work and the possibility of a thousand-year tranquility of the Yellow River's situation, see various articles in Tan (1986) and Yao (2003: 155–175).

of silt made certain parts of the river increasingly vulnerable to flood-ing. In the tenth century, bank ruptures and floods occurred in twenty-four individual years. Most of them happened within a small area in the Huazhou 滑州 and Chanzhou 澶州 prefectures, where the river's channel zigzagged, the earth supporting the dykes was loose and fragile, and the currents tended to be turbulent. Through the tenth and eleventh centuries, this dangerous section of the river saw the most major flooding and course shifts.

Meanwhile, from the late tenth century on, sediments began to deposit at the river's estuary and block river water from entering the sea. Dizhou 棣州 prefecture, for instance, was close to the ocean and saw the river flowing through the southern half of its domain. In the 980s, this district carried 56,178 registered households, roughly 280,890 people.[25] Here, the riverbed of the Yellow River had risen nearly ten meters above its surrounding ground. The dykes could no longer be built higher, and the increasing pressure of water occasionally crashed through them. Between 1007 and 1014, floods struck the capital city of the prefecture every year. In 1014, a flood nearly submerged the entire city, forcing local officials to petition to the imperial court to abandon the city and remove its residents. Soon after people evacuated, the city of Dizhou was completely sub-merged by a second flood.[26]

This eastward movement of flooding problems toward the river mouth did not alleviate pressure on the river's upstream sections. Rather, by the beginning of the eleventh century, the entire 700 kilometers of the river's lower reaches had become highly problematic; its various sections were troubled by different kinds of hydrological mechanisms. The blockage of the river mouth must have jeopardized the river's normal flow and caused both water and silt to surge backward. There is no historical source to demonstrate this phenomenon, but with basic hydrological knowledge, one may imagine that the counter-directional flow from the coastal area surged westward to clash with the river's eastward-flowing mainstream. Wherever these two hydrological forces met saw great damage. In the early eleventh century, these clashes happened again and again in the Huazhou-Chanzhou area. In the years 1015, 1019–1021, 1034, and eventually in 1048, the river provoked its most serious bank ruptures and floods precisely in this area.

[25] Liang (1980: 134).
[26] XCB, 83: 1839.

This brief survey of the river's history charts a gradual end to the thousand years of tranquility, both in terms of the river's conditions and the North China Plain's experiences of environmental stability and disturbance. The catastrophic events that began to occur in the eleventh century were in fact a culmination of a growing trend of river disasters. Situating the momentary environmental event in 1048 in a complex temporal-spatial context helps us see clearly how the currents of history had been preparing its actors – the river, the land of north China and the people residing there, and governmental and political figures – for the dramatic outbreak of a catastrophe like the 1048 event. Hence, the environmental drama presented in this book did not come about as some random event; rather, it was the result of a series of causal relations complicated by both natural factors and human activities.

1.2 The Autonomous Plain

Hebei as a Geographical Entity

Before the Yellow River's penetration in 1048, Hebei was a land "north of the Yellow River." For nearly a millennium, not only did Hebei experience limited environmental impact from the river, it utilized the river's broad, heavy body as a natural barrier to shield itself from the rest of China. The river endowed Hebei with a geographical boundary as well as a sense of separation and independence – both Hebei and the rest of China saw Hebei as its own entity, distinct from other regions.

Geographically, the plain resides at the northeastern corner of traditional Chinese territory. In the east, it abuts on the Gulf of Bohai, where the sea cuts off its connection with any other landmass, such as the peninsulas of Shandong, Liaoning 遼寧, and Korea. In the west, the plain leans against the Taihang Mountains 太行山, which stretch north–south over four hundred kilometers and stand over a thousand meters in altitude, high enough to block Hebei from the highland of Shanxi 山西. To the north, Hebei's geographical division from its neighbor is not as sharp as in the other three directions. The century-long battles between the Han Chinese and the Khitan 契丹 took place here, resulting in the display of troops and fortresses on both sides of the Juma 拒馬 River. The political and military situation had long established the Juma River as the *de facto* northern boundary of Song-occupied Hebei. In 1005, the Song and Khitan's Liao 遼 (907–1125) states issued a peace treaty and officially declared the Juma River a border between the two states. Hence, the

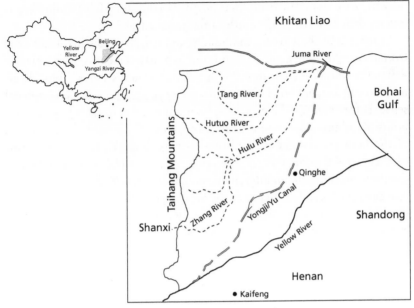

ILLUSTRATION 5. Hebei in the Tenth Century

medium-size Juma River served as both the political and the geographical
northern edge of the plain.

Given this geographical contour, the "Hebei" plain at question in this
book refers roughly to the land called the "Jizhou 冀州" region during
the Han and Three Kingdoms 三國 periods (the second century BCE
through the third century CE), the southern half of the "Hebei dao"
during the Tang period (the early seventh through early tenth century),
and the southern half of the "Zhili 直隸" region in the Ming 明 and
Qing 清 periods (the early fifteenth through the early twentieth century).

This region, thus, is also different from modern Hebei Province whose
territory includes a vast area north of the Juma River, where modern
Beijing 北京 is located. Hebei in the tenth to twelfth centuries refers to
the southern half of modern Hebei Province, the region administered
under the name of "Hebei lu" by the Northern Song Dynasty. The land
to its north, the northern half of modern Hebei that includes the city of
Beijing today, was under the control of the Liao Dynasty as the Liao's
"Nanjing 南京" district during the tenth to twelfth centuries. Its land
and people underwent a drastic political, socio-economic, and cultural
transformation due to nomadic influences. Readers should note that the

present book does not study that northern land; the Hebei Plain here is strictly defined as the land south of the Juma River.[27]

Bracketed by these rivers, mountains, and sea, Hebei distinguishes itself from its neighboring areas. It stands out as a material entity with a clearly defined geophysical enclosure. This book foregrounds a geographical definition of Hebei, acknowledging it foremost as a plain in the geographical sense, before regarding it as a socio-economic and cultural region, or as a political, administrative unit of the Song empire. These three definitions of the land are correlated, and they often overlap each other in terms of their spatial coverage. In this book, the term Hebei often refers to the three meanings in an interchangeable manner, with an understanding that the geophysical existence of the land lays the foundation for its other significances. In places where more clarity is needed, I shall explain in exactly which sense the term is being used.

By emphasizing Hebei as an enclosed geographical entity that enjoys rather uniform materiality, I highlight Hebei's image as an environmental entity equal to but distinct from other environmental entities, like the Yellow River and the imperial state. I honor Hebei's roles as a participant and actor in history, which performed and interacted with other historical actors in the complex process of making north China's environmental history. Hebei did not participate in the historical process nominally, as an abstract political unit bearing an administrative title, nor did it participate merely as a conceptual substitute for anthropocentric subjects like people, their society, and their collective culture. As a geophysical entity, Hebei not only served as a material site where various environmental changes and exchanges as well as political and economic activities took place, it also acted as both a recipient and an object of these changes and activities, which modified the land's physicality in various ways. Most importantly, the land responded to the movement of the Yellow River and the interventions of human activities by setting limitations or provoking reactions. It defined the ways in which the river behaved within its territory; it shaped and reshaped the livelihood of the people who were affected by every change to the land's materiality. The land itself kept changing and took part in the endless making and unfolding of the historical drama. By playing participatory roles in the environmental

---

[27] This book does not extend the range of the Hebei Plain toward the land in the north not only because the Juma River sufficiently served as Hebei's geographical, political, socio-economic, and cultural boundary, but also because historical sources associated with the Liao-controlled northern land are scant and do not support an in-depth study of its environmental history.

process, and by way of its constant reciprocation with other entities, the plain of Hebei made itself a prominent historical actor.

This geographical entity distinguishes itself through its internal geophysical singularity. First, although it covers a vast area of roughly 120,000 square kilometers (back in the Northern Song period[28]), nearly as large as modern-day England, the land sees little variation in elevation. Being a typical plain, Hebei lacks fluctuation of its surface; it spreads out smoothly, seeing no significant obstacle, like mountains, to divide the land into distinctively different sections.

Second, nearly the entire area is uniformly low-lying. Born as a tectonic sink millions of years ago, it has continued to sink, as the mountainous terrains around it continue their uplift. Except for a narrow strip along the foot of the Taihang Mountains where the terrain is relatively high, the plain stands only 50–20 meters above sea level on average, much lower than other areas in north China. From western Hebei to the eastern coast, a distance of 400 kilometers, the land's altitude gradually drops from 100 to 2 meters. The change in gradient is so minor that across Hebei one may not observe much topographic difference.

Third, Hebei is climactically varied: the eastern coastal area receives more oceanic influence; the western mountainous area traps higher humidity and thereby enjoys more rainfall in the rainy season; while the central plain suffers higher aridity and lacks any shield against summer heat, strong winds, or cold fronts. Nevertheless, in general, the plain shares a relatively uniform continental temperate climate. Located between latitudes 35° and 39° north, this area is dominated by interplays between the southward movement of cold, dry air masses from Siberia–Mongolia and the northwestward movement of warm, moist air masses from the Pacific. When the northern forces rule, they produce a cool, dry Hebei during a large portion of the year. Spring and summer are usually short, but the temperature can go up to 35°C in most places.

Throughout Hebei, the temperature drops under the freezing point in winter, now as back in the Song period. Heavy snow is common. When spring arrives and the land heats quickly, most of Hebei experiences the "hot dry wind (*ganrefeng* 乾熱風)," which blows the earth so dry that it often kills winter-spring crops. The rainy season does not start until mid or late May. In general, precipitation is low throughout Hebei, with regional variations for annual rainfall between 400 and 600 millimeters. This small amount of rain nourishes the land in a peculiar way: about

[28] Liang (1980: 164).

70 percent of it hits the ground during three summer months, which creates downpours that fill up rivers, cause floods, and wash away the dry, loose soil from the land surface. During the rest of the year, the other 30 percent of the rainwater sprinkles down sparsely, far from enough to relieve aridity. This climatic pattern makes Hebei subject to certain natural disasters. Excessive rain causes floods, while a lack of rain causes drought. Historical records show that this seasonal contrast was evident in the Northern Song period as well as today.

Lastly, Hebei's geophysical singularity is also manifested in the characteristics of its water resources. Most of Hebei's natural streams originate from the western mountainous area. Supplied by underground water and snowmelts in spring, the rivers follow the smooth descent of the gradient toward northeast Hebei. In the vicinity of modern Tianjin where the land is lowest and was covered by swamps in the tenth to twelfth centuries, the rivers merge with each other before discharging into the sea. Back in the Northern Song period, some of these rivers were known for being muddy due to their heavy silt load. Their water volumes changed often and, due to Hebei's rain patterns, were prone to floods. Therefore, navigation by boat to travel from western Hebei downstream to eastern Hebei was a challenge.

Thanks to the flat low ground, water accumulates easily. Meanwhile, the underground water table sits merely 1 or 2 meters under the land surface; with even a little infiltration of rainwater, it rises quickly to form lakes, ponds, and springs. In early China, western and northern Hebei were festooned by extensive lakes. Many of them had shrunk or disappeared by the ninth century; the bottoms of these lakes had been cultivated as fields by farmers.[29] With the addition of more water, however, these lowlands could still trap water and turn back into swamps and lakes. This is exactly what happened in the late tenth century. Under heavy rains, the local rivers ran wild and flooded, and a considerable portion of northern Hebei was submerged in stagnant water.

From the first century until the Yellow River's entry into the plain in 1048, Hebei's water system functioned as a largely independent, self-reliant entity. Rain, snow, surface runoffs, and the underground water circulated and replenished each other. These waters stretched toward every corner of the land to organize a vibrant, self-sufficient geographical entity, which formed the underpinning of the environmental life for both humans and non-humans on the Hebei Plain.

[29] Zou (1987: 25–39).

Cultural, Socio-Economic, and Political Autonomy

For readers who have learnt about Hebei through the scholarship of late imperial China, Hebei was a "land of famine" in its recent history.[30] Located south of the metropolitan area of Beijing, capital to the Jin 金, Yuan 元, Ming, and Qing dynasties and present People's Republic of China, Hebei was where these late imperial states deployed massive amounts of soldiers and conscripted large numbers of corvée laborers, where roads and waterways spread all over not to benefit the locals but to deliver grain and wealth from south China straight to Beijing. In recent centuries, the land increasingly suffered from hydraulic breakdowns and environmental disasters; its human population was frequently struck by agricultural failures, hunger, and demographic losses. For many recent centuries, this region was not a significant player in the arena of political and socio-economic contestations among various regions; rather, it has become one of the poorest, most powerless parts of China. This impoverished image of Hebei is very different from how the region looked before the eleventh century. In the following pages, we shall trace the historical evolution of a militarily strong, politically independent, and economically self-sufficient Hebei before the eleventh century. For many early centuries prior to the eleventh, the geographical enclosedness of Hebei had interacted with the people living there and produced a society that enjoyed a history and culture quite different from people in neighboring regions. Hebei's uniqueness lies in its ethnic, economic, and cultural hybridity, its military tradition, and its political autonomy.

Back in early China, the land of Hebei was a contested region where multiple feudal states of the Spring and Autumn 春秋 (700–476 BCE) and Warring States 戰國 (476–221 BCE) periods vied. It was a borderland – an ethnic, economic, and cultural melting pot – between the sedentary, farming Han Chinese and non-Han peoples, including the horse-riding nomads and semi-nomadic hunter-gatherers who arrived from the Mongolian Steppe and northeast Asia. Either through violent territorial disputes and military struggles or through peaceful economic exchanges and intermarriages, these ethnic groups intermingled to produce a population that was known as the "men of Yan and Zhao (*Yan Zhao zhishi* 燕趙之士)" in many later centuries. These people, also known as the Hebei people after the geographical name "Hebei" came into common use, were a kind of hybrid between two ethnic, socio-economic, and cultural traditions.

---

[30] Lillian M. Li (2007).

Before the imperial times, the early Hebei people were distant descen-
dants and subjects of the Han Chinese culture. In comparison with those
living to their south and west, they did not strictly observe state rituals
and social norms derived from the tradition of the Zhou 周 Dynasty that
had dominated the lives on the central North China Plain. They were
not well acquainted with Confucian philosophy, ethics, and literature,
which had formed a basic ethos for the men of China's ruling classes.
Hebei men did not produce famous thinkers or writers like Confucius
and Mencius, whose moral and political teachings defined the Chinese
society and its individuals since the second century BCE. Neither did they
produce powerful politicians like Guan Zhong 管仲 (of the Qi 齊 state
in Shandong) and Lord Shang 商鞅 (of the Qin state in Shaanxi 陝西),
whose political sophistication helped build strong states that led toward
the rise of imperial China.

Instead, the early Hebei people were known for their martial and
heroic characters. King Wuling of the Zhao Kingdom 趙武靈王 (340–
295 BCE) was famously known for promoting non-Han culture, such
as horse riding, archery, and nomadic styles of clothing, in order to
improve his state's military strength. Jing Ke 荊軻, a strong man from the
northern land of Hebei, became one of the most renowned individuals
in the literature of this era for his assassination attempt of the king of
the Qin, later the First Emperor of the Qin Dynasty. Literature from
early China gives us a general impression that, in the land of Hebei, even
ordinary farmers knew how to ride horses and shoot an arrow. When
not farming, they hunted or practiced martial arts, or sauntered around
with swords hanging from their belts. These men were born soldiers
because of the region's martial tradition and strong sense of honor and
personal worth. Open, friendly, and blunt, they made acquaintance with
strangers easily and often developed their social lives through drinking.
These qualities, however, could get them into trouble too. When offended,
they would not hesitate to provoke a fight. They would avenge any slight
of family or personal honor and were known to become outlaws.[31]

Teeming with heroes and strongmen, Hebei had for centuries been
the breeding ground for fearless warriors and powerful military leaders.
Their armies could provide the force for the rise of a central authority.

---

[31] Literature of early China, such as *Zuozhuan* 左傳, *Zhanguo ce* 戰國策, and *Shi ji* 史記,
offer many stories and anecdotes about warriors, assassins, and remarkable figures of the
sort from the Hebei area. They give us a general impression of the martial characteristic
of early Hebei people.

The founding emperor of the Eastern Han 東漢 Dynasty, Liu Xiu 劉秀 (6–57 CE), for instance, pacified rebellions and unified China under one central rule. He achieved this because he gained support from Hebei warlords and built a political and military foundation inside Hebei. From the late Han through the Three Kingdoms period, Hebei acted like a military powerhouse. Prominent contenders for the imperial throne, like Yuan Shao 袁紹 (d. 202), Cao Cao 曹操 (155–220, whose family established the Wei 魏 Dynasty), and many others, established their military and political careers here and used Hebei as the base for their military expansion toward the rest of north China. Dominating the civil war in north China, Hebei warlords often resisted centralized control coming from the outside; they cared more about their own interests and political autonomy. In this sense, Hebei men were the most disobedient subjects an imperial state had to deal with. Even worse, an ambitious Hebei warlord could easily rally his own troops and expand beyond Hebei to challenge the state in central north China, while the central state often experienced difficulties in entering highly independent Hebei: the land's geographical barriers, in particular the Yellow River, effectively blocked most invasions from the south.

Through the early seventh century, China was wracked with civil war. Various non-Han ethnic groups streamed into China proper from the Mongolian Steppe and northeastern Asia to participate in political and military competitions. Both disturbed by and forced to absorb these populations, Hebei's military culture and tradition of political autonomy were further strengthened. Households of wealth and high social status amassed weaponry, raised horses, and trained their own militants for self-protection. In this period, a manorial economy thrived. Large estates owned enormous plots of land and commanded the labor of multiple households to engage in various kinds of production. The manor produced both agricultural and non-agricultural products to guarantee a highly self-sufficient economy, which relied very little on exchanges with the outside world. This economy allowed estate owners to develop their military forces and gave them enough freedom to emerge as local political leaders and compete for power at higher levels both within Hebei and in interregional or even national arenas. These "strongmen from east of the [Taihang] mountains (*Shandong haojie* 山東豪傑)"[32] in Hebei acquired extraordinary political and military power in north China from the third

---

[32] This phrase sometimes referred to "east of the Yao Mountain," meaning the eastern part of the North China Plain, a realm larger than Hebei.

century on. They participated in north China's political contentions and simultaneously protected their homeland from falling prey to any external authority.

From the mid-sixth century, northwest China saw the rise of strong regimes, which eventually suppressed the powers in the northeast and conquered Hebei. The Sui and Tang dynasties both acquired Hebei as a northeastern province of their imperial empires. This repression of the "strongmen from east of the mountain" has long been considered a major transition in Chinese history, representing the political and cultural integration of different regions, like Hebei, into a centralized imperial state.[33] All over China, the manorial economy slowly gave the way to a more diversified agro-market, empire-wide economy. Thanks to a peaceful political environment from the early seventh century, small landowners were released from the control of the large estates and thrived in various specialized modes of production.[34]

By the mid-eighth century, Hebei had become a major agricultural producer in the empire and contributed greatly to the state's finances.[35] Its grain products traveled over a thousand kilometers westward to feed the population in the imperial capital of Chang'an in Shaanxi; it was also known as the largest supplier of refined silk in the empire. Meanwhile, trade boomed and market towns mushroomed, especially along streams that provided convenient water-based transportation. Inside Hebei, the Yongji 永濟 Canal (known as the Yuhe 御河 Canal in the Northern Song period) was built in the early seventh century. This north–south waterway linked Hebei's local rivers with the Yellow River that skirted Hebei's southern border; it carried goods in and out of Hebei and distributed them to various parts of the plain. With this additional means of transportation, commerce flourished. Qinghe 清河 County in central Hebei, for instance, gained so much wealth that people called it the "northern warehouse of the empire."[36] Hebei's booming regional economy, considered the strongest in the Tang empire, led to an increase in population, and by the mid-eighth century, it enjoyed the largest regional population among the empire's various provinces.[37] Its registered households accounted for

[33] Chen (1997).

[34] McDermott and Shiba offer a survey on the transformation of economy during the Tang period, in Chaffee and Twitchett (2015: 321–325).

[35] Pulleyblank (1955: 33). See figures of annual tributes that provincial circuits presented to the Tang court, in Du You, *Tong dian*, 6: 34–38.

[36] *Zizhi tongjian*, 217: 6957.

[37] See Shi's (1991: 53–59 and 168–191)'s study on Hebei's economy in the Sui and Tang dynasties.

20 percent of the entire empire, and its population density was the second highest in the empire, just barely behind the metropolis of Chang'an (see Illustration 5).[38]

All these political and socio-economic changes, however, did not seem to have fully incorporated Hebei into the rest of China, nor reduced it to a submissive subordinate to the imperial state. As the state remained wary of the burgeoning region, Hebei and its people sustained their regional identity as a geographically distant, economically self-sufficient, and politically semi-independent area. Its vigorous economic growth and population increase enriched its regional authorities and military forces; it endowed Hebei's generals and later warlords with immense confidence and strength in terms of resisting or even challenging state rule. This sense of superiority and political semi-autonomy eventually led to the An Lushan Rebellion in 755.[39]

This rebellion, which nearly tore the Tang empire apart, was initiated by non-Han generals like An Lushan 安祿山 and Shi Siming 史思明 from northern Hebei. It then exploded into a multiplicity of regional warlords and political factions throughout China, who fought with each other and grabbed as much land and population as possible to enlarge their domains. Among them, Hebei warlords were particularly powerful and arrogant. While most other regional powers formed checks and balances in military, civil, or economic terms and helped preserve the central authority of the Tang, Hebei warlords kept full control of their territories and often threatened the stability of the imperial rule. They rejected any intervention from the central authority, demanded honor and gifts from the state, monopolized wealth in their areas, refused to contribute taxes to the central government, summarily expanded their own militaries, and invaded their neighbors and annexed land without heeding the opinion of the central government.[40] Hebei's extraordinary military strength and unbridled ambition to supersede the state were analyzed by the late-Tang poet official, Du Mu 杜牧. The land of north China centering Hebei was something that "A king cannot be a king without owning it; a hegemon cannot be a hegemon without owing it. A cunning thief who wins this land is able to disturb everything under Heaven."[41]

The resurgence of Hebei's military tradition was reinforced by this region's ethnic hybridity and mixed social and cultural practices, which

[38] Based on Liang (1980: 86, 114).
[39] Shi (1991: 191) and Pulleyblank (1955).
[40] Twitchett (1965: 211–232; 1976) and Tackett (2014: 149–154).
[41] "Zuiyan [On My Crime]," *Fanchuan wenji*, 5:87.

continued to produce the kind of "cunning thief" that pro-state, non-Hebei native like Du Mu complained about. The cosmopolitan empire of the Tang drew non-Han ethnics from Inner Asia and North Asia, some conducting trade with the Han Chinese while many settling down in north China to become farmers or join the Tang's armies. For centuries, Hebei, like other north China regions like Shanxi and Shaanxi, hosted a highly mixed population: Han, Sogdian (like An Lushan and his fellow soldiers who originated from central Asia), Bohai (from the modern China–Korea border), and Khitan co-inhabited and intermarried here. Being Han was not necessarily superior in either ethnic or cultural terms; instead, being non-Han sometimes suggested better physical conditions and higher military capacities, which were welcomed and respected in a time of constant war. One's personal worth was considered to be more valuable than ethnic or family background. Social relations were formed in a variety of ways. To trace blood kinships and lineages to common ancestors – a practice that organized the Chinese Confucian society – was just one way. Under the influence of non-Han and especially nomadic practices, sworn brotherhoods and loosely formed social-professional alliances became prominent. This was particularly true within the military, in which the ratio of non-Han was higher than in the civilian population. In armies, due partly to nomadic influence and partly to high mortality, the practice of adoption was popular. People of superior social and political status adopted orphans or inferiors as their children, regardless of their ethnic backgrounds. An adopted son was generally given the same opportunities as his foster siblings and, if he proved himself talented and capable (often in the martial sense), he might make an equal claim to the adoptive father's inheritance, including his political and military power.

In addition to speaking Han Chinese as a common language, it was not unusual for the Hebei people to communicate in other languages, either in the market places or in armies. The average literacy level was low, and the Hebei men in this period were not known for scholarship or literary sophistication, unlike the more educated population in central and south China. A good example is Zhao Pu 趙普 (922–992), a native of Hebei who became a chief advisor to the founding emperors of the Northern Song Dynasty and served as their Grand Councilor for several decades. Although he helped the emperors to establish the state and guided them in nearly every significant political decision, Zhao was said to have gathered his intelligence from merely half a volume of Confucius's *The Analects*. This anecdote might be an exaggeration or a fabrication by political rivals to blemish Zhao's reputation. Nevertheless, it suggests that during the turbulent tenth century, a culture based on the standards of Han Chinese Confucian teachings might not be what the Hebei men valued most. Or, even rather renowned scholars, who were certainly the minority in Hebei, such as Liu Kai 柳開, were best known for their northerner's blunt temperament and martial spirit, very different from refined, delicate southern scholars.[42] In northern Hebei, people often dressed in a nomadic "*zuoren* 左衽" fashion – that is, with the front piece of their garment folded toward the left side of the body – even if they happened to be ethnically Han. Some shaved their hair in various nomadic styles. Practicing martial arts and learning horse riding and archery were a significant part of Hebei culture, which remained vibrant even throughout the eleventh century.[43]

The blurred ethnic and cultural identities of the Hebei people as well as their socio-economic and political pragmatism not only helped them survive the political turbulence, but also strengthened their military autonomy and sense of difference.[44] All this fueled north China's political chaos from the late ninth century through the tenth century. As the Tang Dynasty was replaced by several short-lived regimes, rapid rebellions, and numerous secessions in central China, Hebei warlords actively engaged in the contestation for power and contributed to the frequent dynastic successions.[45] Some of them established dynasties themselves; some served the regimes as leading generals to sustain their solid control over the Hebei military. In an era when "Those who possess mighty soldiers and strong horses will become the Son of Heaven!"[46] as the domineering, Late-Tang general An Zhongrong 安重榮 (?–942) claimed, the person

---

[42] Wu (2006: 295–344). For Hebei's distinct, isolated culture, see Tackett (2013: 251–281).

[43] Standen (2007) studies the great diversity of ethnicities and identities across the Song–Liao border in the Hebei area. However, in his study of a man traveling across China in the tenth century, Dudbridge (2013) reminds us that we should not overestimate the cultural hybridity of people in northeastern regions like Hebei; Han Chinese's cultural and ethnic identity still remained strong. We should certainly note that, while literati (scholarly officials) maintained their strong Han identity particularly in times of political, social, and cultural crises, ordinary people like peasants and soldiers might have been more practical and drawn toward social and cultural practices that could better preserve their lives in extreme hardship, such as practicing martial arts and adopting non-Han lifestyles.

[44] Mao (1990: 99–112). Such sense of difference did not only come from Hebei people's self-image, but also from the perceptions of non-Hebei people. See Tackett (2013: 255–260).

[45] For the political and military turbulence during the tenth century, see Naomi Standen and Hugh Clark in Twitchett and Smith (2009) and Lorge (2011: 38–205).

[46] *Jiu wudaishi*, 98: 3005.

who "owned" Hebei seemed to be in a good position to vie for the throne. That An was able to make such remark and contemplate the idea of arrogation was due to his status as a major commander of Hebei's military forces. His declaration echoed perfectly with Du Mu's assessment of Hebei's strategic significance in the ninth century.

Entering the tenth century, Hebei's military prominence skyrocketed especially because of its geopolitical position between the Han Chinese regimes and the Khitan's Liao Dynasty. The Khitan originated in southeastern Inner Mongolia and expanded rapidly in the late ninth century. In the early tenth century, this equestrian people had established a nomadic empire, not only dominating a great part of the Mongolian Steppe and northeastern Asia, but also pressing upon land that had traditionally belonged to China. For years, the Khitan raided the land north of the Juma River; in 937 and 947, their troops marched all the way through Hebei, crossed the Yellow River to enter Henan, and even captured several imperial capitals of different Chinese regimes. The Khitan's overwhelming military strength defeated several Chinese rulers, who were forced to give up land north to the Juma River, where sixteen military prefectures (including modern Beijing) were located, to the Khitan and fulfill its demands for wealth.

The Khitan's military superiority and, for a period, political oversight of a Chinese regime endowed the land of Hebei with a tremendous strategic significance.[47] On the one hand, Hebei suffered as the battlefield for multiple regimes, and its society, population, and economy were ruined by the prolonged period of war. On the other hand, this land became an indispensable military base and buffer zone for any Chinese regime, which had no choice but to support Hebei and reinforce its military in order for the region to serve its role against the Khitan. Hence, ironically, the socio-economic decline of Hebei went along with its strong hold on political and military power. Its regional military leaders used the Khitan as leverage to contest the central authorities in the south and negotiate to their advantage. When they felt pressure from the south or resisted being centralized by a Chinese regime, they turned to the Khitan in the north for protection. The regional forces in Hebei swung back and forth between the regimes on either side and switched their loyalties as would benefit them. To the Khitan, it made sense to help maintain a relatively

---

[47] For the Khitan's military and political interactions with the Late Tang Dynasty and the Late Jin Dynasty, see Naomi Standen in Twitchett and Smith (2009: 38–132) and Lorge (2011).

strong and autonomous Hebei. Although it was capable of launching an attack on central China, the Khitan's several attempts had proven that it could not occupy Chinese land for long, since the culture, economy, and society were too different from its own, and the resistance against foreign rule was too strong. The Khitan needed Han-Chinese agents to preserve and maximize its interests, for instance, protecting the frontier trade and the importation of Chinese goods. A semi-autonomous Hebei, not fully yielding to the Chinese regimes, served the Khitan well.

The Chinese regimes rooted in Henan, south of the Yellow River, had mixed feelings about Hebei's military power, autonomous inclination, and ambiguous relationship with the Khitan. They relied on support from the Hebei warlords, and they needed Hebei to be strong and intact to fend off Khitan invasions. It was not in these regimes' interests to see the dissolution of Hebei's military strength. Yet, when Hebei acted as a decentralizing force, it might challenge the Chinese states' rule or even assist the Khitan in a conquest of north China. These regimes could only fill up Hebei's military positions with relatives and trustworthy men, in order to ensure Hebei's loyalty and to curb its separatist tendencies. Yet, during the chaotic, opportunist Five Dynasties 五代 (907–959) period, nobody, even a brother, was trustworthy and consistently loyal. The aforementioned An Zhongrong was not the only one who expressed the desire to become an emperor. In this sense, Hebei continued to produce potential rivals to the existing regimes. This ambivalent relationship between the Chinese regimes and Hebei helped sustain Hebei's semi-autonomous status throughout the tenth century. When the Northern Song Dynasty came to power in 960, it inherited this complicated relationship with Hebei.

Before we move on to introduce the arrival of the Northern Song state, let us briefly return to the Yellow River. What was the river's position in the long history of Hebei? In a less visible, marginal way, the river contributed to the formation and sustainment of Hebei's geographical, political, and cultural singularity. It formed Hebei's southern border, provided it a geographical division, and served it as a defensive barrier. It contributed to reinforce Hebei's cultural, socio-economic, and political separation from the rest of China. Hence, it may seem shocking to modern readers that, after a thousand years of relative benignity and a marginal relationship with Hebei, the river chose this plain as its flooding victim and the geographical base of its new delta. Instead of continuing to guard Hebei and reinforce the long history of Hebei, the river crashed into the plain, transformed its environment, and contributed to the ending of Hebei's self-sufficient, autonomous tradition. Before the eleventh century, the Hebei people had carried out a vibrant social, economic, political, and cultural life, with little influence from the environmental entity of the Yellow River. They had been oblivious to the river's bad temper and violent tendencies; history had not prepared them – either materially or mentally – for a deadly attack by the river. So what brought the river's catastrophic impact upon these men and women?

This book suggests that the shift of the river's course into Hebei in 1048 was a matter of probability. The probability is not evident in the present chapter, as the river and the plain had sustained a marginal relationship for a long time. But the next three chapters will show that, as time moved on to the late tenth century when the Northern Song state started to play a prominent historical role, the probability began to rise. I shall anatomize the history of the early Northern Song to demonstrate how the land of Hebei evolved from a region of political, socio-economic, and environmental autonomy to a region highly dependent on the state, which had less and less control over its own fate. I will point out that this fall in Hebei's status made the region susceptible to environmental attacks, in particular when the state sought to channel the Yellow River's disasters to plague Hebei. In order to unravel this trialectic relationship among the river, the plain, and the state, let us first look at the rise of the imperial state of the Northern Song, as another prominent actor in the making of history. The state's need to manage Hebei and the Yellow River simultaneously, a story that will unfold over the next three chapters, eventually broke down the marginal relationship between the plain and the river and drew the two into an environmental co-inhabitance.

2

The State's Hebei Project

Compared to the Yellow River and Hebei, the Northern Song (960–1127) state came upon the scene relatively late. Yet, even as a newcomer, the state forcefully took steps to transform Hebei into a subordinate periphery and turn the Yellow River from an environmental outlaw into the state's manageable geopolitical property. The present and following two chapters explore these state desires and efforts. They question how the state's interventions in the life of a region as well as the life of a major river provided possibilities for these two entities to encounter each other and for the environmental drama to take place in 1048. The state's active interventions derived from its strong sense of anxiety about its survival in the midst of political, military, and environmental challenges. In this chapter, we shall first take a brief look at how the state's perception of the world – a geopolitical chaos it was born into – shaped the state's survivor mentality. We will then elaborate how the young state sought to secure its survival by grabbing the control of power from the hands of decentralized regional forces like Hebei, and how it strengthened its core political area on the southern side of the Yellow River by downgrading powerful regions like Hebei to a servile and dependent periphery. This chapter analyzes a multi-dimensional project the state launched to transform Hebei into a political, military, socio-economic, and even environmental periphery.

When the Northern Song state ascended the stage of history in 960, it succeeded the short-lived Five Dynasties, which altogether lasted a mere fifty-three years. The Song could not anticipate how long its rule would last, whether or not its military leaders would usurp the throne to form a new dynasty, just as its own founding emperor did to his predecessor, or whether or not it would follow the pattern of frequent dynastic secessions and become a sixth truncated dynasty. The recent history haunted the young, insecure state, imbuing it with a strong distrust of others, including the individuals who served it. Such feelings defined the state's everyday political practices: its state-building was not directed toward unrealistic dreams or fantasies of imperial glory, but rather was designed to guard its existence, to survive crisis after crisis, and to extend its rule a little longer than its predecessors.[1]

We, as modern readers who have the advantage of hindsight, know that this imperial state prospered until 1127. Thanks to Song scholarship, we praise the Song for having the most affluent economy in its contemporary world, for its relatively benevolent Confucius rule, for its sophisticated literature and arts, as well as for the high literacy level among its populace. Given its unprecedented growth in terms of its economy and technology, we feel we might legitimately entertain the idea that Song China, as early as the eleventh century, was taking a leap toward an early modern era. Yet this revolutionary transition in history seems to have sputtered out in the thirteenth century. Even given the springboard of the Song's high-level development, China failed to ascend to the next level of progress. Was this a waste, and a shame to the Song glory?[2] Such views are retrospective impositions of our modern desire, anxiety, and grievance. They are expressions of our longing to find China a noteworthy spot in a Eurocentric world history and to place it in the tide of a single lineal mode of historical progression. These concerns were certainly not what the Song state worried about in its early years. As a young, vulnerable state, it saw the world around it treacherous; each step forward was full of danger. Any success in consolidating and extending its rule would only arrive due

---

[1] See Chaffee and Twitchett's (2015: 7–9) discussion on "the pragmatic character of Sung institution building."

[2] Many Song historians endorse the Naitō hypothesis on a unique Tang–Song transition era, whose successful experience was not replicable in later periods. Two seminal works in English language are Elvin (1973) and Hartwell (1982). An increasing number of scholars have begun to challenge this view by arguing for historical continuation from the Song through the Yuan and the Ming period. They suggest that the remarkable growth during the Tang–Song transition sustained and transformed in various ways during an extended Song–Yuan–Ming transition. See Smith and von Glahn (2003). Yet, these two periods and their historiographies are not equally studied. The lack of large-scale economic, social, and demographic assessments for the thirteenth to fifteenth centuries and certainly the shortage of studies about north China make it hard to challenge the distinct status of the Tang–Song transition or to bridge the disjuncture between the Tang–Song scholarship and another rather developed field, the scholarship for late imperial China.

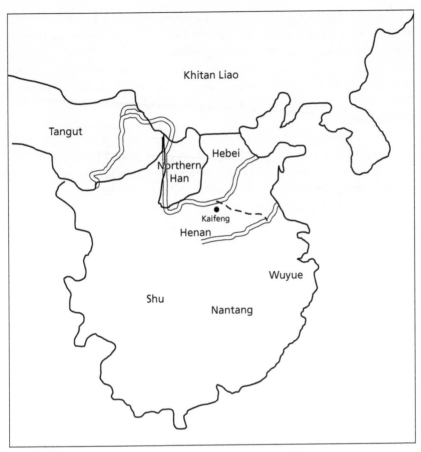

ILLUSTRATION 6. Early Song's Geopolitical Situation

to careful calculation; meanwhile, every decision carried potential risk. It was such perception of itself and its position in the world that gave the state the "tentative nature of early Sung political life."[3]

The Song began with the control of a small territory centered in Henan on the southern side of the Yellow River. During the next twenty years, this land was besieged by multiple states. To emerge triumphant in this multi-state rivalry required that the Song engage strategically in diplomacy and warfare with each of its neighbors. By 980, the Song defeated most of its enemies and had successfully reunited most of the traditionally

---

[3] Hartman in Chaffee and Twitchett (2015: 29).

Han Chinese land under its rule.[4] Despite such territorial expansion, by the turn of the millennium, the state had still failed to regain the land of northwest China. Once under the control of the Tang Dynasty, that part of China now remained distant from the Song's central authority and was occupied by some Tangut tribes. These semi-nomadic tribes established a Xixia 西夏 empire three decades later and had since become the Song's archenemy.

Forty years after its establishment, the state still experienced constant threat from its northern neighbor. Almost every year, Khitan horses carried warriors, arrows, and bows southward, overwhelming the Song's frontier troops, plundering the land of Hebei, and setting fire to human settlements. In the 980s and 990s, the Song's second emperor, Taizong 太宗 (939–997), attempted two expeditions, each crossing Hebei to approach the far northeast. He hoped to give the Khitan a decisive defeat and to regain the swath of land on the northern side of the Juma River that was considered a traditional land of the Han Chinese. That area, where modern Beijing is located, once belonged to the Tang Dynasty but was annexed by the Khitan in the early tenth century, much to the humiliation of the Han Chinese. Both military actions failed horribly, nearly costing the emperor's life and toppling his regime. The Song's military weakness in the face of the Khitan led to a large-scale invasion by the Khitan in 1004. The Khitan army swept through Hebei, flaunted its military forces in southern Hebei against the northern bank of the Yellow River, and threatened the Song with further invasion. In early 1005, the two states eventually reached a peace agreement that recognized the two states as equal sovereignties. War was subsequently replaced by state-level diplomacy and gift exchanges to the material benefit of the Khitan, who received an indemnity of 200,000 lengths of silk and 100,000 ounces of silver every year.[5]

The peace treaty did not bring a sense of eternal security. For the next 120 years, the Song state continued to see the Khitan as a greedy bully and potential terror. To make the situation worse, the rise of the Tangut as an imperial power in northwest China since the mid-1030s dragged the Song into warfare that lingered over decades. The Song's fear of these foreign enemies strengthened the state's survivor mentality. It made the state

---

[4] For the political and military history of early Song, see Twitchett and Smith (2009: 206–246) and Chaffee and Twitchett (2015: 214–249).

[5] For the Song–Liao relationship, see Rossabi (1983) and Tao (1988). For a discussion on the Song's military weakness, see Lorge (2005: 30–44).

see every problem it encountered as a kind of existential crisis. Hence, throughout its rule, particularly during its early years, the state cautiously assessed the costs and benefits of anything it engaged in, avoided risks and upheavals, eliminated any chance of potential problems, and balanced out the struggles among uneven powers.[6]

A survivor's mentality also dominated the ways in which the state dealt with domestic issues, as it encountered formidable players within its domain, such as the Yellow River and the Hebei Plain. The increasingly flood-prone Yellow River began to wreak havoc at the heart of the state's territory, seriously threatening the stability of the state from the very beginning of its rule. As we shall see in Chapters 3 and 4, the state responded to the mounting environmental pressure by going into crisis mode: it innovated peculiar hydraulic solutions that forced the river to shift northward into the Hebei Plain. The present chapter reveals how the state handled Hebei. The state inherited a heavy historical legacy that portrayed Hebei as a decentralizing force and potential traitor; this legacy haunted the state with a deep sense of fear and distrust of the region. On the one hand, it had no choice but to rely on Hebei's solidarity as a strong military buffer zone, across which Song and Liao diplomats traveled, and in which the state placed soldiers, weapons, and military supplies, as well as constructed fortresses and moats. On the other hand, the state remained suspicious of Hebei for its dubious loyalty to the central authority. This land, given its long-term political, military, and socio-economic autonomy, became a hotbed of spies who leaked security information to the Khitan, smugglers who sold strategic goods like iron and copper coin abroad, and outlaws that the Song's military could easily turn into if they became disenchanted with the court.

For the Song state, the question became how to subdue this wild land and curb its military traditions and political ambitions. More than that, it was also about how to appropriate Hebei into something beneficial and resourceful – as a submissive periphery of the empire and a loyal servant of the state, who would quietly guard the heart of the regime from a northeastern periphery. As the ensuing pages demonstrate, during the first eight decades of the Song period, the state carried out what I call a Hebei project, which appropriated control over life on the Hebei Plain in political, military, and socio-economic terms, and even modified the physical appearance of the land.

[6] For the early Song state's survivor's mentality and the political culture of excessive caution, see Deng (2006).

2.1   Establishing a Military Entity in Demilitarized Hebei

Throughout the Northern Song period, Hebei stood at the forefront of the Song's resistance against the Khitan's Liao Dynasty. Hence, it remained the most heavily militarized region in the empire. Between 960 and early 1004, the two states engaged in many military actions against each other, most of which took place in Hebei. In 1004, within a matter of days, a Khitan army stormed through Hebei all the way to its southern border, the Yellow River. The loss of Hebei terrified the Song imperial court, which, located a mere hundred kilometers south of the Yellow River, could be reached by Khitan cavalry within a day or two. Emperor Zhenzong 真宗 (968–1022) was compelled to journey northward across the Yellow River and entered the soon to be captured southern land of Hebei. This gesture of determination, as demonstrated by setting royal feet on Hebei's soil, if only on its southern tip, bore enormous symbolic meaning. It strengthened the Song's claims over the land and its hold over the entire empire.

The traumatic experience of wars and their associations with Hebei reinforced the Song state's conviction that without Hebei's solidarity, there would be no Song state. The state had to protect and strengthen Hebei's land and people in order for them to function in return as an effective military entity to defend the state. Hence, from the very beginning of its encounters with Hebei, the state showed a strong presence in the region. It invested heavily in shaping Hebei's land, people, and society in accordance with its political and military priorities. In northern Hebei, it constructed a series of walled cities as military garrisons along the southern bank of the Juma River.[7] These cities were surrounded by military settlements run by battle troops – the Imperial Armies. The cities were interconnected by express roads and waterways. During any kind of emergency, troops and military resources could move from one place to another in accordance with need. Hence, the northernmost strip of Hebei, called the "immediate frontier" (*yanbian* 沿邊 or *yuanbian* 緣邊), as vast as it was, could function as a single entity during any military action.[8]

South of the frontier area, the rest of Hebei was divided into a "secondary frontier area" (*cibian* 次邊) in central Hebei and "interior prefectures and commanderies" (*jinli zhoujun* 近里州軍) in southern Hebei, depending on their strategic importance. The administrative districts in

---

[7] *SHY*, "Fangyu," 8: 2a–b and 8: 2b. See Cheng Long's (2012) studies on Hebei's military and strategic geography.

[8] *XCBSB*, 3xia: 141.

ILLUSTRATION 7. Hebei's Administrative Districts in the Early Song Period

the secondary frontier area supplemented the first frontier area and coordinated the distribution of military supplies. The districts in the interior, southern part of Hebei were the region's political and economic bases. Enjoying a relatively larger civilian population, this area engaged in agriculture and produced a considerable portion of basic goods that Hebei's military and civil administration demanded.

This three-tiered strategic system was loosely defined. Extant historical records do not specify which prefectures or commanderies each tier possessed, nor how the districts of the three tiers corresponded to and coordinated with each other in actuality. There is no record of the day-to-day operation of the system. We do know that the placement of the troops was spread throughout various parts of Hebei, rather than being concentrated in specific places along the frontier. A considerable portion of the troops was stationed in more southern districts where access to water transportation and food was convenient.[9] This arrangement made possible a multilayered defense system with an efficient backup for areas on the frontlines of battle. It also reduced the government's need to transport all its military supplies over long distances to the northern frontier. A large amount of supplies could be collected from local areas and stored in nearby prefectures, thus reducing the risk that all supplies could be destroyed at the same time in a war or a natural disaster. When a food shortage occurred in one area of Hebei, troops could be mobilized to access food in another area.[10]

Hebei's military forces kept growing over the decades. After peace returned in 1005, Hebei's military no longer engaged in war. Despite this, by the early 1040s it had acquired an army that included 477,000 men for the Imperial Armies, the District Armies, and various militias.[11] This number continued to grow in the late 1060s, when a reformist government supported policies for "strengthening the military." The heavy military presence served the purpose of intimidating the Khitan and suppressing their ambitions for another invasion. In reality, it might have mainly served the function of assuaging the Song state's sense of insecurity.

The massive military population and the geographic division of their administrative centers was a great drain on military supplies. As we shall discuss later in this chapter, Hebei's civilian population growth and its economy were too slow to meet the soaring demands of its military. In the late eleventh century, Hebei's military demanded six million *dan* (1 *dan* 石 ≈ 67 liters) of grain and other kinds of supplies every year, most of which had to be shipped from southern and central China. To guarantee such external supplies, the state began to build up Hebei's transportation infrastructure as a means of obtaining goods and supplying the military. In particular, the state exploited existing waterways like the Yuhe Canal,

[9] For spatial deployment of Hebei's military, see Cheng (2012: 60–77).
[10] *XCB*, 49:1072 and 166: 3997.
[11] Ouyang Xiu, "Lun Hebei caichan shang shixiang shu [Letter to Chancellors on Hebei's wealth]," *OYXQJ*, 118: 1825–1828. For more about Song's military system, see Wang (1983), Cheng (2012: 60–77), and Wang Tzeng-yu and David Wright in Chaffee and Twitchett (2015: 214–249).

previously the Yongji Canal.[12] Essential to Hebei's economic boom before
the ninth century but declining substantially during the ninth and tenth
centuries due to north China's political chaos and civil war, the canal
was revived in the late tenth century. Running from Hebei's southwestern corner to its northeastern end, with the exception of the frozen winter
months, this canal provided efficient transport to integrate Hebei's military and civil units and to facilitate the exchange of goods between them.
Its northern terminus was linked with frontier and local streams. These
interconnected bodies of water carried boats westward to frontier trading sites in Bazhou 霸州 and Xiongzhou 雄州, and then farther west to
Dingzhou 定州, the region that produced the most precious porcelain
and silk in the Song empire. The canal's southern end crossed the Yellow
River to connect with the Bianhe 汴河 Canal, an economic artery during the Song period. This connection allowed endless shipments of grain
and other bulky goods from the lower Yangtze valley, the breadbasket of
southeast China, to the center of military consumption, Hebei. As Hebei's
military population continued to rise, the role of the southern goods as
military supplies became increasingly crucial. The availability of the Yuhe
Canal itself and its interconnection with other waterways significantly
shortened the distance between Hebei and other parts of Song China. It
helped Hebei to overcome its socio-economic shortage and to maintain
the existence and operation of this frontier land's military system.

In areas around the Yuhe Canal, the state endeavored to modify
the land in order to construct a vast network of supporting transportation infrastructure. Highways were laid down, small canals were
opened, tunnels were constructed, and a series of ponds and ditches were
dredged.[13] Some of this infrastructure was meant to facilitate transportation throughout the frontier provinces; some were erected as manmade
barriers to defend the low-lying plain against the advancement of future
enemies. As will be examined in greater detail shortly, this drastic transformation of Hebei's physical landscape for military purposes, which
led to various economic and environmental implications over the next

---

[12] Zou (1993: 153–157).

[13] For example, in 1002, the Nan and Shuiwen rivers in Zhenzhou prefecture were diverted
southeastward into Zhaozhou prefecture. In 1004, the water of the Tang River was
diverted over a length of 33 *li* to the prefectural seat of Dingzhou, and through a 62-*li*-
long newly dug canal it was connected with the Sha River; the entire flow ran through the
Bianwu Pond and eventually converged with the Juma River. In this way, a water system
supporting an uninterrupted transport route came into shape across frontier prefectures.
XCB, 21: 483; 22: 489; 56: 1228.

century, should be considered a significant component of the state's political and military appropriation of Hebei.

As waterways and roads penetrated the three tiers of the strategic system, weaving every inch of the land into an integral military geography, the state added a lofty layer of governing, supervising, and mediating institutions, such as the Fiscal Commission and the Pacification Commission. These provincial-level institutions were not grounded in Hebei's regional or local bureaucratic structure. The commissioners were appointed by the imperial court; they stayed in Hebei for just a few years and rarely had a chance to become invested in local business. These institutions and officials stood between the central government and Hebei's local authorities to facilitate their vertical communication. Horizontally, they bridged the division between Hebei's military authorities and civil governments, as well as managed interregional exchanges of resources in and out of Hebei. They played essential roles in synchronizing the operation of the entire military hierarchy, from the state-level leadership, to Hebei's commanders, and to ground-level military execution. They certainly organized and oversaw the lateral collaboration of many districts throughout Hebei.

Given this multilayered strategic system, the giant military population, the multiple means of transportation, and the supervising and mediating institutions, the imperial state had established within Hebei a complex, integrated military entity. This fairly thorough militarization of Hebei, however, brought its own risks. Given the autonomous tradition in the region, which we have seen in Chapter 1, how could the imperial state prevent a militarized Hebei from falling back into a self-reliant, independent, and (worse still) anti-state situation? The state had to work equally hard to contain Hebei's decentralizing potentials. To do so, the state employed two main strategies: first, it put Hebei's military power under the direct control of the central government; and second, it demilitarized Hebei socially and culturally by promoting a civil culture.[14]

First and foremost, the effectiveness of Hebei's military entity, as the state anticipated, was embedded within an empire-wide system of resource collection and distribution. Hebei's military force was so massive that its own land and people could not generate enough agricultural

---

[14] Chikusa (2006) closely studies the first two emperors of the Northern Song in terms of their backgrounds, personalities, and military and civil governance. Chen (2010) examines the formation of the political philosophy in the early Song government, which pursued the centralization of the state's military power. Also see Hartman's chapter on Song politics in Chaffee and Twitchett (2015: 19–138).

production to sustain it. The days when a warlord could resist state rule by amassing a few thousand men and dominating the wealth of several counties were over. Hebei had to depend heavily on the importation of food, clothes, and cash from the rest of China. Such interregional transactions could hardly be done without the organization and coordination of state-level institutions. Maintaining the extensive transportation infrastructure was itself expensive; it had to rely on the state's organization and investments. In terms of other kinds of military resources, Hebei civilians were prohibited from large gatherings and from storing weapons; they were discouraged from practicing martial arts and playing with knives and swords. Iron mining and smelting had long been an important industry in western Hebei; it produced the weaponry that had strengthened Hebei's warlords in previous centuries and continued to equip the Song's frontier troops. Now, the state put iron production and circulation under the state's control, allowing only a small amount of iron to flow into the civilian society for use in agricultural tools.[15] Whenever farmers slaughtered cattle, or fishermen harvested fish, they had to turn over to the government the resulting tendons and fish bladders, since these materials could be used to produce strings for bows and glue for weapons.[16] Any resource that could be employed for military uses fell under the state control. Such state control prevented Hebei's military entity from becoming self-sufficient. In this sense, Hebei's troops and military infrastructure become only some components in the overall military apparatus of the imperial state.[17]

Hebei's dependence on the state was also reinforced by the state's insistence on a single military leadership. The central government oversaw Hebei's day-to-day military operations, with the emperor himself and his top officials – Grand Councilors and the Bureau of Military Affairs – as the final decision makers. They designed the plans for how Hebei's military forces should act in any critical circumstance, and they wielded the final power to decide how to allocate Hebei's troops and mobilize other resources. The Song emperors, though many of them did not have actual battle experience, were known for their personal intervention in military affairs that went on hundred kilometers away on the frontier.

[15] For iron production, circulation, and consumption in the Song period, see Wang Lingling (2005).

[16] *QSW*, 694: 2–3.

[17] For more of Song's military history, see Wang (1983) and Wang and David Wright in Chaffee and Twitchett (2015: 214–249).

They prescribed military commanders with secret strategies before the latter departed for war; they did not hesitate to send generals letters in the middle of battle, interrupting their existing plans and instructing them in new tactics. That the emperors tended to act as helicopter commanders was not to the benefit of the Song military, and it may have in fact contributed to the Song's constant military failures. Nevertheless, the virtue of such state intervention was that it allowed the central government a solid control over its frontier forces.

The state increased its control via subtle means as well. Emperor Taizu 太祖 (927–976), founder of the Song Dynasty, persuaded his prominent generals into early retirement and placed talented young leaders of lesser backgrounds in important positions. The military commanders in this new era neither resided in one region over the long term – certainly not in their hometowns – nor were given permanent charge over a certain set of troops, which was different from what Hebei's regional warlords did in the past. Rather, a general was assigned by the state to lead a set of troops for a specific military task. Soon after the task was completed, the commander was sent by the court to another place to take up another position and another task. This arrangement of personnel resulted in a situation in which "commanders know nothing about the soldiers and soldiers recognize no commanders."[18] The commanders were unable to develop personal armies as warlords did in the previous centuries.

Similar changes were made to the lives of soldiers. In previous centuries, the armies relied on local volunteer soldiers, who carried their own equipments and acquired supplies from their families. Their devotion and loyalty rose from their attachment to their people and land; they fought for their own local interests, not for a remote central government. Their sense of the existence of an imperial state was rather weak. These troops gave rise to Hebei's powerful warlords, who were deeply rooted in regional identities and interests. To reverse the situation, the Song state recruited professional soldiers, at least for the Imperial Armies, who came from different parts of north China and were sent to remote garrisons such as in Hebei. Treating their roles as mere jobs, these men earned monthly salaries from the government and were well aware of their employment relationship with the state in the name of an emperor, instead of with individual commanders. Their promotion and demotion were determined by a single set of rules that the state regulated, instead of by their personal

---

[18] For a detailed analysis of the military policies in the early Song, see Lau Nap-yin and Huang K'uan-chung in Twitchett and Smith (2009: 215–220).

ties with commanders. More importantly, the troops' maintenance in terms of various supplies came from state revenues and was centrally planned, arranged, and distributed. The dissociation between a soldier's personal career and the well-being of his family and hometown led to the rise of professional armies, whose loyalty was oriented more to the state than to the region of Hebei. With these measures, the state managed to break down family and regional ties as well as personal affections that had perpetuated Hebei's military autonomy for many centuries. The true military power fell firmly in the hands of the state.

The second strategy to curb Hebei's decentralizing potential was that, along with centralizing military power, the state was dedicated to promoting civil governance and civil culture in order to demilitarize Hebei's local governments and society.[19] The first two emperors, although accomplished generals, were keen to promote their image as learned scholars. They demonstrated their passion and knowledge about books and calligraphy; they urged their generals to learn reading and writing, sometimes by publicly shaming them for being illiterate. The first four decades of the Song period saw a rapid shift in cultural preferences in the government as well as in the broader society. More and more scholars, who discussed war rather than personally participated in war, entered the government. The government's tendency of "emphasizing the civil and repressing the martial (zhongwen qingwu 重文輕武)" encouraged more and more people to acquire high social status, fame, and wealth by assuming civil official positions. The social and political status of military officers continued to decrease. Over time, people who wished to serve in the government began to prefer the civil track to the military track.[20]

This political and cultural shift had a profound influence on Hebei's political life and society. Each of Hebei's jurisdictions was now governed by a civil bureaucratic team and a parallel military organization. Even in the most militarized districts in northern Hebei, civil officials were in place to assist or oversee military commanders. In the 1040s when military tensions soared between the Song and the Liao, the state went a step further to replace Hebei's top-level military commanders with civil officials, who were viewed by the contemporary as "Confucian marshals

---

[19] For the rising prominence of scholarly officials in the Song government and their dependence on the state rather than on their own power bases, see Liu (1962: 137–152) and Bol (1992: 148–175).

[20] See Wang (1983), Deng (2006), and Hartman in Chaffee and Twitchett (2015: 29). For the social composition of the Song bureaucracy and the increasing significance of the examination system in bureaucratic recruitment, see Chaffee (1995: 49–65).

(*rushuai* 儒帥)."[21] In theory, the military and civil leaderships had separate duties that did not overlap on a daily basis. Military commanders had no right to inquire about civilian affairs or revenue collection; equally, civil officials could not access military forces residing within their own districts. This division of responsibilities prevented the concentration of power in individual hands and the emergence of political allies at a local and regional level.

Since Hebei produced only a small number of scholars in the early years of the Song, a large portion of its civil officials came from elsewhere. After peace returned to Hebei in 1005, its people began to settle down and engage in various economic activities to rebuild some kind of civilian livelihood. The preference in the tenth century to train oneself as an independent-minded, self-profiting warrior to join an army gave way to a preference for educating oneself to become a thoughtful person who embraced Confucian values and served his government with political sophistication and morality. Mastery of horseback riding and archery became a less attractive approach than the demonstration of profound civil knowledge to climb the social ladder. More and more young men devoted themselves to reading and writing and considered participation in the civil service examination a more viable career path. Across the empire, an increasing number of southern scholars moved northward; they acquired official positions and served in northern regions like Hebei. As a result, there emerged a new civil, educated population, which began to fill official positions inside Hebei, as across the empire. This new population challenged Hebei's old military establishment: it not only changed the existing power dynamics and political landscape inside Hebei, but also inspired a fashion of civil culture that gradually dissolved Hebei's martial tradition.

The increasing number of scholars entering the government quickly expanded and diversified Hebei's civil bureaucratic system. In response, official positions mushroomed. Each official claimed authority over a small section of governance and asserted checks-and-balances over each other. By the late 1030s, officials and clerks in the Song government had developed into a rather redundant population, who functioned inefficiently and exhausted government resources. Yet, in the early years of the state's rule, the swelling bureaucracy was "intentionally made redundant and inefficient."[22] The fragmentation of duties and the intricate network of political strengths prevented any accumulation of power outside of the

---

[21] *QSW*, 2227: 535.
[22] Mostern (2011: 121).

central government. In Hebei in particular, the excessive civil bureaucracy counterbalanced the continuously expanding military and competed with the latter for control over the population and resources.

As the consequence of the state's military and political appropriation, Hebei underwent two seemingly opposite trends: the expansion of a gigantic, multilayered, hierarchical military entity; and the demilitarization of Hebei's civil society and governing body. These seemingly contradictory trends worked in concert with each other to help transform the region and its people from a warlike, autonomy-seeking political force into a periphery that was subordinate to and served the imperial state.

2.2 Building Tunnels and Digging Ponds in the Northern Land[23]

The state's efforts to turn Hebei into a centrally controlled military entity also involved an environmental aspect, through modifying the physical characteristics of the land. During the Northern Song period, individuals, farming communities, local officials, and military organizations actively changed the conditions of the land throughout China by clearing woods, cultivating arable fields, building irrigation facilities, constructing dams, and setting up military colonies and garrisons. Yet, very few projects were like the one carried out inside Hebei, which came from the direct interventions of the state, well-defined strategic purposes, and multi-dimensional approaches.[24] In Hebei, the state deliberately changed the form and composition of the land and water in order to create a landscape that better suited its military and strategic needs.

---

[23] Part of this section having to do with ponds appears in an article in *The Medieval History Journal*, see Zhang (2011: 21–43).

[24] To compare the state's management of Hebei with that of other regions, readers may refer to the existing scholarship about the Song's spatial expansion toward south China, such as Shiba Yoshinobu's works on the lower Yangze delta, Robert Marks on the Pearl delta, and Richard von Glahn and Paul J. Smith on Sichuan. These studies show that, for various southern regions, the state followed the mass migration of population, collaborated with local powers and played supervisional roles instead of military dominance and multi-dimensional managerial roles as it did for Hebei. Indeed, the state maintained tight military control over other northern frontier regions like Shaanxi and Shanxi, where the Song shared borders with the Liao and the Xiaxia and where most military conflicts between these states took place. But these regions remain understudied; the limited scholarship focuses on the state's military and diplomatic handling of the non-Chinese states. We know very little about what these regions (their environments and human societies) went through. Due to the scarcity of historical sources and scholarship about these northern regions, we may suspect that the kind of multi-dimensional (military, strategic, political, environmental, and economic) appropriations the state conducted in Hebei was unique and incomparable.

One such project, carried out in relative secrecy, was the construction of a series of underground tunnels in northern Hebei. Discovered by archaeologists in present-day Yongqing 永清, Ba 霸, and Xiong 雄 counties, the tunnels spread through the strategic zone along the Song–Liao border, adjacent to or directly under Song garrisons.[25] None of the existing historical records mention them, but uncovered artifacts indicate that they were built during the Northern Song period, most likely in the late tenth and early eleventh centuries when the Song and the Liao were still at war. Since the archaeological digs were conducted sporadically, the overall size of the tunnels remains unknown. Judging from what has been discovered, I suspect that the tunnels stretched widely across the frontier area. In Yongqing County alone, the tunnels were found to cover an area of more than 300 square kilometers.

Many of these tunnels are of identical shape and size. They were built with the same techniques and used the same construction materials – a kind of dark earthen bricks. Furthermore, they were built to such good quality that it seems the construction was carefully designed and carried out over a relatively long time, and that the same design was simultaneously used in different places. This suggests that at least the majority of the tunnels were built via collective efforts, which were organized and funded by people who could employ sophisticated engineers and could maneuver large numbers of workers to undertake construction in various places simultaneously. Given that northern Hebei was a war zone in the early Song period, where the population was sparse, poor, and unstable, we can speculate with a large degree of certainty that these tunnels were government projects and that they were built for military purposes. The lack of both private and governmental records indicates the covert nature of the project. Unlike aboveground strategic infrastructure, the tunnels could remain secret in order to avoid attention and attack from the Khitan. As such, they were the perfect defense system for the Song state.

While the tunnels remained invisible, another state project was carried out in a more forceful, visible way and brought about drastic changes to Hebei's physical landscape. As we discussed earlier, the revival of the Yuhe Canal and its connections with Hebei's local streams created a vast network of water transportation. These efforts resulted in a massive body of standing water, which by itself could serve as a barrier to halt the advancement of the Khitan armies. To a flat lowland like the Hebei

---

[25] These underground tunnels, named as "*zhandao* (戰道, lit., battle paths)" by modern scholars, are unseen in any Song documents. For more studies, see Wang (1991: 332–334) and Liu (2000: 27–42).

Plain that lacked natural barriers of strategic values, the emergence of this watery landscape attracted the attention of military commanders in Hebei's frontier, who decided to appropriate these waters for strategic uses. As a result, a series of ponds and ditches over a length of several hundred kilometers came into being to cover two-thirds of Hebei's border.

Late tenth-century Hebei saw an unusual amount of rain, and the local rivers overflowed from time to time, waterlogging the land. In the meantime, the local rivers were occasionally used strategically by military leaders. In 923 and 1001, some troops broke through the banks of the Hutuo 滹沱 and Bao 鮑 rivers to induce floods to halt the advancement of their enemies.[26] These actions changed the rivers' natural waterways and led to flooding disasters. The unbridled waters flowed freely across the land, sometimes infiltrating local lakes and swamps and causing them to expand. At the turn of the eleventh century, a substantial part of northern Hebei was immersed in stagnant water. Near Xiongzhou 雄州, a major frontier garrison, the waterlogged territory stretched "endlessly."[27] Assuming that the swampy landscape would be difficult for Khitan armies and their horses to cross and that nomadic Khitans were unfamiliar with sailing, Hebei's commanders decided to create a defensive system out of the waters. Their idea was to stabilize the naturally produced swampy landscape and prevent it from disappearing, and meanwhile to enlarge its area and reshape its form in order to meet strategic needs.

He Chengju 何承矩 was the forerunner in the experiments with pond construction. When He first arrived in northern Cangzhou 滄州 as a Military Colony Commissioner in 993, he noted that "the rivers have risen and overflowed due to rain and waterlogging in Hebei in recent years. They have destroyed cities, settlements, and buildings. [Water] has accumulated here and there, generating ponds and obstructing agricultural production."[28] He tried to channel the excessive water to expand existing swamps. In his original idea, the ponds so produced would provide stable irrigation and allow his troops to carry out paddy rice cultivation around the ponds. Although their economic outcome remained questionable, the paddy fields themselves might serve as strategic obstacles to "restrain the [Khitan] cavalry."[29]

---

[26] *Jiu wudaishi*, 29: 401, and *XCB*, 50: 1102.

[27] *XCB*, 34: 756 and 51: 1111.

[28] *XCB*, 34: 747.

[29] *SS*, 279: 9478. See Lorge's (2008: 59–74) discussion on the military, strategic significance of the ponds. But we must be aware that such significance was an assumption of Hebei's military commanders, not a tested result based on any wartime situation. Historical

Over the next two decades, officials and military officers in northern Hebei followed He's practices and continued to develop ponds and ditches. They took various steps to search for water resources: from the east they diverted seawater to infuse the ponds; from the west, they routed water from the rivers and springs that originated in the mountains in western Hebei.[30] With water arriving from all directions, the commanders had laborers dig ponds to contain it. To protect these manmade ponds, they ordered dykes to be erected around the ponds, upon which plants like willows, Chinese mulberry, and hemp were planted to anchor the soil and to consolidate the dykes' foundations.[31]

As the ponds spread and water resources appeared abundant, Hebei's military commanders encouraged their soldiers to carry out agricultural activities suitable for this special watery landscape. Soldiers at the Jingrong 靜戎, Shun'an 順安, and Weilu 威虜 commanderies built "square fields" (fangtian 方田) around the ponds. Approximately 1.56 meters wide and long, and 2.18 meters deep, these small plots produced a small amount of grain and vegetables.[32] In Xiongzhou, soldiers turned a considerable amount of land into vegetable gardens. They dug wells and ditches, shaped deep plots and ridges, set up fences, and planted hedgerows of shrubs and bushes around the gardens.[33] The ponds provided these fields with a convenient source of irrigation.

Observing all the initial efforts made at the local level, the imperial state soon recognized the strategic significance of the ponds and stepped in to patronize the pond construction and maintenance. In 1014, it authorized Hebei's Pacification Commission to establish regulations for dredging the ponds and mapping the dykes. Regulations like the "Code on illegally breaching dykes" made it illegal for people to damage any infrastructure associated with the ponds.[34] Hebei's Commission of Military Colonies, which used to manage agricultural production only, assumed responsibility for overseeing the execution of the regulations. In addition, techniques were invented to monitor physical changes in the ponds. For instance, water loss was a common occurrence, especially in dry years when the Hebei Plain suffered from rapid evaporation. The "water ruler"

geographer Cheng (2012: 34–53) provides an in-depth discussion on the transformation of natural geography around these ponds.

[30] SHY, "Shihuo," 17: 2b and 3a. SS, 279: 9478. XCB, 122: 2887.
[31] XCB, 82: 1880.
[32] XCB, 55: 1214 and 56: 1234.
[33] XCB, 93: 2151; 65: 1455; 55: 1214; 65: 1455; and 93: 2151.
[34] XCB, 117: 2761.

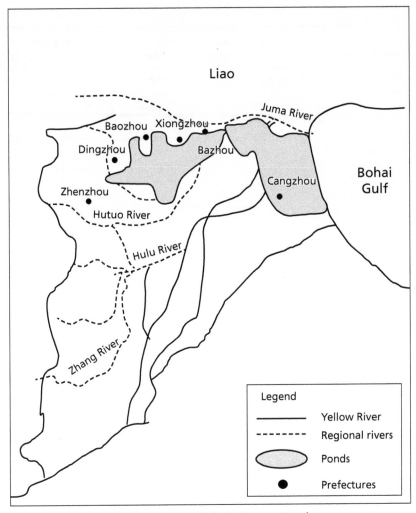

ILLUSTRATION 8. Hebei's Frontier Ponds

(*shuize* 水則), a wooden pole with measurement marks, was installed in a pond to indicate any increase or decrease in its water level. Reports of the ponds' conditions were officially filed and presented to the central government periodically. Clearly, the state had fully claimed the frontier ponds as its property and established a system of management for them.

By the 1030s, Hebei's northern frontier saw the formation of an interconnected system of ponds and ditches (Illustration 8). According to the *Standard History of the Song*, its entire length was 527 *li* (roughly

TABLE 1. *The Size of Hebei's Frontier Ponds in the 1030s[a]*

From East to West	Length (*li*) 1 *li* ≈ 530 m	Width (*li*)	Depth (*chi*) 1 *chi* ≈ 31.2 cm
First water body	120	90–130	5
Second water body	120	30–50	6–10
Third water body	70	50–60	6–7
Fourth water body	27	8	6
Fifth water body	60	15–25	8–9
Sixth water body	70	30–40	6–10
Seventh water body	30	150	10–13
Eighth water body	20	10	3–5
Ninth water body	10	10	3–5

[a] XCB, 112: 2607–2609

260 km), stretching from the coastal area in the east to western areas like Baozhou 保州. Its surface width from north to south ranged between 4 and 70 km, with a mean width of 53 km. Some ponds were deeper than others, but in general they stood at a mean depth of about 2 meters. In order to administrate and maintain these ponds efficiently, the government divided the entire system into nine sections, each designated a "water body" (*shui* 水). Each "water body" was managed by the nearest military administration (see Table 1).

With the underground tunnels and aboveground ponds and many other works, the state modified the land of Hebei to produce some unusual environmental traits that they hoped in wartime might confuse, hinder, or halt the enemy. Functioning in concert with Hebei's transportation system, military personnel, and strategic administrative system, these environmental traits created a multi-dimensional, fluid military landscape within Hebei for the state's military to advance, retreat, or conceal themselves; they provided means for various military components to navigate toward and communicate with each other.

Clearly, before the Yellow River shifted its course in 1048 to drastically change Hebei's physical landscape, the Song state had already acted as a significant environmental force to reshape the land of Hebei. With its interventions in the regional environment, the imperial state transformed the land from an enclosed, singular geographical entity into a military-oriented, state-serving strategic infrastructure. The state established its firm presence inside Hebei. Hebei was no longer its own separate geographical entity, because much of its physical environment had been co-opted into the state's gigantic military apparatus and become the state's strategic property.

2.3 Restoring an Agricultural Economy

The state's emphasis on Hebei's strategic significance also motivated it to pacify the war-ravaged, easily agitated Hebei people, in order to prevent this frontier population from developing any kind of anti-state sentiment or activities. To bring stability back to the people and the society, the state did more than just advocate for the civil culture that I introduced earlier in this chapter. It endeavored to return the people to a land-bound, sedentary livelihood. Helping Hebei restore a basic agricultural economy and granting its people a basic level of economic self-sufficiency was another major agenda in the state's Hebei project.

In the previous two centuries, Hebei had been deeply harmed by civil war; its economy was exhausted by regional warlords and their relentless military actions. The first four or five decades of the Song period were equally chaotic. Military control and battles seesawed between the Song and the Khitan, severely damaging the land and its people. Food shortage was common, and the prices for grain were sometimes so high that commoners were driven to eat wild plants.[35] The only good harvest at the turn of the century was the autumn crop (mainly millet and soybean) in 1003 in southern Hebei.[36] This single harvest, however, could not relieve the shortage of food. So when the Khitan provoked war and marched into Hebei in 1004, the Song state confronted not only a fierce enemy but also the hunger of its own weak army. During those decades Hebei's mortality rate remained high.[37] A great number of the male population died on the battlefield. Many others fled their homes to migrate to southern parts of China or wandered across Hebei's devastated earth to eke out a minimal livelihood. Many turned into outlaws, engaging in banditry and plundering already impoverished villages and towns. Hebei, like other regions in north China during the tenth century, saw numerous houses and villages burned to ashes, countless corpses rotting in the open air, and field after field of arable land teeming with wild grasses.

By the time the Song state set its feet on this land, Hebei was no longer an affluent region with a dense civilian population, as it was in the

[35] XCB, 50: 1102 and 51: 1111.
[36] XCB, 55: 1212.
[37] See Tian Xi's memorial, XCB, 51: 1113.

mid-Tang period. A demographically and economically impoverished Hebei certainly impeded the state's efforts to establish and sustain a powerful military entity there. Without the society to supply enough manpower to the armies, and without the land to produce adequate food and other materials for the soldiers, the carefully designed military system discussed earlier could not have been rooted firmly in Hebei, but would have had to rely excessively on the importation of resources from elsewhere. Such reliance would have made Hebei vulnerable to any change to external conditions and have exhausted the state as its supplier.

To rebuild Hebei, the state put forth a package of economic incentives to help resettle the vagrant population as soon as peace returned in 1005. It released a considerable number of Hebei soldiers from their duties and sent them back home to become farmers.[38] The government distributed famine relief to help them cope with the post-war damage.[39] For those who took up plows to turn wild land into fields, the government granted them exemptions of tax and corvée services for three years, so they could focus exclusively on tending the fields.[40] Realizing that Hebei was full of fallow land, the government encouraged landless people in other provinces to move to Hebei.[41] The policies were so favorable that some famine refugees in the Liao Dynasty secretly crossed the border and settled down in Hebei. The government opened the door to various kinds of people and helped them acquire land.[42]

A large number of the settlers – retired soldiers or sometimes ethnic Khitan – knew little about agricultural production. The government sought advice from experienced farmers and collected and printed agricultural treatises for distribution around Hebei. Hebei's regional officials were charged with the duty to educate those in their jurisdictions about farming practices. The new settlers arrived in Hebei without the basic resources and capital to start a new livelihood, and local governments had very little to offer to them. The state took various measures to supply the settlers with whatever an agrarian subsistence lifestyle required. For instance, the government permitted people to travel out of Hebei to purchase crop seeds without any transit tax.[43] Since much of Hebei's livestock had been killed in the war and farmers faced a severe shortage

---

[38] *XCB*, 59: 1307
[39] *XCB*, 59: 1309, 1318, 1326; and 62: 1384.
[40] *XCB*, 67: 1505.
[41] *SHY*, "Shihuo," 69: 38a. *XCB*, 62: 1383.
[42] *XCB*, 62: 1388.
[43] *SHYBB*, 675a.

of draft animals, the government encouraged the importation of cattle from Henan and other provinces. In the past, cattle from the south were banned from crossing the Yellow River to enter Hebei, because their tendons and hides were the best materials for making weapons. In 1004, 1005, 1009, and 1014, the government not only lifted the ban, but also exempted commercial taxes on cattle sales in order to boost the trade of livestock into Hebei. Government funds were even issued for purchasing cattle for Hebei farmers.[44]

To deal with the severe shortage of draft animals in post-war Hebei, the government explored other technological solutions. It became a big advocate for a farming tool called the "stepping plow" (*tali* 踏犁).[45] Already popular in the Huai River valley in central China, this plow was a long, curved wooden beam, one end of which was a handle, and the other equipped with an iron blade and a foot-board just behind it. By hoeing into the soil with the blade, then stepping on the foot-board to help pull the top of blade back out, the farmer was able to use the leverage created by his body weight to break hard earth. With this tool, a farmer could till his fields, albeit slowly, even without animal power. Considering this a must-have for poor Hebei farmers, the government sent a group of Henan farmers to Hebei to introduce the tool and its manufacture.[46] Furthermore, agricultural tools were generally scant in post-war Hebei, as iron was hard to come by. In 1005, the government issued a policy to allow the importation of cast and wrought iron from Henan into Hebei, tax free.[47] In 1013, a further exemption of the "tax on agricultural implements" was granted specifically to Hebei farmers, which allowed them to purchase tools at lower prices.[48]

After these incentivizing policies were put in place to help people reconnect with their land and to boost their interest and ability in farm, the Song state carefully designed a set of economic institutions, which were both to inspire a long-term, sustainable growth of the economy and to regulate its performances within a stable, balanced economic order. To this end, the state granted the Hebei people substantial economic freedom and restrained government institutions from intervening too much in regional economic activities. It reduced corvée services that were previously imposed upon commoners, so people could spend

[44] *XCB*, 58: 1294; 72: 1630; and 59: 1307.
[45] Song (1981: 63–69).
[46] *SHY*, "Shihuo," 1: 17b.
[47] *XCB*, 59: 1314.
[48] *SHY*, "Shihuo," 1: 18a.

more time tending to their own livelihoods. Civil construction projects like building city walls and bridges now fell almost exclusively to conscripted corvée soldiers and laborers. Local governments and military organizations were prohibited from disturbing ordinary citizens' daily lives and encroaching on their private property. They could no longer "borrow" (i.e., extort) money from citizens in the name of purchasing military supplies, a common practice in the warring tenth century.[49] All financial means for governmental organizations and projects now had to come straight from government revenue, which was carefully budgeted, regulated, and monitored by the central government. Previously, people paid multiple taxes under dozens of titles, which not only was confusing but also created opportunities for corruption among local governments, military organizations, and individual officials. The taxation system became significantly simplified in the early eleventh century; farmers paid mainly summer and autumn taxes associated with harvests from their land.[50]

While giving people considerable economic freedom, the state also acted as a paternal authority, protecting the economy from external shocks while diagnosing and correcting its internal problems. Agriculture was a fragile endeavor; it was subject to many variables. A few months of bad weather or a sudden outbreak of natural disasters, for instance, would destroy crops for an entire season and put farmers under extreme duress. During the first four decades of the eleventh century, seventeen years reported heavy rainfall in the summer, which led to flooding from many of Hebei's local rivers that damaged summer crops. A few years saw very warm winters, and the lack of snow hurt crops like winter wheat. Nineteen years reported unusual summer heat, dryness, and droughts.[51] The 1030s was a particularly dry decade. All of north China suffered from extensive drought and locust infestation. In the worst circumstances, harvests failed completely. Hungry people dug locust eggs out of the dry

---

[49] *SHY*, "Shihuo," 39: 9b.
[50] *XCB*, 59: 1321. *SHY*, "Shihuo," 1: 21b–22a and 70: 7b. For Song's taxation system, see Wang Shengduo (1995) and Bao (2001).
[51] *XCB*, 47: 1017 and 1019; 48: 1045, 1046, and 1052; 51: 1126; 52: 1134 and 1140; 54: 1182; 56: 1248; 58: 1296; 60: 1345; 63: 1406; 65: 1455; 71: 1590; 72: 1630, 1634, and 1639; 76: 1726, 1730, and 1733; 77: 1758, 1759, and 1762; 79: 1807; 80: 1831; 81: 1843 and 1852; 82: 1883; 83: 1901; 84: 1914; 87: 2003 and 2006; 88: 2011, 2017, 2019, 2020, and 2027; 89: 2040; 90: 2089; 94: 2140; 96: 2206; 99: 2305; 104: 2410 and 2411; 105: 2443 and 2447; 106: 2463, 2473, and 2478; 107: 2498; 108: 2518; 112: 2622; 113: 2633; 114: 2663; 115: 2703 and 2711; 118: 2790; and 122: 2887. Also see sources from various chapters in the *SHY* and *SS*.

earth and handed them to officials. As a means of government-sponsored famine relief, refugees exchanged each *sheng* 升 (0.67 liter) of locust eggs for five *dou* 斗 (33.5 liters) of grain and beans or, in another case, for twenty copper coins from government granaries.[52] When such external disturbances happened, the government would step in to provide the distressed people some means of subsistence living.[53]

How did the state deal with the inherent and increasing inequality of Hebei's economic structure? Some people ascended the social ladder to become officials and local elites, while others acquired property and fortunes to become large landowners. The economic freedom that the state granted boosted the free trade of various products, including land and labor forces. Such trade, over time, led to the concentration of wealth in a small number of hands. Ordinary peasants, however, easily lost out in the intense socio-economic competition. When natural disasters occurred, they did not harm everybody equally; the poor took the brunt of it. If harvests failed over a few successive years, the poor had to uproot themselves from the land, abandon their homes, and take a flight. The well-to-do were not only more likely to survive the hardship, they could also take advantage of the situation by seizing land and property from the displaced poor. The economic inequality and social stratification were so stark that the state had to acknowledge the differences among its subjects and divided its taxpayers into five tiers. It asserted a state-level scheme of moral economy, in which the upper tiers of the population were supposed to carry more socio-economic responsibilities in serving both the state and the society, while the poor were exempted from some of tax burden and corvée service.

In a region as strategically significant as Hebei, it was essential for the imperial state to maintain a certain level of economic justice in order to ensure social stability. Every year, the state demanded that local governments update the registrations of their male populations in order to have a clear sense of labor forces available for government uses. Every three years, the state conducted a census to register population and household property and to remake its books, so it could track vertical movements of the population within the socio-economic strata.[54] It issued laws to

---

[52] *XCB*, 114: 2661 and 115: 2705.

[53] For instance, residents in Binzhou and Dizhou in southeastern Hebei and those in the northern frontier received tax exemptions from the government (*SHY*, "Shihuo," 70: 161a). Residents in southern Hebei received disaster relief (*XCB*, 76: 1733).

[54] Wu (2000: 28–29 and 34–44). These policies were applied to most of the Song territory, not only within Hebei.

protect the ownership of land and private property of poorer citizens to soothe social competition and prevent excessive concentration of wealth. In executing these laws, local governments acted as the justice keeper as well as a mediator among various social groups. When a dispute on land ownership, trade, or mortgaging occurred, government officials tended to issue legal rulings that, at least theoretically, favored the original, poor owner of the property.[55] When wealthy families engaged in usury and seized property from the poor, local governments would step in to intervene, providing the poor with some modicum of protection.

Another approach that the state took to mediate economic competition was to directly participate in Hebei's economic life. Multiple state-owned enterprises were set up inside Hebei to compete with wealthy private entities, to the benefit of the poor. For instance, a fair amount of land was designated as "government fields," which the government rented to peasant households at lower rates than what private landlords charged.[56] Knowing that wealthy families loaned out money to the poor at high interest rates and that some families went bankrupt because of their heavy debts, the government also established itself as a creditor that lent money with much lower interests. A related policy, the "Advanced purchase of silk" (*yumaijuan* 預買絹), was applied widely to Hebei. The poor often experienced hardship in spring, when they had exhausted food supplies through the winter and their summer crops had not yet ripened. This was when peasants were forced to turn to the rich, pawning their property and borrowing cash to buy food for survival and seeds for spring cultivation. This was how the poor often ended up deep in debt. Understanding this seasonal economic cycle, the government stepped in and released funds to purchase silk in advance from those who required capital to carry out silk production in the spring time. With the help of this money, the poor could feed themselves as well as gather the capital and labor to produce silk and cultivate their fields through the spring and early summer. When summer arrived, as agricultural harvests brought food to fill their stomachs, the poor were also able to pay back to the government by handing in their silk products.[57]

---

[55] See cases of land ownership disputes in 1021 (*SHY*, "Shihuo," 1: 19b) and in 1028 (*SHY*, "Shihuo," 1: 24a). Also *XCB*, 91: 2108.

[56] According to some quantitative data in the 1080s, Hebei's government fields were 3.41 percent of its entire arable land, a rate higher than in any other provinces. The situation was most likely similar in the first four decades of the eleventh century. See Liang (1980: 290).

[57] *SHY*, "Shihuo," 37: 5a.

By carrying out these various incentivizing policies and by asserting its institutional role in protecting and regulating economic activities, the state helped restore a stable agricultural society and economy in Hebei. From the 980s to 1045, Hebei's population recovered slowly yet steadily; its registered households increased by 23 percent, from 574,502 to 705,700.[58] As the people gained confidence in the Song state and the peaceful political and social environment the state brought about, agricultural production began to rebound. Bumper crops were reported in the fall of 1006 and 1007; in 1008, all of the Hebei Plain enjoyed an excellent harvest. Thanks to the resulting abundance, the prices of various goods dropped immediately. In comparison with the price in the late tenth century of 100 copper coins per *dou* (6.7 liter) of millet, the price for millet was now only seven or eight coins per *dou* (about 4.5 cash per *dou* for unhusked millet); straw and grass, which were used as forage and building materials, cost a mere 1.5 cash per bundle.[59] During the next two decades, climate conditions were rather benign, and there were few natural disasters. Good harvests were reported every year through 1013. The years from 1020 to 1025 also saw decent harvests, which generated a large surplus of agricultural products that quickly filled up Hebei's military granaries in the frontier area. A 1012 report stated that Baozhou's granaries were so full that the grain had begun to rot. Granary managers had to get rid of the old grain by selling it cheap to local markets. In another report, troops complained about the lack of storage space for supplies, because while granaries were full enough to feed the troops for three years, new grain kept flowing in every year.[60]

To be sure, good harvests did not take place throughout Hebei equally. While some parts of Hebei were blessed by repeated good harvests, other areas suffered setbacks and poor yield. From time to time, natural disasters destroyed crops, and state protection and economic interventions offered limited help. An explosion of locusts in 1006 and a sandstorm in 1007, for instance, hit southern Hebei hard. From 1026 to 1030, continuous heavy rains raised the water level in various rivers and caused flooding in southern, western, and central Hebei.[61] By the early 1030s,

[58] Liang (1980: 133–134).
[59] XCB, 70: 1567. According to Hino (1993: 456–466 and 19–74), the ratio of price between millet grain and its kernel was 1: 0.6. Also see his discussion about straw and grass, their usages, measurements, and prices in the Northern Song period.
[60] XCB, 77: 1752. SHYBB, 601a.
[61] XCB, 104: 2410 and 2411; 106: 2463 and 2478; 107: 2498, 2499, and 2506; and 108: 2518. Also SHYBB, 603a.

droughts, most likely caused by climatic dryness, dominated central and southern Hebei. Even the whole of northern China became a breeding ground for locusts, leaving behind complete desolation. Song contemporaries remembered how dreadful the situation was in 1032 and 1033, when hunger killed many and drove many others into flight.[62] As Hebei ran out of food, the central government had to issue multiple tax exemption orders and delivered grain into Hebei as famine relief. Military supplies to Hebei's gigantic armies also ran short. In the 1030s, 70 percent of the military supplies had to be imported, mostly from south China via the long-distance water transportation system.[63]

Northern Hebei, however, was a different story. There, disasters were always associated with excessive water. The ponds and ditches that the state took great pain to maintain inflicted many floods, often ruining the land around them. Water-borne diseases transmitted among domestic animals (perhaps among humans as well) and reduced the number of cattle, the draft animal that the government had painstakingly helped Hebei farmers acquire.[64] It is obvious that where resources were limited, such as in northern Hebei, state interests in military security conflicted with private interests in pursuing a normal livelihood and economic gains. As time passed, these competing interests loomed large and evolved into frequent conflicts between Hebei's military authorities who reinforced their control of the land by expanding the flood-prone ponds and the commoners who protected their livelihood by illegally damaging the state-owned ponds. We shall investigate the increasing clashes between the state and Hebei's local communities in Chapters 5 and 6.

This same period, the early decades of the eleventh century, was also when the Yellow River became turbulent. The river's marginal relationship with Hebei began to evolve into repeated small-scale flooding events, which increasingly struck certain areas in southern Hebei and caused problems to the people there. Chapters 3 and 4 will demonstrate how the river and the plain became more and more physically involved with each other and how the river began to have a negative impact on southern Hebei's social and economic life. Before 1048, the negative impact of the river floods was similar to the troubles caused by the ponds in northern Hebei: it was limited in terms of both scale and severity; it created local, individual problems not yet remarkable enough to reverse the recovery

[62] *XCB*, 133: 3183.
[63] See Cheng Lin's report in 1034, in *XCB*, 114: 2675.
[64] The shortage and disease of cattle were reported in 1004, 1005, 1009, and 1015, see *XCB*, 58: 1294; 59: 1314; 72: 1630; and 85: 1940.

and upward growth of Hebei's population and agricultural economy in the early eleventh century.

The arrival of the Northern Song state to the historical arena brought phenomenal changes to the lives in Hebei, the region's long-term autonomous tradition, and its relationship with the rest of China as well as the imperial state. First, during the early decades of the Song's rule, Hebei evolved from a warzone to a peaceful region where the civilian population engaged in steady human reproduction and robust economic activities. The region experienced an evident socio-economic recovery and growth, which helped its people transcend the devastation and suffering from the previous two centuries. Despite localized setbacks like occasional natural disasters, such recovery and growth, granted more time and continuous efforts and investments from both local sources and state institutions, could have been sustained for a long time and leapt to an even higher level. However, we should certainly not overestimate the economic achievements the state and Hebei had made by the 1040s. The overall agricultural production of Hebei was rather small, just enough for the civilian society and the regional governing body to live a slightly more comfortable lifestyle than what they had had during the previous warring era. Hebei's giant military relied very little on the wealth created by its own land; much of its supplies came from Henan and Shandong, or from as far away as the lower Yangtzi valley, the grain basket of the Song empire. In the meantime, environmental pressure had begun to build in north China; the overwhelming intrusion of the Yellow River in 1048 damaged Hebei and its society profoundly, and crippled – if not completely reversed – Hebei's upward economic development.

Second, during the first eight decades of Song rule, the state poured its efforts into turning the war-oriented, autonomy-seeking Hebei into a settled, agricultural stronghold where people had a stake in maintaining its intimate ties with the imperial state. As a result, Hebei found itself more and more distanced from its traditional self-reliance, martial spirit, and autonomous inclination. By merging into the state's empire-wide military apparatus as a frontier military entity, by transforming its land, water, and people into strategic components constituting that entity, by relying on the imperial state as its military leader, financial patron, and socio-economic sponsor and regulator, Hebei had become a subordinate servant who not only hinged on but also guarded the imperial state from the empire's political and socio-economic periphery. Once the biggest troublemaker to many previous regimes, Hebei's decline of political status within the imperial system contributed to the centralization of power into the hands of the state. It gave rise to a core-periphery structure over the empire, which laid the weight of political, military, and socio-economic powers in the Henan region, the land south to Hebei through the division by the Yellow River, where the imperial court dwelled. Assessing the Song's state building efforts, Charles Hartman maintains: "Never again would regionalism gain enough traction to outpace centralism as a major organizational force in the Chinese mentality."[65]

But, before "the 'new' empire was here to stay," the state had to deal with an increasing destructive, life-threatening physical environment, especially the challenges from the soaring Yellow River. Luckily, the downgrading of Hebei as a political, military, and socio-economic periphery provided a possibility for the state to appropriate the region into an environmental periphery as well – meaning, a region less significant, state-serving, and even self-sacrificing in environmental terms. Such transformation in Hebei's environmental status was evident in the state's small-scaled modification of Hebei's indigenous land and water for strategic purposes, such as the dredging of local canals and the opening of frontier ponds. However, the transformation was significantly actualized when the state searched for viable solutions to quell the flooding of the Yellow River, when the state singled out Hebei as a suitable substitute for the core region Henan as the bearer of flooding disasters. The next two chapters will examine the intensified interactions among the state, Hebei, and the Yellow River, which led toward Hebei's environmental peripheralization and eventual victimization.

[65] Hartman in Chaffee and Twitchett (2015: 22).

3

The 1040s

On the Eve of the Flood

Before we move on to the next chapter to investigate the state's hydraulic policies and practices involving the Yellow River, let us first build upon the previous chapter and take a look at the effects of many of the Song's state-building efforts toward the middle of the dynasty. By curbing the decentralizing forces like the Hebei region to consolidate the state power and prolong the state's rule, what had the Song state become and what did the society look like under its rule? Had the state building process successfully led to a prosperous, powerful imperial regime, shortly before the Yellow River's catastrophic crash into Hebei? Had the state gotten rid of the existential crisis it experienced during its adolescence and become confident in its control of its territory and subjects? The following survey of changing circumstances of the state, the society across China and that of Hebei, and the broad environmental conditions in north China in the decade of 1040s gives an immediate context to the outbreak of the environmental change in 1048.

Before the Yellow River invaded Hebei in 1048, the Northern Song state had just entered its middle age. Its ruler, Emperor Renzong 仁宗 (1010–1063), the fourth emperor of the dynasty, was now a mature adult in the middle of his forty-year-long reign (1022–1063). The analogy of a middle-age man for the state does not derive merely from our retrospective knowledge that the 1040s fell exactly in the middle of the state's duration from 960 to 1127. It comes more from the state's own perception of its growth, fluctuating fortunes, and new challenges, which were quite different from what it faced as a youthful, insecure regime in the previous decades.

By now, both the Song state and the society had achieved many successes. Peace, stability, and economic prosperity, which had long been absent in China, were now firmly established across the empire. While historians now celebrate the Song's many achievements, we must acknowledge that the state building process had also sunk into a multifaceted mid-dynasty crisis. Military impositions of the Xixia Tangut and the Khitan, swollen military and bureaucratic apparatuses, the widening disparity of wealth in the society, strained state finances, failed attempts at top-down political reform, as well as burgeoning environmental disasters throughout the empire, all together imposed on the state a strong sense of crisis. Many of these problems were evident in the land of Hebei and affected the livelihood of people there.

3.1   State and Society in the "Festive Era"

In 1041, Emperor Renzong designated the coming years as a new reign era, Qingli 慶曆 (1041–1048), the name of which meant a time for festive celebration. Indeed, there were many things that the state could celebrate. Now in its eighth decade, far beyond the lifespan of its five short-lived predecessors, and appearing to be stable and strong, the Song demonstrated the potential to last much longer. Perhaps it could even match the longevity and glory of the Tang Dynasty. By 1042, the Song's skirmishes and territorial disputes with the Tangut Xixia and the Khitan Liao had been settled by diplomatic means. By bribing these nomadic regimes with gifts of silver and silk every year, the state purchased peace for its northern borders. The annual gifting was humiliating to the state; yet, pragmatically speaking, it cost much less than any war expenditure and was in fact only a tiny fraction of the state revenue.

The long-term peace had made those who lived along the frontiers like in Hebei "ignorant of battles and weapons." Instead of worrying about their safety and migrating to escape war as people did in the previous centuries, now subjects of the Song state were peacefully settled and could tend their businesses and raise families. Over the previous eighty years, families had welcomed three to four generations, which had increased the overall population of the empire. During the decade between 980 and 989, the state had 6,499,145 registered, taxable households. Shortly before 1048 when the Yellow River's course shift inflicted heavy damage on Hebei, the state encompassed 10,723,695 registered households, which was a 65-percent increase over sixty years.[1]

---

[1] Liang (1980: 122).

In the course of this phenomenal population growth, the major issue facing average peasants had switched from obtaining basic security to managing a subsistence lifestyle and competing for more resources. By the early 1040s, most of the arable land in northern China, including in Hebei, was turned under the plough. Agriculture had been revived even in deeply war-damaged regions like Hebei. To obtain new land to accommodate the ever-growing population, Han Chinese farmers pushed farther south, where mountainous terrains, frequent rainfall, excessive surface water, and tropical and subtropical climates were barriers to settlement. In the face of these challenges, northern immigrants brought in advanced agricultural tools and invented new tools and farming technology to adapt to the resource-rich new environments. Water-abundant Hunan, mountain-covered western Sichuan, and the malaria-plagued Pearl Delta in south China were gradually populated by settlers from all over the country.[2] These regions slowly developed agricultural colonies that not only produced enough food to feed their regional populations but also made increasing contributions to the state revenue.

China's key economic areas were shifting toward the southern half of the country.[3] The lower Yangzi valley adopted early-ripening rice, whose growing season was short enough to guarantee the plantation of an additional crop after the first harvest in mid-summer. By investing enormous labor and time and by managing flood control and irrigation, these regions reduced various kinds of uncertainty inherent in the land. By the middle of the eleventh century, farmers could predictably produce two crops of rice every year.[4] Slightly north, in regions like Henan, Shandong, and Jiangsu south to the Yellow River, winter wheat was widely planted. This winter crop was sown in late autumn and harvested in early summer; it made use of the wintertime when most other crops failed to grow, and thereby dramatically expanded the use of the land throughout the four seasons. Hence, many fields of the North China Plain could produce three crops in two years, rather than one crop per year as in the past. As these high-yield crops spread over China to increase crop rotations on a given swath of land, the growing season of a field was significantly extended. In order for the land to support such a long growing season, farmers took various measures to improve land fertility. By using human night soil and animal manure, as well as planting nitrogen-enriching legume crops like

---

[2] Perdue (1987), von Glahn (1987), Smith (1991), and Marks (1998). For an environmental survey of the Han Chinese expansion toward its peripheries, see Marks (2012).
[3] Chi (1936).
[4] Ho (1956), Shiba (1988), and Elvin (1973).

soybeans, they restored nutrients to their fields fairly quickly and thus shortened the fields' fallow period.

These technological improvements and their wide application – an "agricultural revolution" in Mark Elvin's words – increased the production of staple food all over the empire. The resultant abundance of food supported the growth in the human population. It provided many at least a subsistence lifestyle, reduced the rate of poverty, and enhanced living standards for the general populace. It is most likely that Song people, in comparison with their eleventh-century contemporaries in the rest of the world, ate better and lived a healthier life.

The growth in agriculture provided a solid foundation for the multi-dimensional Chinese "Medieval Economic Revolution," in which the commercial boom was a major component.[5] Enormous agricultural surpluses entered markets at all levels. For instance, the government taxed farmers on their grain and also purchased additional grain from the markets in the Yangzi valley every year. Of this grain, six and half million *dan* were shipped to the capital to feed the giant bureaucratic body and the military.[6] Much of this long-distance trade was conducted by private merchants. Ordinary people, especially those in urban and suburban areas, could access markets and buy goods relatively easier than in the past, thanks to the bounty of goods and their wide circulation. Many people purchased their daily food supply from local urban centers or market towns along roads and waterways, without the need to produce everything themselves.[7]

With the excess production came a diversification of labor, as some peasants no longer needed to till the land. They invested their time in other kinds of specialized, high-income production, such as sericulture, tea plantation, and ceramics production. These non-farming sectors of the economy with their high profits, again, attracted more people to leave traditional farming and become skilled workers. The self-sufficient manorial economy that had dominated medieval China broke down. Producers in various occupations no longer worked mainly to meet their personal needs. A weaver did not weave to dress herself; a porcelain-making

---

[5] Elvin (1973). We should note some recent challenges to Elvin's generalization and optimism, such as McDermott and Shiba's chapter in Chaffee and Twitchett (2015: 321–436).

[6] *XCB*, 104: 2408.

[7] The scholarship on the market economy and urban development in the Tang–Song period is gigantic. See a recent survey by McDermott and Shiba in Chaffee and Twitchett (2015: 379–384).

family used only one set of earthenware for their meals; and a gardener living in the vicinity of a town focused on planting vegetables not just to put on his family's dining table. A great portion of their production was oriented toward the market. They distributed their goods locally to satisfy consumers close by or sold their goods to long-distance merchants who carried them into nationwide circulation and even into international markets. Hebei, for instance, had become a major producer of high-quality silk, internationally renowned porcelain, iron, and sea salt in the 1040s.

Along with the remarkable increase in agricultural production, the proliferation of economic specialization, and a burgeoning population whose soaring demands for goods stimulated production, a robust market economy came into shape. Markets of various sizes mushroomed and became an indispensable component of the lives of many people. They were interconnected by roads and waterways and enjoyed exchanges of both capital and commodities. The Song state minted much more copper coins than its predecessors and the dynasties in the next few centuries to satisfy the demand of trade. More than the heavy, bulky cash, however, it was the growth of credit systems, such as paper money circulating within private sectors and various kinds of value-bearing credit certificates the government issued, that facilitated interregional trade and made large business transactions among different markets fluid and secure.[8] The flow of capital and commodities was also facilitated by flourishing water transportation throughout China. By linking up with each other, the local, regional, and national waterways formed a vast network, stretching out in many directions. Via this network, commodities were able to surmount geographical barriers and became spatially fluid. As a result, while people in Hebei ate rice produced by the farmers in the lower Yangzi valley, the well-to-do in the cities of south China, like Yangzhou 揚州 and Hangzhou 杭州, wore delicate silk and drank tea from white porcelain cups that were manufactured by Hebei workers.[9]

Widespread markets and convenient transportation also drew together people. Merchants, service people, and their consumers aggregated to form urban centers. Undergoing a process of rapid urbanization, traditional jurisdictional centers saw the growth of non-political, economic sectors. Meanwhile, there emerged a large number of cities and towns

---

[8] von Glahn (1996: 43–56). For a detailed study of Song's monetary history, see Gao (2000).
[9] For the development of canals, see Ch'uan (1946), Aoyama (1963), Shi (1988b), and Zou (1993).

that paralleled old jurisdictional centers and existed mainly for economic purposes. The imperial capital Kaifeng 開封, for instance, boasted more than a million households and was the most crowded city in the world at the time.[10] It sat on the Bian Canal and acted as a hub for the streams of people and goods. The scroll "Qingming shanghe tu 清明上河圖," usually attributed to Zhang Zeduan 張擇端 (1085–1145) in the first quarter of the twelfth century, gives us a vivid depiction of how everyday life was carried out in the suburbs of the city. Taverns, teahouses, and food vendors lined up along streets and on bridges, together with small stalls selling shoes, scissors, and knives. Big boats streamed through the Bian Canal and bridges in busy traffic. Horses, donkeys, camels, carts, and human hands carried bulky goods to marketplaces. This vibrant urban life was not unique to the capital. Even in frontier regions like Hebei, market towns blossomed along waterways. Large cities like Daming in the south and Dingzhou in the northwest became known for their large populations and prosperous economic life.

Blessed with social stability and economic growth, the cultural life thrived in the Song society: arts, literature, book production, popular culture, and nightlife in urban areas all flourished. A major indicator of this cultural vibrancy was a general increase in literacy among the populace. An increasing percentage of the male population was released from traditional economic activities and turned to learning.[11] With the increase in paper manufacturing, the wide application of printing technology, and the vigorous book trade, books were no longer the monopoly of state libraries and Buddhist monasteries. Students and scholars could get books fairly easily and at rather cheap prices from the market. Since transportation was more widespread and convenient than before, people corresponded more often by post and even traveled in search of knowledge, teachers, and schools. It seems that by the mid-eleventh century, theoretically nearly every man had the chance to acquire some kind of education and gain a certain level of literacy.

Meanwhile, the diversified economy, especially the commercial sector, required men who were able to read, write, and think. Hence, reading and writing were no longer merely leisure activities, privileges that only the aristocracy could enjoy, means for the elite to cultivate their personal morality and intelligence, or a ladder for a small number of bright young

---

[10] For urban development of Kaifeng, see Zhou (1992).
[11] On books, printing, and reading, see various chapters in Chia and de Weerdt (2011), and Robert Hymes in Chaffee and Twitchett (2015: 542–568).

men to ascend from the bottom of the society to earn a political career in the government. Rather, literacy became a practical occupational skill that brought to men an opportunity for employment.

Of course, the rise of reading and writing to prominence was not only a result of economic demands. As the previous chapter addressed, the Song state actively promoted civil culture; it was certainly a major consumer of the talents this culture generated. The young Song state made institutional efforts to demilitarize its governing body and the society and to cultivate a civil culture among its subjects. It took steps like opening schools in every level of its jurisdictional centers and maintaining tax-free land as a means to generate scholarships. Most significantly, the government endeavored to build a bureaucrat apparatus on the basis of civil servants who were men coming from various kinds of family backgrounds and were dedicated to learning. Given such incentives, the younger generation of men pursued personal worth and professional success not just through family ties or military achievement as the elder generations did in the tenth century, especially in regions like Hebei. Instead, they took a literate approach and spent years learning literature, philosophy, and history, with the hope of struggling through "the thorny gates of learning,"[12] pass the civil service examination, and earn a position in the government. As the government continued to encourage their political and professional ambitions, more and more families and young men saw learning and the civil service examination as an attractive career path.

In the 1040s, scholar-officials produced by the civil service examination dominated various levels of the Song government. Many of them were not satisfied with individual professional successes or economic gains. They sought to elevate the collective worth of the society by forging a set of Neo-Confucian values. "This culture of ours,"[13] as seen in their eyes, sought to restore Confucian teachings and to remedy various transgressions, such as militarism, foreign influences, regional separation and decentralization, and religiosity, which had plagued individuals and the Chinese society for many centuries. These emerging Neo-Confucian scholars believed that they, as a collective whole, could correct faults in every aspect of Song's political, social, and cultural life by promoting Confucian values like loyalty, righteousness, piety, and reason. These men saw various forms of cultural practices not only as the manifestations of,

---

[12] To paraphrase Chaffee's (1995) book title.
[13] To paraphrase Bol's (1992) book title.

but also as the means to, a resurrection of Confucianism. The "*guwen* 古文*"* movement, a renaissance of the classics (lit., ancient style of writing) that was initiated in the ninth century, achieved its height in the 1040s. Its advocators, like Ouyang Xiu 歐陽修 (1007–1072), had gained prominence in various cultural scenes and attracted enormous numbers of followers in young students.[14]

The Neo-Confucians were also activists in the political realm. They considered building a benevolent, rational Confucian state as an ultimate manifestation of their Neo-Confucian agenda, and serving the state as their individual and collective responsibility. This agenda was more significant than their personal worth and career success. Likewise, the well-being and sustainment of the state was more important than that of any individual. Hence, the ideation of the notion "*guojia* 國家," similar to what we call "state," had supplied the key objective that their individual and collective efforts were dedicated to. These scholarly officials defended the *guojia* and its interests against any offense or challenge, although that sometimes led to confrontations with their peers in different political factions or even the emperor himself. By the mid-1040s, these Confucian scholars had filled most of the positions at the imperial court and the offices at the provincial and county levels.

The Song state had journeyed a long way to arrive in this Festive Era.[15] The substantial growth of the population provided the state with a sizable army that guarded its borders, as well as a large corvée service team that maintained the civil and transportation infrastructure around the empire. The prospering economy larded state treasuries with cash, grain, and fine silk. As mentioned, by 1048, the state recorded 10,723,695 legally registered households, or about 54 million people. Its accounting books showed that in 1049, the state obtained a sum of 126,251,964 in revenues, a number that referred to grain, cash, and various kinds of products, regardless of units of measurement.[16] This number is a 71-percent increase from the revenue recorded for 1015. It is hard for us to understand what this number really means, but clearly it indicates a large revenue income that supported a remarkable expansion of the state's military and bureaucratic apparatuses. These interrelated apparatuses grew very quickly. By the early 1040s, they had become so large that

---

[14] For more about Ouyang Xiu, see Liu (1967).

[15] For a recent, comprehensive survey of Song's economic, social, and intellectual history, see Chaffee and Twitchett (2015).

[16] See Liang (1980: 288).

many in the government considered them redundant and inefficient, with the potential to lead to a political and financial crisis.

By this time, the government was no longer run by aristocracy, but mainly by a huge number of professional bureaucrats. They wielded administrative power and spoke learnedly about governance, but they had no access to military force. They dutifully guarded their individual positions, but were prohibited from encroaching on the business of others. Within the expansive, hierarchical bureaucratic structure, individual political powers designated to official positions were so balanced and eventually diluted that they could not form a singular force to challenge state power and the absolute authority of the emperor. This peculiar governing body effectively prevented a coup d'état by military leaders or regional power-holders, as had happened often in the previous few centuries. By the 1040s, the kind of strongmen like An Zhongrong in the tenth century, mentioned in Chapter 1, had disappeared. The state was no longer worried about separatist forces that had once plagued the state from within. For the Song state, the mid-dynasty did seem a Festive Era.

3.2   The Song's Mid-Dynasty Crisis

The peace and prosperity portrayed above, however, is a remarkably simplified image of Song China, as seen in retrospect by our distant eyes. The 1040s brought a series of political, socio-economic, and environmental problems, each of which in its own way challenged the state's sense of stability.[17] Many of the problems occurred in Hebei. The Song state was clearly facing a midlife crisis before the catastrophic flooding of the Yellow River in 1048. The prevailing sentiments of crisis and anxiety shared by the state's ruling members at the time drove many to reflect on the flaws of the state's governance and those of the society and its culture. The movement toward a reform led by statesmen like Fan Zhongyan 范仲淹 (989–1052) and Ouyang Xiu in the mid-1040s was a response to the anxiety and dissatisfactions. Unfortunately, the reform was soon crushed, and the status quo continued. The attempt to reenergize the state eventually yielded to the reality of an inefficient, corrupt government and a society increasingly threatened by financial difficulties and

---

[17] For the administrative, military, and fiscal problems the Song state faced in the mid-eleventh century (not explicitly for the 1040s or for the region of Hebei), see Twitchett and Smith (2009: 289–327; 347–362), and various chapters in Chaffee and Twitchett (2015).

environmental disasters. The following pages will explore the Song's mid-dynasty crisis through two lenses: first, military, financial, and political problems particularly associated with Hebei; second, widespread environmental issues in north China.

Military, Financial, and Political Crisis

In 1038, the Tangut Xixia terminated its tributary relationship with the Song and proclaimed itself an independent empire. Outraged, the Song declared war, and soon found itself being dragged deeply into a costly war on its northwestern frontier, where it was defeated by the Tangut in almost every important battle. The conflict also upset the Song's relationship with the Liao. The Liao capitalized on the situation and displayed a heavy military presence on the Song–Liao border in Hebei, threatening the Song with invasion. Meanwhile, its emissaries showed up at the Song court in 1042 to press the Song to give up its territory in northern Hebei, where key strategic garrisons, frontier ponds, underground tunnels, and state-run trading sites were located.

The prospect of engaging in two wars on two separate fronts terrified the Song. A sense of crisis – about the state's very survival – permeated the court. It drove the emperor and his ministers to seek diplomatic means to handle the Liao and eventually to accept an agreement in 1042, which furthered the humiliating terms imposed by the 1005 peace treaty. According to the new agreement, the Song would increase its annual gift of silver and silk to the Liao, in the official name of a tribute presented by an inferior state to a superior state. The Liao would drop its threats of invasion and, as it enjoyed its political and economic gains, would mediate between the Song and the Xixia. In 1044, after a year-long negotiation, the Song and the Xixia came to a peace agreement. By sending the Xixia a significant amount of silver, silk, and tea, the Song claimed a nominal overlordship over the Xixia and saved itself from total humiliation.[18] Peace returned to the Song's two borders. Yet, the impact of the military tensions and diplomatic humiliation was profound and lasting. The Song state became increasing suspicious of its nomadic neighbors and invested more to strengthen its guard. As a result, we see the expansion of armies and the militarization of frontier civilian populations along the state's northern borders.

In Hebei, officials and military commanders believed that the best way to prevent a future conflict with the nomads was to mobilize civilians

---

[18] For these military tensions and territorial disputes, see Twitchett and Smith (2009).

and organize them into militias. The professional troops, which the state had taken pains to recruit from various parts of north China to suppress Hebei's domestic military traditions, seemed ineffectual when confronting the nomads. By contrast, Hebei's "indigenous men" (*tuding* 土丁) were considered brave, martial, good at riding and shooting, and were excellent soldiers by nature and tradition. Keen to protect their homeland and their own interests, these local men could rely on family ties and local bases to obtain supplies. As such, it would cost less for the government to recruit men for the militias than for the professional armies.[19]

In accordance with this idea, in 1040, the imperial court ordered Hebei's Fiscal and Pacification Commissioners to draft men "secretly" without alarming the Liao, in order to revive a long-declining militia, the "Strong Valiants" (*qiangzhuang* 強壯) in Hebei. By the end of the year, the Strong Valiants militiamen numbered 293,000.[20] The other existing militia, the "Righteous and Brave" (*yiyong* 義勇) was also expanding. By late 1042, it numbered 189,230.[21] These militiamen, together with Hebei's professional Imperial Armies and District Armies, raised the total number of Hebei's troops to 770,000 by the mid-1040s.[22] This number varied over the course of the rest of the Northern Song; in general, over 450,000 men remained in Hebei's Imperial Armies, District Armies, and Righteous and Brave militia.[23] Since 1005, this was the first time that the state drafted soldiers in Hebei on such a large scale.

This drastic conscription induced profound and often negative social and economic consequences. New militiamen were supposed to come from taxpaying, landowning households (*zhuhu* 主戶). A third to a half of the male adults in Hebei's landowning households were drafted into

---

[19] Wang Gongchen's proposal in 1040 and Jia Changchao's comment in 1042, in *XCB*, 127: 3007 and 138: 3317–3318.

[20] *XCB*, 127: 3007; 47: 1036; 127: 3020; and 138: 3317–3318. For more about Song's military system, see Wang (1983) and Wang and Wright in Chaffee and Twitchett (2015).

[21] *XCB*, 138: 3312.

[22] This number is a combination of Hebei's Strong Valiants (293,000 heads) and the total of Hebei's Imperial, District, and Righteous and Braves (477,000 heads). See Ouyang Xiu, "Lun Hebei caichan shang shixiang shu," *OYXQJ*, 118: 1825–1828.

[23] In 1064 Hebei had more than 150,000 Righteous and Braves militia (*XCB*, 203: 4915). In 1066 Hebei had more than 301,000 "battle soldiers," excluding the militia (*XCB*, 208: 5053). In 1069, the registered Righteous and Braves numbered 186,400 (*XCB*, 6: 275). Assuming the scale of Hebei's battle soldiers remained stable, as did Hebei's militia, the sum of these types of troops would have amounted between 450,000 and 500,000 in the 1060s.

the Strong Valiants alone.[24] More had to serve in the Righteous and Brave militia. As a result, in the mid-1040s, over half of the male population in Hebei's landowning households were registered for some kind of military service. Let us use a number from the late 1070s for reference. At that time, 78 percent of Hebei's registered households were landowners.[25] If this ratio was similar thirty years before in the 1040s, it means that about 40 percent of Hebei's male adults were drafted into the militias and had their arms tattooed with a military identity, in part to prevent them from escaping. Looking at this high percentage and understanding that there were also additional Hebei men serving in the professional troops, it is clear that Hebei experienced a radical militarization in the 1040s.

As adult males, these recruits were the main labor force for Hebei's agricultural production.[26] Military service took them away from their land and complicated their lives and the livelihood of their families. In the late fall of every year, they were forced away from their land before the harvest was completed in order to begin military training or service, and they were not discharged from duties until farming started again the following spring, when the land desperately demanded labor. Militia service led to a labor shortage, which by extension imposed a heavy burden of economic activities on the rest of the population – the elderly, women, and children.

Given the reduction of its agricultural labor force, Hebei very likely produced less food. Of its limited agricultural production, a great deal of Hebei's products was consumed by the growing military. Hence, not much was left for civilian consumption to improve living standards or to serve as capital for other economic activities and investments. The

---

[24] According to the conscription policy for Hebei's Strong Valiants militia in 1000, if a household had two or three male adults, one of them would serve the militia. For larger households, two persons from a household with four or five male adults, three from six or seven, and four from eight or more than eight would serve the militia (*XCB*, 47: 1036). In 1064, a court decree ordered to "conscript one out of three, two out of six, and three out of nine male adults of the landowning households" to form the Righteous and Braves militia in Shaanxi, following the example in Hebei (*XCB*, 203: 4915).

[25] Household numbers are based on Liang (1980: 141–149).

[26] We must clarify that not all of Hebei's military were subject to full-time training and military duties. Militiamen divided into groups and rotated to participate in training and other duties. Also, theoretically, most of their military training took place in the winter when they were supposed to be released from economic activities. No historical sources survive to help us understand how exactly military training affected economic activities, especially on the basis of individual activities. In general, the increase in the burden of military services on the society must have to some extent caused disturbance to the society's regular economic life.

kind of revolutionary growth in agricultural productivity and technology
that scholars have depicted for the contemporary lower Yangzi valley,
which depended on heavy investments of manpower and other resources
to carry out intensive farming, could not take place in Hebei. Quite the
opposite, Hebei's countryside presented a rather bleak image in the late
1040s. "Immense fields lie barren," wrote Fan Zhen 范鎮 (1007-1088),
one despairing Hebei official at the time, "and the population is sparse."[27]
Hebei was not given a chance to recover from the harvest failures and
hardship caused by multiple natural disasters in the 1030s. Instead, it proceeded into a troubling new decade, in which it was threatened by war and
shaken by an anxious imperial state that hastened to re-appropriate and
destabilize Hebei's demographic and economic structure. The increase in
the state's demands for labor and material supplies ran parallel to the
decline in the civilian population and agricultural production, both producing anxiety all around. As some Song officials commented a couple of
decades later, the 1040s was the time when the peacefully settled Hebei
people began to be uprooted from their land again.[28]

The military expansion and the depression of Hebei's civilian society
affected the state in negative ways. The military demands skyrocketed.
Although the government expected militiamen to provide their own supplies, in reality the Strong Valiants brought along horses and armor only
under the condition that the government released their households from
paying duties for corvée services.[29] Some well-to-do Righteous and Brave
militiamen prepared their own crossbows, for which the government
rewarded their households with a tax deduction worth two thousand copper coins. The government still had to provide food and make weapons
for men from poor families.[30] When assigning men duties rather than regular military training, the government even paid wages. The Righteous
and Brave were paid according to the scale for the professional District
Armies, that is, a monthly salary of 500 copper coins, 167.5 liters of
grain, and a certain amount of silk and hemp products.[31] The expansion
of Hebei's militia did not save the government money, as its advocates
believed it would. In fact, the government's expenditure on Hebei soared.
By the mid-1040s, the government's annual military expenses for Hebei

---

[27] "Shang Renzong lun yibing kunmin [Memorial to Emperor Renzong about the increasing
military and its burdens on the people]," *SMCZY*, 120: 18a–21a. *XCB*, 179: 4335.
[28] Sima Guang's comment in 1064, *XCB*, 203: 4918.
[29] *XCB*, 47: 1036.
[30] *XCB*, 138: 3312.
[31] *XCB*, 138: 3312 and 161: 3895.

rose to 24,450,000 (of various units) of coins, grain, and fabrics. Beyond this number, as Ouyang Xiu pointed out, the government had various "irregular expenses," such as issuing grants to soldiers at special events as well as awards to those with excellent performance in training.[32]

As expenditures rose, Hebei's agricultural revenues decreased, putting pressure on state coffers.[33] In Jizhou prefecture in central Hebei, for instance, the annual military expenditure in the late 1040s included 380,000 *dan* (1 *dan* ≈ 67 liters) of grain and forage, 103,000 lengths of plain silk, 16,500 lengths of hemp fabrics, 135,000 *liang* 兩 (1 *liang* ≈ 40 grams) of silk floss, and 110,000 strings of coins. But the prefecture's tax income provided only 43,000 *dan* of grain (11 percent of the demand), 5,400 lengths of silk and hemp fabrics (5 percent of the demand), and 27,000 *liang* of silk floss (20 percent of the demand).[34] The majority of its expenditure had to be covered by income from somewhere else. While the districts in southern Hebei might have been able to produce more goods for the armies, the heavily militarized frontier districts must have been in an even worse economic and financial situation than Jizhou. Balancing out the regional differences throughout Hebei, we may use Jizhou's situation as the indicator of Hebei's average. Thus, let us make a rough estimate: Hebei's own revenues might have contributed 15–20 percent of its military expenditure, leaving 80–85 percent to the importation from outside of Hebei.

The massive importation of goods was reliant not only upon the coordination but also on the coffers of the central government. By 1047, it cost the government approximately 10,000,000 strings of copper coins every year to purchase grain and forage to feed its soldiers in the three frontier provinces of Hebei, Hedong, and Shanxi. We may roughly assume that at least one third of this was for Hebei.[35] Indeed, the economic boom across the empire over the previous few decades had filled state treasuries. Yet the war in Shaanxi and rapid militarization in Hebei consumed more than what the state had gathered and quickly depleted imperial coffers.

---

[32] "Lun Hebei caichan shang shixiang shu," *OYXQJ*, 118: 1825–1828.

[33] For a survey on Song's fiscal administration (not specifically for Hebei), see Peter Golas in Chaffee and Twitchett (2015: 139–213).

[34] Bao Zheng, "Qing yi Jizhou jiuliang bingshi gui benzhou [Pleading to return the Jizhou troops that accessed grain supplies in other prefectures]," *XSBGZY*, 8: 105–109.

[35] *XCB*, 161: 3895. Bao Zheng, "Zai qing yinuo Hebei bingma ji ba gongyong huiyi [Second pleading to relocate Hebei's troops and eliminate corresponding costs for governmental purposes]," *XSBGZY*, 9: 119–120.

Let's look at one particular measure the government employed to gather supplies and how it affected state finances. The government had a hard time collecting military supplies with its bureaucratic team, so it collaborated with private merchants and encouraged them to trade and transport supplies. Along the Yuhe Canal and the Bianhe Canal, long-distance trade for military consumption to regions like Hebei flourished. A peculiar kind of commerce blossomed between the state as buyer and merchants as seller and broker. In this relationship, the state rendered enormous economic power to merchants, upon whom the state and its military apparatus became heavily reliant. The merchants, often deemed greedy, engaged in speculation, controlled the market by buying up goods, manipulated market prices, and suppressed the government's purchasing power. Hence, wealth, which was levied on the general populace and used to fill up the state treasuries, flowed into a small number of private hands and deepened the society's economic disparity. Unfortunately, these merchants did not actually provide the state with sufficient military provisions. The particular commercial model that the state had developed to fulfill its military demands turned out to worsen its financial burden.[36]

We observe an increasingly negative spiral in the state's relationship with Hebei: the more the state demanded Hebei be militarized, the less self-sufficient both Hebei's military and civilian society became, the higher the state's costs went up, the more deregulated commercial activities became, and the less market activities remained under the state's control. As a result, even with its immense financial stake, the state found it more and more difficult to obtain food and other supplies. The swollen military in Hebei suffered constant scarcity. In the early 1040s, the troops located in the northern frontier required three to four million *dan* of grain each year. Despite the state's efforts, these troops obtained merely 850,000 *dan* in 1041, 450,000 *dan* in 1042, and 1,040,000 *dan* in 1043.[37] The situation was exacerbated when Hebei's annual demand climbed to seven million *dan* in the late 1040s.[38] In the worst scenarios, as when natural

---

[36] For the transactions between merchants and the state and the state's fiscal challenges, see Wang Shengduo (1995), Bao (2001), and Jiang (2002: 220–283). For Hebei's military strategies and supplies, see Cheng (2012).

[37] *XCB*, 161: 3895. Bao Zheng, "Zai qing yinuo Hebei bingma ji ba gongyong huiyi," *XSBGZY*, 9: 119–120. Ouyang Xiu, "Qi zhan biandihudou xian [Pleading to extend the deadline of grain purchases]," *OYXQJ*, 117: 1800–1801.

[38] Bao Zheng, "Qing zhibo Bianhe lianggang wang Hebei [Pleading to distribute some grain supplies shipped through the Bian Canal to Hebei]," *XSBGZY*, 10: 123–124.

disasters happened, even relatively rich prefectures in southern Hebei had very little food to feed its officials and military.

In the mid-1040s, dealing with the unsustainable growth of Hebei's military and the state's corrupt financial system became two significant and interrelated concerns that were constantly debated at the imperial court. Prominent statesmen like Ouyang Xiu, Han Qi 韓琦 (1008–1075), Fu Bi, and Bao Zheng 包拯 (999–1062) all presented their commentaries and proposals to Emperor Renzong. They were worried about the military's unlimited consumption of the state revenue and, conversely, about the obstacle that the fiscal deficit imposed on the military system's effectiveness. The conflict between the two would eventually lead to a breakdown in either the military system or the state finances, or in the worst case, both.

In Hebei, signs of an impending crisis burgeoned in the military. A mutiny broke out in Baozhou in northern Hebei in 1042. The frontier soldiers protested against corruption among their commanders, who had cut the soldiers' stipends and provoked tremendous resentment.[39] The insurrection was put down by the military. Yet, five years later, soldiers in Beizhou 貝州 (known as Enzhou 恩州 after 1048) in central Hebei organized another mutiny, took control of the walled city, and killed local officials and military commanders.[40] They even secretly communicated with troops in other Hebei garrisons and in southern provinces across the Yellow River to plan for a large-scale, interregional rebellion. The Song court was caught offguard and terrified. It quickly sent officials from the imperial court to Hebei to replace the local leadership and maneuvered in troops from other places that were better paid and more trustworthy. After two months of fierce battles and serious defeats at the hand of the rebels, the government troops besieged the city of Enzhou, cut off food supplies, and lured some rebels to surrender. Soon after the rebels surrendered, officials ordered their execution. More than a thousand rebels were beheaded or buried alive. A purge swept through the Hebei military to identify disloyal individuals and ferret out connections between soldiers and the rebels, leading to the death and punishment of many.

It is clear that during Emperor Renzong's Festive Era reign, the Song state's security crisis caused both by its nomadic enemies and by its own responses to the crisis led to the drastic militarization of Hebei,

[39] *QSW*, 1023: 274.
[40] *XCB*, 161: 3890.

the region's economic downturn, the government's financial stress, and the military instability. External, interstate problems were internalized and triggered hidden domestic issues, which shook the Song's political, social, and economic stability from within. All this did not only happen to Hebei. Throughout the Song empire, civilian-led rebellions, often joined by low-ranking military, became more and more common. Wang Lun 王倫 and his fellow rebels, for instance, who began in the Shandong area and went on to establish alliances with Hebei soldiers, swept through the eastern part of north China and the lower Yangzi valley in 1043. As various social problems exploded, natural disasters caused by large-scale environmental changes, which we shall discuss shortly, also began to mushroom. As the 1040s went on, more problems revealed themselves and combined to challenge the state's rule from various directions. Hebei, apparently, lay at the center of the crisis.

In contrast to the rosy image of a stable state and a prosperous society that historians have portrayed in hindsight, the ruling classes in the 1040s saw a rather disconcerting reality in Song China. In their eyes, the state was burdened by a gigantic military, a redundant bureaucracy, various kinds of corruption, and exhausted state finances.[41] To save the state from these afflictions, a group of moralist and idealist young officials cried for changes in the government. Led by Fan Zhongyan, Ouyang Xiu, Fu Bi, and Han Qi, this new generation of officials persuaded Emperor Renzong to side with them and to launch an institutional reform in 1045.[42]

Unfortunately, the reform did not go very far. As far as senior conservative politicians were concerned, the reformists adopted radical measures to shake up the existing power structure that had overseen and balanced different interest groups; they challenged the status quo that had maintained the old generation of officials in power for decades. Worse yet, the reformists rose very quickly as a political power, which could potentially unite various forces to dominate the court and overrule the emperor's monarchal authority. The accusations that anti-reform officials unleashed toward the reformists portrayed the latter as ill-natured and profiteering. The factional rivalry that featured Song politics had reached its first peak. The flurry of accusations agitated the nerves of the anxious emperor: he wanted some changes that would save his state from dwindling, but he

---

[41] Many Song statesmen and officials expressed their concerns and proposed their prescriptions; most famous was Song Qi's "Shang sanrong sanfei shu [To discuss "three redundancies" and "three wastes"]," *QSW*, 489: 224–226.

[42] For more about the Qingli Reform, see Liu (1957, 1967). For the intellectual underpinning of the reform, see Bol (1992: 176–211).

also feared that radical changes would destroy the fragile stability and cause the state to collapse. Within barely two years, suspicious Emperor Renzong called off the reform and dismissed its leading members from his court.

Underpinning its abolition was the reform's failure to tackle the crisis mentality permeating the state and its ruling members. The reform identified many manifestations of the state's mid-dynasty crisis and confronted them with individual policies. Yet, it was unable to disentangle the anxiety deeply embedded in the way in which the Song state perceived the world and its position in it. The state's crisis mentality was not new: it had evolved from the state's tremendous concerns about its survival as a vulnerable regime in an extremely challenging political, socio-economic, and environmental world, which began with the state's birth in the late tenth century.

Environmental Crisis

We must note, the state's sense of crisis also came from its experience of escalating environmental disasters in the 1040s. The frequent occurrence of disasters made this decade incredibly ominous, despite its designation as a "Festive Era." To begin with, there were several years in which north China reported extensive rain; in Hebei, the rains damaged roads and fields and caused many of the frontier ponds to overflow into nearby villages.[43] Yet, most of the 1040s were very dry. The severe droughts and locust attacks that north China suffered in the early 1030s had returned. In the early 1040s, China "had no rain in subsequent years," due to the remarkable heat. The situation was particularly alarming in 1043. A serious shortage of rainfall destroyed spring, fall, and winter crops, essentially laying waste to the entire agricultural efforts of that year.[44] Then the winter of 1045 in north China was reported as extraordinarily cold. Freezing rain, sleet, and the icicle on plants were seen everywhere. Hebei even saw a very unusual "red snow."[45] The red color may suggest heavy dust and chemical particles in the lower atmosphere, which very likely came from emissions caused by frequent earthquakes during this period.

Between 1044 and 1049, an extensive drought caused many wells and streams to dry up in the lower Yangtze valley and led to widespread

---

[43] XCB, 132: 3153; 135: 3227; and 136: 3269.
[44] XCB, 141: 3377; 143: 3463; and 145: 3520.
[45] XCB, 145: 3518.

epidemics and deaths among livestock. A large number of residents were found dead of thirst due to the severe shortage of water in the capital Kaifeng.[46] Drought and locusts also ravaged the central and southern plain of Hebei. Observing the dreadful situation, an official lamented that "The raging barren land extends over thousands of *li*, putting an end to the livelihood of the commoners."[47] In 1049, Hebei was so severely attacked by drought that Ouyang Xiu claimed, perhaps with exaggeration caused by despair, that 80–90 percent of its population had died and been displaced.[48]

What truly distinguished the 1040s from other decades in terms of disasters was the frequent occurrence of earthquakes. It seems that the subcontinent of China entered a geologically active time. Starting from the mid-1030s, Shanxi, the highland region west to Hebei, experienced a series of earthquakes over five days, causing the deaths of 22,391 people (another report said 60 percent of the local population), injuring 5,655 people, and killing more than 50,000 livestock.[49] In 1037, the earthquakes extended to the metropolitan area of Kaifeng in Henan. Over the next ten years, these places experienced frequent earthquakes. Larger earthquakes caused serious ground ruptures and eruptions of underground water, dust, and other substances.[50]

If the earthquakes in the 1030s were merely regional disruptions, what followed in the 1040s were empire-wide calamities. In 1045 and 1046 in particular, multiple earthquakes broke out simultaneously or closely followed each other in the frontier region and eastern part of Hebei. Roaring tides came from the Bohai Gulf, which indicate earthquakes at the bottom of the ocean. In the Shandong peninsula southeast of Hebei, an earthquake caused a coastal hill to collapse into the ocean. From Shanxi to the west, to Shaanxi where the Song and the Xixia shared borders, and to Henan at the core of the empire, various regions continued to report earthquakes. The southern half of the empire was not quiet either. From the Sichuan basin in the southwest to Hunan and Hubei, and all the way along the middle reaches of the Yangzi valley, earthquakes occurred one after another. As far south as in Guangdong, reports came back to the court about earthquakes both on land and in the ocean. Earthquakes

---

46 *XCB*, 147: 3554 and 158: 3831.
47 Qian Yanyuan, "Shang Renzong dazhao lun hanzai [To respond to Emperor Renzong's edict on discussing the drought]," *SMCZY*, 40: 1a–6b.
48 *OYXQJ*, 126: 1914.
49 *XCB*, 120: 2840 and 2844.
50 *XCB*, 120: 2840 and 145: 3518.

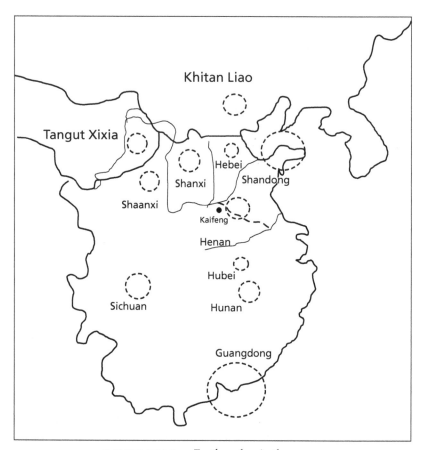

ILLUSTRATION 9. Earthquakes in the 1040s

continued in the highland areas of Shanxi and Shaanxi after 1046, and
in early 1048, they returned to central Hebei, shortly before the Yellow
River shifted its course.[51] In 1048, the land north to Hebei within the
Liao's territory was also reported for earthquake.

There are no detailed descriptions of the severity of each of these
earthquakes.[52] However, by simply pinning down the rough locations
of their occurrences over a map of China, the sheer spatial breadth is

---

[51] *XCB*, 155: 3766; 156: 3792; 157: 3798; 158: 3821, 3823, 3826; and 159: 3844, 3846,
     3849.
[52] Some seismologists and historical geographers used textual materials to reconstruct the
     scale and severity of some of the earthquakes. See Institute of Geophysics et al. (1990).

astonishing. The simultaneous occurrence of multiple earthquakes in various parts of China over several consecutive years was rarely seen in Chinese history. It has not happened in the recent history of China, although modern seismic technology is capable of detecting and measuring earthquakes. Chinese experiences with modern earthquakes like the famous Tangshan 唐山 earthquake in 1973 and the Wenchuan 汶川 earthquake in 2008 do not help us understand the scale of the disasters in the 1040s. However devastating they were, these modern earthquakes were singular events that took place in limited areas, had a limited duration, and did not trigger a series of earthquakes in ensuing years. It is hard for us to conceptualize what it was like for the ground all over China to be shaking at the same time. Therefore, I believe it is not a stretch to claim that the 1040s was an exceptional geological period with extraordinary tectonic movement.

These exceptional geological activities released tremendous energy and emitted enormous substances from the depth of the earth into the air to tint the snow in Hebei in 1045 with a red color. Most likely, such geological turbulence forcefully reshaped the macroclimate over China, which may explain the heat and the climatic dryness in that decade, and perhaps in the previous decade as well. Despite the lack of direct evidence, let me make a bold conjecture: this climatic dryness may have contributed to the reduction in the Yellow River's water volume and thereby its floods for a few years before 1048 – a phenomenon to be mentioned in the next chapter. Meanwhile, the frequent movement of the earth's crust itself, especially in north China, might have shaken and destabilized the old course of the Yellow River and contributed to its dramatic course shift in 1048. Unfortunately, we have no extant evidence to either support or contradict this hypothesis. As I will analyze in greater detail in the next chapter, without knowing to what extent the forces of nature made the river shift its course, we are at least able to appreciate the substantial efforts that humans – in this particular case, the Song state and its institutions – made to push the river northward.

The variety of environmental disasters must have caused tremendous harm to the Song society. Harvests failed because of the prevailing droughts and sudden coldness and floods. Since Hebei witnessed red snow, we also have reason to believe that the emission of chemical substances might have changed the microclimate in this part of China and affected – vert likely polluted – its soil and water to some extent. The dryness and shortage of water might have reduced the water volume in various rivers and made Hebei's water transportation less reliable. All this contributed to a general economic downturn and compounded the hardship that was already caused by various military, political, and socio-economic problems, a situation we examined earlier in the chapter. The hardship was particularly serious in regions like Hebei and Shanxi that were most heavily plagued by the environmental disasters.

The impact of the environmental disasters on the state was multi-dimensional. There was certainly a material impact, which put additional stress on the state revenue and its financial arrangements. But from a non-material perspective, the disasters disturbed the state and its ruling members psychologically. Between the late 1030s and 1048, statesmen and officials hastened to inform Emperor Renzong about what happened outside his imperial court. They fearfully warned him of the menacing signs from the Heaven: the state had never experienced so many disasters in previous decades; the disasters indicated the state's cosmological and moral crisis, for "the will of the Heaven signals change."[53] The kind of "moral meteorology" that Mark Elvin observes for late imperial China, which held the ruling members of the state responsible for climatic-environmental changes, prevailed in Song China too.[54] The state should be frightened; it should reflect upon its morals and conducts and correct its faults. Alarmed, the emperor issued multiple edicts to blame himself for his poor leadership and moral inadequacy. Claiming responsibility, his Grand Councilors ushered in memorials to accuse themselves of faults and begged for resignation and punishment.

It was this sense of an environmental–cosmological crisis, together with other human crises that the state experienced in military, political, and socio-economic realms, that caused the ruling members to reevaluate their governance and prompted many to call for a reform. This sense of crisis also convinced Emperor Renzong to side with the reformists in the early 1040s, because if he chose not to, not only his personal rule but also the imperial state established by his forebearers to which he had dedicated his life would soon meet its demise. Hence, the heightening disasters in the 1040s served as an environmental–cosmological drive to facilitate political changes and sponsor the rise of reformist politicians like Fan Zhongyan, Ouyang Xiu, Fu Bi, and Han Qi. However, the environmental disasters read as portentous signs were open toward various, and even

[53] Bao Zheng's comment, *QSW*, 539: 318.
[54] Elvin (1998: 213–237).

conflicting, interpretations. Conservative, anti-reform officials referred to the disasters – in particular the instability of the earth – as an expression of Heaven's rage toward the radical reformists. They used the earthquakes as evidence for their claim that reform policies destabilized the originally tranquil, harmonious state of the world. These accusations appeared more convincing than the reformists' criticism of the old-fashioned, inefficient, and sluggish system of the state governance. The conservatives' accusations reversed the tide of opinion at the court and changed the emperor's mind; they eventually led to the ouster of reform leaders in 1045.[55]

As the institutional efforts to change the status quo were abolished, the Song's mid-dynasty crises continued to mount and disturb the imperial state and the society. In the previous chapter, we examined some of the state building process that featured the centralization of power and the formation of a core-periphery political structure, which turned Hebei into a political, military, socio-economic, and environmental periphery of the empire. By the 1040s, it had become clear that such power concentration encountered various challenges and the core-periphery structure did not seem very stable. The burgeoning problems in different realms and at different locales – many associated with Hebei – threatened the state's sense of security and stability. The existential crisis and the survivor's mentality the young Song state experienced in the late tenth century did not disappear due to the state's achievements in its early decades. Rather, they transformed into a new set of crisis and anxiety in the middle of the dynasty.

Into this context, suddenly, there came the catastrophic flood and course shift of the Yellow River in the summer of 1048. The environmental drama that this book opens with in the Prologue, after a lengthy prelude, would finally deliver its most ferocious blow. So far we have focused the discussion on the changing relationship between the imperial state and Hebei and suggested that a politically and socio-economically peripheralized Hebei would pave the way for the abrupt surge of the river's course into its land. How had Hebei, an environmental entity marginally related to the Yellow River during the previous thousand years, gradually encountered the river, emerged as a potential flooding

---

[55] For factional struggles during the Qingli reform, see Liu (1957, 1967), Bol (1992: 176–211), and Levine (2008: 9–10; 47–56).

ground to bear the river's turbulent body, and eventually suffered the river's intrusion? The next chapter will target these questions by investigating how the state, in order to permanently pacify the disastrous Yellow River, interacted with both the river and Hebei, and brought these two entities together.

4

Creating a Delta Landscape

Imagine you are living in central Hebei on the sixth day of the sixth lunar month in 1048. You may still be experiencing or trying to recover from hardship due to droughts, earthquakes, and harvest failures in the previous few years. You have never seen the Yellow River before; it has always been far away. Family elders may have told you stories about the river, but you have never felt any real connection to it. Whether a peasant or town-dweller, the river has had nothing to do with your daily life. All of a sudden, on that day, you hear a roaring in the distance. It grows louder and louder, screams rising out of its dull thundering. Before you have time to figure out what is happening, the water comes upon you in gigantic torrents. People, livestock, and buildings are all swallowed by the violent waves. Stunned, you are swept away. There is nothing but water all around you. Gasping for air and close to drowning, you begin to paddle as the old, weak, and unlucky are sucked under all around you. You and the other lucky ones grab onto a tree or make it to high ground.

The tremendous flood comes without warning; no one even knows which river has flooded. No one in central Hebei is prepared for a disaster like this one. Over the next several hours, you watch the torrents dismantling villages and sweeping away your neighbors, and even your own children and parents. Only after days pass do the high waters begin to ebb. Dead bodies of people and animals bob in the currents. As you and your fellow survivors desperately wait for rescue and relief, which

Parts of this chapter appear in a book chapter in *Nature, the Environment and Climate Change in East Asia* edited by Carmen Meinhert, see Zhang (2013: 137–162).

may never arrive at all, you look into each other's eyes, already drained of hope. Perhaps the only thing left are the questions, "Why did this happen?" and "Why did this happen to us?"

In the summer of 1048, the question of why must have haunted most of Hebei's flood refugees. This question is equally intriguing to us, modern readers of history. Chapter 1 has informed us that for nearly a thousand years, the river and the plain had maintained a geographically, environmentally marginal relationship. How did this long-term status quo come to an abrupt end? Also, we know in retrospect that, after occupying the Hebei Plain for eighty years, the river shifted out this land in 1128; since then it stayed away from Hebei and restored a marginal relationship with it for almost 900 years. Was this unique, brief episode of history – the eighty-year-long entanglement between the river and the plain – a random incident? If we follow modern hydrologists' explanation of the river's mechanism as "prone to siltation, prone to overflow, and prone to course shifts," and the long-term environmental transformation on the Loess Plateau that I sketched in Chapter 1, it seems that what happened in 1048 was an inevitable, natural outcome of the long-term environmental tendency. It appeared simply as a tragic but "natural" catastrophe brought about by the unfathomable forces of the river itself, or as a dramatic but unforeseeable climax to the Song's mid-dynasty crisis in the 1040s.[1]

Those living in the eleventh century who had experienced the dramatic event reached similar answers. For educated men and officials inside and outside Hebei, and perhaps for Emperor Renzong as well, their search for the answer went beyond the welfare of individuals. Taught to believe in Heaven's Mandate as well as a cosmological view of the resonance between natural phenomena and human behaviors, they might have wondered whether or not this disastrous event was another heavenly punishment for human misconduct or the state's ill governance, following on a series of portentous signs from the previous years, such as earthquakes, red snow, and plagues of locusts.

Among the more scientifically and technologically minded men of the age, there were those who refused to attribute everything to the will of an abstract Heaven or to interpret disasters in purely moral terms.

[1] By collecting historical data of rainfall, Man Zhimin (2014: 20–25) has postulated a positive correlation between increasing rainfall in middle-period China and the increase in the Yellow River's floods. This view certainly contributes to the general understanding of the flooding events as "natural" disasters.

These men observed the pattern of the river's floods and came up with answers that are fairly close to modern hydrological explanations. To Ouyang Xiu, the Yellow River carried such a heavy silt load that it would inevitably build up in the riverbed and clog the river course. Given enough time, this hydrological characteristic would invariably lead to an overflow of the river.[2] Even without knowledge of gravity, people in the Song were convinced by empirical observations that water would flow downward toward the lowland. "It was the form/circumstances of the earth," Liu Chang 劉敞 (1019–1068) explained, which caused the river to breach the dykes.[3] As Hebei was considered low-lying, it was understandable that the river, once free of the constraints of its dykes, would flow northward into Hebei. To these men, the river was subjected to what we might term "natural" forces. It was these forces, rather than cosmological and moral principles, that precipitated the disaster.

However different they appear, these explanations of the 1048 event seem to agree on one point: people were not directly involved in the physical movement of the river; they remained passive before cosmological or natural forces. Similar to our modern assumption, these medieval views also suggested that people, especially those living along the river's lower reaches, were powerless to stop the river from flooding. A catastrophe as gigantic as the 1048 event was merely a hydrological issue. It would occur sooner or later if not precisely in the summer of 1048, and slightly upstream or downstream if not precisely at the site of Shanghu. The river hydrology, similar to the large-scaled geological forces that we discussed in Chapter 1, determined when the river flooded and toward what direction it shifted course. There was not much that manpower could do to cause, intervene in, or avoid the situation.

The present chapter turns from hydrology to hydraulics by bringing the Song state into the long-term marginal environmental relationship between the river and the Hebei Plain, and questioning how the arrival of the state in 960 changed this relationship. By investigating the pattern of the river's movements and imperial states' hydraulic works during the hundred years prior to 1048, the chapter reveals that the river's course shift into Hebei was not an "act of God," as the hydro-geologist Gilbert

---

[2] "Lun xiuhe diyizhuang [The first memorial on repairing the Yellow River]," 109: 1642–1644; "Lun xiuhe dierzhuang [The second memorial on repairing the Yellow River]," 109: 1646–1648; "Lun xiuhe disanzhuang [The third memorial on repairing the Yellow River]," 109: 1650–1652 in *OYXQJ*.

[3] "Shang Renzong lun xiu Shanghukou [Memorial to Emperor Renzong on repairing the bank rupture at Shanghu]," *GSJ*, 31: 12b–13b, p. 1095–1668.

White once famously termed floods.[4] Rather, it was a consequence of trialectic struggles among the river, the Hebei Plain, and the imperial state. In the trialectic relationship, the state's deliberate choices and subtle manipulations pushed the river a little by a little toward the empire's northeastern periphery. To put it plainly, the peripheralized Hebei was chosen by the state to serve as the river's flooding ground, and to bear the immense suffering from the river's overwhelming power. For the crisis-ridden Song state, this peculiar way of dealing with the river bolstered the state's constant efforts to subdue and appropriate Hebei – making this political and socio-economic periphery into an environmental periphery. In this sense, the state's management of the turbulent environment, just like its appropriation of traditionally decentralizing regions like Hebei, contributed to the state building process. Given the state's forceful environmental management, the life of the river, the plain of Hebei, and the imperial state became inextricably entangled.

4.1   Why Hebei?

A brief survey of historical sources leading up to the 1048 flood indicates that the river naturally tended toward Henan – the land in the south – rather than toward Hebei. From various Tang, Five Dynasties, and Song sources, I single out forty-two years from a span of 350 years prior to 1048, in which the river's floods, bank ruptures, and course shifts reportedly took place.[5] Among these forty-two years, thirty-six give us some rough indication of the locations where the events occurred or the areas that the floods affected. They demonstrate the river's tendency to shift between two trajectories, northward into Hebei or southward into the heart of Henan (see Table 2). What is immediately obvious from a cursory glance at this information is that by the late tenth century, the river consistently flooded the area to its south. By the end of the tenth century, however, the river began to flood the area to its north with greater frequency. Does this mean that the river developed a "natural" tendency toward the north, and the 1048 event was merely the culmination of the centuries-long tendency?

---

[4] White (1945: 2).

[5] Two years in the eighth century, three years in the ninth century, twenty-six years in the tenth century, and twelve years in the first forty-seven years of the eleventh century. The data are collected from *Jiu Tang shu*, *Xin Tang shu*, *Jiu Wudai shi*, *Xin Wudai shi*, *Zizhi tongjian*, *Xu Zizhitongjian changbian*, *Song shi*, *Song huiyao*, and various personal diaries and collections between the eighth and early twelfth centuries.

TABLE 2. *The Yellow River's Floods before 1048*

Year	Direction of Flooding	Year	Direction of Flooding	Year	Direction of Flooding	Year	Direction of Flooding
722	North	941	South	972	South	1000	South
813	South	944	South	973	South/North	1011	North
829	South	946	South and North	977	South	1012	North
891	South	954	South and North	978	North	1014	North
918	South	964	South and North	979	North	1015	North
923	South	965	South	982	South/North	1019	South
931	South	966	North	983	South	1028	North
932	South and North	968	North	992	North	1034	North
939	South	971	South	993	North	1041	North

A close examination of these records leads to quite a different picture. First, the records suggest that most northerly floods happened on a small scale; by contrast, the southerly floods led to more destructive, widespread damage. In many cases, the river even shifted its entire course toward the south to affect the Huai River valley. In terms of scale and severity of floods, the river seemed to tend toward the south. Second, the exacerbation of the river's flooding problems went hand in hand with the establishment of strong central authorities in north China centering on the land of Henan. Their increasing commitment to flood control led to the construction of hydraulic works along the southern banks of the river. Such efforts helped prevent southerly floods. But as their unintended consequence, these efforts pushed the river's hydrological force to concentrate on the weaker northern banks, thereby increasing the chance of northerly floods. If the river indeed developed a northward tendency from the end of the tenth century, it was most likely a product of the deliberate hydraulic efforts, which prioritized the south at the expense of the north.

A scrutiny of a few floods and hydraulic practices demonstrates how the states before and including the Song intervened more and more in the movements of the Yellow River. In 918 and 923, two different generals of the Late Liang Dynasty 後梁 (907–923) commanded their armies to breach the river's dykes in order to create floods that would halt the advancement of their enemies from the north.[6] The floods let loose by these actions were supposed to submerge the enemy's land in the north, but in reality, they plagued the core territory of the Late Liang, Henan. Embroiled in the war, the Liang never even tried to ameliorate the disasters. In the following decades, the destabilized Yellow River flooded Henan in 931, 932, 939, 941, 944, and 954, with catastrophic effects.[7]

Only the flood of 954 led to the beginning of strong flood-control efforts from the Chinese state then in power, the Late Zhou Dynasty 後周 (951–960). The Zhou, unlike the negligent Late Liang, immediately recruited corvée laborers to repair the bank rupture and to stop the flood from extending farther south.[8] The Zhou emperor, Shizong 世宗 (921–959), was young, energetic, and capable, and he sought to pacify the violent river as he had conquered his military enemies.[9] Through his efforts, the broken dykes were repaired, the river's tendency toward the south was blocked and its water was pushed northward. These actions created a vast stretch of waterlogged land in southern Hebei and northern Henan. Because these waters did not threaten the political core area of his state, the emperor made no further effort to handle them. Year after year, these stagnant waters ravaged the northern land unchecked, hurting the livelihood of the people, particularly those in southern Hebei.

The troubling situation remained unchanged through 964, four years after the Northern Song Dynasty had replaced the Late Zhou. Local residents and officials in southern Hebei petitioned the Song court to have the water problem fixed.[10] Such requests failed to attract any substantial attention from the court. The court claimed that it could not afford the immense financial and labor costs required for the hydraulic work. It also noted that if the stagnant waters were to leave southern Hebei, it would need to flow somewhere else. Who wanted to take over the waters? Certainly not the core political area in central Henan on the southern side of the river. Like the Late Zhou before it, the Song court chose to ignore the problem and stick with the status quo, much to the detriment of southern Hebei. A hydraulic approach, "protect the south and ignore the north," emerged. Although it was not intended as a deliberate assault on the people in the north, it more or less generated the same effect.

---

[6] *Zizhi tongjian*, 270: 8824 and 272: 8890.
[7] *Jiu Wudai shi*, 141: 1882–1883. *SS*, 91: 2256–2257.
[8] *SS*, 91: 2256–2257.
[9] For the history of the Five Dynasties, see Naomi Standen and Hugh Clark in Twitchett and Smith (2009).
[10] *SS*, 91: 2257.

The Song's southern bias dominated its later hydraulic practices. In 965 alone, a series of bank ruptures and floods broke out in the metropolitan area of Kaifeng as well as Mengzhou 孟州, Chanzhou, and Yunzhou 惲州 – all within a distance of 200 kilometers from Kaifeng. Later, floods occurred in Huazhou in 966 and 967, in Chanzhou in 971, and in Chanzhou, Puzhou 濮州, and Kaifeng in 972.[11] The majority of the territories of these districts were located in Henan, suggesting that the river continued to flood toward the south, thus threatening the capital at Kaifeng. In each case the Song government followed the Late Zhou precedent of 954: it immediately repaired the bank ruptures without any hesitation despite heavy costs. It is obvious that the state had become very sensitive to the river's threat to Henan, the land to the south of the river, and would do whatever it could to protect it.

The Late Zhou and Song states' treatments of the floods suggest four things. First, the river's bank ruptures and floods became increasingly frequent through the tenth century, of which the Song state was well aware. Second, serious floods continued to occur on the southern side of the river, and on several occasions the river even shifted its entire course into Henan. The state fixed the problems promptly and by doing so, pushed the river back to the north. There is no historical or modern scientific evidence to suggest that the river had naturally shifted away from the south. Rather, it was human forces – the imperial state's deployment of certain policies and various resources – that prevented the river from remaining in the south. Third, the state's interventions did far more than block the southerly floods. As historical geographer Li Xiaocong has specified, by repairing and constructing dykes, the state's technical solutions forced the river to press northward, thereby increasing both the chance and severity of northerly floods.[12] The increasing number of the northerly floods, which Table 1 exhibits, was the consequence of both the southerly floods and the state's hydraulic practices – the latter sacrificed the land in the north for the safety of the politically important Henan. Lastly, one may argue about the creditability of the historical records. The records for the southerly floods were perhaps better constructed and preserved; yet, those for the northerly floods might be poor, implying that there were perhaps more northerly floods than that recorded in real history. This argument, in effect, lends credence to my argument by pointing out the state's neglect of the land north of

[11] *SS*, 91: 2257–2258.
[12] Li (1986: 138–144).

the river, a neglect that left Hebei poorly protected and vulnerable to disasters.

As we can see, behind all of these "natural" disasters lurks a series of responses of the imperial state, whose calculus of sacrifice and salvation came to have dire consequences for Hebei. These early approaches of the state to disasters and environmental management drove the further development of the state's hydraulic policies and practices over the next few decades. During that period, Hebei loomed large as the state's chosen environmental victim who, by becoming the river's flooding ground, saved the land in the south and guarded the greater good for the state.

4.2   To Flood South or to Flood North – A Politico-Hydraulic Enterprise

The State Perception of Geopolitics and the River

The Song state was involved with flood control from the moment of its founding. The first emperor, Taizu, immediately assumed the role of "hydraulic leader" (following Karl Wittfogel's notion[13]) and set up official positions in every district along the river's lower reaches to take charge of flood-control works. His government went to great lengths to prevent floods by investing large sums of money, recruiting corvée labor, planting trees along riverbanks, and building and repairing river dykes. When floods and bank ruptures did occur, the government treated them as emergencies, and took prompt actions to cope with them.[14] To Taizu, the institutional and technical efforts were to pacify the river's ferocious torrents and restore its peaceful, tranquil state before the tenth century.

The more the state labored to prevent floods, however, the more hopeless the situation became: flooding events grew more frequent and more severe. The river continued to send down tremendous amounts of silt, and in the lower stretches of the river the extraordinary speed of sedimentation and the resulting increase in the force of water flows overwhelmed any human efforts. The years of 965, 966, 967, and 971 saw the explosion of serial floods and bank ruptures, with most of these floods extending southward toward the capital Kaifeng. 972 was a particularly devastating year. During the fifth and sixth lunar months, north China

---

[13] Wittfogel (1957).

[14] For detailed studies on the Song's water management, especially on its hydraulic institutions, see Yoshioka (1978) and Nagase (1983). For hydraulic technology, see Needham et al. (1971) and Flessel (1974).

suffered extensive rain, which caused water levels to soar and to breach banks at several locations. "There are severe floods in various prefectures on both the southern side and the northern side of the river."[15] Once again, the river's southerly floods threatened the capital. Over all of north China, agriculture was decimated, large numbers of people were forced to flee their land, various supplies ran short, and food supplies in the capital could barely sustain its population for half a year. The demand for food diverted grain through long-distance transportation from the lower Yangzi valley to the north. The flood, the harvest failure, and the difficulty of shipping goods made 972 a year of "great hunger (*daji* 大饑)."[16]

Faced with a crisis of such magnitude, Emperor Taizu and his young imperial state discovered that more than a decade of battling the river had yielded only frustration, insecurity, and anxiety. Before long, the state came to grasp its vulnerable position within north China's unstable environmental system. Such awareness urged the ruling members of the state to evaluate the significance of the Yellow River against the state's geopolitical context. River disasters should no longer be treated as individual, random incidents to be contained by individual technical solutions; they should now be seen as grave threats to the stability of the fledgling state. The river must be incorporated into the state's holistic geopolitical structure as something so critical as possibly to jeopardize the fate of the newly established Song state. This new realization forced the state to accept that the power of the physical environment often surpassed that of the state, to ground the state's geopolitical considerations within a broader environmental context and to take serious any environmental challenges imposed by the recalcitrant river upon its political and socio-economic advancement.

To understand how this realization of the entwined relationship of the state and the Yellow River shaped the state's hydraulic policies, let us read the geopolitics in the late tenth century through the state's eyes. In the late tenth century, the Song state, led by Emperor Taizu, saw the world around it as complicated and hostile. Following the precedent set by its short-lived predecessors of the Five Dynasties, the Song settled its political core in the Henan area. There, the plain of Henan provided an economic, political, and military base to the state, with Kaifeng in northern Henan as its capital. The great strength of this imperial city was

---

[15] XCB, 13: 283–285.
[16] XCB, 13: 293.

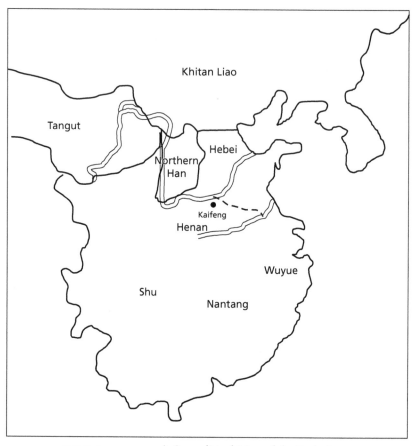

ILLUSTRATION 10. A Geopolitical Map of the Early Song

its proximity to convenient water transportation. The Bian Canal, whose northern end was connected with the Yellow River and southern end with the Huai River and the Yangzi valley, ran directly through the city. As the central artery of an empire-wide transportation system, the canal shipped wealth and goods from the south to supply the heavily populated metropolitan area of Kaifeng and the enormous military forces spread throughout north China. But the tie between Kaifeng and the canal also posed a serious danger.[17] Located less than a hundred kilometers south to the Yellow River, the city faced increasing flooding threats from the latter. Any danger the river inflicted toward the south would not only harm the city itself, but also jeopardize the canal. Flooding that damaged

---

[17] For environmental conditions of Kaifeng, see Cheng (2002).

the canal and clogged its channel with silt would render the canal unnavigable.

A decade into its rule, Henan was still the sole region solidly under Song control. Beyond this political core area, the land all around remained a politically and militarily contested zone. In south China, the Wuyue 吳越 (907–978) and Southern Tang 南唐 (937–975) kingdoms in the Yangzi valley were still independent from the Northern Song. In the southwest, Sichuan had just surrendered to the Song but was not yet under the Song's solid control. In north China, the political situation was even less clear and stable. In the far northwest, Shaanxi had fallen in the hands of the semi-nomadic Tangut, who later grew to be a major enemy of the Song. Shanxi remained under the control of the Northern Han 北漢 (951–979) kingdom, whose ruler relied on the overlordship of the nomadic regime of the Khitan for protection. In 969, Emperor Taizu attempted to conquer the Northern Han, but his military expedition ended in defeat. In the northeast, from the mid-tenth century onward, the central government had developed better control over Hebei, whose warlords gradually submitted to the state. Yet, as I discussed in Chapters 1 and 2, Hebei's autonomous tradition remained strong; regional leaders, if dissatisfied with the Song state, might easily divorce the state and claim independency. Beyond the northern border of Hebei, the Khitan was the Song's fearsome enemy. Nearly every year through the end of the tenth century the Khitan cavalry marched southwards to plunder Hebei, posing a constant threat to the Song's frontier security.[18] Besieged on almost all sides, the leaders of the Song must have wondered if the young state could survive the threats posed by the hostile neighbors or if it would follow in the unfortunate footsteps of its five predecessors and become the sixth short-lived regime.

Adding to this worrisome geopolitical situation, the state could not escape the dangers of a destabilized environment. In the 970s, in order to survive any inter-state conflicts, the Song required, at the very least, a strong home base. Yet, its core area lay in a low-lying plain, without natural barriers. To make the situation even worse, the monstrous Yellow River attacked this area with constant floods. The southerly floods and course shifts undermined Henan's – hence the state's – economic growth, labor capacity, and political solidarity. The environmental challenges at the heart of the Song's territory, just like the political and

---

[18] For a political and military history of north China, see Lau Nap-yin and Huang K'uan-chung in Twitchett and Smith (2009: 206–278). For a discussion on the early Song's administrative geography, see Mostern (2011: 103–165).

military enemies surrounding its borders, were a major component of the hostile world that the state was born into in the late tenth century. Hence, the Yellow River became a major player in the state politics. Any hydraulic management that the state conducted with regard to the river would invariably incur serious political implications. The river had become a matter of "national security."[19]

Given such geopolitical-environmental realities, the state was forced to reflect on its existing flood control practices, which had heretofore dealt with individual floods by means of individual technical solutions, be it constructing dykes to block water or opening a small channel to drain water. These practices needed to be embedded in a systematic politico-hydraulic enterprise, which balanced the state's political demands and its environmental constraints. Hence, in order for a hydraulic plan to work, the state needed not only to understand the plan's technological challenges but also to rationalize the plan's potential political benefits and costs. This meant that the state had to make hydraulic choices and decisions in both environmental and political terms.

Emperor Taizu's Politico-Hydraulic Landscape
Against this backdrop, after the outbreak of flood and famine in 972, Emperor Taizu issued an edict to lay out his understanding of the Yellow River issues:

Lately, it has been raining in the prefectures of Chan, Pu, and others. The torrential river has caused disasters. We have suffered so much flooding, which has severely troubled the people. Therefore, whenever reading past literature, I attentively study river issues. As for the records of the Xia period, they mention only diverting the river to the sea and smoothing its stream in accordance with mountainous terrains. It is never heard [in those records] that [people] managed the torrents by force and by constructing extensive high embankments. In the Warring States period, various states pursued their own interests by clogging the old river courses [in Hebei]. Small interests obstructed large affairs, and the private harmed the public. Therefore, the system of the "Nine Rivers" [i.e., various branches of

---

[19] In the rest of the book I will compare our case study with studies on hydraulics in late-imperial China by scholars such as Pierre-Etienne Will (1980, 1985) and Peter Perdue (1987), and point out their differences, especially in terms of the relationship between hydraulics and state power. A fundamental difference lies in different waterbodies and imperial states' differing perceptions toward them. Unlike the Yellow River in the Song period as a national-security issue that directly threatened the state's sense of survival, many water issues in late-imperial China that scholars have studied were regional or local issues, but not necessarily a state affair from the state's point of view.

the river's lower reaches in the Hebei Plain that were said to be dredged by the legendary Yu] was eliminated. Since then, river disasters continued without an end throughout later dynasties.[20]

The emperor expressed his regret over the river's endless damage, and criticized the uselessness of conventional approaches in dealing with the floods. Using the conduct and achievements of the legendary sage king Yu the Great 大禹 as a yardstick for contemporary flood-control activities, Emperor Taizu conveyed five logically interconnected messages.[21]

First, Taizu contrasted the hydraulic techniques of blocking water by erecting dykes, as was often done in history, to Yu's method of diverting water to the sea through various channels. To Emperor Taizu, the former used human forces to go against the natural tendency of the river, and had led to repeated failures. The latter was deemed natural, since it respected the geophysical features of the land. The naturalness of the latter technique led to Yu's success. Hence, the Song state should use the latter as the principle for its hydraulic works.

Second, Hebei was deemed a natural lowland. Only by directing the Yellow River into the so-called "Nine Rivers" through Hebei did the sage king succeed in his hydraulic works. Yu's victory seemed the only recorded and "proven" (albeit mythological according to our modern views) one in the history of Yellow River flood control. With such understanding, the emperor hinted that a successful hydraulic plan should follow the tracks of the Nine Rivers and let the river flow northward to Hebei, rather than southward to Henan, the Song state's political core region. Hebei, therefore, was discursively constructed as a naturally, technically, and historically legitimate bearer of the disastrous river.

Third, although being a legitimate bearer of the river, Hebei would unavoidably be harmed by a shifting river, and such potential harm must be addressed by the state. The emperor implied that allowing the river to flood Hebei would not terribly damage the land and people there, because Hebei's harm was minor in comparison with the greater good it could bring about to the imperial state. Here, the emperor rationalized his political philosophy on the state-society relationship, advocating a "state first and society second" ideology. He employed the legend of Yu

---

[20] *SS*, 91: 2258.
[21] For studies about Yu the Great, see Lewis (2006). Heping Liu (2012: 91–126) examines how the legend of Yu the Great influenced the Northern Song state's governance. Ruth Mostern (2011) discusses the development of geographic scholarship on the text, "Tribute of Yu," in the Song period.

as an ideological tool to justify the state's demand for Hebei's sacrifice in political and moral terms. The emperor used the territorial separation and political unrest of early China as a historical analogy to signify the social, political, and environmental uncertainty of his own time. The political decentralization that hurt state interests caused the failure of any holistic, systematic treatment of the river; conversely, the dysfunction of the river system deepened the breakdown of political unity and centrality of a state. Hence, political conditions and the river's hydraulic works were not only entwined but also mutually constitutive. Only by integrating political and moral correctness with technical soundness did Yu achieve both the hydraulic success and the state's centrality. Without such integration, not only would any hydraulic work be doomed to fail, but the state itself would also face demise.

For Emperor Taizu, the river hydraulics bore extraordinary political significance precisely because hydraulics was politically productive – a tamed environment would not only strengthen the state but also, through and only through the growth of the state, protect and promote the well-being of the people. Given such understanding, the emperor called on his subjects to surrender their private interests to the common interests and the greater good for the imperial state, and to conduct hydraulic works in ways to prioritize the state's interests. Only by doing so, he implied, the state would legitimately trump private and regional interests, consolidate itself, and ultimately deliver equal care to its society. Given all this, the emperor called for Hebei's sacrifice and justified the river's harm to Hebei.[22]

---

[22] For a detailed analysis on the emperor's edict, especially on contrasting notions like "public" and "private" in the light of the state-society relationship, see Zhang (2013: 137–162). Emperor Taizu's perception of the state–society relationship influenced Northern Song politics throughout the dynasty; it was strongly echoed and further strengthened by reformist political thinkers like Wang Anshi in the 1060s–1070s, who advocated a powerful, activist state that superseded, led, regulated, and delivered care to the society. See further discussion about this in Chapter 5. In this book, I acknowledge the state as a self-conscious, self-preserving entity with bounded autonomy and capacity. Thinking along with various statist theorists (e.g., Evans, Rueschemeyer, and Skocpol in *Bringing the State Back In*; and Joel S. Migdal for the "state-in-society" approach and the emphasis on the state's everyday life), I consider the state as a compromised, partially autonomous entity that strives to behave rationally and to formulate self-promoting intentions, but in reality it constantly suffers from bounded rationality and external complications Such a state is incapable of forming or asserting lucid and coherent intentions; it has to collaborate, negotiate, and conflict with the society, thus sharing blurry boundaries with the society. Despite such limitation, the state still maintains consciousness of its own existence and well-being. It distinguishes its core values and interests from those of the society. And it strives to keep its self-identity and

Fourth, built on the previous point, the emperor hinted that none of the Song state's previous hydraulic efforts were able to bring to north China permanent environmental peace. Even Yu did not achieve a total success in taming the river. Yu had to sacrifice Hebei in the north as the river's flooding ground in order to preserve the greater good. Based on this understanding, the emperor implied that a "limited state" like the early Northern Song should admit its constraints and abandon its hope for a complete, permanent success.[23] Instead, it should aim at a partial success by producing a pragmatic, compromised environment, in which not everyone would equally benefit from the state's hydraulic care; rather, the political core area would receive better protection, and the imperial state as a whole would survive its troubled youth. Given this logic, sacrifices had to be made; the state had to rationalize its decision and choose its victim. Obviously, Yu's legend helped Emperor Taizu to justify the sacrifice of Hebei, the land in the north.

Last, in a somewhat buried message, the edict sought to strengthen the legitimacy of the Song state. In the late tenth century, anyone who had concerns about the legitimacy of their ruler must have wondered why Emperor Taizu and his Song state were chosen to receive the Mandate of Heaven and, if they were virtuous enough to keep it, why their rule over north China was so frequently and severely challenged by river disasters.

self-image even when burdened by external complications and facing constant encroachment from societal forces. Throughout the Northern Song period, the awareness and emphasis of the state (*guojia*) remained strong among its ruling members. Such awareness of the existence of a state and the pursuit of statehood were especially strong when challenges to the state arose and its conflicts with the society became intensified. This was when, such as in the early Song, the state rulers prioritized the state's interests and sacrificed the needs and interests of the society. This understanding of the state resonates with Chaffee and Twitchett's (2015: 7) judgment of the pragmatic nature of the Song state. Emphasizing the state's self-consciousness and self-protection, I regard Emperor Taizu's utilization of the legend of Yu as an ideological tool for the purpose of preserving the state, not foremost and ultimately for the purpose of caring for the people. This understanding differs from Heping Liu's (2012: 91–126) interpretation that Song rulers used the legend of Yu as inspiration for ideal rulership and benevolent governance. In her study on famine relief and flood control during the Qing and Republican periods, Kathryn Edgerton-Tarpley (2014: 447–469) discusses the legend of Yu and holds a similar interpretation as Heping Liu. But she also suggests a shift of state emphasis "from 'nourish the people' to 'sacrifice for the nation'" during the late imperial-modern transition. The Song history demonstrates that there was never such a shift in the Song period. As the present and next two chapters continue to show, the state prioritized self-protection and self-promotion by demanding the society's sacrifice; it always put its survival and prosperity before the well-being of the society.

[23] To follow Peter Perdue's (1987) argument on the limited capacity of state power based on his study in the Ming-Qing period.

The early Song state could not ignore the cosmological link between river disasters as messages from Heaven and its ruler's insecurity in his role as the monarch. After all, by 972 the Song had just entered its second decade; memories of the frequent failures and dynastic successions of its predecessors remained fresh among the ruling members and in the society. There was no evidence that the Song would last any longer than the previous regimes. Furthermore, Emperor Taizu's usurpation of the throne from the Late Zhou Dynasty through a mutiny did not lend him much moral power.

Bringing the sage king Yu into the Song's politico-hydraulic discourse helped mediate the Song's cosmological and legitimacy crisis. The edict reminded people – or at the very least comforted Emperor Taizu's own heart – that even under the rule of Yu, the river flooded terribly and people suffered.[24] Disasters and suffering did not prevent Yu from becoming one of the most virtuous and successful rulers in history. River disasters might not be Heaven's punishment for poor governance; rather, they were tests Heaven issued to evaluate and train its chosen candidate. The Mandate of Heaven was not a static object given to a ruler without testing or challenging him. Rather, it was something to be acquired through efforts; it was gained and secured through reflections on and corrections of wrong deeds. Emperor Taizu faced exactly the same test Yu faced; therefore, he had the potential to become another sage ruler as great as Yu. By following Yu's methods of managing the river, the emperor would be able to extract moral strength, curb the river disasters, and consolidate his cosmological connection with the supreme power of Heaven.

Using Yu the Great to construct a hydraulic, political, and moral discourse, Emperor Taizu politicized and moralized Yellow River hydraulics, and pinpointed the ultimate goal of hydraulics as the preservation of the imperial state. This discourse conceptualized a new landscape of north China, a revival of the legendary landscape created by Yu in which the river was channeled through the "Nine Rivers" inside Hebei.[25] This ideal

---

[24] Heping Liu (2012: 99) suggests that "Yu's leadership in the flood myth became a powerful paradigm to epitomize Song emperorship, good government, and the efficiency and effectiveness of state organization." Building on a previous footnote [Note 22], I argue that the early Song state and its rulers used the legend not idealistically, but pragmatically. It is less about how Song emperors could become perfect rulers by modeling sages like Yu; it is more about how they construct a particular discourse around the legend to help them cope with the contemporary, critical challenges.

[25] To ask what this landscape did politically, we may think with W.J.T. Mitchell (2002: 17), "These semiotic features of landscape, and the historical narratives they generate, are tailor-mae for the discourse of imperialism, which conceives itself precisely

landscape enacted Hebei as its key element; only through Hebei's sacrifice would Yu's landscape be actualized, the Yellow River tamed, and the imperial state consolidated. The state, the river, and the plain of Hebei trialectically interacted with each other. Hence, to a ruler like himself, the emperor must adopt Yu's politico-hydraulic-moral model by designating Hebei as the river's future victim. To his subjects and ministers, they should follow the state's perception and conception (instead of seeing the situation like individuals) and comply with the state's hydraulic decisions, even if the decisions demanded that they sacrifice themselves.

But, even if Emperor Taizu's idea was legitimate and technically viable how could the state anticipate that Hebei would comply and sacrifice its land and people willingly? The Hebei of Yu's legendary time was most likely a marshland without many human inhabitants, but the Hebei of the tenth and many previous centuries was one of the strongest regional powers that resisted state control. This question reminds us that we must read the state's politico-hydraulic discourse against the changing relationship between the state and Hebei that we have examined in Chapters 2 and 3. We have already observed that, while struggling with the turbulent Yellow River, the Song state simultaneously carried out a multi-dimensional project that, gradually, appropriated Hebei into the empire's political, military, and socio-economic periphery, a state-serving and self-sacrificing entity. Hebei's incorporation into the state apparatus and its increasing dependence on the state made possible the state's transformation of the region into an environmental periphery. From the late tenth century through the mid-eleventh century, three paralleling processes – the descendence of Hebei's status within the empire's core-periphery power structure, the growth of a centralized imperial state, and the rise of Yellow River hydraulics as a "national security"-level state affair – proceeded side by side and mutually reinforced one another. It is this river–plain–state trialectic complexity that produced the political, moral, ideological, and technical conditions for Emperor Taizu and his followers to create a dependent, submissive, and weak Hebei and to designate it as the river's future flooding ground.

Not limited to just bringing up an abstract conception, Emperor Taizu meant to materialize the conception by actual hydraulic practices. To reproduce Yu's landscape, Emperor Taizu urged his subjects to

(and simultaneously) as an expansion of landscape understood as an inevitable, progressive development in history, an expansion of 'culture' and 'civilization' into a 'natural' space in a process that is itself narrated as 'natural.'"

contribute hydraulic knowledge that introduced Yu's "method of diverting and channeling the river."[26] His call solicited the submission of a
twelve-chapter-long text, entitled "The Original Canon of Yu," compiled by a commoner named Tian Gao 田告. The Emperor met Tian in
person, consulted him, and honored him. Most importantly, he delivered Tian's text to hydraulic managers who worked at various hydraulic
sites on the river, treating it as the emperor's instructions to "personally
supervise laborers." By applying this "Original Canon of Yu" to actual
hydraulic practices, the hydraulic works were said to have "fixed all the
bank ruptures very soon." This implies that the flooding problems in 972
were resolved by diverting and channeling the river's water toward the
north. Unfortunately, because the "Canon" was not preserved, we have
no idea what sort of technological counsel it offered, how exactly it was
applied to the hydraulic sites, or whether or not it was truly read by
officials and workers on the river.

From conceptualizing certain hydraulic ideas to practicing hydraulic
activities accordingly, what Emperor Taizu provided in 972 was not
merely some political rhetoric, which criticized the existing situation
and advocated symbolic values of land and water as well as Yu's legend. Rather, his edict and ensuing practices initiated a politico-hydraulic
enterprise that set the basic guideline for future hydraulic policies and
practices throughout the Northern Song period. This enterprise envisioned an imaginary landscape that through its verbal invocation and
material substantiation, step by step, exerted material power to transform the existing geophysical environment into a beneficial, state-serving
one. Such an imaginary landscape, as literature theorist and art historian
W. J. T. Mitchell sees it, "is woven into the fabric of real places and
symbolic spaces."[27] Through interweaving the real (Hebei and the river
in the Song period) and the symbolic (the Nine Rivers inside Hebei and
their political significance that Yu endowed), the emperor discursively
constructed a landscape that would eventually lead to both the transformation of the physical land of north China and the remaking of the land's
symbolic meaning during the Song.

Li Chui's Proposals to Shift the River Northward
The politico-hydraulic enterprise that Emperor Taizu initiated was further developed by Song officials in later times. Their concrete hydraulic

[26] *SS*, 91: 2258.
[27] Mitchell (2002: xi).

proposals substantiated the imaginary landscape the emperor conceptualized, and detailed technical measures to move the Yellow River out of Henan and into Hebei. Li Chui 李垂 (965–1033), an eighth-rank assistant staff writer and revising editor of the Institutes and Archives, was a major advocate of such plans.

In 1015, the Yellow River broke its bank and flooded multiple locations in Henan. As the imperial court was troubled by the dreadful situation, Li Chui handed in a lengthy memorial, "Essay on the Geographic Advantages of a Diversion of the Yellow River."[28] Li claimed that the river "inundates Yan and Qi [generally referring to Henan and Shandong], and spreads its damage over the Central Kingdom." Thinking geopolitically, the river "leaves out the flat, fertile land over thousands of *li* in Hebei, and allows the frontier gangsters [the Khitan] to plunder it." Building upon Emperor Taizu's conception, Li argued that the river's damage to Henan harmed the state as a whole and provided the Khitan with real socio-political advantages. Such harm could be reversed if the state diverted the river to the north to let the river harm Hebei instead. A northward-flowing river would both "benefit the common people" in the south, and turn the river into a defensive barrier within Hebei to prevent any invasion from the Khitan.[29]

According to this cost-benefit rationale, Li proposed channeling the river northward into western Hebei. In that case, the river would first converge with various local rivers, then run through the central plain of Hebei, and finally enter the Bohai Gulf. That was precisely the route, Li specified, that Yu the Great constructed. Along with his textual specification, Li also presented pictorial illustrations to demonstrate his plan. His textual description and images, by naming and depicting mountains, streams, and administrative territorial realms, attributed concrete, material substances to the abstract, moralistic landscape Emperor Taizu conceptualized.

The court did not accept Li's proposal, technically citing its complexity and immense cost. Despite rejecting the proposal, the court nevertheless agreed with the essence of Li's idea and approved an alternative, small-scaled hydraulic plan, that is, to open a diversionary "small river" to channel some of the river's water to the north.[30] Li had proven that he aligned himself with Emperor Taizu. When another huge flood occurred

---

[28] *SS*, 91: 2261–2262.
[29] *SS*, 91: 2261.
[30] *XCB*, 84: 1917.

in 1019, he took the advantage of the event and presented his proposal
again. An unprecedented catastrophe, the 1019 flood wrought havoc on
thirty-two districts south of the river.[31] It was said at the time that a
dragon, the divine creature that controlled the river and caused floods,
had emerged from the Yellow River.[32] The city of Xuzhou 徐州, about
300 kilometers south to the river, was said to be fully submerged by
water.[33] The flood took over many local streams to its south, including the Bian Canal, and extended all the way southward to affect the
Huai River. To handle the catastrophe and repair the bank rupture, the
imperial state would have to use sixteen million units of raw materials
and 90,000 laborers. The crisis forced Emperor Zhenzong to compose an
essay to memorialize the occurrence of the disaster.[34] It also urged the
court to recall Li's hydraulic proposal in 1015. Li himself, now promoted
to a lower sixth-rank court official, was recognized by the court for his
hydraulic talent and granted the opportunity to travel to Hebei, where
he would inspect the physical landscape and discuss his proposal with
Hebei's regional officials.

  After his Hebei trip, Li Chui submitted a report, in which he pointed
out the brutal reality: "Now the river has burst and gone southward, and
it has done great harm"; due to various technical reasons, all hydraulic
work to block the river from surging farther south was unsuccessful.[35]
To him, the only solution the state could take was to reroute the river's
course to the north. But Hebei's regional officials opposed Li's idea, for a
changed river course would surely endanger Hebei's military landscape.
Hebei authorities certainly did not want to sacrifice their districts as the
river's flooding ground. The conflicting interests between the state and
the regional powers of Hebei, just as Emperor Taizu implied in his 972
edict, were evident. Realizing that his original proposal was too bold and
unacceptable to many, Li offered a less ambitious proposal. No longer
advocating shifting the entire river to Hebei, he proposed relocating only
a short section of the river's course into Hebei, so the river would avoid
going through some vulnerable places where many serious bank ruptures
had occurred.[36]

[31] *XCB*, 93: 2153.
[32] *XCB*, 94: 2164.
[33] *XCB*, 94: 2164.
[34] *SS*, 91: 2263.
[35] *SS*, 91: 2263.
[36] "The tomb epitaph of Li Chui," *QSW*, 590: 121–122.

Just as four years before, Li's second proposal was declined. Referring to the proposal as "troublesome," the imperial court did not leave
behind an explicit explanation on the dismissal. Christian Lamouroux
considers the rejection of Li's proposal as a result of the state's pursuit
for stability (*anjing* 安靜, lit. quiet), a status quo in which people pre-
ferred not to stir things up.[37] As sound as it is, this explanation reveals
only part of the truth. Indeed, the Song state and its officials talked about
the stability principle rhetorically from time to time. Yet, in their everyday political life, they constantly put forth new policies and proactively
launched new projects, certainly including enormous hydraulic projects
at very high costs on the southern side of the Yellow River. To the Song
officials, "stability" was a relative matter; its significance shifted depending on circumstances. Officials used this notion often as political rhetoric
during their factional competition, not to guard the principle itself but
to silence the opposite party. My own explanation for the court's rejection of Li's proposals is that the proposals met resistance from Hebei's
regional authorities.

Let us look at an instance in 1015. When the river flooded toward the
south, the Fiscal Commissioner of Henan in the south proposed opening
a channel to divert some of the floodwater northward. This proposal
was strongly opposed by the Fiscal Commissioner of Hebei in the north,
who feared that a northerly channel would spread the river's flooding
damage to his districts.[38] The imperial court intervened to carry forth
the proposal, which resulted in the opening of a northerly channel. From
this instance, we can tell that the Song state was an extremely activist
state; everyday, mundane political practices took place in a busy and
fuzzy fashion through subtle negotiations between the state and regional
authorities; various powers constantly interplayed to make things happen. "The state's pursuit for stability" by not initiating things – a lofty
political philosophy that Song politicians rhetorically cited as Lamouroux
observes – did not dictate actual political practices.

The court rejected Li Chui's proposals because Hebei's regional authorities rallied support from its sympathizers at the court and won the debate.
We must remember that, in the first few decades of the Song period, Hebei
natives dominated high-ranking official positions at the imperial court,
including the position of Grand Councilor.[39] They might have boycotted

---

[37] Lamouroux (1998: 554–555).
[38] *XCB*, 84: 1917.
[39] Wang Gungwu (1967: 208–215) argues that Hebei military leaders and politicians
dominated political power and political life in the early Song period.

any plan to divert the Yellow River into their homeland where their families and property were located. These people very likely represented the group who, as Emperor Taizu criticized in his 972 edict, prioritized their private, small interests over the state's public, greater interests.

Hydraulic Practices between 972 and 1048

Despite the dismissal of Li Chui's proposals, the landscape envisioned by Emperor Taizu and Li Chui – the revival of Yu's landscape – was not dismissed; rather, it was quietly under production. The state, following Li's approach, took better care of the river's southern banks while directing small portions of the river water northward into Hebei. These two techniques of river hydraulics – treating both sides of the river differently – were not declared officially. But they were undertaken in reality. A scrutiny of hydraulic policies and practices in the next few decades shows how the state applied different attitudes and technical solutions to the two sides of the river; as as a result, Hebei continued to fall into an environmentally inferior situation and became more and more susceptible to the Yellow River's attacks. The politico-hydraulic enterprise Emperor Taizu initiated continued to rule the ways in which the state dealt with the river and the Hebei Plain.

In the years of 982, 983, 984, 1000, 1004, 1019–1021, and 1027 when the river threatened its southern banks and Henan, the court promptly acted to repair bank ruptures and build new dykes.[40] Twice it ordered its ministers to perform the highest level of state rituals at the sites of the bank ruptures, offering the *Tailao* 太牢 sacrifice and jade plates to the river god. These actions, imitating the ritual that Emperor Wu of the Western Han Dynasty dedicated to the Yellow River at the end of the second century BCE, aimed not only to pacify the floods but also to consolidate the newly built embankments.[41] The treatment of the river's northern banks was the opposite. We do not see the extensive construction of dykes to protect the northern banks; there was no sacrifice dedicated to any northerly flood. Instead, hydraulic efforts focused on opening diversionary channels: the first one in 993, the second in 994, the third in 1012, the fourth in 1015, and several more during 1019–1021. These channels directed some of the river water to the north.

Blocking water from spreading south and diverting water toward the north were referred as two opposite techniques. The term *sai* (塞, to block)

[40] *SS*, 91: 2259–2264.
[41] *Shi ji*, 29: 1412–1413.

was frequently used to describe the works on the river's southern banks, while terms like *fen* (分, to divert) or *kai* (開, to open) dominated the works on the northern banks. The latter was considered as the techniques Yu innovated, the "method of diverting and channeling" that Emperor Taizu advocated in 972. Rooted in the state's politico-hydraulic enterprise to prioritize Henan and sacrifice Hebei, these opposite techniques complemented each other and formed a systematic treatment of the Yellow River.

As a result of these political decisions and hydraulic practices, "the river's flow gradually turned toward its northern bank," as one contemporary observed after the completion of a northerly diversionary channel in 1021.[42] It is understandable that the concentration of hydrological force pressed upon the river's northern banks; without adequate infrastructure construction and maintenance, the vulnerable northern banks were subject to future ruptures. When summer storms brought excess water and raised the water level in the river, a flood surging northward could be anticipated.

In 1034, the river breached its northern banks, surging into southern Hebei.[43] Drowning much of the southeastern corner of the Hebei Plain, the water formed several meandering streams. In contrast to its prompt reactions to previous southerly floods, the government did not rush to fix this northerly bank rupture. Instead, from 1034 to 1041, the imperial court held extensive, repeated debates on whether or not to fix it.[44] The political and technical language the debates employed did not favor the welfare of Hebei and its people. Although a few voices advocated routing the river out of southern Hebei to relieve the locals' suffering, in the end the court decided not to repair the banks.[45]

There were many reasons for the decision. Geographically, the river's old course in northern Henan was heavily silted up and could no longer accommodate the river. More important reasons were provided in 1041 by Yao Zhongsun 姚仲孫, who had just completed his tenure as Hebei's Fiscal Commissioner-in-Chief and returned to the court.[46] With more knowledge of Hebei's geography and the river situation than his colleagues in the capital, Yao recommended against repairing the bank

---

[42] *XCB*, 97: 2247.
[43] *XCB*, 114: 2682; 115: 2691; and 115: 2703. For detailed studies on the 1034 bank rupture and shift of the course, see Zou (1986b).
[44] *XCB*, 115: 2703; 116: 2724; 118: 2785; 118: 2787; 122: 2887; and 131: 3109.
[45] *SS*, 91: 2267.
[46] *XCB*, 131: 3109.

rupture. He pleaded with the court to construct set-back dykes, widen old dykes, and straightjacket some meandering sections of the river's course in southern Hebei. These steps would give the river a considerable swath of land in southern Hebei, in which the river's unbridled body could move around freely. As a result, Yao expected to contain the river within southern Hebei rather than to bring it back to northern Henan.

Yao's proposal promised many advantages, three of which were particularly attractive to the state. First, although the river ran through southern Hebei, it was Yao's optimistic belief and cost-benefit rationale that the river would not impose much negative impact on Hebei. This echoed Emperor Taizu and Li Chui's opinions that the river's harm was lighter on Hebei than on Henan. Second, the proposal would lessen the financial and labor burdens on the state. This point was particularly important in the early 1040s, when the midlife Song state was sunk in a deep fiscal crisis. As we have seen in Chapter 3, financial troubles forced the emperor and his officials to consider all actions in light of financial constraints; any economical solution was appealing to the state. Third and most importantly, as the river was relocated, Kaifeng and the entire Henan area – the core region of the state – would be forever set free from disasters.

With no intention to over-interpret the minds of the Song officials, I would like to raise a hypothesis: the Song state must have been pleased to see the river and its floods move northward after 1034. By approving Yao Zhongsun's proposal, the imperial court surely recognized the environmental and political implications of Yao's ideas. In 1041, the court once again confirmed the decision not to repair the bank rupture created in 1034. To encourage the river to remain in southern Hebei, the state ordered hydraulic workers to open an additional diversionary channel, which shared the hydrological force from the mainstream and channeled more water further to the interior of Hebei.[47] The landscape that Emperor Taizu conceptualized on the basis of the legend of Yu and Li Chui envisioned was steadily taking shape.

In 1042, the government contemplated taking a further step, when Guo Zi 郭諮, a commissioner in charge of inspecting various Yellow River embankments, proposed channeling the entire river course into the central part of Hebei. To Guo, the river was already inside southern Hebei, so why not push it to move a little further northward to

[47] XCB, 133: 3160.

materialize Emperor Taizu and Li Chui's vision? As a military officer, Guo elaborated on various military advantages a northerly flowing river would provide.[48] Guo's proposal appeared timely, as in that year a territorial dispute between the Song and the Khitan's Liao was growing into serious military tensions. The talk of the Yellow River's strategic value, as a natural barrier to halt any advancement of the Khitan armies, sounded attractive to the court. Later, when the Song and the Liao settled the territorial dispute through diplomatic means and the military tensions eased, Guo's proposal was set aside. Nevertheless, the imperial court indeed once approved the proposal, going so far as to "store up materials to carry out the project."

Clearly, from the early 970s to the early 1040s, a current of ideas had continued to develop and inform several generations of the state leadership in their ways of handling the river. Building on top of each other and elaborating and strengthening each other, these ideas formulated specific hydraulic policies and practices. These ideas and practices altogether enhanced the possibility of transforming Hebei into a potential flooding ground. Both discursively and materially, the state's politico-hydraulic enterprise encouraged the river to tend northward.

4.3 State Building through Landscape Transformation

The river's situation remains unclear between 1042 and 1047, due to the lack of historical records. Only a few flooding events were reported, all on a small scale. This seeming decrease in flooding was due partly to climate changes; the reduce in rainfall kept the river's water level low. As Chapter 3 discussed, both northern and southern China suffered from extensive droughts along with periodic earthquakes and outbreaks of locusts. The lower reaches of the Yellow River in the realm of southern Hebei were said to contain little water, and by 1043 the water had become so shallow in some places that people could cross the river on foot. The remaining water moved about on the land surface; it did not carry a hydrological force strong enough to cut through the ground and to form a deep, stable channel.

The Song state might have congratulated itself on the absence of floods during these years. It might even have attributed such absence to its wise application of different hydraulic techniques to the two sides of the river,

---

[48] XCB, 136: 3247–3248.

as well as to the resultant shift of the river's course into southern Hebei in 1034. The absence of serious floods might also have helped to justify the state's decision not to repair the 1034 bank rupture. In hindsight it seemed a correct decision to allow the river to remain in southern Hebei, instead of bringing it back to northern Henan.

This absence of disasters, however, did not mark the end of the calamitous history of the Yellow River in the Song period. Rather, it offered six years for the river to keep silting up its riverbed, building up its hydrological force, and waiting for the right moment to explode. This moment came with a heavy rainfall in the summer of 1048. After years of drought, the rain poured down in a sudden deluge on the thirsty Loess Plateau and washed down enormous silt and mud from the middle range of the Yellow River. Water and silt quickly filled up the shallow riverbed in the lower reaches, where sediments deposited in the riverbed over the past several years were thick and deep. The combination of the massive volume of water and the elevated riverbed forced the torrents up against the riverbanks.

Without scientific data and scientific measures to assess the literary descriptions of our sources, we cannot quantify to what extent non-human factors and state-organized hydraulic works each impacted the river's movement. What remains certain to us is that both joined hands to destabilize the river. This time, thanks to the better protection of the southern banks, the flow did not surge toward the south as it did many times in the early Song period. Instead, it targeted the less protected northern banks and surged into the multiple northerly diversionary channels that the state's hydraulic projects opened in the previous decades. Hence, the majority of the river's hydrological force amassed on the northern banks, in particular in fragile sections where the river course bent and twisted, such as the site of Shanghu. As a result, the roaring torrents destroyed the bank on the northern side of Shanghu; they surged toward the north to cause a complete shift of the river course in 1048.

This dramatic event reversed the river's long-term tendency toward the south, and relocated most of the river water and flooding problems to the heart of Hebei. As the two giant environmental entities – the river and the plain – collided and merged into each other, the Hebei Plain turned instantly into a delta of the river's lower reaches. This transformation of geographical composition of north China and the appearance of the land coincidentally matched Emperor Taizu's vision of a beneficial landscape and the hydraulic designs that Li Chui and Guo Zi proposed. All of a sudden, the legendary landscape Yu the Great created came to life in north China. "The tracks of Yu the Great are restored!" – so cheered the ministers and historians of the Yuan Dynasty in the early fourteenth century. These compilers of *The Standard History of the Song Dynasty* examined the history of the Northern Song state's Yellow River management and interpreted the 1048 event as a landmark to this history. They, as officials of the Yuan Dynasty who witnessed the Yellow River's frequent disasters in their own time and their government's repeated failures in controlling the monstrous river, seem to have perfectly understood the difficulties the Song rulers faced and resonated with their anxiety and desires. Hence, they grasped the significance of the 1048 landscape transformation and celebrated it as a major achievement of the Song's environmental management.[49]

The shift of the river's course was by no means an incidental revival of the legendary landscape, as the Yuan historians celebrated. It was a result of the Song state's sense of environmental crisis, of Emperor Taizu's politicization of river hydraulics, of the development of his conception through the technical designs by Li Chun, Yao Zhongsun, and Guo Zi, and of the state's deliberate hydraulic policies and practices. At the core of all this lay the history of Hebei being downgraded into an environmental periphery. Focusing on the court's dismissal of Li Chui's proposals, Christian Lamouroux holds that the Song government insisted on maintaining the status quo of the river's hydraulic conditions by not letting the river run northward. It was not until 1048 that "nature had decided and imposed its choice on the authorities," and it was nature that made the river shift its course.[50] My analysis of the state's perceptions, conceptions, and conducts toward both river hydraulics and Hebei has pointed to the opposite conclusion.

The encounter and clash between the river and the plain – two only marginally related entities in the past – and their entangled co-inhabitance in the next eighty years was not a random, natural event. Surely, the imperial state was not the only actor behind the environmental change; as Chapters 1 and 3 suggested, river hydrology, the geology of north China, and climatic conditions all played roles in the changing situation of the river. Yet, the state's forceful interventions in both the river and the plain supplied significant "probabilistic causation" that had, slowly and

---

[49] *SS*, 91: 2256.
[50] Lamouroux (1998: 555).

over a long time, diminished the river's southward-flooding tendency and increased favorable technical and environmental conditions that brought the disastrous river to the Hebei Plain. The decades-long process of the state's management of the river was the operation of the state's politico-hydraulic enterprise. It was a process of Hebei being reduced to a peripheral region and singled out to become a potential flooding ground of the river; it was also the process of the state's soaring desire and painstaking pursuit of empowerment and centralization. In the trialectic negotiations and struggles among the river, the plain, and the imperial state, Hebei – the land and its people – was not simply unfortunate when it was attacked by the river in 1048. It was not the river's instantaneous violence – as a force of nature in Lamouroux's belief – that crushed this land. Rather, it was the state orchestrated "slow violence" (in Rob Nixon's words) through a series of rationalization, policy-making, hydraulic practices, and appropriation of Hebei that caused harm to Hebei.[51] This is what Hebei's flood refugees never knew, as they desperately asked themselves: "Why did this happen?" and "Why did this happen to us?" in the summer of 1048. If we had to answer for them, the answer would be: "Because your state, your emperor and his imperial court located hundreds of kilometers away in Kaifeng, needed you to bear the brunt of this disaster for the greater good!"

At the end of the chapter, let us briefly analyze some political implications of the state's hydraulic efforts and the environmental change

---

[51] Nixon's (2011) notion brilliantly captures the kind of interventions that the Song state performed on both the Yellow River and the region of Hebei. Such interventions and their catastrophic consequences take place over a long time and show no obvious, evil intention. The absence of a clearly articulated intention and of causal links between various steps during the process makes the resultant catastrophe appear inevitable, random, and "natural." Thereby, such absence makes invisible and untraceable the profound violence grounded within the entire process. In our case, none of the Song emperors and officials stated an intention to purposefully harm Hebei and its people; in their political reasoning and hydraulic ideas, they avoided specifying the potential harm Hebei would receive if the river shifted northward. This absence of bad intention cannot obscure the reality that step by step the state reasoned and acted to prioritize its own interests while ignoring negative consequences to Hebei. Such slow violence contrasts with instant, apparent violence. The latter can be seen in many historical cases; for instance, as Chapter 5 and the Epilogue will show, at the end of the Northern Song the governor of Kaifeng ordered a breach of the Yellow River's bank in order to inflict a flood to halt the invasion of the Jurchen army. A similar case is from 1938 when the Republican government bombed the Yellow River's dykes to create a flood in order to halt the Japanese invasion. These two later cases differed from the early Song case, because their intentions were articulated, and they operated within short periods of time. For the 1938 case, see Muscolino (2011: 291–311) and (2015).

in 1048. The state and its ruling members highly politicized the river hydraulics – not only to interpret existing hydraulic practices in political terms but also to design its hydraulic policies and practices in order to promote political gains. As this chapter analyzed earlier, the Yellow River wreaked havoc right at the state's political core and threatened the state's stability or even survival as a "national security" issue. Hence, the state building for power consolidation and expansion had to derive from the state's successful management of river problems. At least in the state's and its ruling members' wishful conception, such state's "hydraulic mode of production" (in line with Karl Wittfogel's productive logic) would not only lead to a benign environment but, ultimately, strong state power. In other words, the Song's state building resulted from its deliberate management of the environment.

To a young imperial state like the Northern Song, the process of state formation and building was by necessity multi-dimensional. As previous Song scholarship has demonstrated, this process involved the choice and establishment of the state's political core; the organization and promotion of the civil bureaucracy; the centralization of military power and institutions; the systematic exploitation of social wealth and various resources; the advocacy of Neo-Confucianism that reshaped political culture, ethics, and social and cultural practices. All these dimensions were simultaneously pursued by the state, each tackling certain political, strategic, socio-economic, and cultural issues the young state inherited. With regard to Hebei, Chapter 2 discussed how state building proceeded through the state's political, military, and socio-economic appropriations of this region.

What historians have consistently overlooked, however, is the environmental crisis that the state faced and struggled to overcome. From the state's point of view, the environmental crisis was just as serious and destructive as the political decentralization and a broken economy. Without handling the Yellow River properly, the young state would not have gone as far as it did; thus, the river and various environmental problems were a crucial part of the state building agenda. Thinking with philosopher and sociologist Henri Lefebvre, to whom states "attempt at once to homogenize, to hierarchize, and to fragment social spaces" and there is "the state mode of production" of social spaces, this chapter has demonstrated that the Song state operated a state mode of production of natural space and environmental relationships.[52] More than space, this

---

[52] Lefebver (2009: 223).

state mode of production created a new kind of physicality for environment entities like the river and the land of Hebei; it endowed the environment of north China with both new geophysical attributes and new political and symbolic meanings. Both the Yellow River and the Hebei Plain became the state's environmental-political property that, granted certain appropriations, would serve the state's interests. Hence, the land of north China was hierarchized into some indispensable parts and some dispensable parts, into a strengthening core where the state's power resided in opposite to a downgrading periphery like the river-plagued Hebei.

By viewing the region of Huaibei as a "sacrificed portion," historian Ma Junya examines how the self-profiting Ming and Qing states intentionally locked the lower reaches of the Yellow River, together with its environmental harm, within Huaibei. Such environmental management sought to protect other geopolitically more significant entities, such as the ancestral tombs of Ming's royal family and the Grand Canal.[53] In his study of the Huang-Yun area between the mid-nineteenth and the mid-twentieth century, Kenneth Pomeranz holds that the state survived the turbulent transition from pre-modern to modern times thanks to its selective investment of resources and the resultant development of certain regions. The regional development entailed political, socio-economic, and ecological marginalization and even degradation of a hinterland area, the Huang-Yun.[54] In that particular case, the state withdrew its attention and investments from the hinterland, including its hydraulic management of the Yellow River; it thereby abandoned the hinterland from the empire's pursuit of modernity. These later states' environmental management – through the prioritization of certain parts of its domain, the shift of its engagement and investments, and the redistribution and concentration of its resources – resonates strongly with the history of the early Song's dealing with the Yellow River and Hebei.

What makes the history of the Yellow River and Hebei different from and perhaps more disturbing than the history of Huaibei or the Huang-Yun is how proactively the state designed and manufactured the destruction of Hebei. The Song state did not simply abandon Hebei by leaving this peripheral region alone or exploiting its resources. It compounded the abandonment by relocating disasters and damage into Hebei, and by reshaping the geophysical composition of the land itself. The creation of a Yellow River delta in Hebei was an outcome of the state's politico-hydraulic deliberation, not merely the unintended consequence or side effect of state negligence. To the state in the nineteenth and twentieth centuries, it redistributed limited productive resources in order not only to prolong its dwindling power but also to join the club of modern states and the modern economy. To the young Song state that carried a survivor's mentality, it redistributed the boundless, destructive environmental forces in order to preserve state power and prevent its own premature death.

The course shift of the Yellow River contributed to the Song's state building explicitly through transforming the geopolitical landscape of north China. The previous chapters have articulated how the Song state tried to undermine Hebei's autonomous tradition and bring it back under the state's central control. With the geographical relocation of the river and its tremendous disasters into Hebei, the state saw the further downgrading of Hebei to an environmental victim and self-sacrificing periphery. From the mid-eighth century to 1048, for the first time Hebei merged into the imperial state as its political, socio-economic, and environmental subordinate. From the state's point of view, its empire now rested in a core-periphery structure that was perfectly mirrored by environmental conditions: the centrality of the state power was solidly situated in and guarded by the environmentally conserved Henan; it exerted control over and offered indispensable support to the environmental periphery, Hebei. This environmental core-periphery structure was a perfect manifestation of a political philosophy that dominated the everyday life of the early Song state: "Strengthening the trunk [or, main body] and weakening the branches [or, limbs] (*qianggan ruozhi* 強幹弱枝)."[55]

Without the operation of a politico-hydraulic enterprise to shift the river northward, the history of Hebei and Henan would have been entirely different. If that were the case, the political history of the Northern Song would have been different as well, and the imperial state might have dissolved much earlier. Through the transformation of the landscape, we see the building of a well-structured, integrated, centralized imperial state – certainly a strong one, in the state's own hope. W. J. T. Mitchel's famous

---

[55] For the early Song state's sense of center-periphery structure from the perspective of political philosophy, see Deng (2006). From the perspective of territorial administration, see Mostern (2011: 294) and note 2.

claim for landscape as "the dreamwork of imperialism" – a medium carrying and producing imperialist power (at least in the power's dreamful thought) – finds a perfect historical manifestation in eleventh-century north China.[56]

---

[56] Deriving from an interrogation of landscape painting in colonial and postcolonial contexts, W. J. T. Mitchell (2002: 9–14) broadens the definition of "landscape" to be "a physical and multisensory medium (earth, stone, vegetation, water, sky, sound and silence, light and darkness, etc.) in which cultural meanings and values are encoded," and thereby encoded with power. He consciously extends this theorization to question the landscape-power relationship in other forms of imperialism, "including Chinese imperial experiences."

PART II

POST-1048

The Unfolding of the
Environmental Drama

In the next four chapters, we shall tackle these questions:

How did the river, the state, and the plain respond to the changing environmental circumstances after 1048? How were they affected by continuous changes and repeated disasters, as they vied with each other to occupy physical space and acquire resources?

5

Managing the Yellow River–Hebei Environmental Complex

By this time, the Hebei Plain had become the Yellow River's delta. Within a same space, the environmental entities of the river and the plain now converged to form a gigantic environmental complex. In a geopolitical sense, the imperial state saw the departure of the violent river from Henan and the reduction of environmental harm at its political core, along with the continued peripheralization of the regional power of Hebei, and the consolidation of the state's political centrality – as Emperor Taizu and his followers anticipated.

This production of a favorable physical environment, a subdued regional society, and strengthened state power seem to have resonated very well with what Karl Wittfogel's theory of the "hydraulic mode of production" sought to capture. This mode of production features a symbiotic, mutually constitutive relationship between political power and hydraulics. "No matter whether traditionally nonhydraulic leaders initiated or seized the incipient hydraulic 'apparatus,' or whether the masters of this apparatus became the motive force behind all important public functions, there can be no doubt that in all these cases the resulting regime was decisively shaped by the leadership and social control required by hydraulic agriculture."[1] Although this line triggers a question of whether the growth of state power precedes state-sponsored hydraulic works or vice versa, it is the production process and its end products that seem to matter more. As historian Donald Worster suggests, "Do chickens make eggs, or eggs make chickens? It hardly matters when we sit down to

---

[1] Wittfogel (1957: 3). See a thorough critique of this theory in Chapter 5.3.

dinner."[2] Our previous chapter has followed Worster to demonstrate the decades-long preparation for such a "dinner" and the presentation of its products in 1048.

Yet, as history moved on to a new stage, we confront different questions: did this "hydraulic mode of production" yield a good dinner as Emperor Taizu and Li Chui desired, or as Wittfogel promised? Did the formation of the Yellow River–Hebei environmental complex bring about environmental stability to north China and, by extension, both a sense and a reality of the state's political security? To everyone's disappointment, as soon as the river shifted into Hebei, the state realized that the new delta landscape was not as beneficial as Emperor Taizu, Li Chui, and others envisaged. The Yellow River–Hebei environmental complex engendered a series of unexpected disasters, and threatened the state with a different kind of uncertainty and anxiety. Ironically, during the next eight decades of its rule, the Song state and its ruling members were busy debating whether or not to undo the "dinner" by reversing the efforts the state had painstakingly made before 1048, and rerouting the river out of Hebei to return it to its pre-1048 or even its pre-1034 course. Two hydraulic leaderships emerged in the government: one focusing on taming and rerouting the Yellow River at high costs and the other prioritizing Hebei's strategic qualities and socio-economic well-being. They competed for resources and the state attention in order to dominate the environmental management inside Hebei. The new Yellow River delta thereby became both a target and a site of intense contestations not only between humans and hydrological forces but also among the state's various political forces.

The present chapter explores the continuous unfolding of the environmental drama by focusing on the state's management of two waterbodies in the Yellow River–Hebei environmental complex – the Yellow River and Hebei's frontier ponds, which were not in any way connected in the past, but became geographically overlapping and physically colliding and conflicting after 1048 as the river's northerly courses overran the ponds. Dealing with the new environmental conditions troubled the imperial state and demanded unending contributions of human lives and resources. Unexpectedly, the state was entrapped by a "hydraulic mode of consumption" that, over the course of the next eighty years, had made the state the supplier and servant of the needs of the Yellow River–Hebei environmental complex – rather than the other way around – and

[2] Worster (1985: 39).

gradually wore down the state power. It is through this consumptive mode that we investigate how the state's environmental management (a pre-modern case for the kind of state-sponsored "schemes to improve the human condition" as James C. Scott studies) failed and also failed its main actor, the imperial state itself.

5.1   Eight Decades of the "Northern Flows"

When the news about the river's bank rupture and course shift arrived at the court in 1048, Emperor Renzong and his ministers were perhaps taken aback, but they did not panic. This result had been carefully contemplated and secretly hoped for over the previous decades. Their sentiment might have been discerned by fourteenth-century historians who, in *The Standard History of the Song Dynasty* they compiled, interpreted this environmental change in such cheerful tones – "The tracks of Yu the Great are now restored!"[3]

As the flood spread farther into central and northern Hebei, however, its disastrous impact began to worry the government. Reports from Hebei told of villages and buildings being swept away, people losing their families and belongings, and crops being ruined. Famine and infectious diseases started to take over the land. More alarming to the state, the environmental changes might have a catastrophic impact on Hebei's strategic landscape, altering several key components in the Song's frontier strategic system. First, the Yuhe Canal was so damaged that it lost its navigational function; this jeopardized the transportation of military supplies and threatened Hebei's military entity. Second, the frontier ponds built and maintained at great expenses as a defense system for the flat land of northern Hebei were endangered by the torrents of the Yellow River. Third, the Yellow River used to function (or at least was hoped to) as a second natural barrier, after the Juma River, to prevent a northern enemy from marching farther into Song territory. Now the river had merged in the Juma, and the double barriers had been reduced to a single one. Not only that, but the Yellow-Juma combination would possibly lend its open watery surface to the Khitan, who could easily enter Hebei and the rest of China by sailing across the water or walking over the ice cover in winter.

The early advocates of a northward-flowing Yellow River like Emperor Taizu and Li Chui did not anticipate any harmful consequences of a northward shift of the river. But Emperor Renzong and his ministers faced

[3] *SS*, 91: 2256.

a cruel prospect: this newly generated Yellow River delta in the land of Hebei would potentially induce invasions from the Khitan. Hence, after 1048, the Yellow River continued to be seen as a national-security issue, so critical that it could cause the downfall of the state itself.

As this prospect loomed large, opinions on hydraulic solutions at the court were divided. They fell into three main camps: returning the river to its original course between Hebei and Henan; dividing the river into several small divergent channels to reduce its hydrological power; and leaving the river alone as it was in Hebei. For instance, Jia Changchao, a former Grand Councilor and now prefect of Daming in southern Hebei, worried that the river would destroy his district and, by extension, all of Hebei. So he urged the government to repair the bank rupture immediately, and to turn the river back to its pre-1034 course that it had followed for the previous nine centuries. Sharing Jia's concerns, most hydrocrats (*shuiguan* 水官), who usually served in the Ministry of Water Conservancy (*dushuijian* 都水監), considered a large-scale project to shift the river back to an old course both technologically and financial challenging. They became the leading voice for the second hydraulic idea: dividing the river. The third group, including statesmen like Ouyang Xiu and Liu Chang, believed that the first two solutions were both unviable, because the costs would be too high for the state to bear. Meanwhile, since "[w]ater flows toward the lowland," Ouyang claimed, the Yellow River had chosen Hebei as its destination. The state should not violate the river's natural tendency by turning it back to the southern highland.[4]

These three ideas persisted through the next eighty years to define the political discourse on the Yellow River hydraulics.[5] In 1049, they simply caused confusion to Emperor Renzong. Without comprehending the whole situation, he hastened to launch a giant hydraulic project, seeking to reroute the river out of Hebei. This decision put forth an urgent conscription of a labor force up to 300,000 men and all sorts of raw materials (like wood, bamboo, grass, and stone) up to 18,000,000 (of various units).[6] Both Hebei and its neighboring provinces were mobilized to prepare for the project.

[4] "Lun xiuhe di'erzhuang," *OYXQJ*, 109: 1646–1648. "Shang Renzong lun xiu Shang-hukou," *GSJ*, 31: 12b–13b, pp. 1095–1668.
[5] For a chronological survey of the hydraulic debates at the Song court, see Lamouroux (1998: 545–584).
[6] "Lun xiuhe diyizhuang," *OYXQJ*, 108: 5b–7b.

Yet a few months later, the emperor had become increasingly suspicious of a full-scale return of the river. He was convinced that his disaster-struck subjects in Hebei were too weak to participate in the giant project; overexploitation of the refugees might trigger social and political tumult. In the light of these concerns, he found the less radical solution suggested by the second group more reasonable. Impetuously, the emperor dropped the early decision, ordering a stop to the conscription and the dismissal of the laborers. Instead, he instructed his hydrocrats to open small divergent channels inside Hebei.

This abrupt change to the hydraulic policy incurred sharp criticism from the third group of officials. They saw the court swinging between panic and hesitation. Its vacillating policies suggested that the court had no self-confidence in making the right decision, and it also distrusted that its advisory bodies were knowledgeable, transparent, and loyal. To officials like Ouyang Xiu, given an ignorant and soft-minded leader like Emperor Renzong, the state would be exploited by ill-intentioned hydrocrats, who cared about nothing but their own political and economic gains.

These political disputes were volleyed back and forth for eight years. All the while, the river was left to run a meandering course and to spread stagnant water across central Hebei. Eventually, a hydraulic project to open a divergent channel was carried out, led by hydrocrats including Li Zhongchang 李仲昌, son of Li Chui who advocated for the river's northern flow in the 1010s. On the first day of the fourth lunar month in 1056, Li's team blocked up the 1048 bank rupture, and forced a portion of the river water into a channel they had dredged. Unfortunately, the channel was too narrow and shallow to accommodate the torrents, so the very same night, the river crashed through the newly repaired dykes and exploded in a massive flood. Tens of thousands of workers drowned, and countless tools and construction materials were swept away. The project was an unmitigated disaster, and southern Hebei was once again swallowed by violent water. This time, the disaster was clearly caused by the mismanagement of the government's hydraulic project.

The court threw Li Zhongchang into exile and punished other hydrocrats accordingly. Frightened and defeated, the hydrocrats, other officials, and even the emperor himself avoided touching upon the river's hydraulic issues for years. Although the river continued to inflict floods, the court simply approved the construction of lengthy "set-back dykes (*yaodi* 遙堤)" in central Hebei. These dykes stood tens of kilometers away from the river and its natural banks, flanking the river from afar.[7] The court had essentially conceded the battle against the river, giving the latter an enormous territory over which the river wandered, meandered, overflowed, and eventually placated its rage.

In 1060, the river burst through its eastern banks at some point in southern Hebei, and carved out a channel that headed toward eastern Hebei, effectively splitting into two streams – a new eastern course and the old northern course. For a while, it seemed that what Li Zhongchang tried but failed to do in 1056 – to divide the river into multiple channels – had come into being naturally. But soon, nature proved that the "divide the river" strategy did not solve the river problems. Once the river was divided into several small streams, each carrying less hydrological force, its silt deposited more easily. Over the next seven years, the riverbeds were quickly silted up to cause both courses to be dysfunctional; hence, floods continued to take place in central Hebei.

The year of 1068 was particularly catastrophic. It was when young Emperor Shenzong 神宗 (1048–1085) just ascended to the throne. After many years of cool, gloomy weather and extensive rainfall, north China observed an intense explosion of sunspots, which might suggest a decrease in temperature and humidity on the earth. In the 1060s, north China also experienced severe dryness. In the worst situation, "there is no rain within a distance of a thousand *li* ... the wild teems with locusts and various pests."[8] Once again, as in the 1040s, earthquakes broke out throughout north China. In the summer of 1068, central Hebei was shaken by strong earthquakes that some modern research rates at a magnitude of 6° or 6.5°.[9]

By now, both courses of the river were heavily silted. When the rainy season arrived and bought about heavy downpours, the river could not contain the excessive water; the torrents burst through its banks. In the sixth and seventh months, first in Enzhou, then in Jizhou, and then in Yingzhou 瀛州, and then all over central Hebei, the river crushed its banks and flooded. Even worse, it was not only the Yellow River that overflowed its banks; Hebei's local rivers also became turbulent with the excess of water. These rivers were caught up by the northern flow of the Yellow River. Their waters either joined the Yellow River to create

[7] *SS*, 91: 2273–2274.
[8] *XCBSB*, 1: 33.
[9] Institute of Geophysics (1990: 125–126).

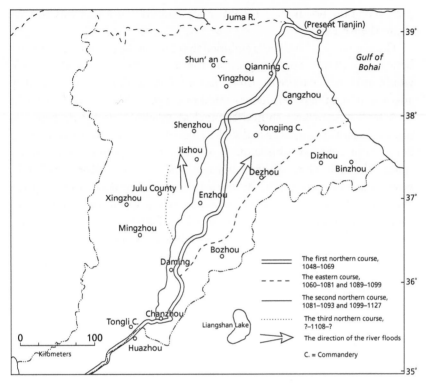

ILLUSTRATION 11. Changing Courses of the Yellow River, 1048–1128

immense floods in central Hebei, or were jammed by the Yellow River and forced back toward their upper streams to inundate the land and people there. Western Hebei, a relative highland area that rarely saw flooding issues, turned into swampy land as well. Its people joined the rush of refugees from the central plain out of Hebei.

The new emperor "was worried about the situation." Once again, the court was thrown back to the situation its predecessor faced in 1048. Opinions split into three factions, following the similar hydraulic ideas as in 1048. The "let the river be" group suggested accepting the reality and accentuating the positive side of the misery. They argued that by discharging straight into the frontier river and the ocean, the Yellow River expanded the overall surface area of water in northern Hebei. Nobody, including the Khitan, could overcome such a treacherous landscape. Although the river killed civilians and damaged Hebei's economy, its presence in the northeastern frontier was indeed "Heaven's way to constrain the Khitan!"[10]

The opponents, however, reminded the court of the twenty-year history between 1048 and 1068, suggesting that the "let the river be" solution would only induce more disasters. Rather than yielding to the river, they advocated that the government should invest more human efforts to fight it. A hydraulic project should channel as much of the river's water as possible eastward, to eventually close up the 1048 northern course. By doing so they wished to free much of Hebei from the river's impact and restore the region back to the environmental situation before 1048. But, how to do this? Questions of when to start the project, how long the work would need to continue, and how much it would cost were causes for contention. There was also the question of who would bear the brunt of the costs in terms of financial and labor provisions – the people of central and western Hebei, or those in southeastern Hebei?

As these issues came to a fore, there emerged a group of officials who supported a conservative approach and demanded caution to any hydraulic project. Famous statesmen like Sima Guang, for instance, doubted that the state and its people were ready for any massive hydraulic work.[11] The land of north China was so ravaged, its people were so exhausted, and the government was so financially strained that the costs for a gigantic hydraulic project could be ruinous. Sima suggested postponing the project for two or three years until such an ambitious project could be reasonably undertaken. He also reminded the emperor that people in central Hebei and southeastern Hebei were both subjects of His Majesty; one should not be sacrificed for the other. Any hydraulic solution to release central Hebei from the disasters should not impose the danger on southeastern Hebei. The state should guard everybody's interests equally.

The activist group of officials saw things differently. To their mind, without quelling the disasters, any effort toward social or economic recovery or any talk about political and strategic solidarity would end in vain. In contrast to the egalitarian humanists like Sima Guang, the pragmatic hydrocrats believed that "wherever the Yellow River arrived, it invariably cast damage in the past as it does in the present days."[12] No hydraulic project could protect everyone equally. The court had to "compare costs

---

[10] *SS*, 91: 2275.
[11] For Sima Guang and his influence on the conservative faction, see Ji (2005).
[12] *SS*, 91: 2277.

and benefits, and weigh the importance" of various solutions, and decide on prioritizing some areas over others, in order to preserve the greater good. This was the same rationale that Emperor Taizu used in 972 to argue for moving the river northward. But, given the changed political and environmental circumstances, this rationale was now applied to justify an opposite hydraulic idea – shifting the river out of Hebei, back to its old, eastward course.

By 1069, the political atmosphere had changed at the Song court. At the tender age of twenty-one and still quite new to the throne, Emperor Shenzong was young, energetic, and ambitious, and he held control over an empire of nearly one hundred million subjects. Yet the empire he inherited was rife with challenges, both internal and external. His subjects were plagued with disasters, diseases, and hunger, and the increasingly impoverished populace could not refill his depleted state coffers. Moreover, his government was largely dysfunctional, filled with professional politicians who appeared old, conservative, and inefficient. They arrogantly lectured the young emperor on how things were done in the past, pushed their interpretations of what the Confucian classics dictated, and urged him to tread carefully so as to not upset either Heaven or his subjects. Their internal conflicts meant that they could not come to consensus on nearly anything, including on how to deal with the Yellow River.

Seeking to gain control over his empire, Emperor Shenzong was attracted to the radical, idealistic political thinker Wang Anshi 王安石 (1021–1086), who at the time was already a rising star in the political scene. Unlike his opponents like Sima Guang, who perceived the state and society to be two dichotomous and competing sides, Wang Anshi saw the two as intertwined and interdependent strings of a developmental spiral leading toward a common goal, with the state as the leading force of its movement. A strong state would not cause damage to or a suppression of the society; rather, if the state were assertive of its own rights and interests, it would be able to address the needs of the society and would eventually guide and contribute to the society's growth.[13] According to this view, even if a state-run hydraulic project caused harm to some people temporarily, the peace and security it brought would benefit the entire society permanently. Wang called for putting faith in the state and letting

---

[13] This analysis complements Paul J. Smith's (1993: 84–88) opinion that Wang Anshi's ideology obliterated barriers between public and private sectors and collapsed distinctions between state and society.

it take the lead, in order to achieve a win-win situation for both the state and its people.

Above all, the activist state Wang envisioned depended upon a courageous, foresighted, and equally idealistic monarch, who was determined to lead the fight against the status quo. In 1069, Wang's powerful call for change spoke directly to the frustrated, anxious young emperor, and Shenzong enthusiastically responded to it. He ousted conservatives like Sima Guang, and cleared the way for Wang Anshi and his followers to organize a new government. Soon, Wang's "New Policies" spread across the empire, provoking reforms at every level of the government and changing the economic and social situation of those even at the bottom level of the society.

Historians have written extensively on Wang Anshi's reforms, and I shall not repeat the details of this extraordinary episode in the Song's political history.[14] What is significant here, and often neglected by previous scholarship, is the relationship between the changing political tide and the hydraulic policies and practices with regard to the Yellow River and Hebei. The state activism that Wang Anshi's reforms precipitated was not limited to politics, institutions, the military, and the economy – various human realms that have been the foci of the previous scholarship. The state activism extended to the control and regulation of the physical environment. The reformists were determined to move the entire Yellow River out of central Hebei and bring it back to its old eastern course. This aggressive hydraulic approach manifested the reformists' political philosophy. To Emperor Shenzong, this fight against the river provided an opportunity to make his rule as powerful and prosperous as the great dynasties through history, and to add his own name to the list of the most successful and wise monarchs China had seen.

Due to the political polarization in this period, the Yellow River hydraulics became highly political. It shaped the politics and contributed to the widening gap between reformists and conservatives. Those who were involved in politics could not avoid participating in the debate about the river hydraulics. Not only did politicians elaborate their political philosophies to rationalize their hydraulic ideas, they used their hydraulic

---

[14] For studies on Wang Anshi, his relationship with Emperor Shenzong and conservative statesmen like Sima Guang, and Wang Anshi's reforms, see Liu (1959), Higashi (1970, 1982), Bol (1992: 212–253), Deng (1997), Li Jinshui (2007), Ji (2005), and Levine (2008). Focusing on the tea-horse trade in the Sichuan area and the government's Green Sprouts Loan policy, Paul J. Smith (1993: 96–127) provides an in-depth discussion on state activism during the reform era.

ideas to demonstrate and substantiate their lofty political beliefs, values, and agendas. They used hydraulic ideas as parameters to judge each other's political stance, so as to categorize allies and opponents. Actively engaging in the hydraulic debates also provided budding politicians with an expedited path into the central government. Hence, the Yellow River and the disastrous landscape of Hebei became both a pawn and an actor in the Song's political games.

Yet, the river itself remained unpredictable. It refused to conform to politicians' wishes. As soon as the hydraulic project had managed to block the northern course in late 1069, the river overflowed and surged toward eastern Hebei, "inundating prefectures such as Daming, Enzhou, Dezhou 德州, Cangzhou, and Yongjing 永靜 Commandery."[15] After years of plaguing eastern Hebei, in 1072, the river broke through its banks in multiple places in southern Hebei. Its torrents once again converged with the Yuhe Canal, ran through central Hebei, and surged toward the northern frontier. So the northern course created in 1048 simply refused to be rerouted by human forces. Years of hydraulic efforts by the reformist government only made the river's water "overflow violently and wander extensively, and cause constant worries about its jamming and blockage."

The activist approach failed to bring about environmental stability. Gradually, the emperor's confidence began to waver. In 1072, he asked Wang Anshi: "Regardless of how the river overflows, it occupies the same size of area that the river requires. Whether the river moves anti-clockwise toward the west or clockwise toward the east, it incurs a similar amount of benefit and harm. Why don't we just leave the river alone?"[16] The emperor had also become aware that the ongoing hydraulic works in Hebei had inflicted tremendous damage, and that the hydrocrats had covered up the situation. In 1074, due both to the exacerbating situation in Hebei and to the emperor's accusation, Cheng Fang 程昉, a leading hydrocrat whom Wang Anshi patronized, was said to die from anxiety. Later that year, under severe attack from the conservatives and having lost the confidence of the emperor, even Wang Anshi himself resigned from the position of Grand Councilor.

The river continued to rage. In the summer of 1077, it overflowed in six different places in southern Hebei. In the seventh month, it suddenly crushed the southern banks at a fascine site called Caocun 曹村 and poured southward into Henan. Its torrents ran over the Liangshan

[15] *SS*, 91: 2278.
[16] *SS*, 91: 2282.

梁山 and Zhangze 張澤 lakes, overtook the Nanqing 南清 and Beiqing 北清 rivers, and surged into the course of the Huai River. Over the next few days, floods swept through forty-five prefectures and ravaged arable fields over three hundred thousand *qing* 頃 (approximately 18,400 square kilometers).[17] All of Henan to the east of the capital Kaifeng was deluged, resembling the situation in 989, 1015, and 1019. The river attacked the state's core political area, with the imperial court barely a hundred kilometers away.

Emperor Shenzong was horrified. He immediately ordered a project to block up the bank rupture and push the flooding waters back to the north. After a year's hard work at enormous costs, in the early summer of 1078, "the river once again returned to the north," namely back to central Hebei.[18] All this negated the previous hydraulic works that the emperor and Wang Anshi supported – to shift the river to an eastern course. The conservatives found this a perfect occasion to unleash their criticism, demanding that the court punish the reform-inclining hydrocrats. As Wen Yanbo 文彥博 (1006–1097) cried, "This is not a natural disaster! It is the inadequacy of human forces!"[19]

By now, the river's 1048 northern course and 1060 eastern course had become dysfunctional. Its older, abandoned riverbeds between Hebei and Henan had disappeared. The river refused to be stabilized into a single flow, but surged toward various directions across central Hebei. In this situation, Yu the Great and the legendary "Nine Rivers" he had created re-emerged in the hydraulic debate at the Song court. Even Li Chui's hydraulic proposals from back in 1015 and 1019, which advocated for the restoration of Yu's courses and the channeling of the Yellow River farther into Hebei's interior, were brought back for discussion. In 1080, the emperor sent several officials to western Hebei to investigate the geography in order to evaluate if Yu's courses or Li Chui's hydraulic proposals were applicable.[20]

All of a sudden, the hydraulic inclination of the court flipped. The idea of "let the river be" – namely, inside Hebei – prevailed. Between 1080 and 1084, several names were brought to the fore of the hydraulic debate: deceased Li Chui, Sun Minxian 孫民先 (prefect of Shenzhou 深州 in central Hebei), and Li Lizhi 李立之 (the chief director of the

---

[17] *SS*, 91: 2284.
[18] *SS*, 91: 2885.
[19] *SS*, 91: 2884.
[20] *QSW*, 2114: 131.

Water Conservancy). These people advocated allowing the river to flow through Hebei, as Yu the Great did in antiquity. Following this idea, the court instructed to evacuate cities, towns, and villages from central Hebei, leaving to the river whatever land it demanded.

In this battle of will, the activist state lost against the river, and even Emperor Shenzong accepted his failure. In 1081, in front of his Grand Councilors and ministers, he lamented:

The Yellow River has been causing harm for long. People of recent generations have tried to manage it by treating it like an object. This is why their efforts were constantly frustrated. Flowing downward is water's nature. Managing water should accord with the Way, which means not to violate water's nature. As long as we follow the river's natural tendency, why should we be concerned about relocating some cities and towns? Even if the divine Yu the Great came back to life, this is the only thing he could do.[21]

And his ministers responded, "Indeed according to your sagely instruction."

Out of frustration, Emperor Shenzong called off the project of returning the river to an eastern course. An activist approach toward the Yellow River, however, revived after he died. In 1085, his son, Emperor Zhezong 哲宗 (1077–1100), stepped onto the throne at age nine. He was welcomed by excessive rain in north China, which drove the river to inundate southern and central Hebei. Districts in those areas protested, urging the state to rescue Hebei. The prefect of Daming warned the court, "The river water has arrived with ferocity. Hundreds of thousands of people are crying for rescue." The prefect of Jizhou, which was located in the center of Hebei, pleaded to the court to do something to remove the river from his district. And the prefect of Chanzhou, where most bank ruptures took place, brought up the old idea of returning the river to its pre-1048, old eastern course.[22] The pressing environmental problems suggested that the hydraulic solution in the early 1080s, which let the river occupy Hebei without putting many constraints on it, caused tremendous damage to Hebei.

The late 1080s was the era known as the restoration of conservatism. Conservative officials came back to power and abolished Wang Anshi's reforms nearly wholesale. Yet, within the conservative faction, officials disagreed with each other on many things. A faction of them, in fact, sided one of Wang Anshi's policies. They wanted, as Wang Anshi did, to move

[21] *SS*, 91: 2286.
[22] *SS*, 91: 2288–2289.

the river out of central Hebei.[23] There emerged a group of self-important hydrocrats in the Water Conservancy like Wang Xiaoxian 王孝先, Li Wei 李偉, and also Wu Anchi 吳安持 who was Wang Anshi's son-in-law and was not persecuted by the new conservative government thanks to his hydraulic talents. They proposed resuming Wang Anshi's hydraulic policy and returning the river to its pre-1048 eastward course. Supporting them were not only some senior, powerful statesmen at the court, such as Left Grand Councilor Lü Dafang 呂大防 (1027–1097), Wen Yanbo, Wang Di 王覿 (1036–1103), Wang Yansou 王嚴叟 (1043–1093), and An Tao 安燾, head of the Bureau of Military Affairs, but also the emperor's grandmother, Empress Dowager Gao, who possessed tremendous political capital and acted as regent in making all final decisions.

Opposite to them was another group of conservative statesmen, including Right Grand Councilor Fan Chunren 范純仁 (1027–1101) and financial ministers Su Zhe 蘇轍 (1039–1112) and Wang Cun 王存 (1023–1101). Endorsing Sima Guang's idea in 1069, these men were both humanitarian oriented and concerned with the state's financial situation. They warned the court that a large hydraulic project would inevitably "burden the people and exhaust [the state's] wealth."[24] Su Zhe, for instance, criticized his opponents for having not learnt their lesson from the failure of Emperor Shenzong: "The late Emperor (Shenzong) could not return the river [to the east], and you gentlemen want to do it. Do you consider your wisdom, courage, and strength superior to that of the late Emperor?"[25] Fan Chunren elevated the Yellow River hydraulics to the level of political and moral philosophy. He reminded the court that "Sages possess three virtues: benevolence, modesty, and restrained from acting before All-Under-Heaven (i.e., the society, the people) maneuvers first."[26] Meaning, the government should be reactive, not proactive. To Fan and his fellows, the activist approach toward the river hydraulics, regardless being sponsored by Wang Anshi's government in the 1070s or by the anti-reform conservative government in the late 1080s, would lead to the state's encroachment of the society, which would eventually hurt the state in return.

From 1086 to 1094, the imperial court was torn by these two groups of hydraulic ideas and political factions. One day it would decide to

---

[23] As Ari Daniel Levine (2008: 12) correctly points out that the political factions in the Northern Song were not monolithic blocks, but rather fluid and complex entities.

[24] *SS*, 91: 2291.

[25] *SS*, 91: 2290.

[26] *SS*, 91: 2291.

support the activist group and hasten to conscript laborers and collect construction materials. Then a few days later it would be persuaded by the conservative group, and call off the previous decision. Such oscillation in hydraulic policies caused officials to complain that the court confused and disgruntled the subjects of the empire. In the midst of such confusion, however, hydraulic works did carry out in Hebei to various degrees.

In 1094, when the Empress Dowager passed away and Emperor Zhezong took control of his court, the hydraulic projects were given new life. At age seventeen, the emperor resented that he had been patronized and repressed by the royal family and senior politicians and that his father, who had supported Wang Anshi's reforms, had been continually denigrated. He lost no time in avenging these transgressions by quickly ousting conservative politicians such as Su Zhe and restoring Wang Anshi's fellow reformists to important government positions. The new government deified both the late Emperor Shenzong and Wang Anshi. The political atmosphere had turned full circle. One of a few people that remained untouched was the hydrocrat Wu Anshi. Wu survived two rounds of political purges, as the emperor could use both his personal connections with the reformists and his hydraulic talents.

Emperor Zhezong revived many of his father's old policies, including the return of the Yellow River to its eastern course. If he succeeded, not only could the young emperor "follow the Sage (Shenzong)" as the name of his new reign era "*shaosheng* 紹聖" indicated, but he would also deserve sagehood himself. With this mission in mind, the emperor pushed the hydraulic works to advance at full speed. In a mere few months, felicitous news came from Hebei. The river's northern course had been blocked, and its flow had been completely turned eastward onto an "old course," although exactly which one, we do not know. Congratulations and adulation flew in from the hydrocrats who supervised the works in Hebei: "This was achieved because of your sagely, wise, and independent determination from the beginning of the 'Following the Sage' era. Please have this historic event recorded by historians."[27]

All seemed to happen just as Emperor Zhezong desired. Yet the reality was that the northern course had not completely vanished, and there was no well-established eastern course to accommodate the water. As a result, the water surged wherever it liked, breaching banks and submerging large areas of land. Southern Hebei was inundated. For years the hydrocrats and their teams were busy rushing among different locations, trying to

[27] *SS*, 91: 2307.

stop the bank ruptures and prevent a total collapse of the river system.[28] People in Hebei were uprooted, fleeing southward into the capital and other regions. In the meantime, nature did not smile upon the ambitious emperor and his hydrocrats. The turn of the century was very cold and wet, and heavy snow descended in the winters of 1091, 1093, and 1101, killing many, including refugees from Hebei who lacked food, clothes, and firewood. After the snow melted into the rivers, the following springs and summers in those years (also in 1094 and 1099) saw excessive rainfall. All the waters caused the Yellow River and other local rivers in Hebei to swell. Constraining them proved impossible.[29] Meanwhile, the whole of north China underwent strong earthquakes in 1099 and 1100, exacerbating the catastrophic situation.[30]

In the midst of the tremendous hydraulic efforts, human costs, and continuous natural disasters, in the summer of 1099, the river burst into a giant flood along its lower reaches. At the site of Three-Gates, southwest of Hebei, the torrents rose tens of meters to destroy a shrine of Yu the Great that was located on the top of a mountain.[31] In southern Hebei, the so-called eastern course was completely overrun: "One hundred percent of the river's torrents are now surging northward."[32] After five years of following his father's footsteps, Emperor Zhezong had come to the same failure and sense of despair. Human forces, even with the strongest support and leadership from an activist state, could not compete with the mighty river. Defeated, the emperor died half a year later, shortly after his twenty-fourth birthday.

In the context of this catastrophic hydraulic failure, we stand at the turn of the new century, watching how history continued to unfold during the last quarter of a century of Song rule. We might anticipate a new emperor who had learnt the lessons of the previous two emperors, and a government that discarded state activism and embraced conservatism. Indeed, at least in regard to the Yellow River, the new emperor, Huizong 徽宗 (1082–1135), and his court remained quite passive for a decade.

---

[28] Some hydrocrats knew that the dykes they constructed were unstable and that if the dykes were destroyed by the river, they would have to face punishment from the court. To avoid any bank failure and consequential punishment, they would secretly breach the dykes to discharge some of the water to release the river's hydrological power. See "The Epitaph of Wang Shuo," *QSW*, 2845: 41.

[29] *XCB*, 511: 12170–12171 and 512: 12182.

[30] *XCB*, 505: 12046 and 514: 12211.

[31] *Shuofu*, 18a.

[32] *SS*, 91: 2309.

In 1108, for instance, the river drowned the entire city of Julu 巨鹿 County and carved out a new course deeper into western Hebei.[33] Even at this critical moment, the court refused to be agonized or react aggressively; instead, it simply ordered the relocation of the city and refugees away from the disaster area. The reports of floods and bank ruptures never stopped coming in those years, but the court remained calm, passive, and reactive, and no one mentioned the idea of returning the river to an eastern course.

None of this suggests that Emperor Huizong was subdued by the hydraulic legacy he inherited, nor does it mean that state activism as a political philosophy guiding the state's hydraulic practices for three decades had completely faded away. As other historians have shown us, Huizong gradually demonstrated a much bigger ego than that of his elder brother Zhezong, or probably even bigger than that of any of his forefathers.[34] Soon after he stepped onto the throne, he restored many of his father's and brother's reformist policies. He patronized a new generation of reformists who quickly occupied every important official position and seized full political power.

State activism as a political philosophy and means of governance prevailed again, but this time it was for a different purpose – to empower and enrich the monarch and individuals in the bureaucracy. Although calling themselves reformists, Huizong's officials cared very little about Wang Anshi's dream of "enriching the state and strengthening the military." As professional politicians, their overriding goal was power itself. They employed two main methods to achieve that goal. One was to win over and control the emperor by indulging him with flattery and drowning him in extravagant presents that they misappropriated from every corner of the empire. The flattery and presents gave the emperor a false impression that he was an excellent monarch and his empire was thriving. The other method these politicians used came in the form of factional struggles and persecution. Skilled propagandists, they deployed a successful ideological campaign to demonize conservatives, including those who had long passed away, like Sima Guang. They intensified the factional division between reformists and conservatives, and blacklisted all the names associated with the latter. By purging officials of different opinions and bringing together similar power-hungry men, they established a quite homogenous government, in which any dissenting voice

---

[33] *SS*, 91: 2312.
[34] Ebrey and Bickford (2006) and Ebrey (2014).

was silenced. As James T. C. Liu observed, such increased conformity "far exceeded normal limits."[35]

It is no wonder Huizong's court appeared more and more harmonious. As the emperor was increasingly shielded from reality, he took pride in this false sense of unity, using it to name his later reign eras: "Harmony of Governance (*zhenghe* 政和)," "Double Harmony (*chonghe* 重和)," and "Advocating Harmony (*xuanhe* 宣和)." Since his loyal and capable ministers were able to deal with the mundane business of the state, as the supreme leader of the state, Huizong could retreat to his artistic and spiritual world, which was full of the glory of worldly successes and fantasies of otherworldly immorality – something his late father and brother dared not dream of.

These fantasies were certainly boosted by the resurgence of the activist approach toward the Yellow River hydraulics. By 1114, the head of the Water Conservancy, Meng Changling 孟昌齡, came up with a new hydraulic plan that Huizong's court "was pleased with and approved." Instead of trying to fix the river's banks, block up its overflows, or shift the river's course toward an eastern direction, Meng instead planned to appropriate the river's upper reaches farther to the west. He eyed the Dapi 大伾 Mountain at the southernmost tip of the Taihang Mountains in southwestern Hebei. He suggested cutting through this mountain to create a channel that the Yellow River could wind through before reaching southern Hebei. With this new course, the river would avoid flowing along its existing flood-prone courses in southern Hebei.[36] In this way, the river would be rerouted northward into western Hebei, most closely in accord with the legendary river courses Yu the Great created in antiquity.

This idea may sound familiar to us: to revive the hydraulic achievement and physical landscape of the ancient sage king. This is precisely what Emperor Taizu conceptualized in 972. It is also very close to the hydraulic proposal Li Chui advocated in 1015, as well as to the idea that frustrated Emperor Shenzong resorted to in 1080. None of these earlier figures were able to put the idea forth in open political debates and develop systematic hydraulic actions for it. Ten years before the downfall of the Song state, Emperor Huizong and his court not only found this idea appealing, but also trusted their capability to execute it. Huizong heralded the new hydraulic project in 1115: "To gouge the mountains to smooth out channels is to follow the tracks of the Nine Rivers [produced by Yu

[35] Liu (1959: 88–90).
[36] *SS*, 91: 2312.

the Great]. To construct bridges to rest upon the toes [of the mountains] is to achieve work that ten thousand generations will rely upon."[37] It was Huizong's belief that he would revive the legendary landscape of north China, and tame the unruly river permanently.

The hydraulic work began immediately with very little planning. It was the middle of summer, at the height of the rainy season when the Yellow River was rising. The torrents smashed through the mountains and valleys, as well as the gullies that hydraulic workers tried to dig, provoking tremendous floods and killing numerous laborers. Southwestern Hebei turned into a landscape of vast lakes and swamps. Yet, none of this made it to the ears of the emperor. What Huizong heard by the end of 1115 was all about success and glory:

> The tracks of Yu the Great disappeared thousands of years ago. It is only Your Majesty who has exerted divine wisdom to restore Yu's tracks and channel the Yellow River through the three mountains. The lengthy dykes are winding and sturdy, forcefully stopping the giant stream. Building bridges on the river to link up the mountains, this work accords with the design of Heaven and Earth. Your power illuminates both the north and the south [of the river across the empire]; it transcends and exceeds anything in the ancient past.[38]

A few months later, there was another piece of cheerful news. In central Hebei, the muddy water of the Yellow River appeared to be running "clear," for the first time in the Song history. By 1119, the river was reported to flow through the "midway"; meaning, it was contained within its channel rather than overflowing its banks. This desirable situation was ascribed to the eminence of the emperor's "sagely virtues" and the assistance of "the divine."[39] In 1120, the court approved a project to open a divergent channel, but just as the Hebei hydrocrats were about to start work, "suddenly a divergent channel came into being automatically. The river flowed smoothly toward the Cunjin Pond. Everybody at the site of the project gathered and sighed [in wonder]." Ministers and officials at the court urged the emperor to have this miraculous event recorded for history, as they competed with each other to usher in their congratulations.[40]

Living amidst this frenzy of hydraulic achievements and adulations, Emperor Huizong dreamt that he would surpass his ancestors and be

---

[37] *SS*, 91: 2313.
[38] *SS*, 91: 2314.
[39] *SS*, 91: 2315.
[40] *SS*, 91: 2315.

memorialized with legendary sage kings like Yu the Great. Envisioning a thorough transformation of the landscape of north China, he antici- pated a coming of a celestial world in which he would ascend to become an immortal. As the emperor was less and less concerned with earthly problems, not much was written about the actual situation of the Yellow River and Hebei during his later years. Scant materials provide glimpses of a rather tragic story. The river continued to shatter banks, submerge cities and towns, and kill men and women there. The hydrocrats found no rest. They still ran from one location to another, busy fixing ruptures and opening straight jacketing channels. What they had promised the emperor and the emperor had believed – that the Yellow River would be pacified once and for ever – had not been actualized.

The Song state had tried everything it could to pacify the river and handle the environmental problems in Hebei, but nothing had suc- ceeded. In 1125, news came from the north that a group of semi-nomads from northeast Asia, called the Jurchen 女真, had overthrown the Liao Dynasty. Months later, the Jurchen army crossed the Juma River and the frontier ponds in northern Hebei, as if the frontier defense system the state had painstakingly maintained for more than a hundred years did not exist at all. Neither the vagrant body of the Yellow River nor the extensive stretch of the frontier ponds seemed to have bothered them.

Startled and panicked, Emperor Huizong hastened to hand over the throne to his son, Emperor Qinzong 欽宗 (1100–1156), thereby releasing himself from any responsibility. Qinzong, though responsible and coura- geous, had few options to save the empire. Exiling corrupt officials was not enough to pacify the rage of morally upright officials or to reestablish a functioning government. Demoting hydrocrats like Meng Changling and downsizing the hydraulic works in Hebei could neither bring back the tens of thousands of lives that were lost, nor recover the immense wealth that had been wasted and embezzled. The court made efforts to relieve famine and help war refugees, especially those in Hebei, hoping they would side with the government in fighting against the Jurchen. But the state's treasuries were so drained by the self-indulgent Huizong and corrupt officials that not much was left behind to use either for the people or for the state's military actions.

In 1127, after the capital had been besieged by the Jurchen for six months, the young emperor and empress surrendered. Huizong joined them shortly after, captured by the Jurchen on his way escaping the capital. With the royal family being whisked away into Jurchen territory in northeast Asia and the dynasty imperiled, the Yellow River became the state's last bid for survival. The governor of the capital, Du Chong 杜充 (died in 1141), ordered his soldiers to breach the river's banks in order to create a massive flood to halt the southward advancement of the Jurchan army. Bursting through the ruptures in the banks, the entire Yellow River poured toward the south, turning the eastern half of Henan into a swamp, resembling what had happened in 989, 1015, 1019, and 1077. But the Jurchen were undaunted. This last strike saw the Northern Song Dynasty coming to a dramatic end.

With the fall of the Northern Song state, the Yellow River turned to its southerly course. Up to the present day, the river has never shifted back to Hebei. The landscape of the Yellow River delta inside Hebei that the state had created in 1048, and that the state had doubted, tried to modify in various ways, and invested in heavily until 1127, had dissolved within days and was gone forever. The eighty years of the river's northern flows were a mere blip in the river's many thousands of years of history. Even historians have generally overlooked it, despite its profound import in the political drama of the Song Dynasty.

5.2   Ponds and the Northern "Watery Land"[41]

The formation of the Yellow River–Hebei environmental complex brought the Yellow River and Hebei's indigenous environmental entities into direct connection and even conflicts, something we shall examine fully in Chapter 8. These new environmental phenomena – seen through the eyes of the imperial state – caused the entwinement and complication of two originally separate political agendas, the river's pacification and Hebei's strategic and military stability. Before 1048, the state handled these agendas individually in two distant geographical zones. It was the idealistic belief of Li Chui and many others that a northerly flowing Yellow River would serve as a natural defensive barrier inside Hebei; meaning, the river would supplement and enrich Hebei's existing strategic apparatus. After 1048, whether or not the river served such purpose remained untested. What appeared absolute was that the river's meandering courses and floods destroyed much of Hebei's strategic apparatus that the state took great pain to construct in the previous decades. Unavoidably, the state's hydraulic activities to tame the river had to intervene in and, often, compete with the maintenance of Hebei's strategic apparatus.

---

[41] An early version of this section appears in *The Medieval History Journal*, see Zhang (2011: 21–43).

Hence, a significant dilemma the state faced throughout the second half of its rule was whether to prioritize the river hydraulics or prioritize the maintenance of Hebei's strategic apparatus; or how the state could treat both with equal attention. To understand the state's management of the Yellow River–Hebei environmental complex is to investigate the Yellow River hydraulics on the one hand and the state's management of Hebei's strategic apparatus in the new circumstances on the other hand. Lying at the heart of the latter was the situation of Hebei's frontier ponds after 1048.

The ponds formed before the 1040s did not remain intact through the rest of the eleventh century. As noted earlier, the climate turned drier in the second half of the eleventh century, and north China was increasingly susceptible to drought. This led to inadequate water supplies in Hebei, so some of the ponds began to shrink or even dry up completely. Meanwhile, due to the long-standing peace between the Song and the Liao, the ponds and other defense systems were never actually tested, so their significance began to be overlooked. Growing negligence and corruption among frontier officials and military leaders led to poor care of this strategic entity. Most importantly, the waters of the Yellow River tore apart the existing structure of Hebei's land, depositing silt in the ponds and exacerbating both the siltage and shrinkage problems that the ponds had already been experiencing.[42] In the 1070s, some ponds were reported to have shrunk so much that local peasants could farm on their exposed shores and bottoms.[43] The defense system that the Song government took such pain to build had begun to collapse.

The situation presented the government with a serious dilemma: whether or not to maintain the ponds against both the forces of nature and the state's political calculation, such as keeping the Yellow River inside Hebei. The maintenance incurred high costs in terms of labor, capital, and materials. As discussed, there was always a faction in the court who suggested letting the river flow where it wanted, even at the expense of the ponds; to statesmen like Sima Guang, the ponds did not seem capable of defending the empire against the Khitan army, and might even offer the Khitan easy, open access to the entire north China when their water froze in the winter.[44] Other officials stressed the economic harm the ponds had caused to Hebei when they overflowed and damaged

[42] XCB, 248: 6053; 396: 9661; and 399: 9733. SS, 95: 2362.
[43] XCB, 240: 5834 and 280: 6852.
[44] XCB, 235: 7207. *Sushui jiwen*, 4: 73–74.

large stretches of farmland. The resulting decrease in agricultural production not only jeopardized the well-being of the Hebei people, but it also endangered the state's revenue income. These anti-pond officials equated the costly maintenance of the ponds with "giving up arable fields," which was not economically viable.[45] With or without the negative impact from the Yellow River, these officials did not favor the maintenance of the ponds.

More people in the government, however, advocated for the crucial role that Hebei's ponds could play in defending the state. For local commanders in Hebei, their careers were closely tied with the existence of the ponds, since the financial subsidies and resources assigned for pond maintenance, which came down from the central and provincial governments, would translate into political and economic power in the hands of these local leaders. In the words of pro-pond officials and officers, the ponds were "not deep enough for boats to float on and not shallow enough for people to walk through. So even with a mighty army, [the Khitan] are unable to pass through [the ponds]."[46] They used the potentiality rather than a tested outcome to define the significance of the ponds.

Occasional military tensions between the Song and its northern neighbor reinforced such rhetoric, demonstrating that the Liao was a continuing threat. For instance, in the early 1040s when the Song was dragged into war with the Xixia Tanguts, the Liao saw it as a good opportunity to harass the Song. The tension did not escalate into war, but it made many in the Song government and in Hebei's military distrust the Liao and believe in the necessity of maintaining an effective defense system in Hebei. Hence, rather than withdrawing its efforts, the state decided to increase its investments in the ponds in the mid-1040s. It approved proposals from Hebei's military commanders, who suggested not only refilling dried-up ponds with water, but also creating new ponds in northwest Hebei, where the high terrain had previously discouraged construction. Yang Huaimin 楊懷敏, who was in charge of frontier security and military colonies in several northwestern Hebei districts, was said to have been "particularly keen on preparing the dykes [for the ponds] in the frontier area."[47]

Two decades later, Wang Anshi and his fellow reformists came to power, and enthusiastically pursued the policy of "strengthening the

[45] *SS*, 95: 2359.
[46] *SS*, 95: 2359.
[47] *XCB*, 156: 3792.

military." They hoped to change the image and reality of the Song as a military dwarf in front of its nomadic neighbors. Such zeal turned into actual military action, as along the empire's northwestern border in the 1070s, Song troops provoked a war to recover the disputed territory occupied by the Xixia Tanguts. No war broke out in Hebei, but a call to reclaim the historically Chinese territory north of the Juma River from the Khitan's occupation was in the air. Meanwhile, the state was concerned that while it was engaged in a war with the Xixia, the Liao might take advantage of the situation and threaten a war against Hebei, as it did in the 1040s. The combination of enthusiasm and anxiety revitalized interest in Hebei's ponds within the reformist government and among the military leaders in Hebei.[48] In the 1070s and 1080s, various projects were carried out to fix the old ponds and produce a more complex "watery" landscape.

There were two major challenges to the maintenance of the ponds. First, there was the rapid depositing of silt from the Yellow River, and in order to prevent that, local commanders and their corvée laborers spent much energy to reroute the river's course and channel away its water. The second challenge was the shortage of water in the generally dry Hebei plain. To deal with the issue, the commanders and laborers channeled clean water from springs in the western mountainous area, and also directed rather muddy water from some local rivers such as the Hutuo River and the Juma River.[49] Cheng Fang, a major technocrat in the reformist faction, made enormous efforts in this regard. He commanded soldiers to "open and repair" the Zhang 漳 River in southwestern Hebei, to "open up" the Hutuo River in northwestern Hebei, to "open up" the Pipa Bay 琵琶灣, and to divert the course of the Yellow River. By taking up these projects nearly simultaneously, Cheng sought to increase water supplies and produce more ponds. He also breached the Hulu 葫蘆 River and channeled its water into the Sha 沙 River, and by doing so, their streams were eventually connected to the ponds.[50]

The famous scholar and scientist Shen Gua 沈括 (1031–1095) also actively promoted the maintenance and expansion of the ponds. When he served as Hebei's Fiscal Commissioner in the mid-1070s, he toured around northwestern Hebei and found that "there was no longer any trace of the ponds and marshes." Deeply concerned about the frontier

[48] XCB, 191: 4622 and 194; 4690. XCBSB, 9: 381.
[49] SHY, "Shihuo," 63: 46a.
[50] XCB, 223: 5421; 245: 5951; 248: 6053; 249: 6073–6074; 254: 6221; and 262: 6400.

security, he petitioned the court to restore the old ponds by infusing them with water channeled down from the western mountainous areas.[51] With his support, local officials spent "government funds" to purchase low-lying fields from private land owners, and turned them into new ponds.[52] Just north of the northwestern city of Dingzhou, Shen supervised the dredging of a pond that eventually expanded to a perimeter of several *li*.[53] To make the best use of this new landscape and its abundant water resources, Shen followed in the steps of He Chengju of the late tenth century and encouraged locals to farm paddy rice around the pond.[54]

The efforts that took place at the local level and were sponsored by civil and military leaders in northern Hebei went hand-in-hand with the financial, administrative, and legal support from the central government. No historical figure is available as to indicate exactly how much it cost to fix the old ponds, create new ponds, introduce various water resources, and support the laborers working on those projects. But it is certain that without the approval of the central government, none of these projects could be easily carried out, and certainly not at the same time. Much of the materials used for construction and the funds used to purchase them was not generated locally, but was arranged and sent down by the provincial financial institutions like the Fiscal Commission. These institutions had to obtain a great portion of the resources from outside of Hebei, because Hebei's own production and tax incomes were too modest to fulfill its expenses. It was the central government that determined and coordinated how much resources were assigned to Hebei and how in general they should be used.

In 1083, the state issued new regulations on pond maintenance. It ordered the water levels of the ponds to be measured regularly and the results to be reported to the imperial court every season.[55] In 1098 the court reaffirmed the regulation, and specified more details on how it should be carried out. It ordered Hebei's frontier officers and pond-managing organizations to measure the scale of any expansion or shrinkage of the ponds, and to submit reports to the Military Colonies Commission in the first month of every season, that is, in the first, fourth, seventh,

[51] *XCB*, 260: 6349–6350.
[52] *XCB*, 260: 6350. *SHY*, "Shihuo," 63: 46a.
[53] *XCB*, 267: 6542.
[54] Wu Chuhou, "Dingwu jun shuitian ji [On the rice paddies in Dingzhou]," *Dingzhou zhi*, 19: 9a–10a.
[55] *XCB*, 333: 8022.

and tenth lunar months.[56] The government also employed a considerable number of soldiers to undertake daily surveillance and dyke repair.[57] These steps, reinforcing the old regulations set earlier in the century and gathering the local efforts by individual officers and officials, installed a systematic management of the ponds.

The support from the central government was also demonstrated by its defense of pro-pond officials when disputes arose between the pro-pond and the conservative anti-pond faction. A case in point was the dispute about Cheng Fang. Conservatives at the court pictured him as a quintessential figure of local reformists, the executor of Wang Anshi's reform agendas. They charged him with abusing power, wasting government money and other resources, pursuing unnecessary projects that were deemed unhelpful for frontier defense, and disturbing the regular livelihood of locals. When these charges turned into personal and moral attacks against Cheng, as the conservatives demonized the reformists as cruel and greedy, it is clear that such disputes were no longer about the ponds *per se*, but more about political and ideological struggles between the two factions. Just like the Yellow River, the ponds became a pawn and the embodiment of the conflicts within the Song state; their existence, enlargement, and shrinkage asserted tremendous political power.

By the end of the 1070s, the manmade ponds spread over "nearly eight hundred *li*" from the west to the east, one third longer than the size in the 1030s.[58] Throughout the rest of the Northern Song Dynasty, the massive construction of artificial ponds seems to have continued, although historical sources do not indicate any obvious enlargement of the ponds. Despite the constant challenges imposed by the muddy Yellow River, the climate, and political upheavals caused by factional competitions, Hebei's ponds maintained its importance in the minds of many people who sought psychological security in the face of potential invasion; they continued to play a key role in the Song's political-environmental life until the fall of the dynasty. This history of the ponds shows that facing the dilemma of prioritizing the river hydraulics or prioritizing Hebei's strategic stability, the Song state could not give up either but had to do both. But the efforts to maintain the geographically overlapped and environmental conflictive agendas were costly. The section on "Hydraulic

[56] *XCB*, 494: 11748.

[57] Although soldiers were assigned to maintain the ponds, there was a constant shortage of labor in Hebei's Ministry of Military Colonies. In 1100, the court approved an increase in the number of soldiers to perform this particular service (*SHY*, "Shihuo," 63: 50a).

[58] *MXBT*, 13: 145.

Politics" in later this chapter will analyze how these agendas politically, financially, and environmentally entrapped the state in an unfortunate "hydraulic mode of consumption."

Environmental and Economic Impact of the Ponds

Despite the century-long costly efforts to construct and maintain the ponds, the strategic value of the ponds was never tested by war during the Song period. Despite the brief tensions between the Song and the Liao in the 1040s and the early 1070s, the Liao never attempted a real attack, although we cannot say whether or not the absence of war was because of the Khitan's awareness and fear of the ponds.

The real test of the ponds did not come until the end of the dynasty, when the Jurchen marched southward into northern Hebei in 1125. We have no historical record indicating how the Jurchen dealt with Hebei's watery landscape and if the ponds caused them trouble or deterred their expedition, but it appears that the Jurchen encountered few obstacles as they crossed the Juma River and conquered central Hebei rapidly. Not only did the Song troops collapse immediately in front of the Jurchen's strong assault, but the ponds that the troops relied upon soon fell under the Jurchen's occupation. In retrospect, the suspicion of the usefulness of the ponds held by those like Sima Guang turned out to be correct. Still, although not effective as a military defense as the state and Hebei's officials and officers wished, the ponds indeed cast enormous influence on Hebei. Their existence – expansion and shrinkage – led to a set of unexpected changes to Hebei's environmental conditions and the economic life of Hebei natives.

Imagine a time-lapse bird's-eye view of northern Hebei from the late tenth century through the first quarter of the twelfth century. Skirted by the Juma River, the land first consists of extensive dry farms and patches of disconnected small swamps and lakes. Over time, an increasing number of wet areas begin appearing. This watery surface continues to enlarge, and by the 1030s it appears like a watery belt that covers the eastern half of the Song–Liao border and connects with the vast coastal swamps by the Bohai Gulf. Despite its temporary shrinkage, by the late 1070s, this watery belt has extended westward to cover more than two-thirds of the entire frontier, over four hundred kilometers and only missing from the mountainous terrain in the west. So how did this change in landscape and ponds' spatial expansion affect the people, flora, and fauna in this area?

In Xiongzhou, where the pond construction began, the land presented stunningly beautiful scenery. Where the ponds stretched several tens of *li*, lotus flowers blossomed in the summer and waterfowl gathered on the shores. When He Chengju was the prefect here in the late tenth century, he took pleasure rides on small boats with his fellow officials, drinking wine and reciting poems. "Even the land in the lower Yangtze valley (*jiangxiang* 江鄉) does not have such scenery," commented a contemporary.[59] Similar appreciation was dedicated to the watery landscape in Dingzhou in the late 1070s, after Shen Gua and his fellow officials transformed the vicinity of the prefecture seat into ponds and streams.

The visual pleasure, particularly of the elites, was not necessarily universal. For locals who had to deal with excessive water on a daily basis, it was a different story. The new swampy landscape would have modified the microclimate in northern Hebei, and affected local precipitation and temperature. In ecological terms, the new landscape (or waterscape) must have remarkably enriched the aquatic life. Various kinds of water plants emerged, and fish and crabs thrived. Locals benefited from these new food sources and, as lotus roots and waterweeds entered the local cuisine, they developed a more diversified diet. Pickled crab, for instance, became a renowned delicacy and specialty of Hebei. Traditionally associated with humid places like the lower Yangze valley, these foodstuffs were once part of the daily life of people in northern Hebei in the eleventh century.

The widespread water also became an ideal breeding ground for insects and bacteria. As Shen Gua observed in the 1070s, exceptionally large mosquitoes and horseflies were active in the Cangzhou, Xin'an 信安, and Qianning 乾寧 commanderies.[60] In summer, locals had to cover their cattle and horses with layers of mud paste to ward off mosquitoes; otherwise the livestock would be bitten to death. People dared not ride horses in the wild, because once "poisoned" by the insects, the horses would gallop out of control. Passengers in carriages and their drivers had to wrap themselves in thick clothes to fend off bugs. We have no sources to tell us exactly how human health was affected by the changed environment, but I suspect that, given limited medical knowledge and supplies, the locals had a hard time adjusting to the new environment. This perhaps explains why the population was sparse in these wet frontier districts.

For locals who traditionally made a living from dryland farming, their displacement and loss of the traditional livelihood were evident. In the early 1040s, Zhang Fangping 張方平 (1007–1091), speaking in his

---

[59] *Wenchang zalu*, 4: 45.
[60] *MXBT*, 23: 229.

capacity as a Minister of Finance, estimated that two-thirds of the land in northern Hebei, much of it formerly arable fields, were occupied by the ponds. Ouyang Xiu put this figure even higher in the late 1050s, claiming that 80 or 90 percent of the arable land was lost to stagnant water from the ponds and the Yellow River.[61] When the government sponsored the further extension of the ponds in the 1070s and 1080s, more private land was dug open and turned into ponds, and the decrease in arable land led to a reduction in the scale of agricultural production across that area.

There was a general decline in locals' sense of security and well-being. Life next to the ponds was not safe or stable, because the waters overflowed unpredictably. When snow and ice melted in the mountainous areas in spring and early summer, the resultant increase of water caused the rivers and streams to rise, and they discharged into the ponds at high speed to cause floods in the low plain areas. The authorities in charge of pond maintenance usually welcomed such floods, because it was the only way the manmade ponds got natural refills. Not only did these officials wait for natural forces to deliver water each spring, they also deliberately channeled water from afar to fill up the ponds, whenever they observed a drop in the ponds' water volume. These activities invariably raised the chance of flooding in northern Hebei. Theoretically, the introduction of water and the wide spread of ponds should have benefited Hebei's agriculture, as it made irrigation to Hebei's dryland possible. Both He Chengju and Shen Gua encouraged irrigation by using the ponds. Yet, as the next chapter will show, these water resources were used mainly for military colonies, whose actual production was very small in scale. The common people benefited very little from the state-owned, military-driven irrigation schemes.

When the maintenance of the ponds took priority, the livelihood of common people had to be sacrificed. From the mid-1030s, the government received reports from time to time, stating that fields, buildings, and even graveyards near the ponds were flooded.[62] In 1042, in the Shun'an Commandery alone, 6,000 households were affected by floods caused by the ponds nearby.[63] When Tang Jie 唐介 (1010–1069) was the magistrate of Renqiu 任丘 County in Mozhou 莫州 in the late 1040s, he had to mobilize local residents to build dykes to encircle the entire county in order

[61] *XCB*, 150: 3658. "Lun Hebei caichan shang shixiang shu," *OYXQJ*, 118: 1825–1828.
[62] *XCB*, 117: 2761. Han Qi, "Tuntiansi yu Hebei zengzhan tangbo weihai zou [Report about the Ministry of Military Colonies' occupation of Hebei's ponds and its harm]," *Anyangji biannian jianzhu*, 1655–1656. Sima Guang in *Sushui jiwen*, 4: 73–74.
[63] *XCB*, 136: 3269.

to protect its land and people from being submerged.[64] In most places of Hebei, where responsible and daring officials like Tang were absent, the locals reacted to the ponds threat by threat instead of pursuing systematic solutions. Sometimes they took illegal steps, such as damaging the ponds, breaching their dykes, or diverting their waters in order to prevent floods.[65] Clearly, there emerged a conflict between the pond-maintenance organizations, which had the strategically-minded state at their back, and local communities, who only occasionally gained support from their local civil leaders. The former group had a stake in keeping Hebei flooded and swampy, while the latter group fought for their minimal rights in guarding their small holdings and sustaining farming activities. In eleventh-century Hebei, the former, pro-pond group usually won out in such conflicts.

The ponds' impact on locals' livelihood and their agricultural productivity showed itself in a subtle way, in terms of the deterioration in the quality of the land. With the very low elevation in northern Hebei, excessive water filtered through the ground and brought up the underground water level, worsening the drainage problem that northern Hebei had long suffered. Mineral contents, in particular salinity, were not washed away but concentrated in the earth and, through the vertical movement of water, moved upward to affect the top soil. When the soil became very briny and toxic to most grain crops such as millet, wheat, and beans, local farmers had either to leave their land and search for more arable land elsewhere, or they had to adapt to the new environmental conditions and switch to other means of livelihood.

As a result, in this part of Hebei, some people started living on the ponds. As observed in the mid-1050s, they "planted lotus and gordon euryale," and in some cases they fished.[66] But reliance on the ponds for food was unstable, since it depended on the government, either at the central level or the local level, to decide whether or not to open the ponds for local economic activities. There was never a certain, consistent policy. Sometimes local military authorities regarded the ponds as state property and monopolized the extraction of resources from the ponds, thus preventing the locals from accessing them. Further, because the ponds existed mainly for strategic purposes, any public access could lead to breaches in security. Zhao Zi 趙滋, for instance, a commander in Xiangzhou 相州 in the 1070s, was very concerned about security issues over the open

---

[64] "The Spirit Path Stele for Tang Zhisu," *QSW*, 1679: 120.
[65] *XCB*, 117: 2761.
[66] Liu Chang, "Chucheng [Exiting the city]," *GSJ*, 4: 15, pp. 1095–1434.

water of the ponds, and believed that spies from the Liao Dynasty would dress up like local fishermen and sneak into Song territory. Zhao's fleet sailed up and down the Juma River in order to capture and expel the Liao spies. Such policing actions must have scared away ordinary people who were there simply to gather food. It is reasonable to suspect that the state may have issued bans on any public access to the ponds for its security concerns. In any case, we should not overestimate the locals' access to the ponds and the ponds' reliability as a new supplier of food resources. In places where the earth was highly salinized, people made their living from small-scale salt production.[67] Such "earthen salt" (*tuyan* 土鹽) was produced across Hebei. With very little investment of capital, with an iron wok and some firewood, a Hebei household could easily set up a stove, collect briny water, and boil the water down to extract salt.

Recognizing these local adaptations to Hebei's environmental and economic conditions, the Song government was forced to accept the difference of Hebei from other parts of the country as an economic entity, and it modified its economic policies accordingly. Instead of taxing agricultural production as it did in other parts of Hebei and the rest of the empire, the government collected taxes on fishing and the gathering of wild plants.[68] It gave up its monopoly on salt production and trade in Hebei, allowing private salt production to provide a subsistence livelihood to those who had lost their land and were mired in poverty.[69]

Whatever alternative means the Hebei natives found to sustain their lives, they were only individual, localized measures that were either unreliable or incapable of supporting a large population. By constructing the ponds and significantly transforming the physical landscape in Hebei's frontier, the Song state decided to sacrifice the lives and the livelihood of the locals, and to largely give up agricultural production in the area. Its choice ranked military security over demographic stability and food security of the people. As a consequence, this northern part of Hebei suffered serious socio-economic decline. In a story recorded by twelfth-century writer Hong Mai 洪邁 (1123–1202), there was a Sanya 三鴉 township (lit., three crows) in this part of Hebei. Its land was covered by ponds, and produced nothing but aquatic plants and fish. Only a few people lived there; its market appeared desolate. Even civil officials appointed by the government to manage the town had to suffer poverty, since their

---

[67] Ouyang Xiu's comment, *XCB*, 159: 3853.
[68] *XCB*, 34: 747; 106: 2481; and 155: 3772.
[69] *XCB*, 159: 3858; 283: 6928–6929; and 360: 8612.

salaries could hardly support their family expenditure. Unable to bear such an impoverished, humiliating life, the local officials abandoned their jobs and ran away, one leaving behind this sarcastic poem:

> During two years of miserable life in Sanya,
> With no grain and no money how can I raise a family?
> For two meals a day I eat only lotus roots.
> Look, my mouth spits out lotus flowers.[70]

5.3   The Hydraulic Politics and the Hydraulic Mode of Consumption

The following few pages bring us to some further analysis on the complexity of the Song state's management of the Yellow River–Hebei environmental complex. Before 1048, the Yellow River and the Hebei Plain were two spatially lateral and marginally related entities. The state engaged with them in terms of two separate agendas, overseeing each with an independent leadership. Hebei's regional governments and military authorities took charge of what happened inside Hebei, such as the construction of the frontier ponds. They played minor, supporting roles in the Yellow River hydraulics. The central government and its hydraulic institution, the Water Conservancy, held the exclusive power in dealing with the Yellow River. These two sets of agendas and leaderships proceeded side by side, without much connection or conflict with each other.

The advent of the environmental drama in 1048 forced the two environmental entities to merge into a Yellow River–Hebei environmental complex. With the disappearance of their geographical division, the two entities now co-inhabited a single space, not only overlapping with each other but geographically intersecting with, clashing with, and merging into each other. This drastic reconfiguration of the environmental reality also brought together the two hydraulic agendas and leaderships into Hebei – they began to interplay with each other and often compete for space and resources, as well as for the state's attention. During the intense reconfiguration of their relationship, these compartmentalized state institutions aggressively quested for more power. Hence, the imperial state was thrown in a serious dilemma: how could it demand the land of Hebei to sacrifice itself and serve as the river's flooding ground, but in the meantime hope its environment and human society would remain strategically effective, economically productive, and socially stable? How could the state balance the two agendas and the competing leaderships

---

[70] "Sanya zhen [The Sanya township]," *Yijian zhi*, vol. 2, 682.

behind them? After 1048, the environmental drama staged and unfolding inside Hebei provided a perfect arena for intense political contestations between the two sets of state institutions.[71]

From 1048, the Water Conservancy turned its eyes toward Hebei. Its institutional extension, the External Executive (*dushui waicheng* 都水外丞), which followed the physical migration of the river and conducted actual work on the ground, relocated its office, bureaucratic team, and workers into Hebei. It considered its agenda – to tame the Yellow River – the top priority in that land, far more important than Hebei's indigenous environmental issues and various socio-economic issues. With the end justifying its means, the External Executive ignored the heavy socio-economic costs that their hydraulic works inflicted on Hebei. Moreover, since the land should give way to the river and river hydraulics, Hebei's indigenous hydraulic leadership – its civil governments and military authorities – should yield to the Water Conservancy. It is the Water Conservancy and its External Executive that should control human and material resources and determine what hydraulic project should take priority. This pro-Yellow River leadership attracted a wide array of members and sympathizers in the government, such as hydrocrats serving the External Executive inside Hebei; bureaucrats serving the Water Conservancy at the imperial court; and military leaders and statesmen at the court who were concerned about geopolitical and strategic stability of north China. None of these men had strong personal ties with the land of Hebei. Whatever political factions they were identified with (either Wang Anshi and his fellow reformists in the early 1070s or conservatives like Lü Dafang and Wang Yansou in the late 1080s), they shared a common understanding about how to deal with the Yellow River–Hebei environmental complex, namely, to prioritize the river issues at any cost.

Facing this external, top-down imposition, Hebei's regional authorities voiced a different opinion: Hebei had the right to exist and prosper, and its own environmental issues deserved great attention. By crashing into Hebei, the Yellow River had become a mere component of Hebei's giant environmental entity, rather than something superior to it. Hence, to Hebei's indigenous hydraulic leadership, any treatment of the river should be grounded within a holistic plan for the environmental management of

---

[71] Hydraulic-induced competition for political power and resources is certainly not a Northern Song monopoly; it is seen in other historical times. For instance, Jane Kate Leonard (1996) gives a detailed account on the negotiations between the court of the Qing Dynasty and its provincial and regional officials on water management.

Hebei; by extension, the External Executive of the Water Conservancy must collaborate with, consult, and respect the regional authorities (if not completely merging into the latter). Supporting such regional claims were Hebei's local officials, military officers, and senior officials like the Fiscal Commissioner, who resented that their authorities were challenged by the intrusive power of the Water Conservancy. Siding with them were humanitarian-minded statesmen like Sima Guang and Fan Chunren as well as financial ministers at the court who were cautious about hydraulic expenditures. To this group, whatever approaches the state took to cope with the Yellow River–Hebei environmental complex, it should always bear in mind the interests of Hebei and its people.

Between 1048 and 1128, these two hydraulic leaderships competed ferociously. The External Executive dominated most of human and material resources and refused to share with Hebei's regional authorities. In one instance when the Zhang River flooded terribly in western Hebei, local authorities desperately needed laborers, cash, and materials to fix the riverbanks. While their districts were impoverished and their treasuries were empty, they found enormous corvée laborers situated nearby, and some storage areas were stuffed with construction materials. Yet, they could not touch on those resources, because they belonged exclusively to the External Executive for the Yellow River hydraulics, prohibited for local access. In another case, in the 1070s when Cheng Fang, a powerful hydrocrat of the External Executive, sought to maneuver a great number of local corvée laborers from the local government to engage in a hydraulic project that he managed, a local official and famous Confucian scholar Cheng Hao 程顥 (1032–1085) refused to release the laborers. The imperial court had to step in to mediate the dispute. It ordered both sides to compromise: Cheng Hao had to hand over 800 local laborers to the External Executive, a number lower than Cheng Fang's original request.[72] Clearly, the struggles with environmental problems were not merely a human-vs.-nature struggle, but one between different human needs and political preferences.

The conflicts between the two leaderships extended from practical matters to abstract political ideas, and even to vicious personal attacks. The pro-Yellow River leadership usually criticized the pro-Hebei group for being blind toward the destruction caused by the river and toward the large picture of the state's interests. Pushing back equally hard, the pro-Hebei group accused the hydrocrats of not caring about human lives,

---

[72] "The Epitaph of Cheng Hao," *QSW*, 1071: 245.

of abusing resources, and of undermining the state's human and economic foundation. Leading hydrocrats like Li Zhongchang in the 1050s,
Cheng Fang in the 1070s, Wu Anchi in the 1080s–1090s, and Meng
Changling in the late 1110s, were all eyed as "petty men" (*xiaoren* 小人)
by Confucian scholar-officials, such as Ouyang Xiu, Sima Guang, Fan
Chunren, and Su Zhe who considered themselves upright "gentlemen"
(*junzi* 君子).[73] The environmental and hydraulic management served as
both a perfect arena and an active medium – in addition to conventional
political, philosophical, or intellectual debates that Song historians have
focused their studies on – for both the production and manifestation of
the Song's factional differences and conflicts. This certainly complicates
our conventional understanding of the distinction between a conservative and a reformist faction in this period; during the politico-hydraulic
contestation, the factional differentiation was complex and fluid.

During Wang Anshi's reforms, the state activism that the reformists
advocated energized both the Yellow River leadership and Hebei's indigenous hydraulic leadership. Be it a petty men or a gentlemen, everyone in
Hebei passionately engaged in hydraulic works and got their hands dirty
with water and mud.[74] The External Executive of the Water Conservancy
expanded its business beyond the Yellow River hydraulics to intervene in
the environmental management of Hebei's local rivers, which traditionally were overseen by Hebei's regional authorities. For instance, because
the Yellow River had messed up the water system of the Zhang River in
western Hebei, the External Executive saw managing the Zhang River as a
natural extension of the hydraulic agenda for the Yellow River. By taking
over the control of managing the Zhang River from the local authorities,
the External Executive spread its power spatially to places originally not
affected by the Yellow River.

Hebei's regional authorities resisted such encroachment. Led by the
Fiscal Commission, they fought back. In the late 1080s, for instance, the
Vice Commissioner Du Chun 杜純 (1032–1095) specified the transfer of
the duties and authorities of Hebei's water management from his office

---

[73] *QSW*, 2218: 371; 2023: 140; and 2023: 146–147. These "petty men" were called
"malicious ministers (*jianchen* 奸臣)" by historians in the Yuan Dynasty who compiled
The Standard History of the Song Dynasty (*SS*, 91: 2256). For the discourse on political
factions during the Northern Song period, see Levine (2008).

[74] Guided by the "measure of agricultural fields and water benefits," a major policy of
Wang Anshi's reform, regional and local officials engaged in hydraulic works across the
empire. For instance, see Pierre-Etienne Will's (1998: 294–297) study of the revival of
the irrigation system of the Zhengbai Canal.

to the External Executive of the Water Conservancy. He claimed: "When the water management was overseen by our office, flooding events were no more than today. Since it has been managed by the External Executive, flooding events have not become less than before."[75] Du indicated that such transfer of power and resources did not improve Hebei's environmental conditions; the intrusion of the External Executive in Hebei's regional business was considered unnecessary. To Du, the division of environmental agendas and institutions prevented any holistic management of environmental issues and certainly harmed the efficiency of any hydraulic work. "Let them [the two institutions] return to a combination as one institution," he recommended. This "one institution" meant Hebei's Fiscal Commission which, to Du and his colleagues, should monopolize institutional and financial powers in dealing with the Yellow River–Hebei environmental complex.

Underlying Du Chun's criticism of the Yellow River hydraulic leadership was an issue of environmental ownership and the ownership of political power entailed and manifested by environmental struggles. Who owned Hebei's environment and environmental management? Who controlled resources and claimed economic and political powers in Hebei? By extension, who was the best representative of the state as the hydraulic leader to wield state power on the ground? After the river provoked a catastrophic flood in 1098–1099, more people joined Du Chun in attacking the External Executive of the Water Conservancy. Cai Dao 蔡蹈, in his memorial to Emperor Zhezong, condemned the External Executive for poor preparation and for causing the catastrophe.[76] Zeng Xiaoguang 曾孝廣 (1040–1100) capitalized on the disaster, pleading with the court to strip the External Executive of its duties and institutional power, and to subject the latter to the leadership of Hebei's Fiscal Commission.[77] So agitated by the environmental reality and its incapable officials, the imperial court came to the same conclusion: the expansion of the External Executive in Hebei failed to quell the violent river or bring to the land environmental tranquility. The court abolished this hydraulic institution in 1099. For the next fifteen years, the environmental management of the Yellow River–Hebei complex fell into the hands of the Fiscal Commission, Hebei's regional authorities, until the mid-1110s when Emperor Huizong restored the External Executive and had it carry out his monumental project – channeling the river through the the Dapi mountain.

[75] "Record of the Conducts of Du Chun," *QSW*, 2741: 55–58.
[76] *QSW*, 2235: 700.
[77] *QSW*, 2569: 247.

So the physical environment and the human politics had became intimately entangled. The environmental drama during 1048–1128 not only opened up a contested physical landscape, in which the river and Hebei's indigenous environmental entities competed to occupy the space and provoked a variety of environmental problems. It also opened up a political, human landscape, where different hydraulic leaderships and political individuals flocked in to assert their preferences, compete for political dominance, and demand the state's attention. The convergence of the Yellow River and the Hebei Plain into a gigantic environmental complex did not give rise to a single hydraulic agenda or a single political authority. Quite the opposite, it intensified the contradiction among various (at least two) agendas, the divergence between their goals, and the competition among different leaderships within the imperial state. It caused differentiation and division of state power rather than its centralization and reinforcement.

This environmental-political history of the second half of the Northern Song period urges us to complicate the chicken-egg metaphor for Karl Wittfogel's productive mode of relationship between political power and hydraulic works, which I quoted at the beginning of this chapter. Regardless of what the chicken or the egg stands for, either power or hydraulics, the history of the Yellow River–Hebei environmental complex did not see a monolithic, integral state as a conceptual whole chicken, but saw a liver, two claws, tips of wings, and a handful of scattered feathers. Neither did it hold a singular, lucidly defined environmental agenda analogous to an intact egg. Lying in front of the master chef – history – was a deformed yolk and liquid white that splashed over hundreds of cracks in the eggshell. How would these ingredients – a multiplicity of historical actors of competing interests – produce a decent dinner, as Wittfogel idealistically envisioned, a neatly tamed environment and the despotic state power of a hydraulic regime?

The Yellow River–Hebei environmental complex became too complicated and costly a meal for the Song state to swallow. The pro-Yellow River group rarely cared about the lives in Hebei, while the pro-Hebei group failed to grasp the state's anxiety about the river problems and their impact on "national security." Rejecting each other, they shared a partisan attitude like "It's your misfortune but not my own" (to paraphrase Richard White's book title).[78] The state, however, could not think in such a partisan way. Whatever happened inside Hebei would in one way or another affect the survival and prosperity of the state. Whoever's

[78] White (1991).

misfortune, either Hebei's, or Henan's, or the Yellow River's, would eventually develop to become the state's misfortune. The state had to continue its investments in the river hydraulics to prevent the river from running wild, and in the meantime tended to Hebei's environment, such as protecting the frontier ponds, to prevent a total devastation of the frontier region.

This is why the imperial state was entrapped in the Yellow River–Hebei environmental complex, why its emperors, without exception, felt torn by and vacillated between contradicting policies, and why none of its frequently swinging, polarized decisions brought about environmental stability and political consensus. The state was unable to make a right decision, yet also unable not to make any decision or not to do anything. The game that the state played with the Yellow River–Hebei environmental complex was not a zero-sum one; rather, it fell in a zone of ambiguity and uncertainty. However calculating and rational the court and its officials tried to be, they were unable to uncover all the blind spots, accommodate all the conflicting interests, or prevent potential backlash from both its politicians and the environment. Between 1048 and 1128, the state's engagement with the Yellow River–Hebei environmental complex followed this cycle: tackling uncertainty – making a decision – taking actions – panicking at the failure – flipping policies – tackling another round of uncertainty. This cycle trapped the state at the table for an unending unpleasant dinner, from which the state could neither withdraw, nor start anew with a package of different ingredients.

The Hydraulic Mode of Consumption

The above analysis compels us to challenge Karl Wittfogel's logic of conceptualization, the "hydraulic mode of production," which has informed most of the scholarship of Chinese hydraulic history and historical relationships between political power and hydraulic management.[79] This

---

[79] Wittfogel (1957) postulated that state-sponsored hydraulic works gave rise to a despotic state and caught countries like China within a kind of "hydraulic society." Since its appearance in the 1950s, this thesis has received enormous criticism from Chinese political, hydraulic, and technological historians. Based on studies mainly about late-imperial China, historians have made two main critiques, respectively from a spatial and a temporal perspective. For the spatial critique, scholars point out that the state was often not the prime hydraulic leader; most of hydraulic works in China were small-scale and carried out by regional and local hydraulic leaders. Localized and scattered hydraulic works gave rise to separate and diffuse regional powers that not only did not congeal into a total power for the imperial state, but also competed with and checked the growth of the state power. Hence, in the state-society equation through the hydraulic lens, there appeared a strong society that the weak state power could not thoroughly penetrate

mode of production operates through three mutually constitutive processes. First, a hydraulic leader utilizes societal forces to manage water and thereby produces a sound environment for the society. Second, although being exploited by the hydraulic leader of growing political power, the society enjoys a certain level of well-being by benefiting from the hydraulic leadership and the tamed environment. Third, through the successful management of water, the regime extracts resources from the society, delivers care to it, and asserts control over it; by so doing the state establishes itself as a despotic regime over the society.

Our exploration of the Song history has so far demonstrated that the first productive process – the Song state's environmental management – often failed. Even though the state served as a proactive hydraulic leader and was capable of amassing enormous human and material resources from the society, and even though the state had benign intentions to

and control, but had constantly to negotiate with, collaborate with, and even rely on. Therefore, a true Wittfogelian despotic state never took place in China. For the temporal critique, scholars point that even when the state functioned as the prime, responsible hydraulic leader to successfully manage water problems, ensure the society's environmental security, and thereby gain strong control over the society, such state efforts could not last forever. Through a cyclical process, the state would invariably neglect hydraulic works; such negligence would cause destruction to the hydraulic works, and inflict environmental disasters to the society. Consequentially, the suffering and resentful society resisted the corrupt state; through disobedience and rebellion, the society challenged the state's control and caused the state to fall. This brought history back to the beginning of a new cycle as a new state emerged and took up hydraulic responsibilities. Throughout this cycle, even if a true Wittfogelian despotic state emerged in historical times, its total power did not last long and did not trap China in a hydraulic society infinitely. These two critiques have led to the creation of two notions, "hydraulic community" and "hydraulic cycle." The former was coined by Japanese scholars and best elaborated by Akira Morita (1974 and 1990) in his studies on regional hydraulic histories in the Qing Dynasty. The latter was coined by Pierre-Etienne Will (1980) in his studies of the hydraulic history in Ming-Qing China. Despite their criticism of Wittfogel's reductive theorization, both "hydraulic community" and "hydraulic cycle" are derivative concepts and empirical revisions of Wittfogel's ideal-typical theorization. Both notions have inherited and followed Wittfogel's logic of reasoning, the "hydraulic mode of production," which essentializes the mutually constitutive relationship between power and hydraulics. The "hydraulic community" scholarship does not deny the constitution of political power through hydraulics; it simply argues a limited scale of the power and its location in various hydraulic communities, instead of in a state-level hydraulic regime. The "hydraulic cycle" scholarship endorses the mutual constitution between power and hydraulics at both the state level and the local level. But it insists that the brief, inconsistent hydraulic commitment from the hydraulic leader would invariably turn the first half-cycle of mutual production between power and hydraulics into an ensuing half-cycle of mutual destruction – the trigger for the downturn was the absence of the state attention and efforts. My critique of both Wittfogel and these Wittfogel-influenced scholarships in the following pages targets their productive logic; it does not target the validity of their empirical cases.

undertake environmental agendas "to improve the human condition" for the majority of the society (as James C. Scott phrases it), it did not pacify the hostile environment – the end result of its efforts was not productive. In fact, the more it tried, the more environmental complications it provoked, and the more environmental disasters ravaged north China. The Yellow River–Hebei environmental complex was too lively, unpredictable, and overwhelming for even a most environmentally engaged state like the Northern Song to handle.[80]

The second productive process did not go through either. As the next two chapters will show, the more the state maneuvered the society to manage the environment, the more human costs the state-society joint force engendered. Given all the resources the society inside and outside Hebei poured into the hydraulic works, not much positive outcome was produced; the hydraulic mode of production did not function well. People in Hebei and, by extension, many in north China suffered increasing damage. The following pages will show that it was not the state's negligence that led to hydraulic destruction, the society's socio-economic decline, and the rise of societal resentment toward the state, as prescribed by the model of "hydraulic cycle" that historian Pierre-Etienne Will coins and many hydraulic historians of late imperial China have adopted. In our case, it was the state's enthusiastic, diligent, and unstoppable engagement with the hydraulics that generated environmental instability, social destruction, and, as to be shown in the final few pages of this chapter, societal upheavals and rebellions.[81]

---

[80] Note that although I ask similar questions to Scott – how well intended schemes led to unintended, disastrous consequences – I do not emphasize his conclusion, that is the schemes' disrespect and ignorance of local knowledge and local practices. I certainly do not provide the converse assumption that schemes employing local knowledge and practices would have a better chance to handle environmental problems. Chapter 6 will show that people's individual, local strategies were inadequate to deal with the overwhelming Yellow River–Hebei environmental complex. What I stress here is that, while tackling the trialectic complexity involving the physical environment, the state, and the society, any focus on the state-versus-society dialectics without acknowledging the spontaneity of non-human environmental entities is not adequate.

[81] We should carefully distinguish the hydraulics oriented toward flood control from that toward irrigation, as well as hydraulic agendas of gigantic, medium, or small scales. Agendas of different natures and scales do not necessarily follow the same model of hydraulic cycle. The kind of "hydraulic cycle" that Will proposes explains very well water issues of regional or local scales in late-imperial China, such as Peter Perdue's study of the Dongting Lake area in Hunan. But it does not explain the irony seen in state-sponsored Yellow River hydraulics in the Northern Song and in the Yuan-Ming period, when, despite increasing investments from the state, the hydraulic works continued to break down, and the society did not benefit from state investments but suffered increasing destruction.

The third productive process obviously pointed to an opposite direction. The transition from the pre-1048 environmental situation to the post-1048 situation did not produce an all-powerful state as Wittfogel's "hydraulic mode of production" logically promised. Rather, every episode of the eighty-year environmental drama reinforced an anxiety-ridden, undetermined, often defeated state; at every stage of its life, the Song state was forced to face some new environment-related crisis. As the state endeavored to gain more power in other aspects of its rule (political, military, financial, demographical, intellectual, etc. as Song historians have lavishly shown), its state power was continuously translated into human and material resources that were channeled toward and depleted in Hebei. Such consumption of the state power was necessitated by the overwhelming environmental power of the Yellow River–Hebei complex as well as by the state's unbreakable entrenchment with the complex and its inescapable commitment to the often failed efforts of environmental management. For example, after the flood in 1056, the river's abrupt southward shift in 1077–1078, and the catastrophe in 1099, the state was so exhausted by river problems that it wanted to end its environmental involvement with the Yellow River–Hebei complex altogether. Nevertheless, it was unable to break from such entanglement; its hydraulic practices and its investment of resources had to continue until the fall of the dynasty. It was not the destruction of hydraulics that led to the social and political breakdown of the state as the notion "hydraulic cycle" observes. Quite the opposite, it was the destruction of the state in the early twelfth century that released the state and the society from their enslavement by their environmental commitment. Through its engagement with the Yellow River, the state sank deeper and deeper into various crises: not only did environmental disasters continue to occur, but also more and more human labor and resources were drained away, factional politics and political conflicts were intensified, the military became harder to control, and the civilian society suffered increasing disasters and hardship.

The history of the Song state's interactions with the Yellow River and Hebei demonstrates the invalidity of Wittfogel's productive mode of theorization. Here, I propose a new theoretical formula that more faithfully conceptualizes the historical reality in our case, which with adjustment may be applicable to many other historical circumstances. This formula – the "hydraulic mode of consumption" – postulates that while the state, the society, and the environment intertwined with each other to produce an eighty-year environmental drama, they were simultaneously burdened, consumed, and even exhausted by their activities and interactions. Most evidently, the state's desire and efforts to tame the river and to create a benign environment for both the state and the majority of the society led to unexpected consequences, including the continuous degradation of environmental systems, catastrophic experiences to the human society, and even the dissolution and depletion of state power.

The consumptive formula provides a general argument for both this chapter and the three forthcoming chapters. What happened in north China from 1048 to 1128 took a heavy toll on its historical players: politically, financially, and mentally on the imperial state; demographically and socio-economically on the people in Hebei; and environmentally and even ecologically on the land and water in north China. None of this was anticipated by the imperial state (the "hydraulic leader" to use Wittfogel's term), when it worked to transform north China's physical landscape and tame the Yellow River. In Chapters 6 and 7, I will analyze how the environmental drama damaged Hebei's population and caused its dominant form of economy, namely agriculture, to decline. In Chapter 8, I will reveal how the environmental drama and state-led hydraulic activities had a long-term negative impact on Hebei's landscape, waterscape, soil, and vegetation.

The following few pages will only briefly discuss three aspects in which, by committing to environmental management, the imperial state was entrapped in a hydraulic mode of consumption and worn down by it. First, the state finances. Modern historians applauded the Song for developing a fiscal administration that "surpassed in sophistication and effectiveness anything previously seen in China," and that efficiently collected wealth from the society.[82] Based on some estimates, the state might have extracted 15% of the national income as its revenue, far higher than estimates for states in later historical periods and in Europe up to the nineteenth century.[83] Despite such impressive revenue income, the state was constantly troubled by heavy deficits due to its uncontrollable expending. In the late eleventh century, the state spent its revenues mainly on three things: its military, its bureaucratic apparatus, and its hydraulic works on the Yellow River. To a substantial extent, after 1048, the state finances operated around the hydraulic demands in Hebei. The Yellow River–Hebei environmental complex consumed such a large chunk of the state's wealth that its financial ministers often complained about the exhaustion of state finances. In the late 1080s, for instance, the state project to

---

[82] Golas in Chaffee and Twitchett (2015: 139–140).
[83] Golas (1998: 90–94).

"return the river" to southern Hebei consumed enormous resources, and statesmen at Emperor Zhezong's court declared that the wealth Emperor Shenzong and his reformist government had painstakingly accumulated over the previous two decades had been depleted. Consequently, the state could not rely solely on its central reserves to sustain the large-scale hydraulic works. It demanded contributions from various regional governments in southern parts of China. This means regions that previously had no obligation toward either the Yellow River or Hebei were now expected to contribute their own reserves to the ongoing projects inside Hebei.

Second, labor. Manpower was another major resource the hydraulic works demanded. After 1048, hydraulic laborers came not only from Hebei, but also from all over north China. The government's conscription policy demanded that every household contribute labor at a rate of one out of every two or three male adults.[84] In emergencies, or for large projects such as in 1088, tens of thousands of laborers were drafted even from the Huai River valley in the south. These men traveled over a distance of hundreds of kilometers to serve in Hebei.[85] During Wang Anshi's reforms, non-Hebei laborers either went to Hebei to perform their duties in person, or they offset their labor with cash so that the government could use the money to hire workers in their stead. In either case, laborers, their livelihoods, and their family activities outside Hebei were conditioned by the hydraulic works, even though a great portion of them lived far away from Hebei and were physically disconnected from the Yellow River–Hebei environmental complex.

During and after Wang Anshi's reforms, the Song government experienced several rounds of policy change in terms of how to recruit labor services.[86] Irrespective of how the administration varied, what remained real and constant was Hebei's and the Yellow River's demand for tremendous numbers of human bodies and their labor force. The hydraulic mode of consumption continued to take the lives of adult men of north China. Originally farmers, urbanites, and soldiers, they were sent to Hebei to conduct manual labor next to the turbulent Yellow River. Many drowned and were flushed away by torrents; a great number suffered from epidemic diseases, which plagued their work sites during the hot and humid summer months. While many died on the trip between their homes and

[84] *QSW*, 2381: 94.
[85] *QSW*, 1517: 13–16.
[86] Golas in Chaffee and Twitchett (2015: 167–172).

work sites, many also escaped their duties and absconded as disaster refugees or outlaws.[87] From the 1070s on, after years of attempting to reroute the river into an eastern course, the government noticed a sharp increase in bandits in both Hebei and Henan. Those men looted cities and towns, killed officials, and attracted followers among the commoners. Many were said to be former hydraulic workers. Toward the end of the eleventh century, the situation worsened further, as several thousand runaways dispersed and hid in the hills and forests of Henan, where no government offices had been established to control the area.[88] Clearly, the Yellow River–Hebei environmental complex not only consumed manpower and deprived the society of a productive force that was traditionally dedicated to human reproduction and economic activities. It also turned a substantial part of that manpower into a destructive social force – in the form of bandits and rebels – that challenged the stability of the society and shook the state's control.

Third, a similar story with other resources. The hydraulic works demanded tremendous amounts of construction materials. As Chapter 8 will discuss in greater detail, Hebei ran out of such resources, so a great portion of the materials had to be imported from elsewhere. Lumber often came from southern Shanxi and Shaanxi more than a thousand kilometers west of Hebei, where mountainous areas were once covered with dense forests. Throughout the eleventh century, trees were felled in order to supply hydraulic construction in Hebei. Local people in these western regions knew nothing about what was happening far away in Hebei; they never saw a single Yellow River flood and would not relate their tree-felling business to the environmental complex in Hebei. Yet, each year they had to go deep into mountains to cut trees as additional corvée service for their local governments. Their governments, meantime, received enormous pressure from the central government that issued them annual lumber quotas. To meet the quotas, local officials developed various strategies to motivate people to provide service, either coercing them or paying them to gather wood.[89] Shipping large amounts of wood through the turbulent Yellow River downstream to Hebei was not easy. Every year, many men involved in shipping were killed by the river's torrents; many households undertaking the job went into bankruptcy.[90] Local governments found it increasingly difficult to recruit sailors for the

---

[87] *QSW* 2480: 122; 2479: 96; and 2472: 323.
[88] *QSW*, 2276: 209.
[89] *QSW*, 2673: 62; 2744: 118–119; and 2427: 224–229. For logging and transportation of vegetative materials to Hebei, see Chapter 8.4.
[90] *QSW*, 644: 176.

job. The central government had to set up offices along the Yellow River to monitor the transportation and to make sure that sailors would not decamp. Here, we observe the operation of a whole institution along the course of the Yellow River to link up the empire's wood-rich northwestern regions in the southern part of the Loess Plateau and wood-deficient Hebei – the wood producer and the consumer – in order to sustain the state-organized hydraulic works.

Regions like Henan and Shandong did not produce large trees, but thanks to successful agriculture, their extensive farmland yielded a large amount of grass and straw every year, which could be used as construction materials as well. The financial authorities in those regions, the Fiscal Commission, were obligated to submit an annual "wood-grass fee (*shao-cao qian* 梢草錢)" to the Water Conservancy, and the latter used this money to purchase hydraulic materials. Sometimes, the regional authorities were unable to meet their quotas, or experienced it as a serious financial burden, because they often struggled to satisfy other financial obligations, such as paying for their own military and bureaucratic teams.[91] Clearly, the financial competition discussed earlier between the Water Conservancy and Hebei's regional authorities also took place between the state's hydraulic leadership and the authorities in other regions across north China.

Hence, the environmental drama taking place within Hebei not only led to the transformation of the land and society of Hebei itself, but it also shaped the socio-economic and environmental relationships among various regions across north China. On certain occasions, such as the "returning the river" project in 1088, the central government ordered the collection of construction materials from as far away as Zhejiang 浙江 in the lower Yangzi valley and Jiangxi 江西 in the middle Yangzi valley.[92] These regions in south China, located nearly a thousand kilometers away from Hebei, were maneuvered by the state to join their northern neighbors in providing goods and services to the Yellow River–Hebei environmental complex. Correspondingly, their socio-economic lives also became conditioned by the unstoppable hydraulic mode of consumption. What happened at specific locales extended to involve and implicate vast regions; multiple spaces co-occurred, allied, merged, and operated in concert.

Elaborating on his famous thesis on China's "Medieval Economic Revolution," Mark Elvin states: "Political pressure acted as a pumping mechanism to create a circulation of goods of which economic demand by

[91] *QSW*, 2703: 153.
[92] *QSW*, 1517: 13–16.

itself was incapable."[93] Our study shows that such "political pressure" derived substantially from the environmental pressure that the Yellow River–Hebei complex imposed upon the state. Managing the environmental crisis drove the transregional goods and resources, while the state functioned as both a manager and a medium. Asking "How Big" the Song's economy was, Peter Golas estimates that the Song state levied 15.6 percent of total national income as revenue, at a rate much higher than that in any Chinese state of a later period. Such understanding suggests that the Song was blessed with strong state power and had enormous wealth to spend.[94] Assuming both Elvin and Golas are right, we need to ask: what was the end goal of this circulation of goods and abundant wealth and who benefited? Did the circulation of goods and a large revenue collection invariably fuel revolutional economic growth as Elvin and Golas optimistically suggest, or signify the formation of a despotic state power as Wittfogel idealistically envisioned?

Clearly not. Between 1048 and 1128, Hebei, as the new delta of the Yellow River's northern courses, became the site of environmental, political, and financial contestations among state-level and regional-level powers. The Yellow River–Hebei environmental complex sat at the center of consumption, spreading its disastrous influence and demanding political attention, human capital, and material resources. Like a black hole, it absorbed everything the state and its various institutions provided, without returning the environmental stability that the state desperately pursued. Rather than the environment to be regulated by an all-powerful state as Wittfogel envisioned, the converse was true: the particular environmental world centered on the Yellow River–Hebei environmental complex organized the state's daily political and financial practices, and demanded the state's service. The core-periphery structure that the state laid down for its empire – for the maximization of state interests at the cost of its various peripheries – saw a gradual inversion that led to the exhaustion of state power. We shall discuss this core-periphery inversion in greater detail in Chapter 7. Consequentially, the Yellow River–Hebei environmental complex governed the Song state within its own "environmental regime," enrolling the state in an environmental drama that it was then unable to end. In its peculiar environmental-political-economic equation, the "hydraulic mode of consumption" placed the imperial state

---

[93] Elvin (1973: 165).
[94] Golas (1988: 90–94).

not in the position of a beneficiary who would profit from both the pacification of water and the appropriation of the human society, as Wittfogel
has suggested, but rather on the opposite end of being entrapped by the
constantly changing environment.

In his seminal work on landscape and power, W. J. T. Mitchell views
landscape as the "dreamwork of imperialism," not only the target but
also the medium of power production and expansion.[95] What happened
in Northern Song China prior to 1048 seems to have perfectly material-
ized this idea. The imperial state's political desires and ambitious actions
sought to appropriate not only a peripheral region like Hebei and its
people, but also the waters and land that molded the people for the
preservation and empowerment of the state itself. Yet, despite its best
efforts to dream up a tame, profitable landscape, the state unexpectedly
slipped into a nightmare: the year to year management of the mounting environmental problems disturbed the state, haunted it, and wore it
down. It seems this history of the Song state's interactions with the Yellow
River–Hebei environmental complex offers us a chance not just to ask
the question political scientist James C. Scott seeks to tackle: how certain,
and in particular state sponsored, schemes to improve the human condition failed. It inspires a further inquiry about how by engaging in such
schemes, the state, as the conductor of these schemes and presumably
their prime beneficiary, got itself entrapped in a failing process.

[95] Mitchell (2002: 10).

6

Life in the Yellow River Delta

As the imperial state created its version of the battle with the Yellow River–Hebei environmental complex between 1048 and 1128, there was another struggle unfolding in Hebei – the new Yellow River delta – where individuals and the entire society were thrown into repetitive turmoil. The costly and extensive hydraulic works taking place inside Hebei did not produce a benign physical environment for its people; rather, they continued to harm the population, consume its wealth, and deprive many of the people of even a subsistence livelihood.

The state related to the environmental drama from a distance. Its concerns about harm done to the state's stability by environmental factors were conceptual and futuristic. Most of its political figures never saw the Yellow River or traveled to Hebei. When debating and making decisions about hydraulic policies, they referenced each other's words and consulted classics, histories, and accounting books. Their delicate, pen-holding hands barely touched the troubled water and earth. Farmers in the Yangzi valley and loggers in Shanxi and Shaanxi could not conceptualize the connection between the fruit of their labors and its consumption inside Hebei. These active participants in the environmental drama did not witness how the river's torrents crushed banks and destroyed buildings. Their ears heard no screams, and their families were not plagued by deaths and the loss of livelihoods.

In contrast, the experiences of the Hebei people were physical, material, and concrete. Their bodies were injured, their loved ones drowned, their roofs and walls collapsed, grain supplies and already sown fields were lost in the floods. As a disaster receded, the survivors stood in their devastated gardens, looking at a land scarred with broken trees, construction debris, and stagnant water. Entire roads disappeared without a trace, along with supplies meant to sustain them during the winter or make spring planting possible. Some wondered if the salinized soil could support crops, while others considered leaving Hebei altogether.

The ordinary people in Hebei did not share the state's grand vision of a carefully designed geopolitical landscape in north China. What benefited the state did not necessarily benefit the people in Hebei – in fact, the people often suffered from it. They could not visualize a vast region called Hebei versus one called Henan, or a giant body of water called the Yellow River. What appeared real to them were flooding waters, dreadful scenes of deaths and hardship, and frightening rumors that haunted their daily lives. This embodied, experiential reality shaped how these men and women made sense of the environmental changes, and how they made choices to cope with the disasters. The state's projects did not address the needs of people in Hebei, but instead often called upon them to sacrifice for the state's desire and ambition. Hence, to those trying to survive in Hebei, the battle against the environmental power of the Yellow River–Hebei complex was often a battle against the political power of the imperial state.

In this chapter, we will piece together a general picture of the suffering and damage in Hebei. This effort is to reveal how the hydraulic mode of consumption took a heavy toll on the Hebei society, not only from the imperial state as seen in the previous chapter. We shall then observe the different choices the Hebei people faced and the strategies they took to preserve their subsistence livelihood. By doing so, we may catch a glimpse of their everyday resistance to both the destructive environment and the indifferent state.

6.1   People, Villages, Towns

Let us begin with some demographics.

The long-term demographic trend in middle-period China shows a clear growth in the overall population, manifested in an increase in the number of registered households. Given that the highest number on record had occurred in the mid-Tang period (specifically in 754), from then on the Chinese population had suffered a drastic decline due to the centuries-long political turmoil and civil war, and it only started to recover in the early Northern Song Dynasty. Although its starting point was rather low in the 980s, the Song population experienced a steady rise during the early eleventh century; in the mid-eleventh century, the population

TABLE 3. *Hebei's Registered Households*

Year	Hebei's Households	Total Households in the Country	Hebei's Percentage of Total Households
754	1,410,793	9,069,154	15.6
circa 980	574,502	6,499,145	8.84
1045	705,700	10,682,947	6.6
1078	1,232,659	16,569,874	7.44
circa 1080	984,195	14,041,980	7
1102	1,192,285	20,264,307	5.9

Notes: The household figures are collected from *Xin tangshu*, Chapters 37–43; *Taiping huanyu ji*; Ouyang Xiu's "Lun Hebei caichan shang shixiang shu," *OYXQJ*, 118: 1825–1828; *XCB*, 157: 3814; *Yuanfeng jiuyu zhi*; *Wenxian tongkao*, Chapter 11; and *SS*, Chapters 85–90. They are comparatively used along with the statistics made by Liang (1980: 86–94, 122, 132–137, 141–148, and 152–160). The area of the Hebei Circuit in the Tang Dynasty was a third larger than the size of Hebei in the Northern Song; the northern third remained under the control of the Liao Dynasty. To compare the household numbers in Tang Hebei and Song Hebei on a same geographic basis, the 754 figures shown in Table 3 exclude the household numbers of the districts in the northern third of Tang Hebei. We must be aware that these household figures reflect more about the government's household registration than actual birth rate among the population.

surpassed the Tang's highest level. Considering that the Song territory was a mere two-thirds of the mid-Tang territory, we must say that this population growth was rather impressive. Not only was the Song's overall population count higher, but its average population density was also much higher than that in the Tang. As previous scholarship has shown, much of this dramatic growth was due to migration to southeast and southwest China, the incorporation of native populations, and an enormous increase in reproductive rates in the southern parts of China enabled largely by burgeoning agricultural production.[1]

Hebei's regional situation was not as impressive as the Song's empire-wide growth. Chapters 1 and 2 showed that Hebei's population recovered steadily from war damage in the early Song period. The numbers in Table 3 indicate that the recovery and growth seem to have carried over all the way through the eleventh century. Yet, irrespective of how the numbers look, the overall size of Hebei's population in the Song period

[1] Hartwell (1982: 365–442) and Kuhn (2009). McDermott and Shibu offer an overall assessment of Song population and its regional variations, in Chaffee and Twitchett (2015: 326–335). For detailed studies about population growth in south China during the Tang-Song period, see Dong (2002) and Wu (2000).

failed to match its mid-Tang level. Moreover, while the entire population in the empire exploded, Hebei's demographic growth seems to have taken place at a much slower pace.[2] This slow growth is seen in the continuous drop in Hebei's share of the empire-wide population, from 15.6 percent in 754 to 5.9 percent in 1102. In comparison with the up-and-coming southern parts of China, Hebei was no longer the empire's top reproducer.

Look closely at Hebei's household numbers: the sharp surge in 1078 is startling. This might indicate a pure natural growth of the population from its 1045 demographic basis. But, it was more likely the result of Wang Anshi's reforms, which sought to ferret out unregistered households. By so doing, the number of legal taxpayers and corvée laborers increased in the government's accounting books. Ironically, this absurdly large number might also be a result of people's deliberate resistance to the reforms. By breaking down one large household into several small ones and a large chunk of property into several small lots, a Hebei household could reduce its obligation for corvée service, and enjoy a lower tax bracket. This means that although the state added a large number of households on paper, it did not necessarily gain more revenue or labor force in actuality. The 1080 number might also have been influenced by the reforms. The 1102 number from the early years of Emperor Huizong, who restored many reform policies as soon as he took the throne, was very likely a result of political manipulation as well. In comparison with these later numbers, the numbers from the 980s and 1045 were rather small. It is possible that they were a result of underestimation, because the government failed to register some households in the rather unstable social circumstances as in the 980s, or it failed to count many illegal, unregistered households who physically lived in Hebei but avoided tax responsibilities. In the aggregate, the five numbers for Hebei suggest that Hebei's population grew slowly after the 1040s, certainly not at a rate as high as the empire-wide growth.

To complicate these numbers and their surface value, the following pages will discuss the impact of environmental changes on the population. The eleventh century was blessed by the absence of major social chaos like war; such peace should have led to greater human reproduction. The chaotic environmental conditions, however, made reproduction hard to sustain. Our non-quantitative, descriptive sources give us a picture of a high mortality rate as well as a high emigration rate in Hebei during the last eight decades of the Song period. It is also possible that

---

[2] For Hebei population's reduced growth rate and density, see Wu (2000: 432–438).

Hebei's birth rate was below replacement rate. These three factors must have engendered a continuous population loss. Since we do not have any numbers for the overall natality, I will conclude my assessment of Hebei's population by suggesting that the birth rate at best remained stable after the 1040s, if it did not in fact decline.

Shortly before the Yellow River entered Hebei, Ouyang Xiu, then Hebei's Fiscal Commissioner, made an estimate of Hebei's population. Around 1045, Hebei had 705,700 registered civilian households, about 1,200 officials who were most likely under a separate household registration, and 477,000 soldiers for the Imperial Armies, the District Armies, and the Righteous and Brave troops.[3] Included in this latter number, the soldiers of Imperial Armies were counted at about 180,000. These individuals fell under an independent military registration, which I assume involved their households; this is to say that there were 180,000 military households.[4] Combining civilian, official, and military households, we can calculate an overall household number for Hebei to be 886,900. Historians usually assume that each household was made up of an average of five members in middle-period China.[5] Accepting this assumption and combining it with the non-Imperial Armies militia members (477,000 minus 180,000), we reach a population number for Hebei of 4,731,500 heads. This figure certainly does not reflect the actual population at the time, but it is statistically valuable to indicate the rough size of the legally registered population.

Beginning with this demographic baseline – roughly five million people – Hebei experienced repeated depopulation during the next eight decades. Its death and emigration rates rose for the first time in 1048, after the Yellow River surged into central Hebei in the summer and a severe drought broke out in the winter and into 1049.[6] The prolonged effects, including harvest failure, food shortages, and a dearth of various resources, drove enormous numbers of people onto the road. According to Liu Chang, the refugees "amounted to one million."[7] Ouyang Xiu made an even higher, most likely exaggerated, estimate, suggesting that 80–90 percent of the people in the region affected by the disasters turned to migration.[8] Starving and exhausted, not many could make it through their journey toward

[3] "Lun Hebei caichan shang shixiang shu," *OYXQJ*, 118: 1825–1828.
[4] For separate registrations for military households, see Wu (2000: 93–94).
[5] Wu (2000: 155).
[6] *Songchao shishi*, 2: 29.
[7] "Shang Renzong lun xiu Shanghukou," *GSJ*, 31: 375–376.
[8] "Lun xiuhe diyizhuang," *OYXQJ*, 108: 1642–1644.

security, and many perished on the road. In Ouyang's words: "Over a distance of more than a thousand *li*, the roads are full of the corpses of men."⁹ In an equally despairing, though perhaps exaggerated claim, Sima Guang cried that "fathers and sons consumed each other" in the ensuing famine.¹⁰

Refugees from central Hebei flowed in any direction offering food and safety. In Dingzhou in northwestern Hebei alone, the local government distributed relief to reportedly several million people.¹¹ Jia Changchao, Prefect of Daming in southern Hebei, was said to have received and given relief to nearly a million refugees.¹² In Heyang 河陽 in southwest Hebei, "fields and buildings were thoroughly washed away," and more than 100,000 people were uprooted.¹³ Crossing southern Hebei, the refugees continued further south, where the government set up relief stations at ports on the Yellow River, bestowing every adult with two *sheng* (1.33 liters) of grain per day and every child half that amount so that they could survive the rest of the trip into Henan. At least half a million people were said to have ended up in Qingzhou in Shangdong, where Prefect Fu Bi witnessed the congregation of refugees in urban slums.¹⁴ Hunger, fatigue, poor hygienic conditions, and infectious diseases were rife. Despite the efforts of benevolent officials like Fu to set up temporary lodgings for them, and to recruit adult males into local armies, the refugee mortality rate was still high.

Suffering and resentful, many refugees banded together and became unpredictable players who could cause potential social and political problems. Fearing subversion, the government encouraged the refugees to disperse or to go back to Hebei. Over time, some indeed chose to return home, hoping that the disasters had receded and they could go back to their old lives. We have no idea how many made their way back home successfully. The return journey was treacherous; according to Ouyang Xiu, only "a few survived."¹⁵ For those who made it back, it was uncertain what would await them. Some returned to find either their land overtaken by the Yellow River's waters, or their property occupied by wealthy and powerful families.¹⁶

⁹ "Dingzhou Yuegutang xu," *Dingzhou zhi*, 21: 26a–26b, 1823–1824.
¹⁰ XCB, 3:125.
¹¹ *Songchao shishi leiyuan*, 8: 82. XCB, 166: 3985.
¹² XCB, 166: 3985. "The Epitaph of Jia Changchao," QSW, 1160: 286–287.
¹³ "The Epitaph of Chen Anding," QSW, 1091: 245.
¹⁴ XCB, 166: 3984–3985. *Songchao shishi leiyuan*, 8: 82.
¹⁵ "Lun xiuhe diyizhuang," OYXQJ, 108: 5b–7b.
¹⁶ "The Epitaph of Zhang Duanshu," QSW, 2699: 95.

Not all refugees had faith in the restoration of safety in Hebei. To
many, the Yellow River–Hebei environmental complex no longer provided a desirable living space. The family of a prominent official, Li
Qingchen 李清臣 (1032–1102), is one example. Li's family had for generations lived in Daming, the district adjacent to the Yellow River. Li
himself was born there before the Yellow River hit the land, and later
died there as Daming's Prefect at the turn of the twelfth century. After
his father passed away in 1039, his family decided to leave Hebei to
"escape the harm of the Yellow River." After temporarily relocating to
Luoyang 洛陽 in western Henan, both living members of the family and
the graves of their ancestors moved to Anyang 安陽 in western Hebei,
because divination had suggested that the location was secure and aus-
picious. Although Li himself later held official positions in Daming and
remained there, his family never returned to flood-stricken Daming, but
settled in Anyang where the mountainous terrain obstructed any floods.[17]

Elite, well-to-do families like Li's were able to choose between different
options to counteract the disasters; they had the means to move in and out
of Hebei. Ordinary and poorer people were not so lucky. They could not
risk returning to Hebei only to find it devastated. Many chose to establish
new homes and settle down outside of Hebei. Tangzhou 唐州 in Henan,
for instance, was an attractive place to stay. Thinly populated, with a
large area of unclaimed, uncultivated land, Tangzhou also had some
diligent local officials who issued low taxes to attract colonizers. Both
environmental conditions and government policies made places like this
attractive to Hebei refugees, where they could find not only a temporary
haven, but a secure, permanent home.[18]

It is not unreasonable to say that in the middle of the eleventh century at least a million of Hebei's five million people were disturbed in
some way by the environmental changes and uprooted from their normal
livelihood or even killed. If not killed or displaced, they lost property and
freedom, and fell into lesser socio-economic status like tenants, servants,
or outlaws. Given enough time for stability to return to Hebei, the damage inflicted on the people of Hebei could eventually be compensated and
repaired. But Hebei's environmental situation seemed to fight against a
recovery. Seven years later, in 1056, just as the Yellow River was about
to settle in its course through central Hebei, and the refugees had gained
enough strength and faith to return home, a state-sponsored hydraulic

---

[17] "The Epitaph of Li Qingchen," *QSW*, 2741: 60–61.
[18] "The Epitaph of Ren Jue," *QSW*, 2637: 219. Also *QSW*, 2154: 27 and 2030: 249.

project provoked a catastrophic flood in southern Hebei. Following it, the river exploded into a new course in 1060 and swept through the eastern part of Hebei. The restored population, thanks both to natural births and the return of refugees, was again subjected to a heavy loss.

Eight years later, in 1068, a severe drought from the previous year extended through the summer, along with a deadly earthquake and a series of bank ruptures and floods from the Yellow River. At that time, the elderly Zhang Cun 張存 (986–1071) and his extensive, wealthy family lived in Jizhou in central Hebei. Zhang used to be Hebei's Fiscal Commissioner and had retired from prestigious positions; his sons held various official positions in Jizhou and other places. Composed of hundreds of members, Zhang's lineage was one of the most prominent lineages in Jizhou. When the earthquake occurred, Zhang was eating a meal in the living room. Suddenly, the whole house shook, and in the ensuing chaos, his family members and servants urged him to leave the city. They said that Jizhou's residents had already packed up to escape the earthquakes. Rumors were also in the air that the Yellow River was pressing upon the city and would soon crush the city walls. Many of the citizens were heading toward Xingzhou 邢州, a mountainous region in western Hebei.[19] Still, Zhang refused to move his family, maintaining moral commitment to his city and his people. Yet, several tomb epitaphs of the Zhang family suggest that the family relocated the graves of ancestors, including those of Zhang's father's generation and later Zhang Cun himself and his sons, to highland Xingzhou, evidence of their relocation and their urge for self-preservation against the damaging environmental forces.

The 1068 disasters followed a drought that lingered on through 1070. Then another drought plus an explosion of locusts during 1073–1074 afflicted the region. The river flooded almost every year at different locations in central Hebei. In the early fall of 1075, for instance, one bank rupture in the realm of Daming was said to have resulted in the inundation of sixty villages and their 17,000 households.[20] Meanwhile, the large-scale "returning the river" project that Emperor Shenzong and Wang Anshi sponsored also caused disturbance to the already-disaster-ravaged people. All of this sparked off another round of high mortality and emigration.

[19] "The Epitaph of Zhang Cun," *QSW*, 1227: 293–295 and "The Epitaph of Zhang Baosun," *QSW*, 2150: 671.
[20] *QSW*, 656: 17.

The demographic components and pattern of emigration during the 1060s–1070s were different from those after 1048. Not only did disaster refugees – in particular people in central Hebei like Zhang Cun's fellow citizens – uproot their families and flee their hometowns, but those who lived on the western highland and who were not directly affected by the disasters also panicked, frightened by the influx of large numbers of refugees (like those fleeing Jizhou to Xingzhou in the summer of 1068). The locals in western Hebei felt that the refugees would become beggars, robbers, and thieves, consuming local resources while destabilizing the social order. In addition to fearing the migrants, local people at of the bottom level of the society, such as low-ranking landowning households and tenants who made a living by farming for landlords, were also hit hard by extensive droughts. They were not much better off than the incoming refugees. So in the 1070s, they began to join the mass emigration to leave western Hebei, although the Yellow River did not affect western Hebei directly.[21]

Losing their tenants, servants, and the local poor, the upper levels of the society felt insecure as well. The loosely defined social groups – the rich and the poor – were used to co-existing in a deeply entangled moral economy, with the rich offering charity and the poor providing the foundation for labor and security. As this foundation fell apart, the higher-ranking households found that they could not survive without the social bonds and protection. They also resented the increasing socio-economic responsibilities. They had to provide relief for refugees, come up with extra labor and resources to cultivate land, and maintain social security. They also had to carry more institutional responsibilities. As their tenants and the poor left the area, the government expected the rich to pay more taxes and provide more corvée services, including participating in hydraulic works to tame the Yellow River and manage local streams.

It was in those circumstances that Wang Anshi issued his major reform policy, the Guards and Tithings (*baojia* 保甲) system. This policy further upset the well-off. The *baojia* was forcefully carried out in Hebei in the 1070s in order to stabilize social bonds within the society and to strengthen the society's service to the state. Local elites were installed as the heads of "*bao*" units and required to both control and look after poorer households in their units. Unfortunately, since Hebei's rural economy and society had already declined, and the poor continued to become unmoored from the socio-economic bonds, the rich could not stop

[21] *XCBSB*, 3xia: 141.

the dissolution of their "*bao*" units and the broader society. They resisted the state's demands that local elites should make extra contributions in difficult times and take responsibility for the poor who left home.[22] Hence, the activist approaches of state control promoted by Wang Anshi's government encountered not only fierce environmental challenges, but also spontaneous or deliberate resistance from different social groups. It is understandable that the well-off felt the urge to leave Hebei as well. Traveling in style, they packed up their belongings, prepared travel supplies, designed itineraries, and traveled by carriage. When crossing bridges on the Yellow River into Henan and questioned by officials at check points, they stated that Hebei was no longer livable because "they were afraid of raids."[23] Like the families of Li Qingchen and Zhang Cun, those people had means to migrate and, if they wished, could leave Hebei forever.

In 1074, 46,000 Hebei migrants were reported to have crossed the Yellow River to enter Henan, and nearly 30,000 of them crowded into the metropolitan area of Kaifeng.[24] By the mid-1070s, refugees from central, western, and eastern Hebei filled major transportation routes and urban areas in Shandong, eastern Henan, western Henan, and Kaifeng. The central government tried to block them from entering Henan, but when that effort failed, it was forced to use different relief strategies to stabilize the situation and restrain the refugees from going farther south. Such strategies included opening up government granaries, selling official titles and certificates of religious clergy to buy extra grain, encouraging wealthy families to share resources, and recruiting male refugees – potential troublemakers to the state rule – into the military.

When the river suddenly shifted southward into Henan in 1077 and was forced back into Hebei by the government's hydraulic works in 1078, the death toll in north China skyrocketed. The poet-official Huang Tingjian 黃庭堅 (1045–1105) described the situation:

The earth split and the river boiled. Eight or nine out of ten households drowned and turned into fish. Recently I heard that each day tens of thousands of people cross the Yellow River from Chanyuan [the seat of Chanzhou on the Yellow River linking Hebei and Henan] to move southward. There is no way to know how many Hebei prefectures have thus become desolate.[25]

---

[22] *XCB*, 256: 6249 and 262: 6413.
[23] *QSW*, 2027: 212, 2459: 89, and 2460: 108.
[24] *XCB*, 255: 6243 and 256: 6251.
[25] "Liumin tan [A sigh for refugees]," *Huang Tingjian quanji, waiji* 6: 998.

In Henan, a prime destination for Hebei refugees, Gong Dingchen 龔鼎臣 (1010–1086) observed dead bodies lying in piles along the roads.[26] The situation was so dreadful, and the demand for relief so tremendous, that any given policy seemed inadequate. The same trend continued through the 1080s and 1090s.[27] As the Yellow River continued to flood southern and central Hebei, the government pressed harder to recruit more hydraulic workers from Hebei, hoping to shift the river's northern course clockwise toward the east. Refusing this imposition, more people were forced to flee or chose to leave their homeland. By the mid-1080s, in Daming only, the empire's Northern Capital in southern Hebei, "more than a half of the well-off families have fled."[28]

The most deadly threat to the Hebei population occurred at the turn of the twelfth century. After the Yellow River's torrents swept through most of Hebei between 1099 and 1102, "corpses of the dead fill the gullies and number in the millions."[29] Some said that more than half of the Hebei population was displaced.[30] According to Chao Shuozhi 晁説之 (1059–1129), more than a hundred thousand "floating people" gathered in Daming alone; another 30,000–40,000 crowded into the Tongli 通利 Commandery in southwestern Hebei.[31] Ranging from several thousand to hundreds of thousands, swarms of flood and famine refugees wandered in various urban areas. As the cities and towns became exhausted and were unable to provide food or shelter, the refugees moved elsewhere. In southeastern Hebei people died from starvation and the severe winter cold. In some literary accounts, which are perhaps exaggerated, "mothers abandon their infants and fathers eat their grown children."[32] In northern Hebei, refugees flowed northward and even crossed the border to enter Liao territory, at the risk of death penalties.[33] Along the border, the hungry went so far as to "eat one another."[34]

We could continue with many descriptions of this sort: observers of the time were all drawn to the misery across Hebei and the whole of north

---

[26] "The Epitaph of Gong Dingchen," *QSW*, 1680: 145.

[27] Su Zhe's comment in 1094, *Longchuan luezhi*, 9: 58–59.

[28] *QSW*, 2023: 135–136.

[29] Han Zongwu, "Shang Huizong dazhao lun rishi [Response to Emperor Huizong's edict on the sun eclipse]," *SMCZY*, 44: 23b–27b.

[30] *QSW*, 2784: 78.

[31] "Shuowen [Questioning on a *shuo* day (first day of a lunar month)]," *SSWJ*, 2: 26b–27a.

[32] *SHY*, "Shihuo," 68: 115a. Chao Shuozhi, "Yuanfu sannian yingzhao fengshi [Responding to the edict on affairs in the third year of Yuanfu (1100)]," *SSWJ*, 1: 18a.

[33] *QSW*, 2342: 232.

[34] *QSW*, 2784: 80.

China. Yet, we do not need to exhaust such accounts to empathize with Ren Boyu's 任伯雨 (1047–1119) lament: "Throughout history, none of the Yellow River's disasters have been as devastating as what we have now." It is easy to visualize the image Peng Ruli 彭汝礪 (1040–1094) depicts: "Drifting and migrating, Hebei people streamed endlessly over a thousand *li*."[35] This environmental-human landscape, a dreamwork that the imperial state created by imitating Yu's legendary landscape and pushing the Yellow River north in 1048, and that over the following eight decades would prevent the river from turning south into Henan, became a hellish world for Hebei's ordinary people.

The environmental disturbance and damage to the population was so substantial that it forced the state and its administrative system to respond to the heavy human losses. One way to do this was to adjust its administrative governance in Hebei. Qingping 清平 County, for instance, was located at the center of Daming Prefecture. After the Yellow River arrived in this area in 1048, the county suffered repeated floods. From 1048 to 1067, the county seat had to relocate twice to escape floods.[36] Similar situations happened to both Zongcheng 宗城 County in Daming and the prefectural capital of Shenzhou.[37] These towns – including their residents, government offices, granaries, schools, and temples – had to relocate several times to avoid the Yellow River. Every relocation meant breaking apart the old society and communities, abandoning property and wealth, and rebuilding a new social structure from the ground up. It also meant that the local government had to remake itself as a new administrative institution: to reconnect with its subjects, to map out new geographical relations within its domain, and to communicate with and serve the state in new ways. Such relocation and post-disaster reconstruction created chaos. Zongcheng, for instance, used to be an affluent town; it sat on the Yuhe Canal and profited from water transportation. After the mid-eleventh century, repeated floods ravaged the area, and the damage to the canal meant that ships no longer stopped there and goods no longer flowed through the town. As its county seat moved to less advantageous places, the town appeared shabby; its various supplies ran short, so its residents had to rely on neighboring districts to fulfill their daily needs.

[35] *QSW*, 2200: 76 and 2831: 166–167.
[36] QSW, 2738: 3.
[37] "Zongcheng xiuxin miaoxue ji [On the newly renovated Confucius shrine and school in Zongcheng]," *QSW*, 3119: 75. Also, Wang Zudao's memorial, *QSW*, 1839: 282.

In many other places, the population loss was so severe that remaining residents did not even warrant relocation. The Song state had to accept the tragic reality that some districts now held so few people that they could no longer fulfill the state's taxation and corvée requirements. It had become unavoidable that the state cut local offices and bureaucrats in order to reduce administrative costs. In 1070, the household number in Liyang 黎陽 Commandery in southwestern Hebei was said to be "only one tenth of the number in the past," so the state degraded Liyang's status from a commandery-level district to a mere county.[38] Worse was Yiguo 倚郭 County after 1048 and Linming 臨洺 County in 1068. They were hit so hard by floods and their societies so depleted that the state could no longer extract wealth and labor from these areas; it became meaningless for the state to keep offices there. The state stripped these places of their jurisdictory status, and ordered their land and remaining populations to merge into neighboring districts.[39] For the same reason, in Emperor Shenzong and Wang Anshi's government in the 1070s, there was intense discussion about eliminating jurisdictions like Qianning, Baoding 保定, and Shun'an commanderies in northern Hebei.[40]

At the beginning of the twelfth century, Hebei appeared desolate. According to Ren Boyu, in the area north of the Yongjing Commandery, only 30–40 percent of the original population remained; in northern Cangzhou only 10–20 percent survived. Over central and northern Hebei, "there was almost no sign of human habitation within a thousand *li*."[41] Indeed, these descriptive accounts do not help us reach even a rough approximation of Hebei's population toward the end of the Northern Song Dynasty. Did the demographic baseline of five million registered

---

[38] *QSW*, 1076: 319.

[39] *XCB*, 507: 12081, 213: 5180, and 405: 9871. Chao Buzhi, "Qingpingxian xinxiu Kongzimiao ji [On the new Confucius shrine in Qingping County]," *Jilei ji*, 29: 3b–4b. "Xin Zongchengxian Sanqingdian ji [On the Three-Purity Hall in the new Zongcheng County]" and "Daming fu Zongchengxian xinxiu miaoxue ji [On the new Confucius shrine and school in Zongcheng County in Daming Prefecture]," *Weixian zhi*, 18: 1b–2a and 5a–6b.

[40] In the early 1070s, Wang Anshi's government conducted censuses across the empire, abolished redundant administrative offices, and demoted their bureaucrats, in order to reduce the government's financial costs. This policy took place in other parts of China, not necessarily because of any change to their populations. In Hebei, however, it took place precisely because of the drastic reduction in Hebei's population. For the changes to jurisdictions in the reform era, see Mostern (2011: 182–209).

[41] Ren Boyu, "Shang Huizong lun yueyun wei Maobi [Memorial to Emperor Huizong on discussing that the moon halo obscures the Mao and Bi constellations]," *SMCZY*, 45: 3a–8b.

people before 1048 drop precipitously during the following eight decades, down to three million or even less? I have no answer to the question.[42] The disaster narrative, nevertheless, leads me to suggest that at the very least, Hebei's population did not grow after 1048. At best, the population might have remained stagnant, if its heavy losses were compensated by an exceptionally high birth rate that was caused by increased marriage opportunities and fertility among the people. But there is no evidence for any high natality, and it seems to me very unlikely. As the entire Song empire enjoyed a stunning population explosion, as seen in the 200 percent increase in the number of households from 980s to 1102 (Table 3), Hebei's population failed to share in that growth.

The stagnation, or more likely a phenomenal decline, of Hebei's population was not caused by a single environmental catastrophe, and certainly not by the Yellow River's course shift in 1048 alone. It was the continuous unfolding of the eighty-year environmental drama and the imperial state's unstoppable Hebei-sacrificing hydraulic management that repeatedly devastated the population. The short intervals between individual disasters meant that the society was unable to bounce back to its demographic baseline before it was hit by another terrible event. After the 1040s, there was not a single decade that was peaceful and uneventful to allow the people of Hebei to resettle, to rebuild a stable livelihood, and to replenish the population.

Instead of fixing our sights on the fluctuations of the overall size of the population – a daunting effort due to the shortage of historical sources for medieval China – we may find it more meaningful to attend to the state of disturbance and unsettledness that characterized the Hebei people at the time. Such disturbance certainly brought inconvenience to people's daily life. For instance, poet He Zhu 賀鑄 was supposed to travel from Guanshi 冠氏 County in southern Hebei west to the Handan area in western Hebei to visit his friend. The trip had to be cancelled before the Yellow River flooded and damaged roads.[43] Such inconvenience to daily

---

[42] In his study on the Nationalist government's destruction of Yellow River dykes for military purposes in 1938, Muscolino (2015) vividly reconstructs the disastrous impact the resultant flooding inflicted on the society of Henan and how refugees coped with the flood, ensuing famine, and war damage. Due to the limitation of medieval sources, the present study cannot offer the similar kind of historical nuances and precision. But readers may draw analogies from Muscolino's work to help visualize what a terrible flooding disaster of the Yellow River looked alike and how it devastated the human society back a thousand years ago.

[43] *Liang Song mingxian xiaoji*, 121.

life seemed insignificant. But looking at the big picture of the whole of Hebei, we should question how the overarching unsettling situation paralyzed disaster refugees and communities, made them unproductive, broke down previous social mechanisms that held together social relationships, and thereby impeded the functioning of the society and its economy. We may at least contemplate the emergence of human conditions in which a substantial portion of people in Hebei endured constant lack and malnutrition that seriously affected the public health and overall capacity of the population. They suffered not only instant violence from those dramatic disasters but also the kind of banal, less visible, and low-intense "violence of everyday life."[44] It was not the catastrophic attacks, high mortality, and massive emigrations alone that brought the society to a veritable standstill.[45]

The Hebei society headed toward bankruptcy, due largely to the destruction of the existing demographic structure, the collapse of communities, and the fall of individuals out of their established status and relationships. Historical sources show a great variety of displacement in addition to a geographical one: the bottom part of the society fell apart given the repeated disasters and hardship; landless tenants lost their access to arable land; small landowners lost property and descended the socio-economic ladder. Large landowners and elite families relocated and invested their fortunes in places outside Hebei. As various social groups broke their ties with each other and with Hebei's "bad earth" (to paraphrase Vaclav Smil's book title), the traditional moral economy went bankrupt.[46] Previously law-abiding citizens fled into the neighboring Liao empire, becoming traitors and potential spies.[47] More migrants fell in the grey zone between refugees and criminals. After the late 1060s, historical records document how homeless and impoverished people formed gangs of various sizes, living like thieves, robbers, or rebels. They "raided households" in cities and towns, "harmed and killed ordinary people," and even

---

[44] Scheper-Hughes (1992).

[45] Due to the shortage of historical sources, our discussion of the social and human consequences of disasters and famines cannot be as systematic and in-depth as the existing scholarship on late-imperial China, see Will (1990, 1991), Lillian M. Li (2007), Edgerton-Tarpley (2008), and Muscolino (2015). Yet, the studies on later time periods help us envision the general pattern of disasters and human suffering back in the eleventh century.

[46] Smil (1984).

[47] *QSW*, 2629: 94.

"murdered government officials."[48] Starving refugees broke into military granaries, stole grain, and set fire to government storage sites.[49] In the 1070s the criminal refugees gathered and dispersed randomly, without serious organization. Gradually, as the environmental and socio-economic conditions deteriorated and as individual suffering congealed into collective resentment, more and more people joined the groups and led to larger and more organized social unrest. Not only did these groups protest their hardship and material losses, they also challenged the socio-economic and political system that exploited them and failed to rescue them from their misery. As the imperial state addressed various kinds of rebellion in the form of organized crime, "fomenting trouble (*zuoluan* 作亂)" and "change/upheaval (*bian* 變)" took place more and more often, especially in the first quarter of the twelfth century, during the reign of Emperor Huizong.

As the imperial state saw it, Hebei was losing the ability to regulate itself. Social mechanisms such as economic relationship, kinship, culture, and ethics fell apart under the mounting environmental pressure. They became less and less capable of containing men and women within the traditional socio-economic structure. This understanding drove the state to engage more with Hebei's environmental management and Yellow River hydraulics in order to reduce the harm done to the Hebei society. Unfortunately, the state efforts, as shown in the previous two chapters, were not only unsuccessful and costly, but often caused additional damage.

The destabilized and weakening society in Hebei certainly opened up space for interventions by a relatively strong, assertive state. State control of this frontier region had always been tight, and now it became even tighter. After the 1070s, the state strengthened its control by policing and militarizing Hebei. One solution was the aforementioned *baojia* system, which sought to establish – on top of traditional social networks – a quasi-police/military network, in which households formed homogeneous units, practiced martial arts, and performed mutual surveillance and protection. The other solution was to absorb the "floating" – homeless and crime prone – male population into armies. By recruiting those men into the military, the state enmeshed them in professional, legal, and financial bonds with the state. By providing food and clothing to meet their basic needs, the state hoped to prevent these men from becoming anti-state

[48] *QSW*, 2519: 98; 1578: 285; and 2471: 308.
[49] *QSW*, 2242: 834.

criminals. This solution inflated the size of different military organizations in Hebei, including professional troops like the Imperial Armies, militias like the Righteousness and Brave and the Strongmen, and various corvée service armies, including the "River Cleaning" corvée army (*heqing jun* 河清軍) that was committed solely to the Yellow River hydraulics.

The militarization of the society, in effect, went against the state's early demilitarization policy in Hebei. As Chapters 1 and 2 analyzed, the state endeavored to separate the civilian society and the professional military in order to suppress Hebei's military autonomy and Hebei people's martial tradition. During the second half of the Song period, however, the state resorted to quasi-militarization as a means to rescue and regulate the dissolving civilian society. Such state intervention, unfortunately, did not keep the society intact or prevent its population from collapsing. Even supplying refugees with military stipends and giving them legal recognition did not assuage their resentment. Instead, the militarization resulted in what the state always feared, a revival of Hebei's military, anti-state tradition among its civilians. It also returned weapons to the martial and independence-inclined people. A considerable number of sources suggest that beginning in the 1070s, members of the *baojia* units carried weapons and used their martial skills to intimidate people and commit crimes. Soldiers deserted their regiments.[50] The "River Cleaning" soldiers complained about the inadequacy of food, clothing, and medication, and many fled from their hydraulic corvée duties.[51] Mutinies took place from time to time.[52]

While the civilian refugees presented the state with humanitarian, financial, and logistical problems, the military outlaws threatened the state's stability and existence. Hence, as Hebei's civilian society at all economic levels was collapsing, the imperial state was losing control of Hebei's swollen military. Various sectors of Hebei's population fell one after another, despite the state's efforts to stop them. Here, we observe how not only environmental disasters but also the "hydraulic mode of consumption" driven by the state's unbreakable environmental engagement operated to take a heavy toll on Hebei's human population, demographic structure, and social stability. The continuous, increasing state efforts in the environmental management that we read in the previous chapter saw a paralleling process of Hebei's social destruction.

[50] *QSW*, 2439: 56.
[51] *QSW*, 2471: 308 and 3234: 181.
[52] "The Epitaph of Gao Dan," *QSW*, 2742: 79.

8.2   Corvée de L'eau: Local Solutions and Resistance

Living on the Yellow River's delta and facing both the overwhelming environmental pressure and the state's active but often unsuccessful management, did the people of Hebei just give in? If we follow geographer Denis Cosgrove and consider landscape as "a way of seeing projected on land and having its own techniques and compositional forms," both the state and the Yellow River had projected their "seeing" of the land and transformed the land by their peculiar means – the former by hydraulic works and the latter by its hydrological dynamics. Was there also a space in the overwhelming Yellow River–Hebei environmental complex in which ordinary people could assert their "alternative modes of experiencing [their] relations with nature?"[53]

Historical records for north China from the tenth through the twelfth centuries do not give ordinary people many opportunities to speak for themselves or about their environmental experiences.[54] Yet a few fragments extracted from the plethora of official discourse about Hebei provide us a few glimpses into their lives. Between people's traditional, rather peaceful livelihoods, and their radical responses to the environmental changes in the forms of death, emigration, and social displacement, we observe a rather wide space. Within that space, Hebei people negotiated with both the environmental pressure and political impositions on a daily basis. They sought all kinds of possibilities and experimented

---

[53] Cosgrove (1998: 269).

[54] Given richer historical sources, studies on southern parts of China and in later time periods provide more cases and more systematic analyses of local responses and local strategies to environmental disasters and socio-economic hardships. For instance, Keith R. Schoppa (1989) studies the interactions between the changes in the Xiang Lake and the hydraulic and socio-economic activities of the local population; Peter Perdue (1987) reveals the shrinkage and enlargement of the Dongting Lake and the local population's coping strategies; Robert Marks (1998) examines how the migration and expansion of a northern population dealt with harsh environmental conditions in the Lingnan area to create a more livable, economically productive land; Lillian M. Li (2007) studies how the population in Qing-period Hebei constantly suffered from and dealt with environmental disasters and famines; Jiayan Zhang (2015) explores the marshy environment in the Jianghan Plain in central Hubei and the local population's socio-economic adaptation to the environment; and Micah Muscolino (2015) tells various "stories of survival" in which refugees responded to the 1938 Yellow River flood through mass migration and ecological adaptation.

The local strategies observed in our Northern Song case studies resonate with much of what these scholarships on late-imperial and modern China have investigated. By consulting these late-imperial and modern histories, readers may be able to visualize a fuller image of local strategies around the individual, fragmentary cases that the Northern Song sources reveal to us.

with a variety of survival strategies. Many of them decided to remain in their hometowns, trying to adapt to and live with the intrusive river, the expanding frontier ponds, and the heavy hydraulic works imposed by the government. They searched for their own solutions for self-protection. Localized, small-scale, and aiming at individual, practical problems, their solutions sometimes coexisted with the state's lofty, grand, and futuristic hydraulic schemes. In other cases, they were in conflict with the state's schemes and even secretly undermined them. Hebei people's "corvée de l'eau" – a contemporary notion that refers to ordinary people's daily efforts to handle water, like fetching water in places that suffer from aridity – contrasted with the state's top-down hydraulic agendas. Such daily efforts were both the Hebei people's survival strategies and their small, yet persistent resistance to the environmental and political violence. In this sense, these men and women were more than mere victims of environmental and political powers, they were tough survivors as well.

Many of these local solutions were pursued collectively under the leadership of local elites, especially local government officials. For instance, in Renqiu County in northern Hebei, the frontier ponds covered a large area, and from time to time they overflowed and inundated arable fields. Most local officials did not dare to confront the problem, because the ponds were the state's property and under the control of military authorities. It took the initiative of a daring magistrate, Tang Jie, who stood up to his colleagues and superiors, and utilized the voluntary collaboration of local citizens to construct a dyke. Stretching over ten *li* and surrounding the domain of the county, the dyke stopped the encroachment of the waters and shielded the local civilian area from the inadvertent incursions of the state-owned property.[55]

Sometimes, local interests contradicted the state's interests, and ordinary people protested state solutions to environmental problems because, although well intended, they might not suit local circumstances. In 1082, for instance, Hebei's Fiscal Commissioner put forth a proposal to the imperial court. It proposed that since Qianning Commandery in northeastern Hebei had experienced many floods from the Yellow River, its jurisdictional center should be moved to a different location and it should be reduced to the status of a county-level district. Qianning's residents, however, protested strongly against the proposal, considering it

[55] "The Epitaph of Tang Jie," *QSW*, 1679: 119–124.

"inconvenient."[56] Their voice was expressed to the court via local officials. To these people, having the jurisdictional status of their hometown taken away, and having their homes and property relocated to a less valuable location seemed even worse than to have to confront problems caused by the turbulent river.

I am certainly not trying to paint an overly simplistic picture of a monolithic society struggling against a monolithic state. As the previous chapter made clear, the state carried a variety of hydraulic agendas, which were sometimes internally contradictory. Likewise, within Hebei's complex society, the overwhelming environmental pressure entailed a broad "hierarchy of suffering"[57] and provoked a wide variety of human reactions. Various social groups had different or conflicting interests and environmental pursuits; sometimes, individual interests conflicted with larger societal solutions. One case came from central Hebei. Linghu Duanfu 令狐端夫 was the magistrate of Quzhou 曲周 County in Mingzhou 洺州 Prefecture in the 1060s and 1070s. At that time, the Yellow River had destroyed Hebei's indigenous water systems, causing local rivers like the Zhang River to become unmanageable. The Zhang's torrents often pressed upon the county seat. Linghu proposed building dykes to protect the town, but his superiors in Mingzhou rejected the proposal. Indeed, protecting Quzhou County alone would not protect all of Mingzhou Prefecture, which included several other counties. The dykes intended to shield Quzhou would perhaps push the waters toward other counties, thus causing additional environmental and social issues that the prefecture government did not want to deal with.

Gaining no support from his superiors for a governmental approach, Linhu turned to local elites. But powerful local families also opposed his idea, because they saw it as a potential hardship and feared that they would have to contribute a great deal to the construction. A flood might not necessarily do much harm to the rich and powerful, who most likely had means to save their lives and property. Against all these obstacles, Linhu obtained support from the ordinary people in the county, whose livelihoods were tied up with the security of their physical environment. They gathered local resources to build a lengthy dyke. Year after year, even after Linhsu left the job and the county, local people spontaneously invested labor and resources to maintain the dyke, strengthening it whenever the Zhang River appeared violent. They convinced themselves and

[56] *QSW*, 2241: 824.
[57] Edgerton-Tarpley (2008: 42).

younger generations that "without this dyke, there will be no Quzhou County."[58] We do not know, however, if the rich and powerful families felt they also benefited from the dyke, and if they regretted their previous objection and decided to participate in the dyke's maintenance.

The division between the upper and lower classes affected how people responded to environmental problems. Lateral social divisions, such as between rural and urban, also played a role in people's decision-making processes, as an event in Mingzhou Prefecture demonstrates. In the early 1080s, the turbulent Zhang River was about to break into the prefectural seat, confronting the citizens there with a dilemma.[59] If the water surged northward it would destroy the walled city; if it surged southward it would sweep through the countryside. Apparently, history had placed the people of Mingzhou in a dilemma similar to that which the imperial state had faced with the Yellow River from the late tenth century on: they could not stop the river from flooding, but they could direct the river in a direction that would cause what they perceived to be less harm. In the state's case, encouraging the Yellow River to shift into Hebei instead of Henan more effectively protected its interests. Liang Yantong 梁彦通 (1030–1098), then the prefect of Mingzhou, evaluated the circumstances and made a judgment similar to the one Emperor Taizu made in 972: "We must prioritize the more critical issue." By critical issue, he meant the potential damage to the walled city, along with its urban citizens, governmental institutions, and concentrated dwellings and wealth. Accordingly, his government organized workers to dig a southward channel to direct the river into the countryside. If rural citizens protested against this hydraulic solution, our sources have no evidence of it. The city and its citizens were protected at the expense of their rural cousins.

The competing interests seen above also appeared evident in a vicious clash between two equal districts: Leshou 樂壽 and Nanpi 南皮 counties. As the Yellow River ran through both counties, the External Executive of the Water Conservancy intervened and designed dykes to restrain the floods. The Conservancy's hydrocrats had no local interests and were only concerned with controlling the flood. Ignorant of the social context and relations between these two counties, they drew up a technical design that would benefit Nanpi and harm Leshou. Hoping to have the favorable design implemented, Nanpi's county magistrate secretly tricked some of Leshou's elite into drafting a petition to the hydrocrats and stating their

---

58 "The Epitaph of Linghu Duanfu," *QSW*, 2404: 138.
59 "The Epitaph of Liang Yantong," *QSW*, 2743: 101–103.

support for the design. The letter implied that even Leshou's own people agreed to construct the dykes in a way that would eventually harm
themselves. Leshou's magistrate, Liu Yu 劉禹, called for a public meeting
at the riverside, and revealed the secret petition to his fellow citizens.
Burning the petition, he declared: "The Magistrate of Nanpi wants to
benefit his people, so he does not make a fair plan. We shall respond to
him by showing our virtue."[60] The public meeting generated a report to
the External Executive, which clarified the Leshou people's disapproval
of the unfavorable hydraulic design. What did the hydrocrats do after
receiving the report? Did they change their design so as to treat both
counties equally? Unfortunately, the historical record does not provide
the answer.

All of the above cases show that local officials represented their people and organized collective actions to combat the hostile environment
and sometimes the capricious state. But the people did not always wait
for officials to respond to the environmental threats. Throughout their
everyday lives, Hebei people were sensitive to the changes in their immediate environmental and living conditions. They understood how much
additional water in the earth would destroy the roots of their crops and
leave them hungry, or how a sudden drop in temperature would drive the
price of firewood up and endanger the weaker members of their family
in winter. They trusted what their bodies told them, and acted spontaneously to protect themselves or to exploit the environment for their own
benefit, even without the help of collective leadership. Their efforts to
survive and maintain a livelihood were dispersive, non-organizational,
and contingent upon the constantly changing situation. As soon as the
immediate environment changed, they modified their strategies.

Multiple government reports show how people colonized the abandoned, dried-up riverbeds of the Yellow River and carried out farming in
the sandy soil. The occupation of and competition for that newly created
land even led to lawsuits among the colonizers. In places where floods
caused soil to become salinized, people had to give up farming. This, however, did not mean that they gave up life or their homeland altogether;
many made a living from producing salt from the briny water and salinized soil. Some Hebeiese illegally cut trees from the banks and dykes of
the Yellow River, which had been planted there by government-employed
corvée workers to protect and strengthen the dykes. They burned the trees
as firewood, or sold them for profit. Farmers living near the frontier ponds

[60] "The Epitaph of Liu Yu," *QSW*, 2334: 63.

often drilled holes through the dykes and broke the banks illegally, sometimes in order to obtain the state-owned water for their own use, and sometimes in order to release the water in directions away from their own fields. In many cases, the acts were illegal and perhaps caused damage to others or to the existing hydraulic infrastructure that the state had painstakingly put in place.[61] Nevertheless, those acts provided the Hebei people some kind of subsistence livelihood and helped them survive the widespread hardship.

An exemplary case comes from the prefecture of Daming in southern Hebei, where the northern courses of the Yellow River entered the plain. By the end of the eleventh century, we witness a complicated landscape co-inhabited by the river, dykes, and people. As illustrated in the image below, the Yellow River flowed northward. Flanking the river to the west was the tall Golden Dyke, and between the dyke and the river's natural bank was a vast area of shore, whose surface was level with the river's water. From time to time, the river overflowed onto this land and then retreated to free it. Our conventional understanding is that land differentiates itself from a river, but this shore land was part of the river's extensive body. From a technological point of view, as the Water Conservancy saw it, the state had given the land to the river, so that the river would have a vast space in which it moved around, acted aggressively, adjusted, and finally calmed itself. The locals, however, wanted to reclaim the land from the river. They gathered materials and labor, and built up a "soft dyke (*ruanyan* 軟壖)" that was not very strong and less than a meter high and wide. The dyke stood in the middle of the shore land, splitting it into eastern and western halves. The eastern half still belonged to the river, while the western half was now used for human settlements and farming.[62]

This situation worried the state's hydrocrats. Modern hydrologists may very likely agree with them: straight jacketing the river's course and reducing the river's area to flow in would boost its hydrological power. As that power built, it would eventually explode into bigger and more

---

[61] Some local strategies came into conflict with the interests of the state and were considered illegal. Based on rich regional and local sources, scholars of hydraulic histories in late-imperial China have extensively discussed this issue, for instance, see Will (1985: 295–347) on central Hubei, Perdue (1987) on the Hunan area, and Zhang (2015) on the Jiang-Han Plain.

[62] Chen Cisheng, "Shang Huizong qi wei hexi ruanyan [Memorial to Emperor Huizong pleading for the construction of the soft dyke on the western side of the Yellow River]," *QSW*, 2241: 393–394.

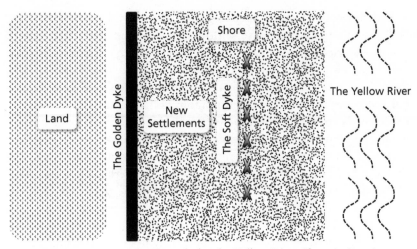

ILLUSTRATION 12. The Struggle for the Yellow River Shore in Daming

harmful floods than its previous moderate overflows. As a consequence, the river would not only crush the soft dyke and destroy the human settlements behind the dyke, it would also flow farther westward against the state-maintained Golden Dyke and perhaps cause a rupture to it. If that was the case, the broader Hebei society, the hydraulic schemes the state's hydrocrats tried to maintain, and by extension the well-being of the state would all be threatened. The state-society contestation was thus manifested through the concrete struggle over the existence or removal of the soft dyke.

The Water Conservancy pressed locals to remove the soft dyke and leave the land. The people, of course, resisted and refused to evacuate: the area had already been their home for years. Meanwhile, some anti-Water Conservancy, less technically driven but more politically minded officials, like Chen Cisheng 陳次升, stepped in to argue on behalf of the people. To Chen, the local people did not intend to do harm; they had not encroached on state property, the Golden Dyke. The soft dyke was a result of their personal efforts enabled by their own investments. Most importantly, the shore land was an open, unclaimed space. Whoever had means to access the common land should have the right to profit from it, and they would be responsible for any consequences of their acts. Let the people stay, Chen suggested. If the river flooded over the soft dyke and harmed the people, it would be their own loss. He advocated that they wait for nature's final judgment, and that the state should do nothing but strengthen the Golden Dyke, the only thing the state had control over.

Did the Water Conservancy insist on the removal of the soft dyke? Did nature's judgment arrive with a gigantic flood? With the lack of extant historical sources, we cannot answer these questions; neither do we know who settled on the land and why they chose to do so. The shore land was certainly productive, but the agricultural gain from it did not come without risk, as a random flood could easily destroy an entire year's crops. It is hard to imagine that families who made a stable living and who owned land outside of the Golden Dyke would risk their lives and livelihoods to move into the disaster-prone shore area. The risk was high; the profit was unpredictable, and perhaps low too. Very likely, this swath of land became a haven for the poor, the landless, absconders, tax-avoiders, and outlaws – in other words, people who had little to lose. Such socio-economic complications remained hidden and unnoticed to technologically minded hydrocrats. Technologically, the Water Conservancy's assessment was reasonable. The settlements on the shore would cause trouble in the long run and potentially harm the bigger, privileged, and protected lawful world outside the Golden Dyke. Indeed, the settlers were being shortsighted.

Understanding the socio-economic and political complications, politician Chen Cisheng pointed out that the poor on the margins of society needed some kind of livelihood. These people were deprived of means of living and could not afford any long-sighted plan. Yet, they not only "have the social right to subsistence" as anthropologist James C. Scott proclaims, but they also demanded such right for subsistence.[63] Where did the state and its privileged bureaucratics expect them to go if driven off this shore land? They would perhaps have no choice but to turn into beggars, thieves, and robbers, or worse, anti-state rebels. We should certainly not overestimate Chen's interest in the cause of social justice. Rather, from a point of political pragmatism, he recommended that the state allow the existence of the settlements and settlers in order to contain them and minimize any future socio-economic complications. Indeed, by the early twelfth century when Chen presented his opinion to Emperor Huizong, Hebei was already a wild land, deeply ravaged by the unruly river, chaotic environmental elements, and a bankrupt society.

The above cases are too fragmentary to produce a complete portrait of the Hebei society, but they do offer some important insights into many lives lived in tremendous hardship. Although victimized by the

[63] Scott (1976: 33).

overwhelming environmental conditions as well as by the state's self-protecting and self-promoting environmental management, ordinary people did not always remain passive or powerless. When their personal interests were at stake – under threat from the physical environment, the state, or other local social groups and individuals – they strove to protect and preserve their interests using a variety of strategies. The continuous unraveling of the environmental drama not only staged catastrophic events like the river's course shift in 1048 and the massive scale of deaths in 1099, but it also brought to bear numerous nameless individuals who tried to survive and, to a small scale, reshaped the hostile environment and confronted the imposing state power.

Given such activism and spontaneity of individuals, Karl Wittforgel's idealistic thesis about the state's despotic power over a submissive hydraulic society seems less than comprehensive; his "hydraulic mode of production" did not operate to yield such a society. The Song state, despite its strict environmental and social control in Hebei, which best represented the Wittfogelian premise for an engaging hydraulic leader, could not guarantee the absolute cooperation of the local people.[64] The resilient and sometimes sly or disobedient people swiftly adapted to the environmental changes; they also negotiated the complex socio-economic and political systems to eke out a livelihood. They did not always rely on a hydraulic leader – either an all-powerful regime or regional authorities – to protect them from environmental pressures.

The Nanpi–Leshou case, in particular, demythologizes the idea of an all-powerful state. Even in situations where the state asserted its tightest control, ordinary citizens voiced their opinions, as shown in the people of Leshou's public meeting and report. Their voices might not have been seen or heard by the top leadership of the state; in this case, they were only documented in Liu Yu's tomb epitaph, and Liu did not rise to political prominence in his career. Nevertheless, their voices and desires had a material effect upon the local environment, and even forced the state's hydraulic apparatus – through its representatives and executors, the hydrocrats of the Water Conservancy – to change its environmental policy. Conservative officials at the Song court gave us the impression that the bullying hydrocrats and a too-powerful Water Conservancy took

---

[64] Such state control was far more tight in terms of hydraulic management than what the late-imperial states could achieve, as seen in studies like Will (1985), Perdue (1987), and Zhang (2015). It is in these later-period cases that Will's (1985: 346) assertion, "hydraulic society was stronger than the hydraulic state," holds much truth.

full control of the hydraulic works and cared nothing about Hebei's local situations. In reality, as the hydraulic tentacle of state power, the hydro-crats not only directly encountered ordinary people but also experienced their resistance. They could not act in a totalitarian manner, but had to open up a space to correspond, discuss, and negotiate with the local peo-ple. When the state and the society met each other on the very material level of the environmental world, in which both the state and the society had a great deal at stake, their relationship became a mixture of intense conflicts and negotiation.

We should not, however, overestimate the strength of ordinary people to combat the environment or to resist the state's impositions. Certainly we should not overstate their successes. Had they been successful often or on a large scale, we would not need to discuss the high mortality, mass migration, and severe displacement that these men and women suffered, nor show how the Hebei society headed toward socio-economic bankruptcy. All of the cases we have seen involve contingent, individual solutions, which addressed the needs of only certain groups of people. Even if they were successful, as seen in the case of urban vs. rural interests, that success sometimes led to a cost paid by others. For the greater Hebei society, the small-scale local solutions could not relieve the suffering of the majority of the population. They were no more than some "weapons of the weak,"[65] which did not directly confront overwhelming powers like the environment and the imperial state. Instead, they searched for the latter's fractures, exploited their negligence, and adapted to them. These everyday forms of resistance helped the disaster-plagued people handle immediate environmental crises and provided them with some kind of subsistence livelihood, but nothing more.

The local solutions were not only dispersive, but also contingent and temporary. Environmental conditions and state policies were constantly changing, often forcing locals to give up previous solutions. In the case of the frontier ponds, although Tang Jie led local people to build a dyke to stop the expansion of the ponds, other officials and military officers responded by expanding the ponds all the more forcefully. The Water Conservancy's plan to remove the soft dyke in Daming was a governmen-tal response to the local solution. Given our knowledge of the primacy of the Water Conservancy during the Song period, it is very likely that it won the argument.

[65] Scott (1985).

If it is inaccurate to view the Hebei people solely as agency-deprived victims or to overestimate the efficacy of their solutions, we should also not reify their resistance or romanticize their relationship with their environment, just as Rey Chow rightly urges us to "find a resistance to the liberal illusion of the autonomy and independence we can 'give' the other" –in our case, the suffering and battling Hebei people.[66] The mounting environmental pressure and social competition divided people into smaller interest groups, each guarding its own position. Their survival strategies often harmed others in one way or another. As Elvin correctly sees it, "River water meant quarrels."[67] The urban citizens of Mingzhou protected themselves by sacrificing their rural cousins; the Nanpi magistrate chose to guard his fellow people against the people next door. By principle, the Hebei people pursued their solutions in a way similar to the way in which the imperial state rationalized its hydraulic strategies about the Yellow River, such as protecting-Henan-by-sacrificing-Hebei. Both, based on their experiences of environmental and social crises, pursued self-protecting, even self-profiting strategies. Just as Chapter 5 shows how the formation of the Yellow River–Hebei environmental complex deepened the division of state institutions and the competition among different political factions, the present chapter reveals the intensification of social and economic struggles among various societal forces inside Hebei.

[66] Chow (1992: 111).
[67] Elvin (2004: 116).

7

Agriculture

A Subsistence-Oriented Economy

As men and women, old and young, abandoned their homes and communities and took flight to search for safe havens, a substantial section of Hebei appeared desolate. Some areas were frequently inundated with Yellow River's floods, while other areas lay fallow and covered with wild grass. The recovery and growth of agricultural production that Hebei had achieved in the first eighty years of the Song period underwent serious damage during the following eighty years. The reduction in the overall size of farming population and arable land, as well as the decrease of land productivity, indicate the decline of this economic form, a situation that contrasts sharply to the spectacular growth of agriculture in southern China at the time.

I will compare three staple crops – millet, winter wheat, and wetland rice – and suggest that certain technological innovations that transformed agricultural production in other regions of China did not bring about dramatic changes to the land of Hebei. Under mounting environmental and socio-economic pressures, Hebei people took a "subsistence-first" attitude toward their economic life.[1] What modern historians consider as indicators of a revolutionary economic growth, such as new species of crops, might not have been regarded as secure and profitable by these people. The disaster-ravaged population had little capital to experiment with new, expensive technology, and did not pursue optimal gains; rather, they simply strove to maintain a stable subsistence at low costs.

A declining Hebei spread hardship and instability toward southern parts of China. It also brought down the imperial state by consuming

---

[1] To follow James C. Scott (1976)'s argument.

its wealth and eroding its power, because to maintain the Yellow River–Hebei environmental complex and keep both the environment and the society from a total collapse, the state kept extracting resources from other parts of the empire and exhausted the state finances. Such resources were mobilized by the "hydraulic mode of consumption," and channeled toward and depleted inside Hebei. The center-periphery structure that the state endeavored to build for its imperial system flipped: from the perspective of resource flows and consumption, disaster-ridden Hebei became the *de facto* center of the empire, the "root of All-Under-Heaven," which demanded continuous and burdensome services from the state.

7.1 Harvests, Labor, and Land

A survey of Hebei's harvest and famine records suggests that Hebei's agricultural growth before the 1040s was undone to a great extent by the frequent occurrence of disasters after 1048. On the surface, historical records report good harvests in three years of the 1040s, three years of the 1050s, two years of the 1060s, three years of the 1070s, four years of the 1080s, and two years of the 1090s.[2] Among them, those in 1050, 1054, 1057, 1069, 1083, and 1098 were considered bumper harvests. The two in 1069 and 1083, particularly, were said to have yielded twice as much as normal.

None of these harvests, however, were common throughout the whole of Hebei. For instance, the 1050 harvest occurred somewhere in eastern Hebei, the 1069 harvest happened in a small area in southern Hebei, and the 1083 harvest was somewhere in the northern frontier area. Good harvests in some areas were always accompanied by poor harvests in other parts of Hebei, so only those in a limited geographical area could enjoy abundant food supplies. Furthermore, good harvests did not occur consecutively; they were often followed and interrupted by bad harvests in intermittent years.

Consider the year 1050. While some places enjoyed a bumper harvest, prefectures like Zhenzhou 鎮州 and Dingzhou in the northwest were struck by floods, which destroyed their autumn crops.[3] Central Hebei was in a dire situation as well. The Yellow River's flooding in 1048 and the subsequent drought through 1049 left many fields covered in stagnant water or left barren. The harvest failure over the next couple

[2] Harvest records are collected from *XCB*, *XCBSB*, *SS*, and *SHY*.
[3] *XCB*, 169: 4065.

of years forced the government to ship two million *dan* of grain from southeast China in disaster relief. Meanwhile, the government recruited some refugees into its armies, because military supplies were relatively adequate.[4] When military supplies ran short, and southeast China itself suffered disasters and famine in 1051 and failed to export grain, the relief to Hebei was reduced.[5] As a result, in the years of 1051–1053 Hebei saw famine and famine-induced emigration. One bad harvest in Dingzhou in 1051, for example, was said to have caused the deaths of one million people.[6] Amid the lingering and widespread misery, a single bumper harvest in 1050 was not sufficient to alleviate the overall suffering.

Hebei welcomed a good harvest in 1054, but this was followed by a series of severe droughts in 1055, a time when, as Ouyang Xiu observed, "Winter wheat [sown in the autumn of 1054] did not sprout and millet had not yet been sown by the end of the spring."[7] The droughts led to a bad harvest that affected not only 1055 but also 1056, when the Yellow River provoked a giant flood in the summer and damaged crops in southern Hebei. Once again, the government had to distribute relief to refugees – a fixed amount of five *dou* (33.5 liters) of grain to each adult and a certain amount of cash to the families of those who were killed in the flood.[8] Similarly, during 1067–1069, the outbreaks of drought, locusts, earthquakes, and Yellow River floods caused a series of harvest failures. According to Sima Guang, in many places of Hebei, standing crops were inundated by flood waters, and grain stored in official granaries rotted. The entire food reserve in Hebei was so small that even its frontier troops could not get adequate supplies.[9]

The 1070s and 1080s saw the intensification of the migration to other regions of north China. Although good harvests were reported sporadically in various places, the overall size of the population and the land dedicated to agricultural production shrank significantly. The situation worsened in the 1090s. Despite good harvests in some parts of Hebei in 1097 and 1098, food shortages and famine were more frequently reported in that decade. When heavy rains caused the Yellow River to soar and inundate southern Hebei in 1094, several hundred square *li*

---

[4] *XCB*, 165: 3974 and 3968.
[5] *XCB*, 165: 3974 and 171: 4119.
[6] *XCB*, 170: 4104. Of course, we should not take this number as its literal meaning. "One million" simply means numerous.
[7] *XCB*, 179: 4327.
[8] *XCB*, 182: 4424.
[9] *XCBSB*, 3xia: 125.

of buildings and graveyards, together with crops, were destroyed.[10] In the most catastrophic years of 1099 and 1100, a large swath of Hebei was waterlogged. Few crops could be planted, so the overall harvest was said to have reached merely 10 or 20 percent of the usual level.[11] The situation was aggravated when the rest of north China reported similar agricultural failure and could not provide relief to Hebei. Across north China, the price for one *dou* (6.7 liters) of millet soared to a thousand copper coins, fourteen to seventeen times its normal price of sixty to one hundred cash.[12]

From 1040 to 1100,[13] Hebei's good harvests were again offset by frequent harvest failures, and the failures and constant food shortages reflected deep, structural problems in Hebei's agricultural system, in particular the reduction of resources allocated to agriculture and the deterioration of production factors like labor and arable land. As the previous chapter concluded, not only did the overall agricultural population decrease, but the remaining population was unsettled. In the new demographic structure, the society's main sources of labor turned into disaster refugees, emigrants, outlaws, or adapted to other modes of production. After the 1040s, immense labor was absorbed into the military and kept from working on the land, thus living off government subsidies instead. After 1048, much of the state-sponsored hydraulic works took place inside Hebei, and a substantial portion of Hebei's labor forces became hydraulic workers. Those people relocated to the river's flooding sites away from their homes and agriculture production, and depended on government support as well. According to Liang Tao 梁燾 (1033–1097), a statesman who served Emperor Zhezong in 1090, regular hydraulic works started on the twelfth day of the second lunar month, so hydraulic laborers left home earlier that month to work on the river and did not return home until late in the third lunar month. The two-month absence from home caused those male laborers to miss the most important agricultural season in Hebei, the period for sowing millet seeds.[14]

---

[10] *XCBSB*, 9: 381.
[11] Ren Boyu, "Shang Huizong lun yueyun wei Maobi," in *SMCZY*, 45: 3a–8b.
[12] Li Xin, "Shang Huangdi wanyan shu [A ten-thousand-word memorial to the Emperor]," *Kuaao ji*, 19: 6b–7a. For a general study on the price increase in the late Song (not specifically for the Hebei area due to the shortage of historical sources), see Ch'uan Han-sheng (1944: 337–394).
[13] Unfortunately existing historical sources do not supply harvest records about Hebei during the first quarter of the twelfth century.
[14] *QSW*, 1787: 258.

Historical records do not reveal the decrease in arable land. Around
1080, Hebei reportedly had 27,906,656 *mu* 畝 of arable fields, including
26,956,008 *mu* of private fields and 950,649 *mu* of official fields. This
number was the second largest among all the provinces in north China,
after Shaanxi where an enormous area of land supported a very small
population and the agricultural production remained lowest among all
north China regions.[15] This means that the number of registered fields
in the government's accounting books, although seemingly very large,
did not necessarily generate an equally large agricultural output.[16] The
number for Hebei, more likely, reflected the fields that the government
expected to levy taxes from, not necessary the actual fields in cultivation.
It certainly did not indicate the percentage of fields that were struck by disasters, covered by stagnant waters, and abandoned by fleeing landowners
and tenants.

Shortly before the Yellow River entered Hebei, Ouyang Xiu commented on the shrinkage of arable land and its low production in Hebei:

The entire land of Hebei is no longer and no wider than a thousand *li*. Along
the northern frontier, in Guangxin 廣信, Ansu 安肅, Shun'an Commanderies,
Xiongzhou, and Bazhou, the land is covered completely by ponds. Eighty to
ninety percent of it is uncultivable by commoners. In Chanzhou, Weizhou 衛州,
Dezhou, Binzhou 濱州, Cangzhou, Tongli Commandery, and the land east and
south to Daming, the Yellow River's disasters strike every year, and fifty to sixty
percent of the land is uncultivable. Even granted a good harvest this year, [the
government] nevertheless had to exempt a million *dan* of grain from the tax
quota [set for those places]. West and north to Daming, the land is very saline
and teems with large and small saline pools, so thirty to forty percent of its
land is uncultivable. Furthermore, there is an immeasurable expanse of lakes and
ponds, barren lands, pasturelands, and fields abandoned by emigrants. From the
mountains and the sea, [the Hebei people] cannot procure profits, and the plain
produces limited wealth.[17]

Ouyang's comment might have exaggerated the negative situation around
1045. Yet, the situation was undoubtedly exacerbated after the Yellow River crashed into Hebei and began its eighty-year-long occupation of the plain. The river's multiple northern courses inundated a large
area in southern, central, and northeastern Hebei. Prefectures in central
Hebei, such as Enzhou, Jizhou, Shenzhou, and Yingzhou that were not

[15] Liang (1980: 290).
[16] Han Maoli (1993: 47–52) argues that although the Hebei Plain covered an immense
    area, the actual acreage of arable land during the Song time was very small.
[17] "Lun Hebei caichan shang shixiang shu," *OYXQJ*, 118: 1825–1828.

mentioned by Ouyang Xiu, had been fairly productive in the past. After 1048, these areas became frequent victims of Yellow River floods. Even worse, the widespread floods, subsequent waterlogging, and their negative impact on Hebei's local rivers magnified the disastrous aftermath spatially, spreading it to other areas to ruin an even larger number of fields that were not directly touched by the Yellow River.

Not only was the size of arable land reduced, but the soil also lost much of its fertility. The floodwaters deposited a layer of silt that covered the cultivable soil with coarse, sandy earth. In Chapter 8, I will scrutinize the changes to Hebei's water systems, and the destructive impact on the composition, texture, and arability of the earth. I will explain in greater detail how the excessive water and inferior soil harmed Hebei's agricultural economy and long-term environmental conditions. Affected by those dramatic environmental changes, the same swath of land, even if still used for agricultural purposes, would most likely generate a smaller yield.

Economic historian Cheng Minsheng studies tax quotas that the central government set up shortly before 1080. Hebei was issued the highest tax quota (9,152,000) among all provinces in the empire – more than twice the amount for the metropolitan area of Kaifeng (4,055,087) and equal to the combination for Huainan 淮南 (4,223,784) and Liangzhe 兩浙 (4,799,122) in the Yangtze valley. Based on these figures, Cheng believes that Hebei enjoyed a steady and solid growth in agriculture; its agricultural production not only satisfied its own troops but also surpassed the level in south China. Hebei, as Cheng maintains, was one of the richest regions, perhaps even the richest region, in the Song empire.[18] I argue that this opinion pays no attention to the massive number of historical sources that I use in this book, which all indicate bad harvests, frequent famines, and high demands for government relief in Hebei. It certainly ignores the prevailing environmental challenges and socio-economic problems that prevented Hebei and its people from conducting normal agricultural activities. Furthermore, Cheng's opinion relies overly on the surface value of the tax figures and ignores the fact that those figures were only quotas, not actual tax payments. As Ouyang Xiu commented in the middle of the eleventh century, "Even given a good harvest this year, [the government]

[18] Cheng (1998: 106–109) and (2004: 267–285; 357–361; and 404). Liang Gengyao (1994: 107–132) has convincingly argued against Cheng's judgment and briefly brought attention to the mounting environmental situation in north China.

nevertheless had to exempt a million *dan* of grain from the tax quota [set for those places]."[19] Obviously, the government had to exempt more when bad harvests and disasters took place. It seems to be a normal occurrence for Hebei's actual production to be far below its tax quota.

Instead of indicating regional production, the figures of tax quotas reflect the government's demand for supplies; more reasonably, they are actually government budgets for regional expenditures. The highest number for Hebei indicates the highest government budget in order to satisfy tremendous consumption occurring inside Hebei.[20] In this sense, Hebei, rather than being a production center as Cheng Minsheng believes, was actually a consumption center within the empire. As the final pages of the present chapter will show, after 1048, Hebei became even more reliant on the state finances and the importation of goods from southern China in order to satisfy the consumption of its disaster-ridden population, its swollen military, and the gigantic hydraulic entity the state maintained in that region. Before we discuss this further, let's take a close look at the production of three staple crops: millet and winter wheat in the next section, and paddy rice in the third section. These studies reveal what Hebei farmers produced to feed themselves in a subsistence-oriented economy, a situation that was different from that of their counterparts in south China.

7.2   Millet and Winter Wheat: Production without Revolution

A predominant discourse in the study of Song history is the thesis of a multi-dimensional Tang–Song transition. In the economic realm, this transition was manifested in a revolutionary growth of various economic sectors, in terms of both an explosion of overall production and a drastic enhancement of productivity. The foundation of this revolutionary growth lay in agriculture, which generated abundant surpluses that supported an enlarging population, boosted trade and market activities, and released enormous amounts of labor from agriculture to engage in non-agricultural modes of production. At the core of this economic thesis is the identification of various revolutionary factors: new agricultural tools, new ways of improving the microenvironment for production, new systems

---

[19] "Lun Hebei caichan shang shixiang shu," *OYXQJ*, 118: 1825–1828.
[20] For the fiscal system and the financial history of the Song Dynasty, see Wang Shengduo (1995), Bao (2001), and Golas in Chaffee and Twitchett (2015: 139–213).

of labor utilization and management, new land tenure systems, and new government institutions and economic policies.[21]

Given all of this, an essential factor that helped to found China's medieval agricultural revolution was the wide adoption of high-yield crops. In south China, this was a species of early-ripening paddy rice.[22] In the next section, I will examine the government's experiments in cultivating paddy rice in Hebei. In north China, the high-yield crop was winter wheat. Here, the question I am about to tackle is whether or not winter wheat was widely planted in Hebei during the eleventh century, in particular after 1048, so as to bring about a revolutionary improvement in land productivity, as well as in Hebei's overall output of staple food. This question is crucial, because its answer implies whether or not the Hebei people could produce enough food to survive the hardship in an extremely challenging environmental era. The answer – that winter wheat was not widely cultivated – will reinforce my argument that there was a *de facto* decline in Hebei's agricultural production that contrasted starkly to the stunning growth in south China.

Millet had dominated dry-land farming in north China for many centuries before wheat became a significant staple grain. Millet was the grain "constantly eaten [by people] in the northern lands (north China in general)."[23] In the Tang Dynasty, millet served as a standard for evaluating the weight and price of other grains.[24] A fall crop, millet was sown by the third lunar month in mid-spring, it sprouted in late spring and ripened in mid-autumn. In Hebei during the eleventh century, the harvesting of millet usually started around the middle of the eighth lunar month and finished by the ninth lunar month, before the frost descended in the tenth month. Given geographical and climatic differences, millet was harvested ten to fifteen days earlier in southern Hebei than in northern Hebei and the western mountainous areas. Millet yields did not improve much even into the mid-twentieth century, when the unit yield was around 60 kilograms per *mu* of land. During the Tang–Song period, the unit yield was

---

[21] Much research has been done in English, Chinese, and Japanese to propose and testify to the "medieval economic revolution" thesis. To grasp the contour of this gigantic amount of scholarship, see Elvin (1973) and Shiba (1970). In Chaffee and Twitchett (2015: 344), McDermott and Shiba critique this overly positive assessment of Song economy by claiming that "any talk of a 'Sung agricultural revolution' is premature."

[22] Ho (1956). Also McDermott and Shiba's discussion on south China's "conquest by rice" in Chaffee and Twitchett (2015: 361–364).

[23] *Tang xinxiu bencao*, 487.

[24] *Wenxian tongkao*, 7: 75.

between 40 and 50 kilograms. In places where labor and water supplies were limited or the weather was cooler, such as in northern Hebei, the production tended to be even smaller. Despite its limited yield, millet was nevertheless the most favored crop for dry-land farmers. Its stability, low water consumption, and high resistance to the dry climate made it a sturdy crop that did not demand much human care.

Millet's predominant role in northern agriculture seemed to be challenged by winter wheat in the Tang period. Agricultural historians have suggested that winter wheat was widely planted; because food produced with wheat flour tasted better, it was more appealing to consumers than millet.[25] More importantly, as a winter crop, winter wheat was sown in the eighth lunar month and harvested in the late fourth and fifth month of the next year. It utilized the winter months, when other grain crops could not grow, and thereby it added one more crop to the land's annual production. Hence, it dramatically extended the land's growing season and sped up the rotation of crops on a same swath of land: in the past, a unit of land could support one grain crop per year, but with winter wheat, it could produce three grain crops in two years, pushing the annual rotation index from 100 percent to 150 percent. Thanks to winter wheat, a unit of land could produce more food every year; such increase in land productivity was remarkable. Given these virtues, scholars have considered winter wheat a revolutionary crop, which gradually replaced millet as north China's leading crop.

Combing through Tang–Song historical sources, however, we find that in comparison with millet, winter wheat had many disadvantages. Given those disadvantages, the lower socio-economic tiers of the population as well as regions like eleventh-century Hebei, which suffered various environmental and socio-economic difficulties, might not be able or willing to pursue large-scale wheat plantation. Without denying that the crop was a technological innovation that could improve land productivity and that was cultivated more in the Tang–Song period than before in some parts of China and by certain kinds of farmers, I argue that previous scholars have idealized the adoption of the crop and disregarded environmental and socio-economic specificities and their constraints. An advanced technology did not make a leap into mass production easily; its application in actual production was confined by various conditions. It was certainly subjected to the opinion of farmers – as individuals in the context of small

[25] Amano (1962: 907), Nishijima (1966: 249–252), Ōsawa (1996: 92–93), and Wang Lihua (1995: 14–17).

farming communities – who judged whether or not they had the capital to pursue the new technology, whether or not their production would be more profitable with the technology, and what costs would incur. In a society like late tenth-century Hebei, where agriculture had just recovered from war damage and was growing at a steady, slow pace, and where environmental and socio-economic challenges led to an economy based on a principle of "subsistence first" rather than "profit maximization," farmers would more likely choose traditional, low-risk crops like millet than high-risk, high-cost crops like winter wheat.[26]

Let us look at winter wheat's disadvantages. Firstly, in comparison with millet, wheat demanded more nutrient and water resources and was more sensitive to climatic variations. In fields of similar soil conditions, millet required less fertilizer than wheat and made more efficient use of water.[27] Wheat was far less drought resistant. It had to be planted in low-lying fields that could be irrigated.[28] On the Hebei Plain where water was constantly in short supply and artificial irrigation was less developed (certainly in middle-period China), dryness threatened all stages of the growth of wheat plants.[29] This meant that cultivating wheat was a challenging and risky business; it required more human care and capital input than millet did.

In spring, when wheat sprouted and desperately needed water, the rainy season had not yet arrived and "dry hot winds" blew across the North China Plain. The rapid rise in temperature and dryness caused the fragile plants to wither. When droughts hit north China (including Hebei) hard in the 1030s, 1040s, 1060s, and 1070s, winter wheat must have been vulnerable. Also, in the 1040s, 1055, 1089, and 1090, warm winters led to a shortage of snow.[30] Without snow to cover the ground and shield the underground seeds from the cold air and retaining moisture, wheat seeds would fail to sprout. After 1048, floods from the Yellow River and Hebei's local rivers took place nearly every year, sometimes

---

[26] Following James Roumasset's "safety first" principle in "Risk and Choice of Technique for Peasant Agriculture," James C. Scott (1976: 22) maintains that, when the "subsistence orientation" structures economic decisions, "[q]uestions of profitability of investment, yield per unit of land, the productivity of labor are in themselves of secondary concern."

[27] Millet is low maintenance and drought resistant in comparison not only with winter wheat but also with other major grain crops. See Zhongguo nongye baike quanshu bianji weiyuanhui (1991: 524).

[28] *Qimin yaosu*, 2: 127. *Sishi zuanyao jiaoshi*, 4: 194. *Wang Zheng Nongshu*, 83.

[29] Zhongguo nongye baike quanshu bianji weiyuanhui (1991: 635).

[30] *Jingwen ji*, 28: 11b–12b. *XCB*, 179: 4327 and 454: 10878.

TABLE 4. *The Unit Yield of Winter Wheat and Millet (in kg)*

Crop	Yield in Hebei 1000s	After D. H. Perkins[a] 1600-1900	After W. Wagner[b] early 1900s	After R. H. Myers[c] 1917-1957	1932[d]	After J. L. Buck[e] 1929-1933	1948-1952[f]	1953[g]
Winter Wheat		33.3		43-73	62	67	46	
Millet	40-50		52.4-66.7		72	96		68.7

Notes:
[a] Perkins (1969: 330); [b] Cited from Bray (1984: 448); [c] cited from Bray (1984: 476); [d] Cressey (1955: 100); [e] Buck (1937: 204); [f] Zhongguo nongye baike quanshu bianji weiyuanhui (1991: 611); [g] Zhongguo nongye baike quanshu bianji weiyuanhui (1991: 523). Bray (1984: 476) finds that Perkins underestimates the yields and believes in higher yields in Hebei and Shandong.

even several times within a single year. While early floods happened in the fourth and fifth lunar months to damage the harvest of winter wheat, later floods often came in the seventh and eighth months to prevent the sowing of winter wheat. Clearly, it was not easy to carry out the cultivation of winter wheat in a sustainable manner in eleventh-century Hebei.

Secondly, while consuming more labor and water resources than millet, winter wheat did not produce a more desirable yield. Based on numbers collected from various sources, winter wheat's unit yield appears to have been ten kilograms lower than millet (see Table 4). Hebei farmers had to reason carefully about whether or not it was worthwhile to pursue a smaller yield for winter wheat at higher costs. Given the escalating environmental pressure and socio-economic hardship, planting winter wheat did not appear to be a secure, profitable practice for ordinary people.

The third disadvantage contradicts previous scholars' belief that winter wheat brought about an improved rotation pattern; that is, three grain crops in two years was achieved in north China since the mid-Tang Dynasty.[31] I do not challenge the technical validity of this rotation pattern. But I argue that, at least in Hebei, this pattern could work only in optimal conditions and was not widely practiced in reality. In this matter, timing was a major obstacle. Winter wheat was sown by the end of the eighth lunar month in Hebei, to be done earlier than in other regions,

[31] Although many scholars argue about when the three-crops-in-two-year rotation system first appeared in the Chinese agricultural history, they in general agree with Amano and Nishijima that millet and winter wheat began to rotate with each other in the same field in the mid-Tang period.

because temperatures dropped quickly in Hebei. The earlier it was sown in that month, the fewer seeds were required and the healthier sprouts would be, meaning lower costs for higher returns.[32] However, in that month the millet harvest had not finished. As fields were still occupied by millet and had not yet been cleared of debris, they were not ready for the plantation of the winter crop. Frequent flooding from the Yellow River and other local rivers in the autumn certainly made the sowing of winter wheat more difficult. In the meantime, most farmers were busily engaged in harvesting and processing fall crops, and managing their payment of autumn taxes. We certainly should not forget that by that time a significant portion of Hebei's male population was getting ready for their winter military training, leaving the elderly, women, and children to handle a great deal of the agricultural work. Thus, it is doubtful that there was sufficient labor for both the fall harvest and wheat plantation at the same time. Now, let us look at the summer time. The harvest of winter wheat was carried out in the fifth lunar month, when young shoots of millet had already broken through the earth in neighboring fields. The wheat fields would only become available for cultivation again in the late fifth month or the sixth month, either for planting a vegetable crop or fast-growing beans, or simply to lie fallow until the eighth month when they could be used for winter wheat again.

Obviously, it is very unlikely that millet and winter wheat were rotated on a same field to achieve the intensified use of land in the three grain harvests over two years system that the previous scholarship has suggested. A more plausible farming practice would have been that in addition to the predominant millet plantation, which rotated at best one crop a year,[33] a certain number of fields was used for winter wheat, with two minor vegetable crops immediately before and after the wheat crop. Such practices would bring the crop rotation in some fields up to three crops within two years, but with only one grain harvest, far less than three grain crops that some previous scholarship has idealistically suggested. In fact, even

---

[32] *Sishi zuanyao jiaoshi*, 4: 194. In the eighth lunar month of 1009, Emperor Zhenzong said: "If the stagnant water is drained soon, there will still be some hope for winter wheat [to be sown in time]. But if the water expands without an end or starts to be drained from the ninth month, the fields cannot bear [the plants of wheat] even if a great deal of seeds are sown." Emperor Zhenzong was referring to the situation in Henan. The frost descended earlier in Hebei than in Henan, the land south of Hebei, so the sowing of seed should be completed before the ninth month. See *XCB*, 72: 1630.

[33] Every few years, the millet field needed to lie fallow to restore fertility. This reality made the rotation index of the millet field lower than 100 percent.

this modest practice – one wheat crop and two vegetable crops in two years – could not be achieved all the time. In 990, for instance, some 680 *qing* (68,000 *mu*) of summer crops (e.g., winter wheat or peas) in southern Hebei were damaged by drought; by the eleventh month of the year, merely 130 *qing* of the fields held fall crops.[34] In this peculiar case of crop rotations, only 19 percent of the fields were utilized again for the next season. The remaining 81 percent lay fallow from the summer through the winter. Across Hebei, the ratio of fields that afforded three crops in two years in a sustainable manner could not be high.

In the eleventh century, especially after 1048, there were many years when crops were harmed by disasters and the land failed to support additional crops. The changes in environmental conditions often led to irregular practices. For fragile crops like winter wheat, a delay in sowing of even ten or fifteen days might cause a substantial reduction in the eventual harvest. Historical records show that farmers often planted spring wheat instead of winter wheat.[35] Like millet, spring wheat was sown in the spring and harvested in the fall. In contemporary China, this crop usually produces a lower yield than winter wheat, and its flour is of an inferior quality.[36] It is only planted in northeastern provinces where temperature is too low for wheat seeds to survive the winter months. In eleventh-century Hebei, however, spring wheat was widely planted. In 1074, for instance, an official document mentioned that there were "households that ought to plant spring wheat (*ying zhong chunmai hu* 應種春麥戶)" in Jizhou of central Hebei.[37] This suggests that spring wheat was not a minor crop, but more likely a major, regular staple crop in the economic life of some people. The significance of spring wheat also suggests the unpopularity of winter wheat in Hebei, due to the crop's fragility and unstable yield against Hebei's peculiar environmental conditions.

We should note that, apart from the timing issues, there were many other factors determining whether or not a more intense crop rotation

---

[34] *SHY*, "Shihuo," 70: 157a.
[35] *XCB*, 68: 1520; 258: 6292, and 280: 6850.
[36] *Zhongguo nongye baike quanshu bianji weiyuanhui* (1991: 613). Also, see the commentary in a Song-period medical treatise, *Chongxiu Zhenghe jingshi zhenglei beiyong bencao*, 492.
[37] *XCB*, 258: 6305. Another interpretation of this phrase is "households who respond to (the government's call) for spring wheat plantation." This interpretation does not undermine my argument that spring wheat cultivation was quite common in this region in the eleventh century.

was possible. As agricultural historian Francesca Bray has pointed out, intensified land utilization can only be realized by "a consequent increase in the use of fertilizer; by more thorough tillage, improving soil structure and fertility; by careful regulation of the water supply; and by better care of plants, weeding frequently, hoeing and watering to ensure that each single stem bears fruit."[38] Not all farming households could afford such inputs of material and labor resources. In practice, "[t]he abbreviated growing season, together with other problems – lack of irrigation, lack of fertilizer, and alkaline soil – has severely limited the possibilities of land use over the winter months."[39] In eleventh-century Hebei, in particular after 1048, the population loss to the military, disasters, and various kinds of socio-economic turmoil sharply reduced labor supplies. The overall impoverishment of the Hebei society, among not only lower levels of the population but also among the landholding, wealthy upper classes, prevented farmers from purchasing seeds and fertilizer or from constructing irrigation infrastructure. A great number of people were at the edge of poverty and suffered frequent food shortages. Those people did not possess much capital. Not many of them could afford to experiment with intensifying land utilization and cultivating high-cost, high-risk crops like winter wheat. They were more likely to rely on traditional technology and produce stable, low-cost crops like millet, despite its low quality and inferior taste.

Given the obstacles imposed by timing, environmental conditions, and resource requirements, a rotation pattern of three grain crops in two years could not be applied widely in real farming practices in eleventh-century Hebei. In fact, this rotation pattern was not achieved in Hebei even in the early twentieth century. Studies show that the rotation index in central Hebei in the 1930s reached only 126 percent, and the average level for all of Hebei was even lower, at a mere 122.56 percent. These numbers suggest a cultivation of five crops over four years.[40] The kind of revolutionary growth in agriculture based on an intensified use of land and a consequential surge in land productivity and overall production – like what previous scholars have believed in winter wheat and what the early-ripening paddy rice brought to southeast China – did not happen in the disaster-ridden land of Hebei. A technological

---

[38] Bray (1984: 133).

[39] Philip C. C. Huang (1985: 58)'s accounts on crop rotation systems in north China.

[40] Hou (2001: 60). At the same time, the rotation index was 143.69 percent in Shandong and 154.2 percent in Henan, south of Hebei. This suggests great regional disparity in the crop rotation system.

innovation, like adopting winter wheat, was unable to blossom into mass production, given the unfavorable environmental and socio-economic conditions.

With all of this in mind, a more realistic assessment can be made about winter wheat. Focusing on the temporal dimension of agricultural practices, previous scholars have considered winter wheat a supplementary crop that filled in the winter gap between two major crops. The above pages have proven this temporal dimension invalid; winter wheat and millet could not rotate one after another on a same patch of field in Hebei. Now stressing a spatial dimension, my analysis suggests a different possibility: winter wheat was a competitor to the dominant grain, millet, because it competed for both land and other resources, like labor, water, and fertilizer. Rather than fitting into the existing rotation pattern that centered on millet, supplementing millet and accelerating the year-round rotation, winter wheat occupied certain fields that were originally for millet cultivation. Hence, the issue becomes that, as the acreage of winter wheat rose, the acreage available to millet decreased. As wheat fields produced wheat (at a smaller unit yield than millet) and two vegetable crops every year, the overall size of millet fields shrank. Moreover, some resources (such as water, fertilizer, and labor) originally dedicated to millet cultivation switched to serve wheat fields, so the remaining resources for millet fields had to decrease. As a result, in an area where the plantation of winter wheat took place, the overall production of millet had to drop. The popularity of winter wheat came at the cost of the millet production. In this situation, the quantity of total staple foods produced from the same land was not doubled or tripled, as happened with the intensified production of paddy rice in the lower Yangzi valley. At best, the total output of staple foods made available to human consumption by the millet-winter wheat combination remained at a similar level as in the past when millet was the dominant staple grain, if not lower, given the fact that winter wheat had a small unit yield.

Therefore, the change to agriculture in north China did not happen in terms of the quantity of staple food – people did not get more food to eat. Rather, it happened to the food structure, the changing composition of various grains and their differentiating consumers. Even given a fairly consistent quantity of staple food, there was a proportional adjustment among various grains. A growing number of the economically well-to-do, in particular urban citizens, began to consume more food made of wheat flour, such as noodles, steamed buns, and

TABLE 5. *Quotas of Summer–Autumn Taxes in 1077*
(Various Measurements)

	Summer Tax	Autumn Tax	Summer–Autumn Ratio
National Total Quota	16,962,695	35,048,334	1:2
Quota for Grain	3,435,785	14,451,472	1:4.2
(*hu, approximately 33.5 liters*)			
Quota for Grass (bundle)	n/a	16,754,844	

Note: Liang (1980: 289).

dumplings.[41] Wheat production and consumption might have increased, but the increase was not revolutionary. In less urban or rural areas, within the lower tiers of the society, and among those who were environmentally and socio-economically challenged, people could neither afford to cultivate winter wheat, nor to consume wheat flour on a daily basis. Millet still dominated their subsistence-oriented staple food production and consumption.[42]

Let's now compare two groups of tax quotas from the late eleventh century to see how significant the two crops contributed to the state finance. In the Northern Song, the state levied two major taxes, respectively in summer and fall. The summer tax included grain (mainly winter wheat and mungbean in north China versus rice and winter wheat in south China), grass (like straw), silk, and cash in copper coin. The autumn tax included grain (mainly millet and soybean in north China versus rice in south China), grass, and cash. Table 5 shows empire-wide summer and autumn tax quotas in 1077. These numbers suggest that, throughout Song China, people were expected to pay double the amount of tax in the fall as in the summer. The grain they submitted to the government in the fall, a combination of millet-beans-rice, was 4.2 times the wheat-beans-rice combination that they submitted in the summer. Table 6 shows the tax quotas for Hebei in 1080, which indicates an even sharper contrast. People of Hebei were supposed to pay an autumn tax 5.6 times

[41] For the popularity of wheat flour in the Tang-Song China, see Wang (2000: 73, 158, 210); and Nishijima (1966: 249).
[42] The situation was similar in Shanxi, the region west to Hebei, where "kaoliang (sorghum) and millet were the circuit's most commonly grown grains, while the more productive grains like barley and wheat remained virtually unplanted in its northern half throughout the Northern Sung." See Chaffee and Twitchett (2015: 357).

TABLE 6. *Quotas of Summer–Autumn Taxes for Hebei in 1080*
(Various Measurements)

	Summer Tax	Autumn Tax	Summer–Autumn Ratio
Hebei Total Quota	1,393,983	7,758,107	1:5.6
Quota for Grain (*hu*)	278,797	3,180,824	1:11
Quota for Grass (bundle)	n/a	3,723,891	

Note: Liang (1980: 290).

the amount of the summer tax. Their autumn tax of grain, namely millet and soybean, was 11 times their summer tax of grains, namely wheat and beans.

These numbers indicate that throughout the Song empire, farmers were supposed to hand over to the government far more millet and rice in the fall than winter wheat in the summer. The millet-wheat ratio was exceptionally high in Hebei during the late eleventh century. The tax payment made in winter wheat was merely a tiny fraction of the payment made in millet. In other words, of the entire amount of staple grain that the government obtained from Hebei within a year, 92 percent was millet. Indeed, tax quotas set by the government reflected the government's taxation preference; they did not strictly reflect actual farming practices and agricultural yields. It is possible that the government imposed a lower tax rate on summer crops and a higher tax rate on fall crops. However, we have no historical evidence to verify such a hypothesis. The previous chapters have suggested that since the 1040s, the Song state experienced serious financial stress; it had particular difficulties in gathering food to feed the growing number of military personnel in Hebei. After 1048, Hebei's military often faced food shortages. In that situation, it seems rather unlikely that the government would choose to levy less wheat if it could. If wheat production were substantial in Hebei, the government would most likely adjust the tax rate to raise its summer revenue in terms of wheat.

These tax quotas and my analysis of the socio-economic conditions in the Northern Song period all together point to a rather minor status of winter wheat in Hebei's agricultural economy. Its production was proportionally insignificant; its contributions to feeding the population in Hebei and supplying revenue to the state were limited. In 1012, Emperor Zhenzong remarked: "Hedong [Shanxi] and Hebei would not work without millet."[43] The dominant status of millet in Hebei's agriculture and mass consumption remained strong throughout the Northern Song period.

As winter wheat failed to take over agricultural practices and dramatically boost land productivity, Hebei's recovery and growth in agriculture based on traditional crop, millet, before the 1040s constituted more of a quantitative, accumulative growth, rather than the kind of qualitative, revolutionary growth that scholars have wished to see. After 1048, because the agricultural population and the arable land both shrank, Hebei's food production declined substantially, not only for winter wheat but for millet as well. Hebei's population and its gigantic military, had to turn to external sources for support. The final pages of this chapter will focus on the roles the imperial state played in feeding Hebei's hungry people.

7.3   Paddy Rice: A Northern Dream of Southern Affluence

As winter wheat failed to improve land productivity and Hebei's agriculture experienced a general decline, food shortages often troubled this region. To the imperial state, perhaps the most serious issue was that it could not obtain adequate food within Hebei to support the massive number of troops there. A significant portion of Hebei's military supplies had come from importation. But importation was not always stable, and heavy reliance on external support put Hebei in a vulnerable position. Had a famine broken out in southern parts of China and thereby reduced exports of grain to the north, Hebei's soldiers would have starved. Any setback in the transportation system either inside or outside Hebei – due to extreme weather, destruction of the canals, Yellow River floods, or broader social and political conditions – could cause shipping delays, reduce supplies, and lead to the exhaustion of Hebei's military granaries. Suffering hunger, soldiers would become resentful of their commanders and the government. As we have discussed in the previous chapters, on many occasions soldiers rose up in protest or even organized mutinies. An unruly military in the frontier province would certainly be Hebei's and the imperial state's worst nightmare.

Well aware of the food shortage issue, some of Hebei's military commanders considered it an inevitable consequence of the construction of the frontier ponds, since the ponds occupied land and squeezed out

[43] XCB, 77: 1751.

agriculture. As much as they believed the existence of the ponds absolutely necessary, they also considered it critical to reduce the military's dependence on long-distance transportation. Facing this dilemma, military leaders suggested reviving agricultural self-sufficiency in northern Hebei by conducting military colonization. Given the fact that the landscape in northern Hebei had changed greatly and the environmental conditions no longer allowed traditional dry-land farming, they began to ponder the possibility of cultivating water-based crops such as paddy rice.

Rice was not a complete stranger to Hebei. Back in the first, third, sixth, seventh, and early eighth centuries some military commanders and officials experimented with it in this region.[44] But the earlier attempts were small-scale and short-lived. The unfavorable natural conditions in this part of China, such as the short growing season and inadequate water supplies, made planting rice costly and unproductive. In the Song period, it seemed that the manmade watery environment in northern Hebei provided at least the abundant water, if not other conditions, that paddy rice required.

In the early 990s when the construction of the ponds commenced, Cangzhou's commander He Chengju decided to institute military colonization, in order for the soldiers to produce their own food.[45] His advisor Huang Mao 黃懋 was a native of paddy rice country in southeast China. Knowing the advantage of the crop, namely its high yield, Huang recommended trying out rice cultivation in the marshlands around the ponds. In the first year of their experiment, the first frost arrived much earlier in Hebei than in traditional paddy rice areas in south China, so the crops were destroyed and the harvest was poor. Huang thereafter imported an early-ripening variety of rice from his native Fujian 福建 province.[46] Thanks to its relatively short growing season, the new variety reportedly produced a bumper harvest, which silenced criticisms of rice cultivation within the government.

From that time through the 1030s, the practice of rice cultivation by military colonies spread westward from northeastern Hebei to central Hebei, wherever the ponds could provide adequate irrigation. In 1034, the central government dispatched an official to Hebei, with the goal of "teaching the common people how to cultivate paddies" in Huaizhou

[44] *Cefu yuangui*, 678.4a; 503.12a; 503.20a; and 497.8a; and *Jiu Tangshu*, 105.3221. For a historical survey of rice plantation in the Yellow River valley, see Zou (1985).
[45] *XCB*, 34: 747.
[46] Perhaps the same early-ripening variety examined in Ho (1956: 200–218).

懷州, Weizhou, Cizhou 磁州, Xiangzhou, Xingzhou, Mingzhou, Zhenzhou, and Zhaozhou 趙州. The result of this government advocacy among the civilians, however, was unclear; no further reports about it appear in historical records.[47] I suspect that production was not successful, because those prefectures were all located at the foot of the Taihang Mountains in western Hebei, where the rugged terrain made controlling water and supplying irrigation difficult. I also doubt that civilian farmers had equal access to the waters in the state-owned ponds.

Among all the places that cultivated paddy rice, Baozhou was their center. In 1020 the military in that district opened more than 10,000 *mu* of paddies and produced 18,000–20,000 *dan* of both non-glutinous and glutinous rice, at a rate of 1.8–2 *dan* per *mu*.[48] Its yield was five times higher than that in neighboring places in Hebei, for example, Shun'an and Qianning commanderies. Its total annual production weighed in at more than half of the entire amount that Hebei's military colonies harvested.[49] Two factors might have contributed to the relatively high production in Baozhou. First, the prefecture was located at the western end of the chain of ponds; its terrain rose gradually and the accumulated water was perhaps able to drain off more easily than in other places to the east. It is likely that good drainage preserved soil fertility, which advanced the growth of crops. Second, Baozhou planters seem to have invested more time and energy in their rice paddies than people in other places. As an official proudly claimed in 1020, Baozhou's successful production was only achieved because its soldiers worked harder and rested less than those in other places.[50] At his suggestion, four out of every ten soldiers who were assigned to farm Hebei's military colonies were sent to Baozhou; their arrival made Baozhou the center of Hebei's military farming.

Obviously, the large labor force was a key factor in Baozhou's high rice yield. However, given the enormous labor inputs, the land productivity seemed rather low. Even at its best, Baozhou's production was far lower than that in traditional rice producing areas in south China. At the time, the unit yield of rice in south China was about 3 *dan* per *mu*, 50–67 percent higher than Baozhou's level – by far the best in Hebei – and certainly much higher than the production level in colonies in other

---

[47] XCB, 114: 2677.
[48] SHY, "Shihuo," 63: 42a.
[49] SHY, "Shihuo," 63: 42a and 63: 41a. *Wenxian tongkao*, 7: 76.
[50] SHY, "Shihuo," 63: 42a and 63: 44a.

places in Hebei. This means that by 1020, Hebei's entire military rice cultivation was very limited, and its productivity was much lower than that in contemporary south China. Hebei's desire to achieve food self-sufficiency by experimenting with the southern crop seemed no more than a case of wishful thinking.

The limited rice production by Hebei's military very likely persisted through the 1060s. During the 1070s and 1080s, Wang Anshi's reformist government sought to "enrich the state and strengthen the military." This agenda, when applied to Hebei, targeted the issue of reducing Hebei's dependence on importation and generating food based on local resources. As Hebei's officials and officers actively performed a major reformist policy, the "Measure of seeking water benefits for arable fields," and proceeded to construct more ponds and collect more water resources, they found the idea of rice cultivation attractive. In 1075, the court approved a proposal to revive the old irrigation system in Baozhou and enlarge its rice paddies.[51] In order to do so, local officials used government fund to purchase dry land (*ludi* 陸地) from private landowners and turn it into water-covered paddy fields (*shuitian* 水田).[52] This practice not only took place in Baozhou, but also spread to other places in Hebei. In Dingzhou in northwestern Hebei, for example, the prefect Xue Xiang 薛向 and the Fiscal Commissioner Shen Gua collaborated to construct an irrigation system and promote paddy rice production. Wu Chuhou 吳處厚 (1053– 1089), a junior official who worked for Xue and Shen, wrote flatteringly about their accomplishment: the semi-arid, bleak land of northwestern Hebei was turned into a "watery land," resembling the lower Yangtze valley where rice paddies offered their bounties.[53]

The reformist efforts arguably increased Hebei's overall rice production. At the height of the state's promotion of rice cultivation, however, conflicts arose over the land and water resources. Planting rice required land and water, and so did maintaining the ponds. Since both resources were limited, would they best be used for the paddies or for the ponds? In the 1070s, for instance, the central government instructed some local officials to reclaim land from some ponds to create paddy fields. They did so by channeling the muddy water of the Yellow River into the ponds and causing the ponds to silt up.[54] In 1077, two officials in Xiongzhou were punished for failing to balance the water supplies for both uses. They

---

[51] *XCB*, 60: 6350.
[52] *XCB*, 262: 6408; 260: 6350; 293: 7146; and 330: 7332.
[53] "Dingwu jun shuitian ji," *Dingzhou zhi*, 21: 35b–37a.
[54] *XCB*, 254: 6206; 260: 6350; 280: 6852; and 501: 11935. *SS*, 95: 2371. *SHY*, "Shihuo," 63: 44a.

"discharged water [from somewhere else] into ponds without planning in advance to reserve water for the paddies."[55] Even in places where local officers and officials did not receive court instructions to expand paddies and were supposed to maintain the ponds, they sometimes were lured by agricultural profit and chose to illegally drain the ponds and plant rice there. Apparently, for a time, rice cultivation, which had originated in Hebei because of the ponds, had now begun to take precedence over the ponds, particularly in its claim over limited resources.

As Nagase Mamoru has correctly pointed out, conflicts over the strategic function of the ponds and the agricultural values associated to them became increasingly evident.[56] Over time, those conflicts tended to favor the ponds. At the imperial court, calls to restore and maintain the ponds never ceased in the reform era; they became even louder after the mid-1080s, when the conservatives came back to power. Those arguments echoed the court debates for whether or not to remove the Yellow River from Hebei, which we examined in Chapter 5. In the debates, Hebei's strategic concerns and the state's security needs rose above anything else – be it the stability and manageability of the river, the hardship of the people, or in this case, the development of rice production to satisfy military demands. As a result, after the mid-1080s, Hebei's rice cultivation fell by the wayside.

Whether the fall of rice cultivation was due to the constraints of resources or to its failure in political competition, the key question is: did paddy rice become a major grain crop, even for just a while, in Hebei during the eleventh century, and thereby improve the life of Hebei's hunger-struck people? Unfortunately, not only was the production short-lived, but it was mainly conducted by government-organized corvée laborers and soldiers, specifically for the military colonies. Despite the government's temporary advocacy, there is little evidence in surviving records to indicate that Hebei's commoners became interested in planting paddy rice. The semi-arid climate in many parts of the Hebei plain made it very costly to manage artificial irrigation for the paddies. The ponds and its water resources were state property, which were not shared by commoners. For ordinary farmers, even if they appreciated that rice had a higher yield than millet or wheat, it would be too big a risk to turn their land into paddies and battle against the unfavorable weather conditions. Securing water supplies also necessitated too much of an investment.

---

[55] *XCB*, 284: 6955.
[56] Nagase (1983: 176–178).

The military-oriented cultivation failed to produce enough food even for the military population, contradicting its initial intention.[57] In 1021, the overall production of Hebei's military colonies was 29,400 *dan*, including rice and other kinds of grain. This number grew very slowly in the following decades; in 1066 it reached a mere 35,468 *dan*.[58] In contrast, Hebei's annual demand for military grain was immense, and it kept rising throughout the Song period. In 1034 the total number of all military items (grain, forage, cash, fabric, and other goods) was 10,200,000, regardless of their different unit measurements.[59] Assuming one fourth of the number referred to grain required to feed Hebei's soldiers – that is, 2,550,000 *dan* of grain – the requirement was 86 times greater than the production from Hebei's military colonies in 1021 and 71 times greater than the production in 1034. In 1055, Xue Xiang, the Fiscal Commissioner, reported that Hebei's fourteen frontier prefectures required five million strings of cash every year to purchase 1.6 million *dan* of grain for military use.[60] Assuming that this amount of grain was for one year's consumption, it was 54 times Hebei's colonial production in 1021 and 45 times the production in 1066. The gigantic consumption that Xue mentioned was only for the fourteen frontier districts. Counting all of Hebei's districts and their military demands, the figure for Hebei's entire military grain consumption would be much higher than 1.6 million *dan*. After Hebei's military expanded rapidly from the early 1040s, its total consumption must have gone far beyond the 1034 number of 2.55 million.

Obviously, Hebei's rice production was far from adequate to feed Hebei's troops. It is no wonder that the ministers of the Military Colony at the imperial court complained: "Even with a good harvest its [rice's] output does not compensate for its expenses."[61] The compilers of the *Standard History of the Song Dynasty* made a perhaps more reasonable, but still damning, judgment: the true benefit of Hebei's paddy rice plantation lay not in agricultural gains but in "storing water to halt the Khitan cavalry."[62]

In southeast China, for example in the lower Yangzi valley, the early-ripening variety of rice shortened the growing season for each individual

---

[57] For more information about Hebei's military colonization and its limited economic value, see Cheng (2012: 78–109).
[58] *SS*, 176: 4266–4267.
[59] *XCB*, 114: 2675.
[60] *XCB*, 181: 4382.
[61] *SHY*, "Shihuo," 63: 44a.
[62] *SS*, 176: 4266.

crop, accelerated the rotation among multiple rice crops on a unit of land, and thereby doubled or even tripled the annual output of the land. This technological innovation drastically boosted land productivity, improved the overall food supplies, and raised living standards among people in southeast China. Yet, when introduced into Hebei in the 990s, even with tremendous government investments and manual care, this variety of rice failed to supplement millet and wheat to become another major crop. It did not boost Hebei's agricultural production, and therefore failed to reverse Hebei's reliance on importation. The dreams of Hebei's military leaders to achieve food self-sufficiency and of Wang Anshi's fellow reformists to "enrich the state" by promoting rice production on the northern land failed to come true. The "watery land" created by the environmental changes in Hebei, and the one in southeast China, produced very different economic stories.

7.4   "The Root of All-Under-Heaven" – Swapping Core and Periphery

At the beginning of 1125, shortly before Emperor Huizong's abdication and the fall of the Northern Song Dynasty, Yuwen Cuizhong 宇文粹中 (?–1139) pleaded with Huizong to fix the dysfunctional state finances. Among various problems the state and the Song society faced, Yuwen pointed out that "Bandits and rebels are burgeoning in Shandong and Hebei. Hebei used to produce clothes and textiles for the whole of All-Under-Heaven, but its silk production and weaving have all been destroyed."[63] The decline of Hebei's economy and collapse of its society were the product of the hydraulic mode of consumption: the unceasing destructive episodes of the environmental drama and the heavy exploitation by the imperial state – in part to remedy the environmental problems – had exhausted Hebei's land and people.

Yet, the suffering was not exclusive to Hebei itself. As Hebei's disaster and famine refugees flowed southward to Henan and then across all of north China, Hebei's environmental and socio-economic disease spread and magnified. Wherever refugees went, they demanded relief and supplies, unsettled the local society, triggered economic hardship, exposed latent social problems, and even instigated mass unrest. In the late eleventh century, rebellions in Shandong and Henan were often sponsored and aided by Hebei's outlaws. The geographical spread of Hebei's problems defied any administrative boundaries and refused to be confined by the state power. Hebei's chronic suffering affected the imperial

[63] *QSW*, 3129: 248.

state and its daily operation, too. As some leaders of the state saw it, the socio-economic degradation of Hebei – a strategically key frontier region that the state could not simply ignore or dismiss from its imperial system but had to protect and hold together – was like "a person with chronic disease."[64] This disease was a gangrenous one. After causing Hebei itself to decay, it spread to other parts of the imperial system, consumed its resources, and gradually wore the entire system down. What happened within Hebei were not only regional affairs signifying a regional history, but also the affairs organizing the empire and constituting the history of the imperial state.

Before 1048, the state expected that despite its limited gross production, Hebei would first satisfy the basic needs of its people, and then submit the excess to the government. The taxes the Hebei people paid were not shipped to the capital Kaifeng to be stored at state treasuries as other southern, wealthy regions were supposed to do. Rather, they remained inside Hebei at the disposal of local governments and troops. Hence, Hebei's production did not contribute much to the state's central reserve. In fact, as the previous chapters have made clear, the state had to channel a certain portion of its revenue, which was collected from central and southern China, to support Hebei's military even before 1048. Therefore, alongside the economic self-sufficiency of Hebei's civilian society, the state assumed the major responsibility for sustaining Hebei's military.

After 1048, the state's financial responsibilities for Hebei multiplied. Not only did it continue to fund Hebei's military, whose size had dramatically increased since the early 1040s, it also had to deal with Hebei's dwindling civilian society and its deteriorating economy. As Hebei's economic self-sufficiency reduced, its tax collections could no longer meet state-issued tax quotas to satisfy the needs of its regional and local governments, to finance civil construction projects and their laborers, or to fill up local granaries as food reserves and famine relief. As I have discussed earlier in this chapter, by 1080, the central government had to set the highest budget (9,152,000) within the state finances to fulfill Hebei's regional consumption, double its expenditures for either Kaifeng (4,055,087), or Huainan (4,223,784) or Liangzhe (4,799,122) in the Yangzi valley. The disaster-ridden, peripheral Hebei sat at the core of the state's financial obligations.

---

[64] Wang Cun, "Qiba huihe jianshui zhiyi [Pleading to end the discussion about returning or dividing the river]," *QSW*, 1517: 16–19.

Take the prefecture Dingzhou as an example. Dingzhou was located in the highland of northwestern Hebei, and was not directly affected by the Yellow River. Beginning in 1048, it had become a major destination for flood refugees from central Hebei. In 1101, Zhang Shunmin 張舜民, a former Financial Minister who became the governor of Dingzhou, stated that the monthly costs for Dingzhou's civil government and military were about ten thousand strings of copper cash. Yet, the total reserve at its "Military Supplies Storage" and Fiscal Commission was only about 730 strings and 200 lengths of silk, which could barely sustain the functioning of the prefecture for a few days. As its metropolitan area experienced a serious shortage of cash and silk, Dingzhou's frontier garrisons lacked basic food supplies, and its soldiers did not even receive the spring uniforms they were promised.[65] Another report was made in 1115: Dingzhou's entire military demanded 1,039,092 *dan* of grain, 225,576 *dan* of horse forage, and 2,104,080 bundles of grass/straw for one year. Its annual tax incomes provided a mere 547,269 *dan* of grain (53 percent of the demand), 96,850 *dan* of horse forage (43 percent of the demand), and 1,181,188 bundles of grass (56 percent of the demand).[66] This means that about 50 percent of Dingzhou's military expenditure depended on the arrangement of institutions like the Fiscal Commission, which collected and purchased grain and other goods from elsewhere.

Dingzhou was Hebei's largest and most strategically important district. It was well funded, and it enjoyed rather stable environmental conditions that guaranteed decent agricultural production. But even this prefecture could barely support itself. As Zhang Shunmin correctly pointed out, it was not hard to imagine how depressed the economic and financial situations were in other parts of Hebei. Hebei, as a whole, could no longer support itself. As a result, the state finances had to pour in to sustain the operation of Hebei's civil governments and military, feed its civilians and disaster refugees, fix its broken land and water, and battle against the burgeoning number of outlaws, bandits, and rebels. As early as in the 1020s, six and half million *dan* of grain were collected annually from the Yangzi valley or along the waterway of the Bian Canal; a considerable portion of that was shipped northward into Hebei.[67] From the mid-eleventh century, Hebei's demands only went up. In the 1070s,

---

[65] *QSW*, 1814: 695–697.
[66] *QSW*, 2869: 109.
[67] *XCB*, 104: 2408.

every year, state treasuries released three million strings of copper cash to purchase grain for Hebei's frontier troops alone.[68]

State interventions and Hebei's importation of goods presented something of a sword of Damocles, which cut both those who supplied the goods and the state – the grand coordinator and biggest buyer in the supply–demand chain. The lower Yangzi valley enjoyed tremendous economic growth during the Tang-Song transition; the agricultural production doubled or even tripled in the eleventh century as compared to the Tang period, so it was capable of producing large quantities of surplus for exportation.[69] Yet, sometimes even this region experienced a reduction in production.[70] In difficult years like 1048, early 1050s, 1068, and 1099–1100, south China experienced environmental disasters and famines, and its ordinary people suffered as much as those in north China. In the mid-1080s when a serious drought and epidemic led to a famine in Hangzhou, the most affluent part of the lower Yangzi valley, its prefect Su Shi 蘇軾 (1036–1101) felt compelled to petition to the imperial court to have its grain export reduced by one-third.[71] Clearly, Hebei had become a burden to regions located a thousand kilometers away.

In such situations, when the state continued to press south China to supply food and cash, regional officials sometimes rose to protest against state exploitation. Some refused to cooperate and shut down food exportation to defend the well-being of their own districts. Tensions between the central government and lower Yangzi regional governments soared, as the latter considered the state's treatments of different regions unequal. Historical sources often mention that shipments of grain from the south were delayed, or the institutions in charge of grain collection and transportation complained they were unable to meet high quotas the central government had set. In 1111, for instance, the central government discovered that the Fiscal Commission in the lower Yangzi area was supposed to ship 6,726,400 *dan* of grain northward to the capital; none of it actually arrived.[72] Even if some of the grain indeed reached northern Henan, ready to be unloaded and reloaded at ports on the Yellow River, a great deal failed to make it further into Hebei's interior and northern frontier. As will be shown in the next chapter, Hebei's waterways were severely affected by the Yellow River's floods and shifting courses.

[68] *QSW*, 1693: 366.
[69] *XCB*, 165: 3968.
[70] *XCB*, 171: 4119.
[71] *QSW*, 2100: 592.
[72] *QSW*, 2674: 75.

The once cheap and smooth water transportation that Hebei benefited from before 1048 lost its routes to meandering waters and a thick cover of sediments.

Whether or not central and south China could produce adequate surpluses and were willing to feed Hebei is one question; whether or not the state could afford to purchase the surplus supplies and organize their distribution is another. As early as 1055, Xue Xiang – who later became Hebei's Fiscal Commissioner and Dingzhou's prefect, and who had engaged in Hebei's pond construction and rice cultivation in the 1070s – remarked that the fourteen prefectures located in northern Hebei completely relied on state finances. To feed these districts, the state annually spent five million strings of copper coins to buy grain worth only two million strings. Three million was embezzled by corrupt officials and speculative merchants.[73] Seeking higher profits even drove some merchants to ship grain from south China to Hebei's northern frontier and trade it to buyers in the Khitan Liao, at the risk of the Song's capital punishment.[74]

Back in 1040, Ouyang Xiu recommended that the state "share profits (*gongli* 共利)" with merchants: by raising grain prices, the government lured private merchants to collect and ship grain to Hebei; the trade benefited the government too, because it could feed Hebei and its military without having to deal with the troubles of purchase and shipping.[75] This peculiar state-merchant business was sustained throughout the Northern Song period. However, the longer it operated, the farther it drifted away from the "profit sharing" ideal. There emerged a seller's market, in which merchants as the supplier capitalized on the business without any constraints. The state, as James T. C. Liu correctly pointed out, became "the largest buyer" in the market.[76] It lost more and more bargaining power, regardless of how it manipulated its fiscal policies to regulate the market. As Hebei's environmental and socio-economic situation worsened, the state desperately relied on private merchants and had to tolerate their speculative behaviors.

In the late 1090s, Su Zhe was in charge of the state's Financial Ministry, and compiled the "Accounting Registry for the Yuanyou 元祐 Reign Era (1086–1094)." His office announced that the state's annual expenditure

---

[73] *XCB*, 181: 4382.
[74] *XCB*, 154: 3748 and 201: 4883. *SHY*, "Shihuo," 39: 15b.
[75] *QSW*, 672: 335–336.
[76] Liu (1959: 111). For the grain trade between the state and private merchants, see Jiang (2002: 220–283; 352–369).

had exceeded its annual income.[77] The situation only became worse over the next three decades. By the time Emperor Huizong took the throne at the turn of the twelfth century, the state's financial deficit was thought to be caused by four major expenses: annual tributes paid to the Liao and the Xixia, the hydraulic works for the Yellow River–Hebei Environmental Complex, military expenses, and the maintenance of the state's bureaucratic system.[78] A great portion of the state's budget, in the form of grain, cash, or human lives, ended up in Hebei. It was devoured by Hebei's environmental disasters, its dysfunctional society, and its swollen military. It was also consumed by the state's continuous mistreatments of issues related to the Yellow River and Hebei, such as the state's last, most ambitious hydraulic project during 1115–1120. As Chapter 5 showed, Emperor Huizong and his hydrocrats tried to imitate Yu the Great and channel the Yellow River toward western Hebei. The deficit of the state finance kept growing toward the end of the dynasty, and eventually led to bankruptcy. When the Jurchen invaded in 1125, the Song state could not even raise enough money to recruit troops to thwart the Jurchen's advancement into Hebei.

Despite the tremendous input of resources that went into managing Hebei and controlling the Yellow River over 160 years, and despite its unprecedented efforts, the Song state did not gain the rewards that it anticipated. It certainly did not produce a total state power that could take solid control of both the environment and the human society. When a real crisis descended, like the Jurchen's invasion, the northern land and people – the state's key strategic entity – did not stand strong to serve the state, as the state had expected them to do. Quite the opposite, over decades, the operation of the Yellow River–Hebei environmental complex had constantly disturbed the state's sense of security and stability, and gradually depleted the state power that the state took pain to build by attaining successes in other territories, such as the increasing economic power in south China and the expanding man power across the empire. The Yellow River-Hebei environmental complex had to a great extent formed the state's "accumulative impoverishment and accumulative weakness (*jipin jiruo* 積貧積弱)," a distinct characteristic featuring this "weak dynasty" that historians since the fourteenth century attributed to the Northern Song state.[79]

---

[77] *QSW*, 2056: 735.

[78] *QSW*, 2241: 821.

[79] Modern historians of Song China tend to challenge this view by emphasizing non-statist, societal achievements in the Song period, see Chaffee and Twitchett (2015: 2–3).

From the beginning of the dynasty, Hebei was a target for the state's political, military, economic, and environmental appropriation, all of which sought to transform the autonomy-inclined region into an integrated, obedient subordinate of the state. When the Yellow River began to wreak havoc, Hebei was singled out by the state as an environmentally periphery that would bear the river's ferocious torrents; its sacrifice rendered security and prosperity to its neighboring regions in the south. The transformation of Hebei's geopolitical and environmental status showed that the Song state was quite successful in ridding Hebei of its long-standing martial tradition, political independency, economic self-reliance, and even its geophysical self-confinement. From the mid-eleventh century on, Hebei was no longer a land that produced strongmen like An Zhongrong in the tenth century, who could rally troops to challenge the imperial throne. It had lost its ability to produce kings or hegemons or rebels whom the people of the late Tang Dynasty, like poet Du Mu, had feared. Hebei had become a defender of the state's northeastern frontier, a political, socio-economic, and environmental periphery that executed Emperor Taizu's geopolitical ideal in 972: as a limb serving the state's main body and the "small good" giving way to the state's "greater good."

Yet, this core-periphery structure, which the state established to hierarchize the imperial system and to centralize its control over its territory and subjects, came with heavy costs. It certainly brought about unintended consequences. Since the mid-eleventh century, the mounting environmental and socio-economic pressures turned Hebei not into a healthy, functioning limb, but a gangrenous one. The main body of the imperial state could not simply amputate Hebei because, in a tightly gridded imperial system, as the periphery goes so goes the core. In order to sustain the core-periphery structure and keep the entire empire functioning, the state had to endlessly nourish the limb with human resources, construction materials, various goods, and financial support, although knowing that its malady was incurable. Even worse, the state's need to prevent Hebei from collapsing allowed its disease to spread in the state's main body and affect its other limbs, such as key economic areas like the lower Yangzi valley.

As the source of the disease, whose maintenance sucked up wealth and resources produced elsewhere, Hebei had grown into a *de facto* center of the empire, the center of consumption rather than a center of economic production like the lower Yangzi valley, or a center of political, institutional, and cultural production like Kaifeng. Hence, within the imperial system, there emerged different sets of core-periphery structures, instead of the single set that the state desired to establish. Or, in other words, from the perspective of resource distribution and consumption, the core-periphery structure that the state sought became inverted. Rather than Hebei being at the state's disposal, the Song empire geared up to serve Hebei's needs, with the state acting as the institutional engine of that service.

After the 1040s, many statesmen at the imperial court began to share an extraordinarily high assessment of Hebei's role within the empire: Hebei became the "root of All-Under-Heaven," the center and foundation of the empire, a geopolitical status that used to be exclusively attributed to the metropolitan area of the capital Kaifeng before the 1040s. In 1044, Fu Bi, a prominent statesman from the mid-1040s to the late 1060s, used this expression and pointed out that Hebei was more significant than other provinces in the empire.[80] Bao Zheng made the same remark twice, in the mid-1040s when he acted as Hebei's Fiscal Commissioner and in 1049 as the state's Financial Minister.[81] He emphasized that Hebei was the foundation to the survival (*cunwang* 存亡) of the Song state. In 1051 and 1053, Wang Ju 王舉 and Song Qi 宋祁 (998–1061) repeated the idea of a foundation, stressing that Hebei was the foundation of the imperial court.[82] The same view was shared by many in the late eleventh century. Wang Yansu, for instance, returned to the same expression at the court in 1085. Even Emperor Renzong issued an edict in 1055, proclaiming that "Hebei is the root of All-Under-Heaven," and deserved special institutional attention.[83]

When a catastrophic flood of the Yellow River destroyed the land of Hebei at the end of the eleventh century and again killed a substantial part of its population, many feared that the collapse of Hebei's environment and society would eventually bring down the state, so the significance of Hebei within the imperial system was further elevated. Chao Shuozhi (1059–1129), who repeatedly professed the significance of Hebei at the court during the last three decades of the Song period, evoked poet Du Mu's writings about Hebei in the early ninth century. In 1126, when the Jurchen were already invading Hebei and shortly before the downfall of the dynasty, Chao once again warned the last emperor about Hebei's critical role to the empire. "For those who rule All-Under-Heaven,"

[80] *XCB*, 153: 3729–3730.
[81] *XSBGZY*, 10: 1. *XCB*, 166: 3991–3995.
[82] *XCB*, 171: 4090 and 174: 4194.
[83] *XCB*, 181: 4370.

he remarked, "they can acquire All-Under-Heaven as long as they own Hebei; once losing Hebei, they will invariably lose All-Under-Heaven."[84]

Clearly, despite the state's painstaking efforts to appropriate Hebei, this frontier land did not assume a subordinate role in the imperial system and serve the state as an obedient, dutiful periphery. It turned into a remarkable player of the imperial history of the Song state, acting both as a trouble-taker whom the state sacrificed to the ferocious Yellow River and as a troublemaker who, while joining force with the Yellow River, increasingly threatened the state's stability. This double-faced Hebei was not the same Hebei as in the Tang Dynasty or in the tenth century. Chao Shuozhi and Du Mu, alive three hundred years apart, were concerned about two different sets of issues. The old Hebei during the Tang–Five Dynasties challenged the imperial state as a rival; its weapons included its sturdy economy, strong local military, powerful political-military leaders, and ambition for independence. The post-1048 Hebei, however, corrupted and dissolved the state slowly from within; its internal environmental and socio-economic disease caused the state to implode before external shocks (like the Jurchen armies) arrived. Ironically, the present book shows that this new, sickly Hebei was the unexpected product of the Song state's centralizing efforts to eliminate the old, powerful, and self-reliant Hebei that commenced with the start of the dynasty. It was certainly a consequence of the "hydraulic mode of consumption" that drove the state's unsuccessful management of the Yellow River–Hebei environmental complex.

---

[84] "Jingkang yuannian shangzhao fengshi [Presenting the memorial to discuss affairs in the first year of Jingkang (1126)]," *SSWJ*, 2: 4a.

8

Land and Water

A Thousand Years of Environmental Trauma

Standing on the Yellow River delta at the turn of the twelfth century, one heard the roaring of water, the cry of hungry mouths, and the crash of buildings collapsing from afar. Homeless women and men gathered where levees rose and fell; corpses were half buried in the mud. Junks and carts careened about, bringing in famine relief and shipping out emigrants and their suffering. Officials wielded whips to extract minimal taxes that had to be squeezed from the already impoverished land. Time and time again, imperial edicts came down to initiate titanic hydraulic projects, only to call them off a few days later. Chained and bent down to the riverbanks, hundreds of thousands of laborers arranged mud and stones to block the surging waters. Much had happened during the eighty-year-long environmental drama, which had shaped the governance of the imperial state, regulated the usage of the empire's resources, and profoundly affected the lives of people across north China, along with their livelihoods.

Various non-human environmental entities that were indigenous to the Hebei Plain were shaken and destabilized by the dramatic changes. They, like the men and women of Hebei, had to deal with the reality that their homeland had become the Yellow River's delta and flooding ground. Not only did they have to reconfigure their positions and relations to each other in the newly formed Yellow River–Hebei environmental complex, but they also had to confront interventions from the activist state and allow the "hydraulic mode of consumption" to take heavy tolls from them. What did the earth see, when its body was carved apart

An early version of this chapter appears in an article published by *Harvard Journal of Asiatic Studies*, see Zhang (2009: 1–36).

by the river's violent flows? What did waters experience, given that they usually moved according to gravity and hydrological dynamics, but were now redirected and reshaped by overwhelming environmental upheavals? How about soil that was covered in water, unable to breathe air and losing its fertility? How about trees and bushes that had once grown wild and were now, under the state's instructions, chopped down to build levees?

The eighty years between 1048 and 1128 constituted a brief moment in the environmental and geological history of both the Hebei Plain and the Yellow River. Yet, the environmental drama and its repetitive episodes hit the land and water so intensely that they created tremendous physical trauma that affected the region for many years to come. The land and water kept their memories not through words, but by leaving marks on the surface and in the depth of the earth: some appeared and vanished quickly like flood waters, while some lasted over a thousand years, like drifting sand and denuded mountains.

8.1 Frantic Streams and the Scarred Earth

As the Yellow River crashed into Hebei in 1048, it encountered multiple local waters, such as the Zhang, the Hulu, the Hutuo, the Juma, and their tributaries, along with the Yuhe Canal and various lakes and ponds. The natural rivers all originated from the Taihang Mountains in western Hebei. Tending eastward or northeastward, they coursed through low-lying central Hebei and the marshy land around modern Tianjin in the northeast. At various points they intersected and converged with each other, before merging into the Juma River that served as the Song-Liao boundary river. There, all the waters gathered, including that of the Yuhe Canal, to discharge into the Bohai Gulf. For a millennium before 1048, these streams collected water resources and distributed them over the majority of the Hebei Plain. Sharing a similar movement pattern, and using a small section of the northeastern coast as their common estuary, they had long formed a giant Hai River system, as the indigenous river system, to dominate the waterscape of Hebei.[1] Much of the Hebei Plain was the alluvial fan – the geological product – of this river system. For a millennium, this river system had not intersected with the 700-kilometer-long lower reaches of the Yellow River. Largely independent, its existence and functioning had not been affected by the Yellow River's flooding events and its hydrological forces.

[1] For the Hai River system, see Zhang (1993) and Zou (1993: 118–147).

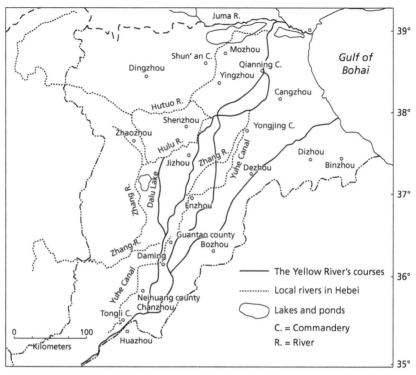

ILLUSTRATION 13. Hebei's Water Systems, 1048–1128

In 1048, the Yellow River invaded. It took over some sections of the Yuhe Canal, cut through the Zhang and the Hulu, ran over the ponds and small local canals that connected with the Hutuo, intersected with their tributaries, and then poured into the Juma River.[2] With its every movement, such as floods and course shifts in 1056, 1060, 1068, 1077–1078, 1081, 1099, and 1108, the Yellow River spread its watery body widely across Hebei and pushed farther toward western Hebei where the local rivers originated. Every step of the expansion of the Yellow's water regime involved a violent encounter with the indigenous environmental entities. During the eighty years, the continuous attacks of this gigantic river crushed the relatively weak indigenous water system, destabilizing and reshaping each of its local streams.

The most immediate effect of the Yellow River's arrival was the dramatic increase in the water volume of the local streams. We do not need

---

[2] *SS*, 95: 2351 and 2364. *XCB*, 313: 7588.

much knowledge about hydrology to imagine the increase in the sheer amount of water over the land of Hebei. Wherever the Yellow River extended, its torrents injected into the local streams and caused them to surge. Unable to accommodate excessive water, those small streams saw their waters burst through banks to overflow the surrounding areas. Hence, many local streams ended their state of stability, and as a result, we find in historical records a substantial rise in the number of flood outbreaks all over Hebei.[3]

What made the situation worse was the redistribution of the massive amount of water. Hebei was unable to accommodate or process so much water. Much of it could not run off into the ocean, because the invasion of the Yellow River destroyed the waterways of many local streams, making their channels dysfunctional. Neither could the water drain off through underground water currents, because Hebei's ground was low and flat; its low gradient slowed down the movement of water. At five to fifteen meters above sea level from central Hebei to its eastern coastal area, and with the underground water table only a few meters underneath, the land surface saw the downward infiltration of surface water and the rapid rise of underground water. As the two water bodies became interconnected and exchanged with each other, neither was able to move around and drain off. Consequently, the land was sandwiched between these waters. This phenomenon was evident to human eyes in the eleventh century. Along the strip of land at the foot of the Taihang Mountains, where the highland met the lowland, a series of water catchments came into being. Water coming down from the mountainous area failed to keep flowing eastward or filter through the ground, but instead accumulated and stagnated in large volumes. It formed a swampy landscape in places like Shenzhou, Zhaozhou, Yingzhou, and Mozhou in western and central Hebei.[4]

Not only did the Yellow River introduce excessive water, it also turned Hebei's local streams into either displaced environmental refugees or its subordinate waterways. The reconfiguration of the hydrological relationship between the two river systems was chaotic and almost always led to the defeat of the indigenous one. Many local channels were destroyed by the Yellow River's floods or rapidly silted up by its sediments; losing channels, their waters were forced to surge in various directions. Other rivers were now occupied by the Yellow River's torrents and surrendered their

3 SS, 95: 2352. XCB, 333: 8015; 323: 7790; and 324: 7810.
4 XCB, 421: 10204.

riverbeds and channels as the Yellow's tributaries to carry the Yellow's muddy water. No longer their own entities, they became components of the Yellow's hydrological system. The local streams' loss of hydrological independence, together with the loss of their hydraulic and navigational functions to serve human needs, became a serious concern to eleventh-century hydrocrats. One of the Water Conservancy's agendas was to release the local streams from the Yellow River's destructive dominance and help them restore their own waterways. But often, the hydrocrats had to accept the reality that the local streams could not cross the central plain of Hebei and travel eastward to reach the ocean without encountering the northward-flowing Yellow River and being overwhelmed by it. Given this geographical and hydrological reality, the hydrocrats had no choice but to create hydraulic works that directed the local streams to enter the Yellow River, and to be overtaken by the latter.[5]

The Yellow's water system and much of Hebei's home river system had now merged into one system – not yet a configured, harmonious one, but instead a chaotic, unruly one that was destructive to both human society and environmental conditions. Many local streams acted as the tentacles and agents of the Yellow's ruthless flooding machine; through them, the Yellow's flooding disasters were magnified and carried down to the local level. People in western Hebei, who were not directly attacked by the Yellow River's torrents, suffered the disastrous impact indirectly through their turbulent local rivers. The Yuhe Canal, for instance, flowed through the walled city of Daming. Due to this spatial setting, when the Yellow River took over parts of the canal's channel, its floods surged straight into the city through the vein of the canal. In 1099, a Yellow-Yuhe joint flood nearly destroyed the city. The disaster prompted the government to block the Yuhe and move its channel outside the city – at the cost of giving up the canal's socio-economic functions – in order to cut the canal off from the Yellow River.[6]

Even worse than the excessive water, the Yellow River brought about another negative impact on the local streams: heavy silt. Modern researchers have considered the eleventh century to be a period when the Yellow River carried one of its heaviest loads of silt. According to their estimates, the river carried and deposited so much sediments that it pushed the river mouth forward and Hebei's coastal line toward the

---

[5] *QSW*, 2624: 10–11.
[6] *QSW*, 2831: 158 and 2016: 15.

ocean 333 meters each year over the course of that century.[7] As a considerable portion of the silt built up new land along the ocean, a great amount of it was carried by both the Yellow's own stream and the local streams to spread and deposit over the Hebei Plain. The geographical features of the Hebei Plain certainly did not help deal with siltage. Its flat, low terrain slowed down the currents and encouraged silt to deposit. Hence, in 1110 when the river burst through its banks in southern Hebei, within merely a year, the flooding water had deposited at the rupture site a layer of sediments that stood higher than one meter.[8] Hebei's local rivers became heavier and muddier, their channels narrowed, and their flows were constantly choked by silt. The Zhang River, for instance, due to the heavy siltage, became vulnerable to environmental triggers such as a heavy rainfall; it flooded more often than in the past, especially in the 1070s.[9]

The hydrocrats in the Song period understood that it was the excess of silt, rather than just the excess of water, that made controlling the Yellow River a nearly impossible task. They tried to tackle the problem with innovative methods, such as trying to dredge the river and remove the sediments. In the 1070s, the reformist government promoted devices like the "iron dragon-claw" (*tielongzhua* 鐵龍爪) and the "river-clearing harrow" (*junchuanpa* 浚川耙) to dig out sediments. Yet, the devices were too small and powerless to combat the massive amount of sediments and high speed of siltation.[10] So the state's hydraulic projects largely had to rely on conventional solutions, like constructing extensive high dykes.

However, the dykes were fragile. They were built of wooden fascine, stone, sand, and mud, rather than the concrete or steel of modern dykes. As historical events had proven again and again, a small breach in a dyke would easily provoke a bank rupture, which would lead to a massive flood and even a shift in the river's course. In 1077, for instance, a bank rupture caused the entire Yellow River to shift southward into Henan, and terminated the river's northern course. In situations like this, not only was there a catastrophic flood, but the event also left behind an enormous deposit of sediments, both in the abandoned northern course and at the site of the bank rupture. Barely half a year after the event, the northern channel was filled up with sediments. When the state maneuvered half a million laborers to push the river's flow back to the north, the flow

[7] Xu (1995: 32–40).
[8] *SS*, 93: 2310.
[9] *SS*, 95: 2351.
[10] *SS*, 92: 2282–2283. *XCB*, 278: 6800. For the technical aspects of these devices, see Needham et al. (1971: 335–336) and Flessel (1974: 63–66).

could no longer find its previous channel and had to carve out a new course. Similar things happened to the local streams. After the Yellow River temporarily retreated from Hebei in 1077 and released the local rivers from its control, many of the rivers could not recover their old courses, which had been ruined by the Yellow's silt. As contemporaries observed in the mid-1070s, the Small Zhang 小漳 River and the Sha River in southwestern Hebei, for instance, had already become too silted to carry water, and their courses had almost dried up.[11]

The fate of the Yuhe Canal is a good example to demonstrate the harm inflicted by the Yellow River's silt. Stretching nearly five hundred kilometers from the plain's southern end to its northeastern corner, the canal had functioned as the imperial state's lifeline. It linked the central plain of north China with the empire's most strategic frontier, and fed the latter with massive military supplies. As analyzed in the previous chapter, Hebei's success in obtaining supplies depended on various factors, including the availability of grain and other materials in southern parts of China, south China's willingness to share resources, and the imperial state's capacity to gather them. It certainly depended on the conditions of transportation that delivered the supplies. Without the Yuhe Canal, the state would find it difficult to ship the supplies to support its giant armies across Hebei. In 1048, the Yellow River cut through the canal and took over a part of its course. After that, the canal not only overflowed more frequently than before, but its waterbed also silted up quickly. By 1076, a stretch of fifty-five kilometers (38,000 paces) of its upper reaches in southwestern Hebei was reportedly heavily silted up.[12] In southern Hebei, parts of its waterbed rose so high that boats could not pass through.[13] After another decade, the majority of the canal was fully blocked by sediments, and had become "entirely useless for shipping things."[14] Having tried unsuccessfully to dredge the canal and remove its sediments with human labor, the Song government and Hebei's residents had to accept the canal's decline as irreversible. After 1128, when the Northern Song Dynasty fell and the Yellow River shifted out of Hebei, the silt-loaded Yuhe Canal was abandoned. Slowly, farmers moved near it and turned its dry waterbed into agricultural fields.[15]

[11] *SS*, 95: 2352, 2354, and 2356.
[12] *SS*, 95: 2356.
[13] *XCB*, 278: 6810.
[14] *XCB*, 393: 9583.
[15] *QSW*, 3050: 375.

The fall of Hebei's major water transport route seriously impeded the delivery of grain and other supplies within Hebei. As a result, grain transport had to rely primarily on more laborious and costly overland means, like draught animals and carts. We should also note that the canal's fall brought down the entire Hebei economy, and in particular caused the decline of market towns and cities along the waterway. Bereft of the benefits of water transportation, the northern capital Daming declined both economically and ecologically.[16] Part of its walled city was gradually buried beneath the Yellow River's silt, and the once glamorous city lost its prosperity beginning in the late eleventh century.[17] The canal itself was not repaired until two centuries later, when the Mongol's Yuan Dynasty established Beijing in the farther north as its capital, and it had to restore the canal as its main route for shipping wealth from south China.

In addition to the streams, other kinds of water, like lakes and ponds, also suffered dramatic attacks from the Yellow River and underwent phenomenal transformation.[18] Take Lake Dalu 大陸 in western Hebei. The largest of the ancient lakes on the Hebei Plain, Lake Dalu had a circumference of about forty kilometers at the end of the tenth century, covering an area of 127 square kilometers.[19] When the Yellow River shifted its course to western Hebei in 1108, it infiltrated the lake and caused a substantial part of the lake to silt up. As the bottom of the lake and the water level rose due to the drastic sedimentation, the water overflowed toward neighboring lowlands and joined small swamps nearby to form another small lake, as Lake Dalu itself shrank noticeably. By the early nineteenth century, this major lake in Hebei had become a small pool, and it eventually vanished in the early twentieth century.[20] The environmental trauma the lake suffered from the Yellow River in the Song period paved the way for its long-term deterioration. We do not know much about other natural lakes in Hebei, but the frontier ponds that the state and Hebei's military maintained clearly underwent great transformation after 1048. As we have discussed in Chapter 5, due to the infiltration of the Yellow's muddy waters, many ponds became shallow and even dried

[16] Zou Hao's plead with the court in order to revive the Yuhe Canal, *QSW*, 2831: 158–159.
[17] Li (1990: 246).
[18] According to Zou Yilin (1987: 25–39), lakes on the North China Plain had changed very little from the sixth to the tenth century; it is in the eleventh century that they began to undergo remarkable changes.
[19] *Taiping huanyu ji*, 59: 11a.
[20] Zou (1987: 32) and Zhang (2006: 404).

up in the 1070s and 1080s.[21] The river's inflow might also have posed similar threats to the extensive underground tunnels that Hebei's military constructed for military defense in northern Hebei.[22]

Over eighty years, the Yellow River forced a new landscape on Hebei with two tools, water and silt. The two phenomena they each caused – respectively, flooding and siltation – did not happen separately. Rather, they took place next to each other both in terms of space and in terms of time: sporadic pockets of dry sediments emerged in the middle of large swaths of water, or once-hidden sandy landscapes appeared soon after a flood retreated. In various locales, the human suffering from flooding in one year soon switched to an experience of drought and the dry earth in the following year. It is hard for us to visualize the entangled coexistence of the two phenomena, which seem in opposition: excessive water does not usually stand alongside excessive dryness of the land; they should remedy or counteract one another. Yet during the dramatic environmental upheavals between 1048 and 1128, they attacked Hebei hand in hand, wounding the face and the depth of the earth simultaneously. In the following pages, we will discuss these two phenomena in greater detail, and explore their environmental and socio-economic implications.

8.2   Too Much Water – Soil Salinization

The excessive water in the Hebei Plain contributed to an unexpected environmental consequence, namely the salinization of Hebei's soil.[23] As explained earlier, water had difficulty draining off due to Hebei's flat terrain and low elevation; it left the land soaked for long periods of time. The saline content and various minerals originally suspended in the underground water were now able to move vertically through the layers of soil. Over time, as the surface water evaporated and the underground water receded, the land dried up. But its soil was no longer the same as in the past: salt, alkalis, and other mineral materials remained inside to change the soil's chemical composition, texture, and appearance.

Before the Yellow River shifted into Hebei, parts of the region had already suffered from soil salinization. Back in the Tang Dynasty, some local officials pursued artificial irrigation, and their "excessive

---

[21] *XCB*, 248: 6053; 396: 9661; and 399: 9733. *SS*, 95: 2362.
[22] Hebei's underground tunnels are discussed in Chapter 2.
[23] The concept of salinization used here follows Edmonds (1994: 124–125).

exploitation of water benefits" and inappropriate methods worsened the poor drainage in the region.[24] The consequential soil salinization turned out to defeat the irrigation's agricultural purpose and interfered with crop cultivation. After the late tenth century, the construction of extensive ponds in northern Hebei and the maintenance of the Yuhe and other small canals together increased the volume of stagnant water on the plain. The invasion of the Yellow River only made the situation worse.

People who visited central and northern Hebei often commented on the poor quality of the soil. Except for supporting the growth of "saline grass" (*yancao* 鹽草), the salinized and alkalinized soil killed most plants. According to Chao Shuozhi, at the end of the eleventh century, "in places where river waters stagnate, no single inch of grass is able to grow. Instead, white alkalis spread everywhere."[25] For people who lived in such areas, farming no longer made sense.[26] They had to change their livelihood, and some switched to exploiting the brine itself. Instead of farming, they extracted salt from the soil and earned a subsistence living from trading the "earthen salt."[27] Even the imperial state had to accept the unfortunate reality that it could not tax these impoverished people based on their agricultural activities. It had no choice but to permit their salt production and trade, and to tax such activities instead – a policy unique to Hebei, in contrast to the strict state monopoly on salt production and trade in other parts of China.[28]

Here, we must bring in Wang Anshi's reforms again. The damage to the soil and the land's failure to produce grain and taxes forced the reformist government to seek technological solutions, hoping to remedy and enrich the soil. In the 1070s and early 1080s, Wang and his fellow reformists enthusiastically advocated a "silting-field measure" (*yutian fa* 淤田法), which would channel the muddy waters from the Yellow River and other local rivers over arable fields. They expected the river silt to deposit there and create on the salty earth a new layer of fertile topsoil.[29] This measure, which was intended to transform the harmful silt into something beneficial and economically productive, was not a new idea. It was practiced in other parts of the world and proven successful on some rivers' flood plains, such as on the Nile in ancient Egypt. Some

---

[24] *XCB*, 159: 3853. See Zou (2005: 47–56).
[25] "Shuowen," *SSWJ*, 2: 29a–b.
[26] *QSW*, 689: 284.
[27] *QSW*, 985: 33 and 2036: 348.
[28] For salt production during the Song, see Guo (1990).
[29] *XCB*, 262: 6400; 263: 6443; and 290: 7085.

modern Chinese historians hold a positive opinion about the measure in eleventh-century north China and believe that it did improve the land quality, just as the Nile did to the land of ancient Egypt.[30] I suggest, however, that although it is theoretically plausible, the "silting-field measure" was problematic and even harmful to much of Hebei.

First, the practicality of the measure depended on whether or not the hydraulic teams and workers could control the direction, scale, and intensity of the flood. The successful story of the ancient Egyptians had to do with the regularity and predictability of the Nile's seasonal floods. In Hebei, once a flood was triggered, it could hardly be contained or stopped; as the previous chapters have made clear, Song hydrocrats failed in most of their flood control attempts. To what extent, then, could they manage the scale of the floods for land-enriching purposes and end the flooding when the land had taken enough water? We should also note that in many places where the measure was applied during the reformist era, the land was inhabited by dense agricultural communities. Without flood-control preparation and capability, any man-made flood and consequential siltation of fields would risk inflicting great damage on existent human settlements, irrespective of whether it did any good. Indeed, in the 1070s and 1080s, Wang Anshi's critics often criticized the damage brought about by the silting-field measure.[31]

The second problem with the measure was, again, the issue of drainage. In agricultural terms, as agricultural historian Francesca Bray has pointed out, drainage "was more important than moisture conservation."[32] By the 1070s, Hebei already suffered from too much water; any additional water introduced by the silting-field measure would only make the burden heavier. The measure might work, but only if the water could successfully be drained off to prevent further salinization of the soil – a phenomenon modern scientists name the "secondary, derivative salinization and alkalinization (*cisheng yanjianhua* 次生鹽鹼化)" that is usually produced by inappropriate irrigation activities.

[30] Comparing to positive cases in ancient Egypt and western parts of Hebei in the third–fourth centuries BCE, some Song historians analogically believe that the silting-field practice in Northern-Song China benefited soil fertility. See Higashi (1970: 434–479), Qi (1987: 79–83), and Han (1993: 44–47). However, by comparing the irrigation practices in ancient Egypt and Mesopotamia, Joachim Radkau (2008: 93) points out that, while Egypt benefited greatly from floods and their sediments, Mesopotamia suffered from poor drainage conditions and resulted in serious environmental degradation. The same technology may lead to opposite results in different environmental settings.
[31] *XCB*, 249: 6073. Su Shi, *Dongpo zhilin*, 4: 24.
[32] Bray (1984: 138).

Let us understand this disastrous phenomenon by looking at a comparative case, which comes from Henan in the 1950s. There, newly established people's communes sought to irrigate the dry land to improve its fertility, and did so by releasing the Yellow River onto the land. The consequences were quite contrary to their intent. The floods induced massive waterlogging as well as soil salinization and alkalinization. In Henan, saline-alkaline fields increased from 2.08 million *mu* to 4.96 million *mu* between 1952 and 1962. In one leading irrigation commune, which practiced the irrigation most intensely, the salinized and alkalinized fields increased from 100 thousand *mu* to 280 thousand *mu*.[33] Rather than improving land fertility, such practices caused agricultural production to drop. Even with good intentions, people's scientific ignorance caused tremendous harm to the environment and to themselves. It took Henan several decades to drain the water away and to rid the soil of its saline contents, and the hard work still continues today. Given this case, we may wonder how much harm Wang Anshi's "silting-field measure" might have inflicted. No historical records show that the Song reformists paid specific attention to drainage, so I am doubtful of the success of the measure in improving the soil quality.

The third problem with the land-enriching measure had to do with the quality of silt that the reformists expected to use to create topsoil. In the case of 1950s Henan, by 1959, the floods had relocated half a billion tons of silt from the Yellow River to the land in the communes, causing massive destruction to arable fields, waterways, and dams. Why is it that this silt did not in fact turn into fertile soil, as the communes' people expected or as Wang Anshi had wished in the eleventh century? The answer is that there is a huge difference between silt and soil suitable for cultivation. According to soil-core analyses, the Yellow River's silt consists of large rocky debris, fine sand, and mud; only the last contains abundant organic matter and is physically and chemically able to transform into arable soil.[34] The soil's maturation process – the transformation of the

---

[33] Shao (1991: 218–219).

[34] Hydrologists have conducted enormous scientific research on the modern Yellow River. Focusing on different sections of the river in various periods, the results that they have achieved vary. Some general conclusions have emerged to help us understand the circumstances of the river in the Northern Song. For example, Han Peng and Ni Jinren (2001) and Zhang Xiaohua et al. (1999) show that when the river flows smoothly, heavy coarse matter of the silt deposits quickly on the riverbed, while fine matter suspends in the current and deposits slowly; as the water flow slows down and tends to evaporate, the suspending fine sand deposits on the surface to generate a layer of smooth and fertile topsoil. But when the river surges, scours, and breached its banks, the heavy coarse

clayey mud and fine sand into something cultivable – is slow, and it takes place only under favorable conditions, such as certain temperature and humidity. This happens over the course of decades or centuries, not in the few years that the Song reformists and the people's communes expected. Meanwhile, in the eleventh and twelfth centuries, river overflows, bank ruptures, and floods occurred frequently. These events tore apart rocks, trees, fascines, and buildings, and threw all of these materials into the river's torrents to become parts of its silt. Hence, the Yellow River did not bring about only smooth mud and fine sand that the simple tools of medieval farmers were able to cope with. It also brought about a mixture of materials including rocks and stones that iron ploughs and hands could not process into cultivable soil. Perhaps quite in contrast to what Wang Anshi and his hydrocrats wished to see, the new topsoil created by the soil-enriching measure was a coarse, raw earth hardly useful for agricultural practices.[35]

Moreover, even fine, smooth silt offers limited fertility. In the eleventh century, farmers sometimes cultivated the river's abandoned dry riverbeds, or the silted land after the retreat of a river flood, or even dangerous shores within the river's dykes, as we saw in Chapter 6. Occasionally, historical records suggest that such silted land was fertile; people strived to own it and even took lawsuits to local governments to dispute the ownership of such land.[36] The state also encouraged Hebei refugees to colonize the empty land that the rivers had already silted over. Yet, does this kind of information justify the effectiveness of Wang Anshi's land-enriching measure? In the *Standard History of the Song Dynasty*, the fourteenth-century compilers included the following passage:

After the [Yellow River's] water recedes, sediments are a fertile glutinous soil in the summer. It then turns into a yellowish dead soil (*huangmietu* 黃滅土) in the early autumn; it is quite loose [in texture]. Later, it turns into a whitish dead soil (*baimietu* 白滅土) in the late autumn. After the first frost, it becomes sand completely.[37]

matter is stirred up by the currents and deposits on the land surface to create a layer of coarse and less fertile topsoil.

[35] Although the silting-field measure was practiced in Hebei, reports about evident land improvement were not from Hebei, but from Henan where people used water from the Bian River, which enjoyed different hydrological characteristics and provided different types of silt. For more discussion on the silting-field measure in Hebei and Henan, see Zhang (2009).

[36] *SHY,* "Shihuo," 1: 27a and 63: 183a–b. *XCB,* 450: 10821 and 518: 12337. *Jilei ji,* 62: 3b, 918.

[37] *SS,* 91: 2265. For a detailed interpretation of this text, see Zhang (2009: 28–29).

This rare account most likely came from some eleventh-century documents, which were available to the fourteenth-century historians but are no longer extant today. It perfectly describes the changing nature of the river's silt over seasons, as the water content in the silt evaporates and its fertility decreases. It suggests that the silt-covered land retained organic nutrients for a short period of time; it might support one or two good harvests. But as the water and organic contents filtered out, land productivity fell rather quickly as well.

As some eleventh-century contemporaries noticed, farmers who planted wheat on the silt-covered land could "barely obtain one harvest to relieve their poverty."[38] They did not get rich from such peculiar land. I suspect that it might have been a sensible survival strategy for Hebei refugees to produce basic food supplies by exploiting the sediments newly deposited on the land. There, they relied on the sediments' limited, quickly fading fertility, and conducted a kind of nomadic shifting farming – cultivating a patch of land, producing a harvest, and then abandoning the nutrient-depleted land to move to a new place. Every cycle of this kind of farming left behind a layer of dry, nutrient-deficit sand. Hence, the siltcovered land did not naturally or quickly turn into mature, cultivable soil to foster the sedentary, long-term farming that Wang Anshi and his fellow reformists pursued. In Yingzhou in central Hebei, for instance, after the Yellow River flooded there repeatedly between 1048 and 1128, the land was devastated rather than improved by the heavy silt the river left behind. By the mid-twelfth century, after the river had retreated from that area for a couple of decades, the local soil was judged to still be sterile.[39]

The "silting-field measure" that Wang Anshi's government promoted, at least in the Yellow River–Hebei environmental complex, did not reverse the salinized, alkalinized conditions of the soil. It failed to improve Hebei's land productivity in general.[40] The situation can be contemplated along with James C. Scott's investigation of "how certain schemes to improve the human condition have failed." To Scott, high-modernist projects that many modern states pursued in recent centuries were founded on "formal, deductive, epistemic knowledge"; they failed because of their leaders' ignorance and dismissal of practical, local knowledge.[41] Similarly, in the case of the eleventh-century Hebei, the state-sponsored land enriching

---

[38] *XCB*, 374: 9078.
[39] *Jin shi*, 73: 1683.
[40] *XCB*, 263: 6440 and 265: 6499.
[41] Scott (1998: 6).

measure was not grounded in an everyday, practical understanding of material environmental conditions. Living with constantly changing conditions, people developed practical knowledge about their land and soil, which led them to give up farming on the briny land and to conduct subsistence, nomadic farming on river sediments. Without such practical knowledge, Wang Anshi and his fellow reformists pursued something theoretically plausible, yet too idealistic to be realized. Not only was the land not enriched by the river silt artificially applied over its surface, but the land-enriching measure might have expedited the soil's deterioration, especially its sandification, as we shall see in the next few pages.

8.3   Too Much Silt – Soil Sandification

Wang Anshi and his contemporaries did not expect, and modern historians of the Song period do not expect to find, the expansion of sandy land in Hebei over a centuries-long process triggered by the Yellow River's dominance of Hebei from 1048 to 1128.[42]

According to the passage in the *Standard History of the Song Dynasty* that I quoted in the previous pages, the river's silt ended up as sand after undergoing an annual cycle of physical, and perhaps chemical, changes.[43] In his hydraulic treatise, preserved in the Yuan Dynasty "General Discussion on the Yellow River Hydraulics," Shen Li 沈立, a hydrocrat who personally worked in Hebei to tame the Yellow River shortly after the river shifted into Hebei in 1048, offered a more detailed description of the changes to the silt.[44] He described the process of the silt's transformation into different types of soil, which he classified according to their compositions and colors. Among various types was one classified as "sand," including subcategories like "active sand," "floating sand," and "running sand." "These three kinds," Shen commented, "are active and movable, so it is hard to succeed [in building flood-control facilities on top of them]." Such sandy land lacked nutrients and could hardly

---

[42] Muscolino (2015: 184–190) discusses the changes to soil caused by Yellow River sedimentation after the 1938 flood. Without scientific tests, we cannot assume that the 1938 flood's effects on Henan's soil were exactly same as the river's effects to Hebei's soil during 1048–1128. But the former supplies an analogous reference that helps us visualize the kind of changes that might have happened nine centuries ago.

[43] The passage does not specify if all the changes took place in a single year, but its context, especially its indication for a temporal subsequence gives a strong hint that these changes took place within a year.

[44] For an introduction of Shen Li and his hydraulic treatise that was compiled as *Hetang tongyi* by Shakeshen in the Yuan Dynasty, see Zhang (2009: 25–30).

support agricultural activities. In 1060, officials conducting land surveys in Hebei witnessed a cluster of "low-rank" fields, which barely generated any agricultural products and had little taxation value. These fields included "land covered by white salt and containing alkalis," "land containing salt and alkalis and encroached on by sand," and the worst of all, "land of dead sand unsuitable for cultivation."[45]

These descriptions of sandy soil have been verified by the results of modern hydrogeological research in southern Hebei. In the area where most of the eleventh-century bank ruptures and floods took place, the Yellow River left behind a stratum of abandoned riverbeds and sediments. These remains, now buried meters underneath the modern land surface, contain an enormous amount of floating and fine sand, rather than solid, muddy earth.[46] Although today we do not see much of this sand on the land surface, people in the eleventh century and many centuries afterward had to cope with it in their daily lives.

There is no way for us to measure the ratio of sandy matter to the entire volume of silt that the river deposited in Hebei. Some Song officials considered it rather high. In 1078, they claimed that silt accumulated on the shores after the river's floods had receded; 80 percent of the silt was sand, and only 20 percent was some kind of solid earth.[47] Due to the preponderance of sandy matter, it was difficult for the silted soil to preserve water and fertility as well as to prevent soil erosion. Farming there was virtually impossible.[48] In effect, after the water evaporated and the soil was exposed to the air, the land started undergoing serious sandification. By 1088, some fascine embankments in Hebei had been named "sand dykes," indicating that they were built either on or by sand, instead of on or by solid earth.[49] In the late eleventh century, Sima Guang sent a poem to his friends living in Huazhou, trying to envision their lives in southern Hebei by the water of the Yellow River. He wrote: "While sand and dust fly, misery and bleakness fill my eyes."[50]

[45] *QSW*, 689: 284.
[46] Xu (1988: 28–29).
[47] *SHY*, "Fangyu," 16: 12a.
[48] In effect, agricultural cultivation in medieval China often damaged vegetation and depleted soil fertility. Poorly planned farming resulted in the exposure of land surface, as Tan Qixiang and Shi Nianhai have convincingly argued for the Yellow River's middle reaches and Zhou Yilin for the river's lower reaches. See various articles in Tan (1986) and Shi (1981, 1988a).
[49] *XCB*, 421: 10205.
[50] *Liang Song mingxian xiaoji*, 45: 2a.

Sandification was a long-term process. It might not have become evident when much of the Hebei Plain was submerged by the Yellow River's frequent floods. But after the river moved out of Hebei in 1128 and the land was exposed to north China's semi-arid climate and started to dry up, sandification began to manifest in more obvious ways. The sandiness of Hebei became very evident in the twelfth century to people like Lou Yao 樓鑰 (1137–1213), a Southern Song 南宋 official. In 1169, on a journey through northern Henan and southern Hebei, Lou saw extensive sandbars standing beside and within the flow of the Yellow River.[51] Place names like "Sandy Inn (*shadian* 沙店)," which indicated the surrounding landscape, showed up in his writing. The circumstances became particularly striking when Lou arrived in Huazhou, a repeated victim of Yellow River floods beginning in the mid-tenth century, where he found "earthen hills lining up on both sides of the road, where the dust is extremely heavy and the air is so thick that one cannot see things even from a very short distance." The locals called that place the "Small Dust Cave" (*xiaohuidong* 小灰洞), a name that makes one suspect the existence of even dustier places down the road. After entering Xiangzhou in southwestern Hebei, Lou journeyed along a tributary of the Zhang River. That small stream was now named the "Little Yellow River," due to its heavy silt. By 1169, the sediments that the stream deposited had produced such a dry landscape that Lou had the illusion of "traveling in a desert." Other parts of Hebei underwent a similar land transformation. In Yingzhou in central Hebei, the land was considered sterile in the mid-twelfth century.[52] In the early thirteenth century, two-thirds of the 30,000 *mu* of arable fields in Shenze 深澤 County of central Hebei, which the state of the Jin Dynasty (1125–1234) granted for military colonization, were reported to have suffered from serious waterlogging, sand coverage, and soil salinization.[53]

The sandification process does not seem to have stopped in the next few centuries. It certainly struck foreigners who visited this part of China. In the late fifteenth century, a Korean visitor, Chhoe Pu, traveled to Hebei in the third lunar month in early spring.[54] In Dezhou in southern Hebei as well as in Tianjin and Beijing in the far north, he saw sand and dust blown about by strong winds; sandstorms were so strong that he could

---

[51] *Beixing rilu, shang:* 14–16.
[52] *Jin shi,* 73: 1683.
[53] *Jin shi,* 106: 2332.
[54] Makita (1959: 239–345).

hardly keep his eyes open. Chhoe seems to have encountered the kind of spring sandstorms that modern Chinese often experienced in Hebei in the post-2000 era. Upon his arrival in Tianjin, where Hebei's streams and the Yellow River converged and entered the sea between 1048 and 1128, Chhoe observed a barren land: "White sand extends without an end. In the wild there is no grass, and crops do not grow. Human settlements are sparse." Curious, he enquired about the land in other parts of Hebei. His Chinese interpreter replied: "In this part of north China, there is an abundance of sandy soil."

Half a century later, a Japanese monk named Sakugen traveled from south China to Hebei in the third and fourth lunar months of 1549, as Chhoe Pu did.[55] In southwestern Hebei, he came upon strong winds and a dull sky that was darkened by heavy sand and dust. His boat had to stop at various places in central Hebei because "fierce winds whirled up sand" and hindered the boat's movement. Similar descriptions are frequently found in Chinese writings of the following centuries.[56] A relatively comprehensive comment on the sandification problem was provided by Lan Dingyuan 藍鼎元 (1680–1733), an official of the Qing Dynasty who once directed the Yellow River hydraulic works. In his "Document on hydraulic benefits in Northern Zhili (central and northern Hebei)" in the 1720s, Lan wrote: "There is no solid earth in north China, and sand is eroded by running waters." For this reason, "river banks cannot be consolidated" by hydraulic works.[57] The banks of the Yellow River, in particular, consisted of floating sand and were unable to support levees.

The tremendous amount of silt transformed into loose, mobile sand; it became the source of sandstorms that have happened in this region since the eleventh century up to today.[58] Take the history of Guantao 館陶

---

[55] Makita (1954: 251–252).

[56] In Yingzhou of central Hebei, a survey in 1499 reported that among 1,120 *qing* (approximately 68.8 square kilometers) of fields, only 418 *qing* were arable, while the others were covered by sand and alkaline. See *Ming shilu leizuan*, 774. Also, see Gu Yanwu's comments on the land in Shandong and Hebei in *Tianxia junguo libing shu*, 2: 9b and 12b.

[57] "Lun Beizhi shuili shu [On water management in Northern Zhili]," in *Jifu tongzhi*, 91: 3652a.

[58] Traditionally, the rapid desertification on the Mongolian steppe or in the farther northwest is considered the major cause of sandstorms in present Beijing. However, "investigations [of the composition of sand and dust matter] suggest that the majority of wind-blown dust which can darken the sky in Beijing several times during the year comes from local river bed sand." See Edmonds (1994: 110), citing Song Jinxi, "Beijing diqu shawuzhi de zhongkuangwu chengfen, jiegoutezheng yu fengsha de shawuzhi laiyuan," *Zhongguo shamo* 1 (1987): 24–33.

County in southern Hebei. In the eleventh century, Guantao was penetrated by the northern courses of the Yellow River, the Yuhe Canal, and
the Zhang River. It was one of several places inside Hebei where various
waters converged and overflowed. In 1051, a bank rupture prompted
the construction of extensive embankments in this area, but despite this
attempt at protection, a flood once again inundated the county seat in
1071.[59] For the next ten years, the county seat was encircled by various
river courses and their embankments; in 1083, the town had to relocate to a higher ground to "escape the water."[60] Nevertheless, in 1103
the Yellow River's torrents inundated and engulfed the new county seat,
inflicting severe damage.[61] After the river shifted out of Hebei in 1128,
its riverbed and embankments inside Guantao stayed behind. Silted and
dry, these heavy sediments have since become a reminder of the county's
tragedy during the Song period.

For centuries, the sandy cover over Guantao's land had not appeared
as an eminent issue in any historical records. The situation changed in
1724, when Zhao Zhixi 趙知希, a new county magistrate, arrived and was
shocked by the desolate landscape. He reported that extensive stretches
of land were under the threat of sandstorms and had become unsuitable
for farming.[62] The source of the sandstorms was traced back to the dykes
built in the eleventh century; within the dykes was an abandoned riverbed
of the Song-period Yellow River, now a course not of water but of sand.
Asked when the sandstorms had begun, the locals of Guantao said they
had no knowledge. Their ignorance of past environmental changes suggests that the sandification dated back to a much earlier origin than the
eighteenth century. Year by year, loose sand was blown about by ferocious winds and spread toward neighboring areas to disastrous effects.

The sites of manors and buildings are buried by sand without a trace. Occasionally, a few buildings have survived to be identified, or their roofs have half
emerged from sand. Sand has spread over an area of more than ten *li*, undulating
up and down to form the shapes of hills and gullies.[63]

The area affected by annual sandstorms was not small, as "for over
seventy or eighty *li* from Zhangsha in the south to Xuedian in the north

[59] *XCB*, 170: 4096. *SS*, 92: 2281.
[60] *XCB*, 335: 8084.
[61] *SS*, 95: 2357.
[62] "Xiaoping shabo jianze ji [Report on sand's occupation of fields and tax reduction in
Xiaoping]," in *Guantao xianzhi*, 6: 303–310.
[63] "Shu Taoshan ji hou [Epilogue to the Prose of Tao Mountain]," in *Guantao xianzhi*, 2:
85–87.

the land is in a similar state."[64] The land survey showed that Guantao's sandy land amounted to no less than a thousand *qing*, approximately 61.4 square kilometers. Defeated by the sand and sandstorms, agricultural efforts often ended in naught. Many local farmers chose to abandon the desolate, sterile land and fled to look for a livelihood elsewhere, hence thinning out the local population.

Such long-lasting environmental and socio-economic tragedy was not unique to Guantao County; it happened in a fair number of places in Hebei. In Neihuang 內黄 County in southern Hebei, for instance, the sandy cover that came into being in the eleventh century remained strikingly visible to the eye in the twentieth century. Also, let us look at Daming County, the Song's northern capital. In its northeastern corner, shortly after the Yellow River turned south in 1128, the dykes along the abandoned riverbed disappeared, buried deeply under "widely diffuse yellow sand."[65] In the county's southeast corner, the river once burst through its banks and created an eastern course in 1060. Over the next few decades, the river kept depositing silt at the site of the bank rupture, which eventually accumulated to form multiple sand dunes, some standing more than ten meters high. Many of the dunes kept evolving and lasted until the twentieth century. For centuries, some of Daming's silt-turned sandy land was ploughed; farmers exploited the already impoverished earth for minimum harvests. Rather than preserving the sandy land to restore its water and nutrients or to cover it with long-lasting vegetation, agriculture depleted the land and exposed it to the open air, thus furthering its sandification process.

In the 1960s when the Communist government encouraged land reclamation to expand agriculture, the local government conducted a land survey in Daming, which finally recorded on paper the damage caused by sandification. Rising and falling and drifting in the wind, the giant sand bodies emitted sand and dust to provoke sandstorms. Just as destructive as those in Guantao County, the sandstorms attacked buildings and killed crops, causing the local economy to languish.[66] Once a vibrant, wealthy city in medieval China, Daming had become one of the poorest districts in Hebei in centuries. Its glory, together with Hebei's glory, had faded away as the sand continued to accumulate.

[64] "Xiaoping shabo jianze ji," in *Guantao xianzhi*, 6: 304.
[65] Shi (1981: 43).
[66] Wu et al. (2001: 18).

8.4   "The Taihang Mountains Are Denuded!"

As the environmental drama kept playing out in Hebei, the land was deeply scarred by turbulent streams, lagoons, and gullies. Drifting sand painted it with patches of brown and yellow, while salt and alkalis sparkled on it with a silvery white. These new elements emerged to participate in and complicate the drama of the Yellow River–Hebei environmental complex; altogether, they complicated the environmental circumstances inside Hebei. In the midst of such environmental tumult, we find things disappearing, such as human lives, crops they planted, animals they reared, boats they used to ship goods, and certainly the fertility of the land the human eyes were unable to see. Here, let us now take a look at the loss of another kind of things – the organic lives of trees, bushes, and grass – Hebei's vegetation in a general sense.

The Northern Song was a period of extraordinary deforestation in Hebei's history.[67] The rapid loss of trees and other kinds of plants was partly associated with people's daily consumption of firewood and building materials. It was also a consequence of the rapid growth of a non-agricultural economy in several small pockets in western Hebei; there, iron mining and smelting and ceramic production flourished. Such economic growth arrived with high energy costs; it drove Hebei's firewood consumption and deforestation to skyrocket. There was also another significant, yet less noticeable cause of the disappearance of vegetation: the hydraulic mode of consumption driven both by the Yellow River's repeated flooding and by the imperial state's unstoppable environmental management. To deal with the river disasters, the state-sponsored hydraulic works utilized a massive amount of trees, bushes, and grass. The usage of vegetative materials to build flood-control infrastructure, like embankments, led to the clear-cutting of both natural forests up in mountains and plants people cultivated in their fields and gardens.

During the tenth to twelfth centuries (and in fact, all the way through the nineteenth century as well), the hydraulic technology that the Chinese state employed for Yellow River flood control was rather simple. Its core technique was to erect embankments along the river. The embankments were constructed with a mixture of pounded earth, rocks, stones, and fascine rolls. This last item refers to large bundles of tree trunks,

---

[67] Several scholars point out the connection between wood consumption for hydraulic purposes and deforestation, such as Yoshioka (1978: 24–26), Menzies (1996: 644–659), and Jiang (1998: 42–50). But none of these studies have examined such connection in adequate details.

wooden sticks, bamboo strips, grass, reeds, and straw. After 1048, as the Yellow River created multiple courses in Hebei and destructed local waterways, the government and the ordinary people of Hebei had to build embankments to contain the problematic waters simultaneously. This meant the sheer quantity of vegetative materials collected and consumed inside Hebei for the hydraulic purposes had to multiply.

So how much vegetative material did a single fascine roll demand according to the Song hydraulic technology? Based on a description most likely written by Shen Li, the hydrocrat previously mentioned who supervised the Yellow River hydraulic works shortly after 1048, a fascine roll (*juansao* 卷埽) consisted of 1,100 bundles of wooden sticks, 2,625 bundles of grass, and 125 pieces of large timber, together amounting to 3,850 total units of raw materials.[68] This mass stood 31.2 meters long and 3.12 meters high, and had a volume of about 230 cubic meters. Hydraulic workers piled up multiple such fascine rolls to build a fascine site (*sao* 埽, a section of embankment) on the river. The size of the fascine site varied; one might stretch over a length from 312 meters to 1,560 meters, and stand at a height of 1–13.48 meters.[69] Depending on how long and how tall it was, the fascine site was comprised of tens or even hundreds of fascine rolls. A small embankment might include only ten fascine rolls and used up 38,500 units of wood and grass, altogether 2,300 cubic meters of vegetative materials. A very large embankment might use up to 770,000 units that when piled up formed a mass of 46,000 cubic meters. Given this information, we know that on average, an embankment in eleventh-century Hebei consumed 404,250 units of wood and grass.

When considering these strikingly large numbers, we must understand that they refer to only the materials found in the final, functioning embankments. Our sources suggest that during the construction process, more than half of the wooden sticks and grass would be washed away. Hence, a tremendous amount of materials was wasted and became invisible costs. In order for the hydraulic teams to construct an average-size embankment, they had to prepare approximately double the amount of materials, or 808,250 units of materials at a giant volume of 48,285 cubic meters.[70]

[68] *Hefang tongyi, shang*: 12–13.
[69] The notion "*sao*" originally refers to a fascine roll made with wood, straw, and stone materials to block a bank rupture; it is then used to mean the hydraulic site along the river where multiple fascine rolls were placed, laborers stationed, and raw materials stored.
[70] *SS*, 91: 2266.

This last number is the size of nearly twenty Olympic-sized swimming pools put together. But it refers to only one embankment. How many embankments of such an average size were built in Hebei between 1048 and 1128? The multiple courses of the Yellow River alone demanded multiple stretches of dykes, each 400–700 kilometers long; moreover, there were other rivers and other waterbodies to deal with. I have found no records of a precise number for the embankments in existence at any given moment during 1048–1128, but there must have been hundreds. The total material costs would have been mind-boggling.

We must remember that the fascine sites were not constructed once to last forever. Even the modern Three Gorges Dam, which was built by most advanced technology and construction materials in the present millennium, cannot be sustained permanently. According to some hydro-engineers, it can only promise a lifespan of stability for about a hundred years. As early as in 2003, before the completion of its construction, the Three Gorges Dam had already seen some minor fractures over its concrete surface. Made of wood and mud, the eleventh-century embankments wore out rapidly and were frequently torn apart by the Yellow River's torrents. Given their very short lifespan, they required constant maintenance and replacement. For instance, a massive flood in the summer of 1056 swept away in a single day the embankments that were constructed in eastern Hebei over the previous years. Beginning in the late tenth century, the maintenance and reconstruction of embankments became a daily task. Look at a rare inscription engraved on a stone incense burner in Huazhou by a lay Buddhist practitioner, some Mr. Zhang, in 1085. Zhang specified that in Huazhou a hydraulic site on the Yellow River's northern bank required constant maintenance. In 1082, eight rounds of renovation were done by using wood and grass; in 1083, three rounds of renovation used wood and grass and another five rounds used grass only; and in 1084, three rounds of renovation used wood and grass and another three rounds used grass only.[71]

In order to fulfill such constant hydraulic maintenance, the Song government established a set of regulations that commanded its hydraulic officials and regional civil officials to collect vegetative materials every year. As early as the end of the tenth century, over ten million bundles of materials were gathered annually and distributed to various fascine sites for their normal maintenance.[72] This amount continued to increase year

---

[71] "Yuanyou yuannian zhuangqiusi shixianglu [The stone incense burner in the Zhuangqiu Temple in the first year of Yuanyou (1986)]," *Huaxian xianzhi*, 6: 2252–2255b.

[72] *SS*, 91: 2265.

after year; the government could not suspend the hydraulic works so as to let the laborers go home or pause the extraction of raw materials. It was this routine, endless demand that made the collection of materials so burdensome, making it a compulsory part of the annual taxes on commoners throughout north China.[73] Taxpayers were compelled to chop down trees, cut bushes, and uproot grass all over north China. In a sense, without knowing the purpose of their actions, they continued to feed and fuel the hydraulic mode of consumption that was centered in Hebei.

Among the various materials needed, a considerable amount of lumber came from the northwestern part of the empire, in particular from the mountainous terrains of Shanxi and Shaanxi. According to Wen Ji 文洎 (died in 1037), who was charged with the transportation of lumber in the 1030s, trees felled in the northwest were packed up in one to two million bundles every year. They were then shipped via the Yellow River on a journey across several hundreds of kilometers, to arrive at downstream areas where they were loaded and distributed to various hydraulic sites.[74] The shipments increased to 3,760,000 bundles in 1029 and then sharply to 7,800,000 bundles in 1030. Compared to this "mountain lumber" that was hard to obtain, materials of smaller sizes such as bamboo, wooden sticks, and grass were easier to gather. These materials came from all over north China, and were collected year-round. All together, the quantity of the smaller vegetative materials might amount to several times that of the lumber.

After 1048, although various north-China regions continued to provide vegetative materials, Hebei overtook those regions as the nearest and most important provider of materials. The river floods, the focus of the state's hydraulic efforts, and the flood-control facilities had largely moved to Hebei. Along with them was the physical movement of vegetative materials; most no longer ended up in Henan, but were shipped to Hebei. Meanwhile, material production sites began to emerge in Hebei. The Taihang Mountains in western Hebei, for instance, began to supply an enormous amount of wood. Of the forty-seven major fascine sites whose names were recorded in Song documents between 1048 and 1128, all but four – that is, 90 percent – were located inside Hebei.[75] Assuming they were each of an average size (the volume of twenty Olympic-size

---

[73] *SHY*, "Shihuo," 140: 8b.
[74] *SHY*, "Fangyu," 14: 14b–15a. *QSW*, 2427: 229. *XCB*, 28: 633.
[75] The names of the fascine sites are collected from the "Monograph of Rivers and Canals," in *SS*, vols. 91–93.

swimming pools) according to Shen Li's hydraulic standards, we are envisioning a gigantic mass of wood and grass of the size of 940 swimming pools. This volume of materials spread along the river courses in Hebei. In reality, there were certainly more embankments than forty-seven; some were named and perhaps many were nameless. Over time, large embankments expanded until they were split into several sub-sites.[76] As the river developed multiple courses in the following decades, the embankments also multiplied. The local streams became chaotic as well, and necessitated more embankments and the corresponding consumption of materials. For example, in one case of repairs made to the banks of the Zhang River in the early 1070s, more than a hundred thousand pieces and bundles of elm and willow wood were logged seemingly overnight from southwestern Hebei.[77] Bringing together the Yellow River's embankments and countless small levees guarding the local streams and ponds, between 1048 and 1128, the entirety of Hebei's hydraulic infrastructure had collected and consumed a massive amount of vegetative materials, so large that it defies calculation.

All of the analysis above concerns the demands of routine hydraulic maintenance. In reality, the rivers and ponds flooded unexpectedly, and the emergencies required additional materials. The emergency consumption was contingent upon how critical the situation was. The annual provision of 10 million bundles that the government ordered to gather at the end of the tenth century was perhaps not enough to handle a single flooding event. After a catastrophic flood in 1019, the government reportedly used 16 million bundles of vegetative materials to fix the river bank's rupture over a time span of nine years.[78] The situation was even worse in 1048. The flood and shift of the river course alone prompted the government to acquire 18 million bundles.[79] During the 1056 incident, due to the miscalculation and poor management by the hydrocrats, one to two million bundles of materials were destroyed or washed away by the flood within a day.[80] Between 1077 and 1078, in order to return the southerly surging river to Hebei, within six months the government assembled nearly 13 million bundles of materials to block up the river's

---

[76] The number of fascine sites kept changing frequently. Some sites were abandoned after a river course eliminated, while some were renewed and multiplied as the river's threats became serious. For a detailed discussion, see Zhang (2009).
[77] *XCB*, 223: 5421.
[78] *XCB*, 105: 2455.
[79] Ouyang Xiu's comment, in *XCB*, 179: 4327.
[80] *Qingxian ji*, 8: 11a–b.

bank rupture.[81] In the late 1080s, the state promoted the hydraulic plan of "returning the river" to southeastern Hebei. The project alone anticipated a budget of 20 million bundles of raw materials; in 1089, the number rose to 30 million and even to 50 million.[82] The project was not carried out at full scale and was eventually dropped. Yet, even the primitive stage of its preparation in 1087 and 1088 had already necessitated the collection of 24 million bundles of materials.[83] This outrageous amount of materials was collected from all over north China and delivered to southern Hebei, where part of it was used in actual hydraulic works, and the rest was abandoned after the abolition of the project. The materials sat at the hydraulic sites and exposed to air and floodwaters; due to bureaucratic negligence, they gradually rotted away.[84] Hence, when trying to imagine the total volume of materials consumed in Hebei, we must not neglect the tremendous random costs and waste. A great deal of the trees and grass taken from the increasingly depleted landscape never actually served the hydraulic works or improved Hebei's environmental situation.

The above numbers are so large that it is hard to comprehend the impact of their consumption on the socio-economic life of the people, as well as on the physical environment. Where did these immense quantities of materials come from? From the point of view of ordinary people, the taxation for such materials imposed a tremendous burden. Usually, farmers paid their taxes with straw left from various crops, handing it in to the local government after harvests. A great portion of straw was then delivered to the hydraulic sites in the winter to prepare for dyke maintenance that usually took place in the early spring. If farmers had a bad harvest and failed to produce enough straw, which happened fairly often in the eleventh century, they would have to resort to other means to fulfill their tax obligations. They had to sacrifice their cash crops by chopping down their fruit and mulberry trees.[85] Alternatively, they were forced to buy the materials from markets, which were often dominated by speculative merchants who manipulated prices to maximize their profits.[86] Paying steep prices in order to fulfill their tax payments for straw placed many farming households under tremendous hardship.

[81] XCB, 289: 7072.
[82] XCB, 415: 10096; 416: 10113; 420: 10179; and 421: 10198.
[83] XCB, 415: 10087 and 416: 10110–10111.
[84] SHY, "Fangyu," 14: 14b–15a.
[85] SHY, "Shihuo," 1: 21b–22a.
[86] QSW, 2012: 108.

In Shaanxi in northwestern China in the 1060s, people were forced to go deep into mountains to log. Year after year, the more trees they felled, the farther the forests retreated, and the more difficult the job became. The hard work plus the difficulty in shipping the lumber drove many households into bankruptcy.[87] In Hebei, the External Executive of the Water Conservancy set up an annual quota of vegetative materials for every local district; the local government was responsible for producing and submitting enough to fulfill the quota. In Qinghe and Qingyang 清陽 counties in central Hebei, county governments appointed nineteen households as leaders to supervise other local families in collecting reeds and grass. These leading households were exhausted by the job; for six years they were unable to meet the quotas and owed 140,000 bundles of materials to the External Executive of the Water Conservancy.[88] They suffered enormous pressure and harassment from the External Executive and the local governments.

The soaring demand for prodigious amounts of raw materials became a tremendous financial burden on the state, too. Taxation did not provide all of the necessary materials; the government often had to use extra funds to purchase a large portion of them. It named this purchase the "harmonious purchase" (*hemai* 和買), meaning that peasants sold their materials to the government at their own will, rather than by force. As the demand for vegetative materials rose quickly, the government constantly went over budget and experienced financial stress. In 1093, for instance, the Fiscal Commissioner of Jingxi 京西 in western Henan reported that its district suffered from poor harvests and it failed to collect taxes, and at the same time, its military consumption was exceptionally high. It fell far behind in its payment of the "wood-grass money" that the Water Conservancy demanded in order to carry out the hydraulic works inside Hebei.[89] As regional governments failed to produce materials, the central government had to use state treasuries.[90] In the late eleventh century, expenses related to Yellow River flood control, including the purchase of vegetative materials, equalled the state's military and bureaucratic expenses, and became a major financial burden on the Song state.

The essential question remains: was the land of north China, especially in Hebei, able to produce the materials in such gigantic quantity, and in a

---

[87] *QSW*, 2387: 186.
[88] *QSW*, 1644: 248–249.
[89] *QSW*, 2703: 151.
[90] Lamouroux (1998) has offered a detailed account on government funds that were used for the Yellow River hydraulic works.

sustainable way? In 1088, the project to return the river to southeastern Hebei anticipated the use of 58,848,082 bundles of vegetative materials. Treating this as a critical project, the government spent three months promoting the "harmonious purchase" and levying taxes on ordinary people. As a result, it obtained only 49,000 bundles, merely 0.8 percent of what it needed; this severe lack of construction materials turned out to jeopardize the hydraulic project.[91] The failure in acquisition was not because hydrocrats and civil officials did not work hard enough, or did not coerce or terrorize ordinary people into compliance. Rather, it was due to the reality that the land was unable to produce so much wood and grass within such a short time.

While draining human society and the imperial state, the hydraulic mode of consumption rapidly depleted the vegetation across north China. As early as the 1030s, forests in the mountains of Henan, Shanxi, and Shaanxi had been "gradually thinned out."[92] In Hebei, the vast plain saw no hills or forests; human settlements were "far from mountains and valleys" where natural vegetation was relatively thick. Under tremendous pressure to make a living, Hebei people often "cut trees at the wrong time and destroyed what was created by Heaven and Earth."[93] In the worst scenarios, when the imperial state issued urgent orders for wood collection in the 1070s and 1080s, people were driven to sell their property to acquire materials from markets and went bankrupt, or they were forced to fell trees in graveyards that were meant to protect ancestral graves.[94] In some harsh winters, many could hardly get firewood to meet their basic needs.

Not surprisingly, natural forests in the Taihang Mountains on Hebei's western border increasingly came under the axe. As early as the late tenth century, the government set up timber workshops on the edge of the mountains to conduct logging. Most of the products went to the state-monopolized iron mining sites nearby as firewood or they were used as construction materials and for tools. After 1048, a considerable portion of the wood went to various hydraulic sites along the Yellow River to build embankments. Due to such large-scale, continuous wood collection, the Taihang Mountains began to lose much of their pine forests. When Shen Gua, Hebei's Fiscal Commissioner, traveled there in the mid-1070s, he lamented that the mountains had become largely bald.[95]

Equally falling victim to the hydraulic mode of consumption was a peculiar kind of vegetation. Trees, bushes, and grass grew along

[91] *XCB*, 420: 10179.
[92] *XCB*, 420: 10179.
[93] *XCB*, 434: 10459.
[94] *XCB*, 223: 542; 416: 10110–10111; and 434: 10460.
[95] *MXBT*, 24: 233–234.

riverbanks and dykes: some were natural born, but many were deliberately cultivated by human labor. From the late tenth century, the Song government ordered the planting of elms and willows along the banks and dykes of both the Yellow River and local rivers. Around the frontier ponds, it is said that the military and corvée laborers planted three million trees.[96] The roots of the plants spread widely and interconnected with each other to fasten the loose, silt-based earth, to hold together the banks, and to prevent erosion and rupture.[97] The plants were government property, or more explicitly, the property of the hydraulic infrastructure administered by the External Executive of the Water Conservancy. Any damage to them by private parties (e.g., theft) would incur severe punishment.[98] Occasionally Hebei's regional and local governments used those trees to construct city walls. As river floods intensified, those plants assumed important roles in protecting the banks, so the state prohibited local governments from using them for other purposes.[99] The hydraulic works controlled by the hydraulic leadership took priority over the civil business conducted by local governments. Despite such regulation, as the environmental problems escalated after 1048, and as the shortage of vegetative materials became more and more evident in north China, the riverside plants could no longer stand alive and remain untouched. One after another, they were chopped down by hydraulic workers and used as construction materials to repair bank ruptures.[100] In 1089, Liang Tao, a statesman at Emperor Zhezong's court, lamented: "The trees previously planted on river banks and dykes have been uprooted completely."[101]

Hence, a painful irony ruled the environment of not only Hebei but also the whole of north China. Inside Hebei, the plants cultivated expressly for the purpose of strengthening the dykes were felled and used for embankment construction. The newly built embankments certainly helped to ease floods, but the old embankments, once deprived of their protective

---

[96] *QSW*, 2674: 79.

[97] The government issued a decree to prompt tree planting along river banks in 962 (*SHY*, "Fangyu," 14: 1a). The same order was reissued in 972 (*SHY*, "Fangyu," 14: 1b), in 1000 (*SHY*, "Shihuo," 1: 17b), in 1016 (*XCB*, 87: 1997), and in 1049 (*XCB*, 167: 4019). In the 1070s, the government again encouraged tree planting along both the Yellow River and Hebei's frontier ponds (*XCB*, 215: 5234; 246: 5987; and 254: 6206).

[98] *SHY*, "Fangyu," 14: 13b. *XCB*, 345: 8280.

[99] *XCB*, 259: 6323.

[100] *XCB*, 223: 5421; 414: 10056; 421: 10204; and 421: 10204.

[101] *QSW*, 1784: 206.

plants, were substantially weakened and became more vulnerable to any future flooding. As a result, the flooding problem was merely shifted from upstream or downstream, or from one river to another. The new floods, once again, triggered another round of logging of the riverside plants and thereby caused more floods elsewhere. For the eighty years between 1048 and 1128, the hydraulic works in Hebei were caught in a downward spiral: although their practices often defeated their own purpose, the hydraulic works could not stop; they had to continue felling the riverside plants.

This irony also dominated the pattern of resource production, distribution, and consumption across all of north China. As I explained in Chapter 1, the key reason behind the Yellow River's floods lay in deforestation and soil erosion in the river's middle reaches. There, in Shaanxi and Shanxi, the untimely, inappropriate depletion of vegetation, either through logging or dry-land farming, uprooted a tremendous amount of loess and sand. The latter contents became river silt and traveled downstream to deposit on the plain of Hebei and Henan, causing the riverbed to rise, blocking the river channel, and forcing the river to flood and shift its course. Song contemporaries had some sense of the causal relationship between the vegetation cover, land erosion, and tranquility of the river. Many were aware that silt coming from the far west had become the ultimate enemy of the river's tranquility. Yet, they were unable to connect the two phenomena that north China was experiencing at the time: the unceasing deforestation and the generation of massive silt in the empire's northwestern frontier, and the flooding disasters and hydraulic works in the empire's northeastern frontier, Hebei. The two geographic units were so far apart that people in the eleventh century, even at the state level, failed to conceptualize their environmental connection.[102] The logging industry in the northwest that the imperial state relied on intensified soil erosion and the river's siltation, and thus contributed to the river's turbulence in Hebei. Yet, in order to tame the river's violent torrents and build extensive dykes in Hebei, the state's increasing demand for construction materials had to turn to the northwest again, causing more trees to fall, more forests to disappear, and more silt to travel downstream to choke the river course. So, the vicious cycle was perpetuated. Once again, we witness the interplay among various environmental

---

[102] Part of the northern Loess Plateau, around the Great Bend of the Yellow River, lay beyond the Song border or was a zone of military contestation between the Song and the Xiaxia. This means that the Song had no control of deforestation activities there and the historical sources of the Song Dynasty do not mention much about the environmental conditions there.

spaces – local,regional, and transregional – that defied the stable structure of the autonomous, self-sufficient macroregions G. William Skinner conceptualized for China. The interplay among multiple environmental spaces swirled north China into the unstoppable hydraulic mode of consumption of resources.

The transregional distribution and consumption issues also manifested in competition and conflicts among different socio-economic uses of resources. Wood produced in northwest China was mobilized and distributed by the state; it then traversed hundreds of kilometers to be consumed in northeast China. Bushes, grass, and straw collected all over north China were funneled toward Hebei as well. All these vegetative materials bore other kinds of use values and offered various socio-economic utilities: they produced food and fruits, they were construction materials, they made tools, they created fire, and they fed domestic animals. From 1048, a large amount of the materials was separated from its traditional uses and was consumed for hydraulic purposes. The competition for vegetation for its domestic use or for dyke construction intensified. As a consequence, in the late eleventh century, there was outcry among poor families who could not gather enough firewood to keep them warm during Hebei's harsh winter.

I do not intend to make the judgment that the Song state should not have engaged in the extensive hydraulic works, so as to avoid exhausting China's vegetative resources. Such retrospective condemnation is meaningless. The Song state in the eleventh century felt that it had no choice. Rather, my point is that in pre-modern eras, only a few kinds of materials were regarded as resources and bore particular utilities. Since their quantities were limited, they were in high demand. Given a same kind of materials, people competed to obtain its different utilities. For instance, wood and straw were the predominant energy resources in the Northern Song period; yet, as construction materials, they carried the capacity for hydraulic utility. These two utilities and people's demands of them were mutually exclusive – a circumstance imposing fundamental material constraints to human activities. As hydraulic works were prioritized by the state, other human activities were jeopardized due to the lack of supplies. Clearly, the hydraulic mode of consumption underpinning the state's environmental management of the Yellow River–Hebei environmental complex led not only to the distributional inequality of resources among different regions, but also to the imbalance of various socio-economic values and functions of resources within a given region or a given society. This phenomenon points to a new possibility to further study the kind of "energy crisis" that scholars of late-imperial China like Kenneth Pomeranz examine. Due to both ecological and political-economy causes, an energy crisis not only comes from the decrease of the overall availability of a particular energy type, but it also derives from the energy type's regional and social unequal distribution and, very importantly, the shifting preferences of different utilities of a given resource. I shall explore this issue fully in other publications.

The above analysis suggests that trees and grass are not merely resources that exist to serve human needs. Instead, they are a part of the material foundation that defines the operation of the environmental world and human lives; they are active entities that both offer and constrain possibilities and, specifically in our case, they were participants in the making of the 1048–1128 environmental drama. Only by seeing trees and grass in this way can we make sense of the entanglement of the environmental and socio-economic changes in north China. We should note that the rapid disappearance of trees, bushes, and grass in north China did not end after the Yellow River left Hebei in 1128. It continued over the next nine hundred years, because all later imperial states followed the Song's footsteps by adopting the Song's hydraulic technology and its mode of consumption of vegetative materials. The continuous thinning-out of vegetation accompanied the deterioration of other aspects of the environment. Without adequate plants to transport and transform mineral contents, to retain water, and to root the earth, the soil salinization and sandification issues we discussed earlier only accelerated and worsened throughout the second millennium.

"The Taihang Mountains are denuded!" Shen Gua lamented in the 1070s. We know that this was only the traumatic beginning of a long-term environmental tragedy, a tragedy that was repeated and reinforced again and again, both by an overwhelming environmental power like the Yellow River and by particular human decisions and practices to contain and regulate the constantly changing environment. The legacy and consequences of the eleventh-century tragedy are still experienced by us today, when we walk down a street in some town of Hebei on a spring day, and when we are blinded by fierce sandstorms and lose our way.

Epilogue

1128: *The Close of the Environmental Drama*

The River and the Plain

On March 20, 1127, after attacking and besieging the capital Kaifeng for fourteen months, a Jurchen army captured Emperor Qinzong and later Emperor Huizong and most of the royal family, and forced them to migrate north toward what is now northeastern China, then the homeland of the Jurchen. The Northern Song Dynasty fell. On June 12 of that year, a younger brother of Qinzong claimed the throne. Emperor Gaozong 高宗 (1107–1187), together with a few remaining officials of the Song court, some troops, and groups of refugees escaped southward. He eventually set up his imperial court in Hangzhou in the lower Yangzi valley in 1131. There began the Southern Song Dynasty (1127–1279).

While Emperor Gaozong was searching for a permanent home in the south, many Song loyalists were left behind, still fighting the Jurchen and hoping to regain control over north China, including Hebei. Some resorted to an environmental solution. In the winter of 1128, the Jurchen continued to advance southeastward. In order to thwart the Jurchen's march, the governor of Kaifeng Du Chong (died in 1141) commanded his troops to breach the dykes of the Yellow River to create a massive flood over northern Henan. This military action seems very similar to the one that Chiang Kai-shek's Nationalist government took in 1938 in the Sino-Japan War. As Micah Muscolino has detailed, the Nationalist troops bombed the Yellow River's dykes to provoke a flood that, according to its strategic plan, would obstruct the Japanese army's use of railways and retard its southward advancement – an action that Kathryn Edgerton-Tarpley calls the "Nationalist state's technologization

280

of disaster."[1] Eight centuries apart, the two actions induced similar social, economic, and environmental consequences: enormous numbers of people were killed and displaced; famine and water-borne epidemics caused widespread hardship; and long-standing water on the land surface caused various environmental conditions to deteriorate. In the 1128 case, the action seems to have been undertaken without a careful strategic plan, a step of utter desperation. As a result, the flooding failed to stop the Jurchen; instead, it only forced Du Chong and his troops to escape south, and drew north China into many years of misery. This environmental disaster was something of a last straw that crushed the hope for Song loyalists to recover the lost territory of north China.[2]

What made the 1128 event different from the 1938 event, and what caused its environmental effects to be more profound, was that in addition to the gigantic flood, the Yellow River's lower reaches burst out of its northern course and poured southward to join various waterbodies in Henan. With this change, the river's course turned 90 degrees clockwise to converge with the Bian Canal, the Si 泗 River, and the Qing 清 River. Through these southward channels, the Yellow River's flow surged into the drainage basin of the Huai River. In 1194, the Yellow River fully took over the Huai's lower reaches, and through them discharged into the Yellow Sea 黃海. As a result, the river's mouth relocated from the coast near modern Tianjin at latitude 39° southward to somewhere close to modern Nanjing 南京 at 32°.[3] All this brought an end to the era of the river's northern flows inside Hebei, and the era of the river's southern flows began. The new era lasted until 1855, when a bank rupture drove the river toward Shandong, and established an eastern course that resembled the river's pre-1048 course. Since then until today, the Yellow River has been disconnected from the Huai River basin. Its lower reaches have remained between Hebei and Henan-Shandong to serve as Hebei's southern border, similar to the situation before 1048.

Just as abruptly as it shifted northward and established a river delta inside the Hebei Plain in 1048, the Yellow River departed from Hebei

---

[1] Muscolino (2015) and Edgerton-Tarpley (2014: 447).

[2] The irony between an intention and its unexpected, opposite outcome is certainly seen in the 1938 flood, as Muscolino (2015: 141) points out, "When they created the Yellow River flood in 1939 and constructed hydraulic works to impede the Japanese, Nationalist military leaders tried to enlist the river as a natural ally. Ironically, their actions also unleashed a natural enemy."

[3] For a detailed study on the Yellow River's southern courses and its effects on the Huai River, see Zou (1993: 107–117), Han Zhaoqing (1999), and Pietz (2002: 3–22).

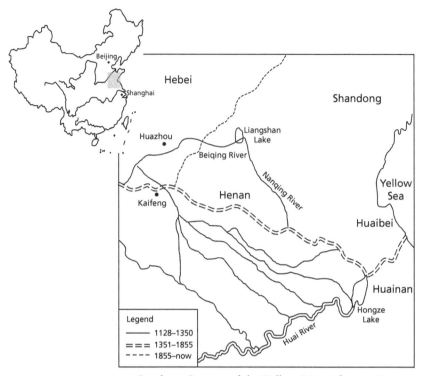

ILLUSTRATION 14. Southern Courses of the Yellow River after 1128

within a day or two in 1128. Suddenly the Yellow River–Hebei environmental complex, which had deeply plagued Hebei and the Northern Song
state, dissolved, and the river's delta landscape in Hebei vanished. The
environmental drama was over, and the river has never entered the heart
of Hebei again.

Compared to the Yellow River's millennia-long history, the eighty-
year environmental drama questioned in this book is indeed a very brief
episode. It is no wonder that people who lived in north China during
the following nine hundred years have forgotten what happened between
1048 and 1128. Even historians have paid little attention to those years.
Nevertheless, this brief episode in history left behind a heavy legacy,
profoundly affecting Hebei of later periods in many ways. Chapter 8
elaborates how its impacts lingered and continued to shape the environmental conditions and human lives in Hebei up to the present day.
Socio-economically, Hebei did not seem to have regained economic and
social vitality after the Yellow River departed from the region. It not only

failed to catch the economic train of a revolutionary growth that southern parts of China had ridden through the late thirteenth century (or over several more centuries, as some Ming-Qing scholars would like to argue). But the environmentally ravaged Hebei continued to experience periodic warfare, political and social turmoil, and economic exploitation and downturn during the Song-Jin transition (a great portion of the twelfth century), Jin-Yuan transition (much of the thirteenth century), and Yuan-Ming transition (the second half of the fourteenth century).

Hebei seems to have had little to do with the highly applauded economic growth in the Ming-Qing period, for which modern historians consider China a leading force of the global economy before the "Great Divergence" took place in the nineteenth century and certain parts of China (such as the lower Yangzi delta) became the breeding bed of "buds of capitalism."[4] In fact, as Lillian M. Li's study on Hebei during the Qing period has sufficiently shown, this region fell to become a "land of famine," which constantly suffered from various disasters and overall environmental degradation. People in this region became heavily reliant on the state for famine relief after the 1690s.[5] The *longue durée* of the regional history of Hebei from the twelfth through the seventeenth century is beyond the scope of this book; we await the emergence of future studies that will fill in this huge gap of knowledge. Nevertheless, our focus on the 1048–1128 environmental drama provides a solid, multi-dimensional historical context for future studies of the continuous deterioration of this region during the later periods.

Let us recall a point made at the beginning of this book (Prologue). After seeing the profound environmental, political, and socio-economic sacrifice the land of Hebei had made, how can we again view the history of middle-period China through a conventional rosy lens without feeling a sense of heaviness or bitterness? How can we continue to take for granted the grandeur of south China and celebrate the illusion of a "medieval economic revolution," which was at best a regional phenomenon? While growth seemed a historical constant and certainly a favored theme of scholarly interests, degradation, destruction, and suffering – the stories of those who lost in the game of history – were the hidden companion

---

[4] The scholarship on the Ming-Qing economic history is gigantic; I shall not list everything here. For the "Great Divergence," see Pomeranz (2001). For the debate on the "buds of capitalism," a hypothesis widely endorsed by Chinese scholars, see Fu (2007a) and (2007b).

[5] Lillian M. Li (2007).

of growth. Dead bodies, hungry refugees, salinized earth, disappeared streams, and vanished trees – they had participated in the making of history long before we were willing to address their existence. Do they not deserve more scholarly passion and compassion? I shall leave these inquiries to my readers and future studies.

Bring the State Back In; Bring the Society Back In – To Their Environmental World

The 1048–1128 environmental drama offers a valuable point of comparison to the environmental and socio-economic history of other regions in later periods. Geologically, between 1048 and 1128, the river discharged its muddy water into the Bohai Gulf, and its silt built up a substantial swath of land around where modern Tianjin is located, pushing the pre-1048 coastal line farther into the ocean.[6] It took the plain of Hebei as its delta and valley. From 1128 to 1855, due to its southward shift, the river discharged its silt through the mouth of the Huai River. Its silt was carried south by ocean tides to the coastal area of the Yangzi River, and continued to build landmass there.[7] During those centuries, the river's lower reaches acquired a new valley, which covered a vast area stretching from eastern Henan to Huaibei and Huainan (both sides of the Huai River), and to the northern edge of the lower Yangzi valley. This area replaced Hebei to become the new bearer and flooding ground of the Yellow River. It became the new "Hebei."

Prior to the mid-nineteenth century, this new river valley had experienced environmental changes and disasters similar to what Hebei experienced between 1048 and 1128. Studies of this lengthy period of the river's history, for instance, by historical geographer Han Zhaoqing, suggest that this new valley area became subjected not only to the Yellow River's frequent floods, but also to long-term environmental issues like disturbance to local water systems, sedimentation, salinization, and deforestation.[8] Socio-economically, this new river valley was so damaged that it suffered an economic decline. It has gradually become the most unstable, poor, underdeveloped region along China's eastern coast. Focusing respectively on its southern and northern parts, Ma Juya and Kenneth Pomeranz have elaborated on this river valley's environmental and socio-economic

---

[6] Xu (1995: 32–40) and Zhao (1984: 8–18).
[7] Elvin and Su in Elvin and Liu (1998).
[8] Han Zhaoqing (1999).

downturn during the Ming, Qing, and Republican periods.[9] Clearly, the environmental drama, which had ravaged Hebei during the Northern Song period, had to a large degree replicated itself in the new valley area in the south. Rather than considering that the brief environmental drama ended in 1128, it seems more appropriate for us to contemplate that the drama spatially migrated from Hebei to the Henan-Huaibei region and took a new stage there. The intricate environmental relationship between the Yellow River and the land that hosted it, as this book has presented, persisted through the following centuries.

Without diving into the geographical migration of the environmental drama too deeply, I would like to further this simplistic regional comparison by bringing forth a hypothesis. Throughout this book I have argued for the mechanism of the "hydraulic mode of consumption," through which a kind of gangrenous disease emanated from the Yellow River–Hebei environmental complex across the broad environmental world. It implicated and affected other regions environmentally and socio-economically during 1048–1128: for instance, through the endless requests for timber from Shaanxi, and the tremendous demands for grain, cash, and manpower from Henan, Shandong, and all the way down to the south in the lower Yangzi valley. Much of the empire had geared up to serve and sustain the Yellow River–Hebei environmental complex. The study of the 1048–1128 environmental drama, therefore, not only tells a regional history of Hebei, but constructs a history of interregional relationships of the empire. It was likely that such mechanism and disease occurred during the Yuan-Ming-Qing period as well. The river's new valley in the Henan-Huaibei region, on the one hand, became the most environmentally and socio-economically compromised area, as Pomeranz and Ma have argued. But on the other hand, it also became a center of consumption that took heavy tolls on its neighboring regions and imperial states.

Ma Junya's study of the southern part of the river valley, the Huaibei region, during the Ming-Qing period focuses on the former issue: that is, how the region's entanglement with the Yellow River led to its multidimensional (even cultural) degradation. Readers may like to engage with Ma's work in the light of my study on the Yellow River–Hebei environmental complex, and question how a sacrificed, declining Huaibei had also imposed enormous environmental and socio-economic costs on other parts of the Ming and Qing empires and entrapped various regions

---

[9] Ma (2011) and Pomeranz (1993).

in extended hardship, even though they were not geophysically involved with the Yellow River. Different from Ma's work, Kenneth Pomeranz investigates the Qing state's "withdrawal" from hydraulics in the valley's northern part, the Huang-Yun (Yellow River-Grand Canal) region, in the dynasty's later years. This suggests the breakdown of the "hydraulic mode of consumption" through the state's intentional disassociation and the rest of the empire's consequential disentanglement from the valley of the Yellow River. Such statist decisions and efforts to disinvest in and abandon the Huang-Yun region show that previously, hydraulic engagement with the region had imposed a huge burden on both the imperial state and other parts of China. Rethinking Pomeranz's study through the lens of the "hydraulic mode of consumption" and comparing it with our case study, readers may contemplate questions such as why the Northern Song state was incapable to break out of its entrapment within the Yellow River–Hebei environmental complex, whether or not the Qing's disinvestment in and abandonment of the Huang-Yun was as successful as it was intended, and what the implications of the disruption of the hydraulic mode of consumption were to both the Huang-Yun and other parts of the Qing empire. Comparing these historical cases, we see that their similarities and differences are both striking. It is beyond the scope of this book to pursue such comparative research. Nevertheless, our exploration of the environmental drama during 1048–1128 helps pave the ground for future studies of those long-term, interregional histories or comparative regional histories.

In the last few pages of the book, let me elaborate on another significant implication that, I hope, the 1048–1128 environmental drama offers to the studies of other regions and later historical periods. That is, how the trialectic complications among various environmental entities and the desires and efforts of a state continued to define the environmental relationships among equivalent historical actors in the following centuries.

During the Jurchen's Jin Dynasty, the state perceived its geopolitical relationship with the Yellow River in a similar way to that of the Northern Song state, except that the environmental structure of north China was reversed: in the Jin Dynasty, the Yellow River flowed southward to join the Jin-Southern Song boundary river – the Huai River, while in the Northern Song Dynasty, it flowed northward to join the Northern Song-Liao boundary river, namely the Juma River. The Jin state adopted the Song state's politico-hydraulic rationales, its hydraulic institutions (e.g., the Water Conservancy and its extensional branches), and its hydraulic technology. Inheriting the Song's hydraulic apparatus, the Jin endeavored to keep the river flowing toward the south, at the expense of the land and people in Henan and Huaibei, in order to prevent the river from shifting back to and damaging Hebei, now a region of higher political significance. As I have examined elsewhere, this adoption of political rationales and hydraulic strategies in one imperial state by another led to opposite environmental constructions in the two consecutive historical periods: the geopolitical core-periphery structure between Henan and Hebei in the Northern Song reversed completely in the Jin period.[10]

The next few centuries saw similar environmental efforts from late imperial states, which followed the footsteps of the Jin Dynasty and continued to restrain the disastrous Yellow River within the geopolitically secondary regions along the river's southern courses. As Ma Junya has pointed out, in order to defend their core political areas in the north (including Hebei), the Ming and the Qing dynasties were both committed to confining the river water within its southern courses and to sacrificing the Huaibei region as the river's flooding ground.[11] The land northwestern of Huaibei, the Huang-Yun region, was socio-economically and environmentally downgraded to a lesser region in the empire system in the later years of the Qing state; the latter decided to cut short its hydraulic investments in the disaster-ridden region and to reallocate its limited resources to foster the development of a modern economy in other prioritized regions. As Pomeranz has analyzed, the state's abandonment of the Huang-Yun region through deinvesting in its hydraulic works made the region a socio-economic and environmental hinterland.[12]

These later regimes adopted and refined the kind of state-prioritizing environmental rationales that the Song state crafted, and inherited the hydraulic apparatus that the Song state installed. For many centuries they had used and perfected the hydraulic technology that Song hydrocrats and workers invented, and relied on the same kind of construction materials that Song hydrocrats employed and exploited. As the Yellow River's lower reaches moved southward, more and more forests, bushes, and bamboo groves in the southern parts of China were depleted for hydraulic purposes. The states and the societies continuously fed immense human and material resources into their often-defeated environmental

[10] Zhang, "Environmentalizing State Politics and Politicizing the Yellow River: The 'State Mode of Environmental Production' in Northern Song and Jin China, 960–1234" (article manuscript).
[11] Ma (2011).
[12] Pomeranz (1993).

management. The burdensome issues that plagued the Song state and Song people continued to manifest in the following centuries: regional disparities, the state's hierarchical treatment of various regions, competition between environmental management and other obligations of the state, political factions and conflicts among various levels of the state's governing body, limited resources and financial strain, momentary crisis and long-term degradation, local resistance to both environmental disasters and the state's mismanagement, and widespread hardship. These issues shaped the daily life of the state, society, and the physical environment, just as they had between 1048 and 1128. The hydraulic mode of consumption, the theoretical formula that I have proposed in this book, ran through the making of China's history during the second millennium. In this sense, the eighty-year environmental drama in middle-period China supplied both the beginning of and the model for a peculiar version of Chinese history throughout the second millennium. This version was not about the historical progress and production that most previous scholarship is concerned with, but about costs, losses, and suffering that the making of history induced and demanded. One effective way to see these costs, losses, and suffering is to bring our conventional discourses about the state and the society – various humanist discourses – back into their environmental worlds that both enable and condition them.

Such trialectic complexity among various environmental entities did not happen only to the Yellow River, a north-China region, or an imperial state in historical times. The 1048–1128 environmental drama resonates with many issues inherent in China's political, socio-economic, and environmental present. These include issues like environmental degradation and resource depletion, the political system's desires and often failures to manage both the environment and human society, the unequal development among different regions, the economic-environmental impoverishment of certain parts of China, and the prevalent, long-lasting suffering of the people there. Once troubling Song China and late-imperial China, these issues are sadly reoccurring in contemporary China.

Think about the developmental strategies that modern China adopts: since the 1950s, it has favored a resource-depleting mode of state building at the expense of environmental sustainability; since 1978, it has prioritized the speedy rise of regions along the eastern coast at the cost of the drastic impoverishment of its western interiors.[13] Certainly think

[13] For studies on environmental destruction and degradation after 1949 that were caused by government policies and economic concerns, see Shapiro (2001 and 2012), Economy (2004), and Pietz (2015).

about mega-projects like the Three Gorges Dam and the South-North Water Transfer. In order to achieve the state-level energy and resource security and to fulfill the resource consumption in socio-economically advanced regions, these projects have not only caused the displacement of millions of people, but also brought profound transformations to the landscape and waterscape across various parts of the Yangzi River valley. Both projects are the congealments and manifestations of the ongoing contestations among the present Chinese state, a titanic hydrological system (or several systems), and contradictory regional realities and interests.[14] Other than some negative consequences we have already witnessed, what else the mechanism of the "hydraulic mode of consumption" has devoured and will continue to devour through the everyday operation of the dam and the water transfer is yet known and awaits our future investigation.

All these modern developments of the trialectic complexity are nothing new. They find a historical analogy or even a historical foundation back in the eleventh century. The politico-environmental decisions made for these cases came from careful deliberations and rational choices, very similar to the reasoning and strategies that the Song state employed to conduct its environmental governance. Surprisingly, the difference between pre-modern eras and the modern era does not seem as significant as we tend to believe. Modernity has obviously not changed the fundamental ways that we – our state and society – interact with non-human environmental entities; it has certainly not changed our wishful perceptions and assumptions that the environment, as a categorical sum of objects, is ready for human appropriation and manipulation for the profit of some social groups (certainly not to everyone).

Yet, will modernity and modern technology spare us from socio-economic struggles, political chaos, resource war, and environmental degradation that the Song state and Hebei's men and women experienced a thousand years ago? Can we break through the curse of the hydraulic mode of consumption? Trapped in and worn down by its hydraulic commitment, the Song state was incapable of seeing beyond its own perceptions and desires and embracing the fundamental constraints the environmental world set upon it. Now, as various environmental problems are looming large in contemporary China, as polluting smog darkens half of China's sky, readers of this book and I – a Chinese and historian

---

[14] For studies on the political discourse, regional struggles, and environmental, socio-economic, and cultural implications of the construction of the Three Gorges Dam, see Chetham (2002).

of China – should ask ourselves: can we see beyond our own perceptions and desires, to honestly face both the complex environmental entanglement that our ongoing activities are producing and the past history that yielded painful lessons we should have but unfortunately have not learnt?

Bibliography

Primary Sources

Anyangji biannian jianzhu 安陽集編年箋注 [*Collection of Anyang and Chronological Annotation*]. Han Qi 韓琦. Annotated by Li Zhiliang 李之亮. Chengdu: Bashu shushe, 2000.

Beixing rilu 北行日錄 [*Diary of the Trip to the North*]. Lou Yao 樓鑰. *Chongshu jicheng chubian* 叢書集成初編, Shanghai: Shangwu yinshuguan, 1935–1940 (hereafter CSJCCB).

Cefu yuangui 冊府元龜 [*Outstanding Models for the Storehouse of Literature*]. Wang Qinruo 王欽若. Beijing: Zhonghua shuju, 1960.

Chongxiu Huaxian zhi 重修滑縣志 [*Revised Gazetteer of Hua County*]. Wang Puyuan 王蒲園. *Zhongguo fangzhi congshu* 中國方誌叢書. Taipei: Chengwen chubanshe, 1966–1989 (hereafter ZGFZCS).

Chongxiu Quyang xianzhi 重修曲陽縣誌 [*Revised Gazetteer of Quyang County*]. Zhou Siyi 周斯億, Wen Liangzhu 溫亮珠, and Dong Tao 董濤. Photolithographic reprint of the 1904 edition, in ZGFZCS. Taipei: Chengwen chubanshe, 1966–1989.

Chongxiu Zhenghe jingshi zhenglei beiyong bencao 重修政和經史證類備用本草 [*Revised Edition of Classified and Practical Materia Medica Based on Historical Classics During the Zhenghe Period, 1111–1118*]. Tang Shenwei 唐慎微. Beijing: Renmin weisheng chubanshe, 1957.

Dingzhou zhi 定州志 [*Gazetteer of Dingzhou*]. Bao Lin 寶琳 and Lao Yuan'en 勞沅恩, in ZGFZCS. Taipei: Chengwen chubanshe, 1966–1989.

Dongpo zhilin 東坡志林 [*Records by Dongpo*]. Su Shi 蘇軾. Shanghai: Huadong shifan daxue chubanshe, 1983.

Fan Zhongyan quanji 范仲淹全集 [*Comprehensive Collection of Fan Zhongyan*]. Fan Zhongyan 范仲淹. Compiled by Li Yongxian 李勇先 and Wang Ronggui 王蓉貴, Chengdu: Sichuan daxue chubanshe, 2002.

Fanchuan wenji 樊川文集 [*An Anthology by Fanchuan*]. Du Mu 杜牧. Annotated by Chen Yunji 陳允吉. Shanghai: Shanghai guji chubanshe, 2009.

Gongshi ji 公是集 [*Collection of Gongshi*]. Liu Chang 劉敞. Wenyuange Sikuquanshu 文淵閣四庫全書, Taipei: Shangwu yinshuguan, 1986 (hereafter SKQS).

Guantao xianzhi 館陶縣志 [*Gazetteer of Guantao County*]. Liu Jiashan 劉家善 et al., Photolithographic reprint of the 1893 edition, in ZGFZCS. Taipei: Chengwen chubanshe, 1966–1989.

Han shu 漢書 [*Standard History of the Former Han*]. Ban Gu 班固. Beijing: Zhonghua shuju, 1962.

Hefang tongyi 河防通議 [*Complete Discussion of Flood Control to the Yellow River*]. Shakeshen 沙克什, in CSJCCB. Shanghai: Shangwu yinshuguan, 1935–1940.

Huang Tingjian quanji 黃庭堅全集 [*Comprehensive Collection of Huang Tingjian*]. Huang Tingjian 黃庭堅. Annotated by Liu Lin 劉琳 et al., Chengdu: Sichuan daxue chubanshe, 2001.

Jifu tongzhi 畿輔通志 [*Complete Gazetteer of the Jifu Region*]. Li Hongzhang 李鴻章. Shanghai: Shangwu yinshuguan, 1934.

Jilei ji 雞肋集 [*Collection of Chicken Ribs*]. Chao Buzhi 晁補之, in SKQS. Taipei: Shangwu yinshuguan, 1986.

Jin shi 金史 [*Standard History of the Jin*]. Tuo Tuo 脫脫. Beijing: Zhonghua shuju, 1975.

Jiu Tangshu 舊唐書 [*Old Standard History of Tang*]. Liu Xu 劉昫. Beijing: Zhonghua shuju, 1975.

Jiu Wudaishi xinji huizheng 舊五代史新輯會證 [*Old Standard History of the Five Dynasties and New Collation*]. Xue Juzheng 薛居正. Annotated by Chen Shangjun 陳尚君. Shanghai: Fudan daxue chubanshe, 2005.

Kuaao ji 跨鼇集 [*Collection of Mount Kuaao*]. Li Xin 李新, in SKQS. Taipei: Shangwu yinshuguan, 1986.

Liang Song mingxian xiaoji 兩宋名賢小集 [*Collection of Renowned Men in the Song Dynasty*]. Chen Si 陳思 and Chen Shilong 陳世隆. Taipei: Shangwu yinshuguan, 1983.

Liao shi 遼史 [*Standard History of the Liao*]. Tuo, Tuo 脫脫. Beijing: Zhonghua shuju, 1974.

Lidai mingchen zouyi 歷代名臣奏議 [*Memorials of Leading Officials of Various Periods*]. Huang Huai 黃淮 and Yang Shiqi 楊士奇, in SKQS. Taipei: Shangwu yinshuguan, 1986.

Longchuan luezhi 龍川略志 [*Brief Records of Longchuan*]. Su Zhe 蘇轍. Beijing: Zhonghua shuju, 1982.

Mengxi bitan 夢溪筆談 [*Jottings from the Mengxi*]. Shen Kuo 沈括. Beijing: Zhonghua shuju, 1958.

Ming shilu leizuan 明實錄類纂 [*Veritable Records of the Ming by Category*]. Edited by Li Guoxiang 李國祥 and Yang Chang 楊昶. Volumes on Hebei and Tianjin. Wuhan: Wuhan chubanshe, 1995.

Ouyang Xiu quanji 歐陽修全集 [*Comprehensive Collection of Ouyang Xiu*]. Ouyang Xiu 歐陽修. Annotated by Li Yi'an 李逸安, Beijing: Zhonghua shuju, 2001.

Qimin yaoshu jiaoshi 齊民要術校釋 [*Techniques Essential for the Subsistence of Common People and Annotation*]. Jia Sixie 賈思勰. Annotated by Miu Qiyu 繆啟愉, Beijing: Zhongguo nongye chubanshe, 1998.

Qingxian ji 清獻集 [*Collection of Qingxian*]. Zhao Bian 趙抃. SKQS. Taipei: Shangwu yinshuguan, 1986.

Quan Songwen 全宋文 [*Complete Song Prose*]. Zeng Zaozhuang 曾棗莊 and Liu Lin 劉琳 et al., Shanghai: Shanghai cishu, 2003.

Shi ji 史記 [*Records of the Grand Historian*]. Sima Qian 司馬遷. Beijing: Zhanghua shuju, 1959.

Shuofu 說郛 [*The Domain of Texts*]. Tao Zongyi 陶宗儀. Shanghai: Shanghai guji chubanshe, 1990.

Sishi zuanyao jiaoshi 四時纂要校釋 [*Essentials of the Four Seasons and Annotation*]. Han E 韓鄂. Annotated by Miu Qiyu 繆啟愉, Beijing: Nongye chubanshe, 1981.

Song huiyao jigao 宋會要輯稿 [*Collated Draft of Important Documents of the Song*]. Xu Song 徐松. Beiping: Beiping tushuguan, 1936.

Song huiyao jigao bubian 宋會要輯稿補編 [*Addition to the Collated Draft of Important Documents of the Song*]. Xu Song 徐松. Compiled by Chen Zhichao 陳智超, Beijing: Quanguo tushuguan wenxian suowei fuzhi zhongxin chuban, 1988.

Song shi 宋史 [*Standard History of the Song*], Tuo Tuo. Beijing: Zhonghua shuju, 1977.

Songchao shishi 宋朝事實 [*Affairs in the Song Dynasty*]. Li You 李攸. Shanghai: Shangwu yinshuguan, 1935.

Songshan wenji 嵩山文集 [*Collection of the Song Mountain*]. Chao Gongsuo 晁公溯, in SKQS. Taipei: Shangwu yinshuguan, 1986.

Sushui jiwen 涑水紀聞 [*Records by the Su River*]. Sima Guang 司馬光. Beijing: Zhonghua shuju, 1989.

Taiping huanyu ji 太平寰宇記 [*Gazetteer of the World During the Taiping Period, 976–83*]. Yue Shi 樂史. Edited by Wan Tinglan 萬廷蘭. Hongye Shanfang cangban 紅葉山房藏版, preface date 1793.

Tang xinxiu bencao 唐新修本草 [*The New Materia Medica of the Tang*]. Su Jing 蘇敬. Annotated by Shang Zhijun 尚志均, Hefei: Anhui kexue jishu chubanshe, 1981.

Wang Zhen Nongshu 王禎農書 [*Agricultural Treatises by Wang Zhen*]. Wang Zhen 王禎. Annotated by Wang Yuhu 王毓瑚, Beijing: Nongye chubanshe, 1981.

Weixian zhi 威縣志 [*Gazetteer of Wei County*]. Cui Zhengchun 崔正春 and Shang Xibin 尚希賓, in ZGFZCS. Taipei: Chengwen chubanshe, 1966–1989.

Wenchang zalu 文昌雜錄 [*Misellaneous Records of Wenchang*]. Pang Yuanying 龐元英. Beijing: Zhonghua shuju, 1958.

Wenxian tongkao 文獻通考 [*General History of Institutions and Critical Examination of Documents and Studies*]. Ma Duanlin 馬端臨. Hangzhou: Zhejiang guji chubanshe, 1988.

Xiaosu Baogong zouyi 孝肅包公奏議 [*Memorials of Bao Xiaosu*]. Bao Zheng 包拯, in CSJCCB. Shanghai: Shangwu yinshuguan, 1935-1940.

Xin Tangshu 新唐書 [*New Standard History of the Tang*]. Ouyang Xiu and Song Qi. Beijing: Zhonghua shuju, 1975.

Xin Wudai shi 新五代史 [*New Standard History of the Five Dynasties*]. Ouyang Xiu. Beijing: Zhonghua shuju, 1981.

Xu Zizhitongjian changbian 續資治通鑑長編 [*Long Draft of the Continuation of the Zizhi tongjian*]. Li Tao 李燾. Beijing: Zhonghua shuju, 1979–1995.
Xu Zizhitongjian changbian shibu 續資治通鑑長編拾補 [*Addition to Long Draft of the Continuation of the Zizhi tongjian*]. Li Tao. Compiled by Huang Yizhou 黃以周, Beijing: Zhonghua shuju, 2004.
Yijian zhi 夷堅志 [*Records of the Listener*]. Hong Mai 洪邁. Beijing: Zhonghua shuju, 1981.
Yu Hai 玉海 [*Ocean of Jade*]. Wang Yinglin 王應麟. Shanghai: Jiangsu guji chubanshe and Shanghai shudian, 1987.
Yuanfeng jiuyu zhi 元豐九域志 [*Gazetteer of the Nine Regions during the Yuanfeng Period, 1078–1086*]. Wang Cun 王存. Beijing: Zhonghua shuju, 1984.
Zhangdefu zhi 彰德府志 [*Gazetteer of Zhangde Prefecture*]. Lu Song 盧崧 and Jiang Dajian 江大鍵 et al., Photolithographic reprint of the 1787 edition, Taipei: Xuesheng shuju, 1968.
Zizhi tongjian 資治通鑑 [*Comprehensive Mirror for Aid in Government*]. Sima Guang. Beijing: Zhonghua shuju, 1982.

Books and Articles

Amano, Motonosuke. *Chūgoku nōgyōshi kenkyū* [*Studies on Chinese Agricultural History*]. Tōkyō: Ochanomizu Shobo, 1962.
Aoyama, Sadao. *Tōsō jidai no kōtsū to chishi chizu no kenkyū* [*Studies on Transportation, Geographical Treatises, and Maps During the Tang-Song Period*]. Tōkyō: Yoshikawa kōbunkan, 1963.
Bao, Weimin. *Songdai difang caizhengshi yanjiu* [*Studies of the Regional Fiscal History During the Song*]. Shanghai: Shanghai guji chubanshe, 2001.
Bray, Francesca and Joseph Needham. *Agriculture, in Science and Civilisation in China, vol. 6, Biology and Biological Technology, Part II*. Cambridge: Cambridge University Press, 1984.
Bol, Peter K. *"This Culture of Ours:" Intellectual Transitions in T'ang and Sung China*. Stanford, CA: Stanford University Press, 1992.
Buck, John Lossing. *Land Utilization in China*. Nanking: University of Nanking, 1937.
Chaffee, John W. *The Thorny Gates of Learning in Sung China: A Social History of Examinations*. 2nd edition. Cambridge and New York: Cambridge University Press, 1995.
Chaffee, John W. and Denise Twitchett. *Cambridge History of China, Vol. 5, Part 2, The Five Dynasties and Sung China, 960–1279 AD*. Cambridge: Cambridge University Press, 2015.
Chen, Feng. *Songdai junzheng yanjiu* [*Studies on the Song's Military Governance*]. Beijing: Zhongguo shehui kexue chubanshe, 2010.
Chen, Yinque. *Tangdai zhengzhishi shulungao* [*Discussion of the Tang's Political History*]. Shanghai: Shanghai guji chubanshe, 1997.
Cheng, Long. *Beisong liangshi choucuo yu bianfang: Yi Huabei zhanqu weili* [*Grain Collection and Frontier Defense during the Northern Song: The*

North-China Military Zone as the Example]. Beijing: Shangwu yinshuguan, 2012.

Cheng, Minsheng. *Songdai diyü jingji* [*Regional Economies during the Song*]. Kaifeng: Henan daxue chubanshe, 1998.

Zhongguo beifang jingjishi [*The Economic History of North China*], Beijing: Renmin chubanshe, 2004.

Cheng, Suiying. *Tang Song Kaifeng shengtai huanjing yanjiu* [*Ecological and Environmental Studies of Kaifeng during the Tang-Song Period*]. Beijing: Zhongguo shehui kexue chubanshe, 2002.

Chetham, Deirdre. *Before the Deluge: The Vanishing World of the Yangtze's Three Gorges.* New York: Palgrave Macmillan, 2002.

Chi, Ch'ao-ting. *Key Economic Areas in Chinese History,* London: G. Allen & Unwin, Ltd., 1936.

Chia, Lucille and Hilde Godelieve Dominique De Weerdt. *Knowledge and Text Production in an Age of Print: China, 900–1400.* Leiden and Boston: Brill, 2011.

Chikusa, Masaaki. *Songchao de Taizu he Taizong: Biange shiqi de diwang* [*Emperors Taizu and Taizong of the Song Dynasty: Monarchs during a Transitional Period*]. Translated by Fang Jianxin. Hangzhou: Zhejiang daxue chubanshe, 2006.

Chow, Rey. "Postmodern Automatons," in *Feminists Theorizing the Political,* edited by Judith Butler and Joan Scott, 101–117. New York: Routledge, 1992.

Ch'uan, Han-sheng. "Beisong wujia de biandong" [Changes to prices of goods in the Northern Song]. *Bulletin of the Institute of History and Philology Academia Sinica* 11 (1944): 337–394.

Tang Song diguo yu yunhe [*The Tang and Song Empires and Canals*], Shanghai: Shangwu yinshuguan, 1946.

Cosgrove, Denis E. *Social Formation and Symbolic Landscape.* 2nd edition. Madison, WI: The University of Wisconsin Press, 1998.

Cressey, George B. *Land of the Five Hundred Million: A Geography of China.* New York: McGraw Hill, 1955.

de Weerdt, Hilde. "Song Studies," in *A Scholarly Review of Chinese Studies in North America,* edited by Haihui Zhang et al., 27–53. Ann Arbor, MI: The Association of Asian Studies, Inc., 2013.

Deng, Guangming. *Beisong zhengzhi gaigejia Wang Anshi* [*Northern Song Political Reformer Wang Anshi*]. Beijing: Renmin chubanshe, 1997.

Deng, Xiaonan. *Zuzong zhifa: Beisong qianqi zhengzhi shulue* [The Measures of Ancestors: Discussion on the Politics in the Early Years of the Northern Song]. Beijing: Sanlianshudian, 2006.

Dodgen, Randall A. *Controlling the Dragon: Confucian Engineers and the Yellow River in Late Imperial China.* Honolulu, HI: University of Hawai'i Press, 2001.

Dong, Guodong. *Zhongguo renkou shi* [History of Chinese Population], volume on the Sui, Tang, and Five Dynasties. Shanghai: Fudan daxue chubanshe, 2002.

Dudbridge, Glen. *A Portrait of Five Dynasties China: From the Memoirs of Wang Renyu (880–956)*. Oxford: Oxford University Press, 2013.

Ebrey, Patricia Buckley and Maggie Bickford, eds. *Emperor Huizong and Late Northern Song China: The Politics of Culture and the Culture of Politics*. Cambridge, MA, and London: Harvard University Asian Center, 2006.

Emperor Huizong. Cambridge, MA, and London: Harvard University Press, 2014.

Economy, Elizabeth. *The River Runs Black: The Environmental Challenge to China's Future*. Ithaca, NY: Cornell University Press, 2004.

Edgerton-Tarpley, Kathryn Jean. "From 'Nourish the People' to 'Sacrifice for the Nation': Changing responses to disaster in late imperial and modern China." *The Journal of Asian Studies*. 73(2) (2014): 447–469.

Tears from Iron: Cultural Responses to Famine in Nineteenth-Century China. Berkeley, CA: University of California Press, 2008.

Edmonds, Richard L. *Patterns of China's Lost Harmony: A Survey of the Country's Environmental Degradation and Protection*, London and New York: Routledge, 1994.

Elvin, Mark. *The Pattern of the Chinese Past*, London: Eyre Methuen, 1973.

"Three Thousand Years of Unsustainable Growth: China's Environment from Archaic Times to the Present." *East Asian History* 6 (1993): 7–46.

"Who Was Responsible for the Weather? Moral Meteorology in Late Imperial China." *Osiris* 12 (1998): 213–237.

The Retreat of the Elephant: An Environmental History of China. New Haven, CT: Yale University Press, 2004.

Elvin, Mark and Tsui-jung Liu, eds. *Sediments of Time: Environmental and Society in Chinese History*. Cambridge: Cambridge University Press, 1998.

Elvin, Mark and Su Ning-Hu. "Action at a Distance: The Influence of the Yellow River on Hangzhou Bay since A. D. 1000." In *Sediments of Time: Environmental and Society in Chinese History*, 344–410. Cambridge: Cambridge University Press, 1998.

Elvin, Mark et al., ed. *Japanese Studies on the History of Water Control in China: A Selected Bibliography*. Canberra and Tokyo: The Institute of Advanced Studies and Tokyo Bunko, 1994.

Evans, Peter B., Dietrich Rueschemeyer, and Theda Skocpol, eds. *Bringing the State Back in*. Cambridge: Cambridge University Press, 1985.

Flessel, Klaus. *Der Huang-ho und die Historische Hydrotechnik in China*. Tübingen: University of Tübingen Press, 1974.

Frank, Andre Gunder. *ReOrient: Global Economy in the Asian Age*. Berkeley, CA: University of California Press, 1998.

Fu, Yiling. *Ming Qing shidai shangren ji shangye ziben* [Merchants and Commercial Capital in the Ming-Qing Period]. Beijing: Zhonghua shuju, 2007a.

Ming Qing nongcun shehui jingji [Rural Society and Economy in the Ming and Qing]. Beijing: Zhonghua shuju, 2007b.

Gao, Congming. *Songdai huobi yu huobi liutong yanjiu* [Studies on Currency and Circulation in the Song]. Baoding: Hebei daxue chubanshe, 2000.

Gao, Guoren. "Su zai Zhongguo gudai nongye zhong de diwei he zuoyong" [Status and Functions of Millet in Chinese Pre-modern Agriculture]. *Nongye kaogu*, 1 (1991): 195–201.

Gates, Hill. *China's Motor: A Thousand Years of Petty Capitalism*. Ithaca, NY: Cornell University Press, 1996.

Golas, Peter J. "The Sung Economy: How Big?" *Bulletin of Sung and Yuan Studies*, 20 (1998): 90–94.

Gong, Gaofa. "Lishi shiqi qihoudai bianqian yu shengwu fenbu jiexian de tuiyi" [Changes to the Climatic Zones and Geographical Divisions of Organisms in Historical Times]. *Lishi dili* 5 (1987).

Guo, Zhengzhong. *Songdai yanye jingjishi* [The Economic History of Salt Industry in the Song]. Beijing: Renmin chubanshe, 1990.

Gupta, Avijit, ed. *Large Rivers: Geomorphology and Management*. Chichester: John Wiley & Sons Ltd., 2007.

Han, Maoli. *Songdai nongye dili* [Agricultural Geography in the Song]. Taiyuan: Shanxi guji chubanshe, 1993.

Han, Peng and Jinren Ni. "Shuitu baochi dui Huanghe zhongyou nisha lijing yingxiang de tongji fenxi" [Statistical analysis on the impact of water and soil preservation on the grain size of silt in the middle reaches of the Yellow River]. *Shuili xuebao* 8 (2001).

Han, Zhaoqing. *Huang Huai guanxi jiqi yanbian guocheng yanjiu: Huanghe changqi duohuai qijian Huaibeipingyuan hupo shuixi de bianqian he Beijing* [The Relationship between the Yellow River and the Huai River and Its Evolution]. Shanghai: Fudan daxue chubanshe, 1999.

Hartwell, Robert M. "Demographic, Political, and Social Transformations of China, 750–1550." *Harvard Journal of Asiatic Studies*. 42(2) (1982): 365–442.

He, Naihua and Xuanqing Zhu. "Huabei Pingyuan qianmai guhedaodai de fenbu he chenji tezheng" [The geographical location of buried old river courses on the North China Plain and their sedimentary characteristics]. In *Huabei pingyuan guhedao yanjiu lunwenji*, edited by Wu Chen. Beijing: Zhongguo kexuejishu chubanshe, 1991.

He, Tonghui and Naiang Wang. *Maowusu shadi lishi shiqi huanjing bianhua yanjiu* [Historical Environmental Changes in the Maowusu Desert]. Beijing: Renmin chubanshe, 2010.

Higashi, Ichio. *Ō Anseki shinpō no kenkyū*; [Studies on Wang Anshi's Reform], Tōkyō: Kazama shobō, 1970.

Ō Anseiki to Shiba Kō: gendai kara tōshi shita Chūgoku shijō no seisōgeki [Wang Anshi and Sima Guang: Political Struggles in Chinese History Seen from a Modern Perspective]. Tōkyō: Chūsekisha, 1982.

Hino, Kaisaburō. "Nōson to toshi" [The Rural and the Urban]. In *Hino Kaisaburō tōyōshigaku ronshū*, vol. 13. Tōkyō: Sanol. 13aburō, 1993.

Ho, Ping-ti. "Early-Ripening Rice in Chinese History." *Economic History Review* 2 (1956): 200–218.

Huangtu yu Zhongguo nongye de qiyuan [The Loess and the Origin of Chinese Agriculture]. Hong Kong: Chinese University of Hong Kong, 1969.

Hou, Jianxin. "Minguo nianjian Jizhong nonghu laodong shengchanlu yanjiu" [Agricultural productivity in central Hebei during Republican China].
Zhongguo nongshi 1 (2001): 57–67.

Hou, Renzhi and Hui Deng, eds. *Zhongguo beifang ganhan banganhan diqu lishi
shiqi huanjing bianqian yanjiu wenti* [Historical Environmental Changes
Corpus in the Arid and Semi-arid Region in Northwest China]. Beijing:
Shangwu chubanshe, 2006.

Hua, Linfu. "Tangdai su mai shengchan de diyu buju chutan" [Geographical distribution of millet and wheat production during the Tang], Part 1. *Zhongguo nongshi* 2 (1990): 33–42; Part 2, *Zhongguo nongshi* 3 (1990): 23–
39.

Huang, Philip C. C. *The Peasant Economy and Social Change in North China.*
Stanford, CA: Stanford University Press, 1985.

Huanghe shuili weiyuanhui Huangshui shuilishi shuyao bianxiezu. *Huanghe
shuilishi shuyao* [An Essential Study on the Yellow River Hydraulics]. Beijing: Shuili chubanshe, 1982.

Huanghe shuili weiyuanhui Huanghe zhi zongbianjishi. *Huanghe liuyu zongshu*
[A Survey of the Yellow River Drainage Area]. Zhengzhou: Huanghe shuili
weiyuanhui, 1995.

Huanghe shuili weiyuanhui, *Zhongguo jianghe fanghong congshu Huanghe juan*
[The Series of Flood Control for Chinese Rivers, the volume for the Yellow
River]. Beijing: Zhongguo shuili shuidian chubanshe, 1996.

Hymes, Robert P. and Conrad Schirokauer, eds. *Ordering the World: Approaches
to State and Society in Sung Dynasty China.* Berkeley, CA, Los Angeles, CA,
and Oxford: University of California Press, 1993.

Institute of Geophysics et al., *Zhongguo lishi dizhen tuji* [Atlas of the historical
earthquakes in China]. Beijing: Zhongguo ditu chubanshe, 1990.

Ji, Xiao-bin. *Politics and Conservatism in Northern Song China: The Career
and Thought of Sima Guang (A.D. 1019–1086).* Hong Kong: The Chinese
University of Hong Kong, 2005.

Jiang, Tianjian. "Beisong Hebeilu zaolin zhi yanjiu" [Forestation in Hebei during
the Northern Song]. *Lishi dili* 14 (1998): 42–50.

Jiang, Xidong. *Songdai shangren he shangye ziben* [Merchants and Commercial
Capital during the Song]. Beijing: Zhonghua shuju, 2002.

Katō, Shigeshi. *Shina keizaishi kōshō* [Examination of Chinese Economic His-
tory], Tōkyō: Tōyō bunko, 1952–1953.

Kawahara, Yoshirō. *Hokusōki tochi shoyū no mondai to shōgyō shihon* [Land
Ownership and Commercial Capital during the Northern Song], Fukuoka:
Nishi Nihon kakujotsu shubansha, 1964.

Kidder, Tristram R., Haiwang Liu, and Minglin Li. "Sanyangzhuang: Early Farming and a Han Settlement Preserved Beneath Yellow River Flood Deposits."
Antiquity 86 (331) (2012): 30–47.

Kuhn, Dieter. *The Age of Confucian Rule: The Song Transformation of China.*
Cambridge, MA, and London: The Belknap Press of Harvard University
Press, 2009.

Lamouroux, Christian. "From the Yellow River to the Huai: New Representations of a River Network and the Hydraulic Crisis of 1128." In *Sediments*

of Time, edited by Mark Elvin and Liu Ts'ui-jung, 545–584. Cambridge: Cambridge University Press, 1998.

Lefebver, Henri. *State, Space, and World: Selected Essays*, edited by Neil Brenner and Stuart Elden, translated by Gerald Moore, Neil Brenner, and Stuart Elden. Minneapolis, MN, and London: University of Minnesota Press, 2009.

Leonard, Jane Kate. *Controlling from Afar: The Daoguang Emperor's Management of the Grand Canal Crisis, 1824–1826*. Ann Arbor, MI: Center for Chinese Studies, The University of Michigan, 1996.

Levine, Ari Daniel. *Divided by a Common Language: Factional Conflict in Late Northern Song China*. Honolulu, HI: University of Hawai'i Press, 2008.

Lewis, Mark E. *Flood Myths of Early China*. Albany, NY: State University of New York Press, 2006.

Li, Huarui, ed. *Tang Song biange lun de youlai yu fazhan* [The Origin and Development of the Tang-Song Transition Thesis]. Tianjin: Tianjin guji chubanshe, 2010.

Li, Jinshui. *Wang Anshi jingji bianfa yanjiu* [Studies on Wang Anshi's Economic Reform]. Fuzhou: Fujian renmin chubanshe, 2007.

Li, Lillian M. *Fighting Famine in North China: State, Markets, and Environmental Decline, 1690s-1990s*. Stanford: Stanford University Press, 2007.

Li, Xiaocong. "Chihe kao" [Studies of the Chi River]. *Lishi dili* 4 (1986): 138–144.

"Gongyuan shi – shi'er shiji Huabei pingyuan beibu yaqu jiaotong yu chengshi dili de yanjiu" [Transportation and urban geography in the northern part of the North China Plain during the tenth to twelfth centuries]. *Lishi dili* 9 (1990): 239–263.

Liang, Fangzhong. *Zhongguo lidai hukou tiandi tianfu tongji* [Statistics of Chinese Historical Household, Land, and Agricultural Incomes]. Shanghai: Shanghai renmin chubanshe, 1980.

Liang, Gengyao. "Songdai nanbei de jingji diwei: Ping Cheng Minsheng zhu Songdai diyu jingji [The Economic Statuses of North and South China in the Song Period: Review of *Regional Economies in the Song Period*, by Cheng Minsheng]." *Xin shixue* 4(1) (1994): 107–132.

Liu, Dongsheng. *Huanghe zhongyou huangtu* [Loess in the Yellow River's Middle Reaches]. Beijing: Kexue chubanshe, 1964.

Huangtu yu huanjing [Loess and the Environment]. Beijing: Kexue chubanshe, 1985.

Liu, Heping. "Picturing Yu Controlling the Flood: Technology, Ecology, and Emperorship in Northern Song China." In *Cultures of Knowledge: Technology in Chinese History*, edited by Dagmar Schafer, 91–126. Leiden and Boston: Brill, 2012.

Liu, James T. C. "An Early Sung Reformer: Fan Chung-yen." In *Chinese Thought and Institutions*, edited by John K. Fairbank, Chicago, IL: University of Chicago Press, 1957.

Reform in Sung China: Wang An-shih (1021–1086) and His New Policies. Cambridge, MA: Harvard University Press, 1959.

"An Administrative Cycle in Chinese History: The Case of Northern Sung Emperors," *Journal of Asian Studies* 21(2) (1962): 137–152.

Ou-yang Hsiu: An Eleventh-Century Neo-Confucianist. Stanford, CA: Stanford University Press, 1967.

Liu, James T. C. and Peter J. Golas. *Change in Sung China: Innovation or Renovation?* Lexington, MA: Heath, 1969.

Liu, Pujiang. "Hebei jingnei de gudidao yiji yu Song Liao Jin shidai de gushi" [Ancient tunnels in Hebei and the history during the Song-Liao-Jin period]. *Dalu zazhi* 1 (2000): 27–42.

Lorge, Peter. *War, Politics, and Society in Early Modern China: 900–1795*. New York: Routledge, 2005.

"The Great Ditch of China and the Song-Liao Border." In *Battlefronts Real and Imagined: War, Border, and Identity in the Chinese Middle Period*, edited by Don J. Wyatt, 59–74. New York: Palgrave Macmillan, 2008.

Five Dynasties and Ten Kingdoms. Hong Kong: The Chinese University Press, 2011.

Ma, Junya. *Bei xisheng de "jubu": Huaibei shehui shengtai bianqian yanjiu (1680–1949)* [The Sacrificed Portion: Ecological Transition of the Huaibei Society]. Beijing: Beijingdaxue chubanshe, 2011.

Ma, Junya and Tim Wright. "Sacrificing Local Interests: Water Control Policies of the Ming and Qing Governments and the Local Economy Huaibei 1495–1949." *Modern Asian Studies* 47.

Makita, Tairyō, *Sakugen nyūminki no kenkyū*; [Studies on Sakugen's Travel in the Ming], vol.1 and 2. Kyōto: Hōzōkan, 1954 and 1959.

Man, Zhimin. "Zhongshiji wennuanqi Huabei jiangshui yu Huanghe fanlan" [Precipitation in north China and the Yellow River flooding during the medieval climatic warm period]. *Zhongguo lishi dili luncong* 29(1) (2014): 20–25.

Mao, Hanguang. "Lun Anshi luanhou Hebei diqu zhi shehui yu wenhua: Ju zaiji dashizu weili" [Hebei's regional society and culture after the An-Shi rebellion]. In *Wantang de shehui yu wenhua*, edited by Danjiang daxue zhongwenxi, 99–112. Taipei: Xuesheng shuju, 1990.

Marks, Robert B. *Tigers, Rice, Silk, and Silt: Environment and Economy in Late Imperial South China*. Cambridge and New York: Cambridge University Press, 1998.

China: Its Environment and History. Lanham, MD: Rowman & Littlefield Publishers, Inc., 2012.

McNeill, John R. "China's Environment in World Perspective." In *Sediments of Time*, edited by Mark Elvin and Ts'ui-Jung Liu, 31–52. Cambridge: Cambridge University Press, 1998.

Menzies, Nicholas K. *Forestry*, in the series of Joseph Needham, *Science and Civilisation in China, vol. 6, Biology and Biological Technology, Part III, Agro-Industries and Forestry*. Cambridge: Cambridge University Press, 1996.

Migdal, Joel S. *Strong Societies and Weak States: State-Society Relations and State Capabilities in the Third World*. Princeton, NJ: Princeton University Press, 1988.

State-in-Society: Studying How States and Societies Transform and Constitute One Another. New York: Cambridge University Press, 2001.

Mitchell, W. J. T., ed. *Landscape and Power* (2nd edition). Chicago, IL, and London: The University of Chicago Press, 2002.

Morita, Akira. *Shindai suirishi kenkyū*; [Studies on the Hydraulic History during the Qing]. Tōkyō: Aki Shobo, 1974.

Shindai suiri shakaishi no kenkyū; [Studies on the Hydraulic and Social history during the Qing]. Tōkyō: Kokusho Kankōkai, 1990.

Morris, Christopher. *The Big Muddy: An Environmental History of the Mississippi and Its People from Hernando de Soto to Hurricane Katrina*. Oxford and New York: Oxford University Press, 2012.

Mostern, Ruth. *"Dividing the Realm in Order to Govern:" The Spatial Organization of the Song State (960–1276 CE)*. Cambridge: Harvard University Asian Center, 2011.

Muscolino, Micah S. "Violence Against People and Land: The Environment and Refugee Migration from China's Henan Province, 1938–1945." *Environment and History*. 17 (2011): 291–311.

The Ecology of War in China: Henan Province, the Yellow River, and beyond, 1938–1950. Cambridge: Cambridge University Press, 2015.

Nagase, Mamoru. *Sōgen suirishi kenkyū*; [Studies on the Hydraulic History during the Song-Yuan Period]. Tōkyō: Kokusho kankōkai, 1983.

Needham, Joseph, Wang Ling and Lu Gwei-djen. *Science and Civilisation in China, vol. 4, Physics and Physical Technology, Part III: Civil Engineering and Nautics*. Cambridge: Cambridge University Press, 1971.

Nishijima, Sadao. *Chūgoku keizaishi kenkyū*; [Studies on Chinese Economic History]. Tōkyō: Tōkyō daigaku, 1966.

Nishiyama, Takeichi. *Ajia teki nōhō to nōgyōshakai* [Asian Agriculture and Agricultural Societies]. Tōkyō: Tōkyō daigaku, 1969.

Nixon, Rob. *Slow Violence and the Environmentalism of the Poor*. Cambridge, MA, and London: Harvard University Press, 2011.

Ōkawa, Yūko. "Koga shitaryūike ni ogeru sachi riyō no rikishi deki hensen" [Historical changes to the utilization of sandy land in the lower Yellow River valley]. In *Kogashitaryūike no rikishi to kankyō*, edited by Tsuruma Kazuyuki, 153–175. Tōkyō: Tōhō shoden, 2007.

Ōsawa, Masaaki. *Tōsō henkakuki nōgyō shakaishi kenkyū*; [Studies on Agriculture and Society during the Tang-Song Transition Era]. Tōkyō: Kyūko shoin, 1996.

Perdue, Peter C. *Exhausting the Earth: State and Peasant in Hunan, 1500–1850*. Cambridge, MA, and London: Council of East Asian Studies, Harvard University, 1987.

Perkins, Dwight H. *Agricultural Development in China, 1368–1968*. Edinburgh: Edinburgh University Press, 1969.

Pietz, David A. *Engineering the State: The Huai River and Reconstruction in Nationalist China, 1927–1937*. New York: Routledge, 2002.

The Yellow River: The Problem of Water in Modern China. Cambridge, MA, and London: Harvard University Press, 2015.

Pomeranz, Kenneth. *The Making of a Hinterland: State, Society, and Economy in Inland North China, 1853–1937*. Berkeley, CA, and Los Angles, CA: University of California Press, 1993.

The Great Divergence: China, Europe, and the Making of the Modern World Economy. Princeton, NJ: Princeton University Press, 2001.

Pulleyblank, Edwin G. *The Background of the Rebellion of An Lu-shan.* London, New York and Toronto: Oxford University Press, 1955.

Qi, Xia. *Songdai jingjishi* [Economic History of the Song]. Shanghai: Shanghai renmin chubanshe, 1987–1988.

Radkau, Joachim. *Nature and Power: A Global History of the Environment.* Cambridge: Cambridge University Press, 2008.

Rossabi, Morris. *China among Equals: The Middle Kingdom and Its Neighbors, 10th–14th Centuries.* Berkeley, CA: University of California Press, 1983.

Scheper-Hughes, Nancy. *Death without Weeping: The Violence of Everyday Life in Brazil.* Berkeley, Los Angles, CA, and London: University of California Press, 1992.

Schoppa, Keith R. *Xiang Lake: Nine Centuries of Chinese Life.* New Haven, CT: Yale University Press, 1989.

Scott, James C. *The Moral Economy of the Peasant: Rebellion and Subsistence in Southeast Asia.* New Haven, CT, and London: Yale University Press, 1976.

Weapons of the Weak: Everyday Forms of Peasant Resistance. New Haven, CT, and London: Yale University Press, 1985.

Seeing like a State: How Certain Schemes to Improve the Human Condition Have Failed. New Haven, CT, and London: Yale University Press, 1998.

Shao, Wenjie. *Henan shengzhi* [Gazetteer of Henan Province]. Zhengzhou: Henan renmin chubanshe, 1991.

Shapiro, Judith. *Mao's War against Nature: Politics and the Environment in Revolutionary China.* Cambridge and New York: Cambridge University Press, 2001.

China's Environmental Challenges. Cambridge and Malden, MA: Polity Press, 2012.

Shi, Nianhai. *Heshan ji* [Collection of Rivers and Mountains], vol. 2. Beijing: Renmin chubanshe, 1981.

Heshan ji, vol. 3. Beijing: Renmin chubanshe, 1988a.

Zhongguo de yunhe [Chinese Canals]. Xi'an: Shaanxi renmin chubanshe, 1988b.

Zhongguo lishi renkou dili he lishi jingji dili [Historical Demographical Geography and Historical Economic Geography in China]. Taipei: Taiwan xuesheng shuju, 1991.

Huangtu gaoyuan lishi dili [Historical Geography of the Loess Plateau]. Zhengzhou: Huanghe shuili chubanshe, 2002.

Shi, Nianhai, Erqin Cao, and Shiguang Zhu. *Huangtu gaoyuan senlin yu caoyuan de bianqian* [Evolution of Forests and Grassland on the Loess Plateau]. Xi'an: Shaanxi renmin chubanshe, 1985.

Shiba, Yoshinobu. *Commerce and Society in Sung China.* Translated by Mark Elvin. Ann Arbor, MI: University of Michigan, 1970.

Sōdai Kōnan keizaishi no kenkyū; [Studies on the Economic History of the Lower Yangzi Valley during the Song]. Tōkyō: Tōkyō daigaku Tōyō bunka kenkyūjo, 1988.

Skinner, G. William. "Marketing and Social Structure in Rural China." *Journal of Asian Studies* 24 (1-3) (1964-1965).

— ed. *The City in Late Imperial China*. Stanford, CA: Stanford University Press, 1977.

Smil, Vaclav. *The Bad Earth: Environmental Degradation in China*. London: Zed Press, 1984.

Smith, Paul Jakov. *Taxing Heaven's Storehouse: Horses, Bureaucrats, and the Destruction of the Sichuan Tea Industry, 1074–1224*. Cambridge, MA: Council on East Asian Studies, 1991.

— "State Power and Economic Activism during the New Policies, 1068-1085: The Tea and Horse Trade and the 'Green Sprout' Loan Policy." In *Ordering the World*, edited by Robert Hymes and Conrad Schirokauer, Berkeley, CA: University of California Press, 1993, 76–127.

Smith, Paul Jakov and Richard von Glahn, eds. *The Song-Yuan-Ming Transition in Chinese History*. Cambridge, MA, and London: Harvard University Asian Center, 2003.

Soja, Edward W. *Thirdspace: Journeys to Los Angeles and Other Real-and-Imagined Place*. Oxford: Wiley-Blackwell, 1996.

Song, Jinxi. "Beijing diqu shawuzhi de zhongkuangwu chengfen, jiegoutezheng yu fengsha de shawuzhi laiyuan" [Mineral composition of the sandy matter and the source of sand to sandstorms in Beijing area]. *Zhongguo shamo* 1 (1987): 24–33.

Song, Yuqin and Lixiao Zhang. "Lishi shiqi woguo shachenbao dongjian de yuanyin fenxi" [Analysis on the eastward movement of sandstorms in Chinese historical times]. *Zhongguo shamo* 6 (2006).

Song, Zhaolin. "Woguo gudai tali kao" [An examination of the stepping plough in ancient China]. *Nongye kaogu* 1 (1981): 63–69.

Standen, Naomi. *Unbounded Loyalty: Frontier Crossings in Liao China*. Honolulu, HI: Hawai'i University Press, 2007.

Su Yongxia. "Tang Song shiqi shizhen yanjiu zongshu" [A literature review about the scholarship of market towns and cities during the Tang-Song period]. *Zhongguoshi yanjiu dongtai*, 4 (2012).

Tackett, Nicolas. "Wantang Hebei ren dui Songchu wenhua de yingxiang: Yi sangzang wenhua yuyin yiji xinxing jingying fengmao weili" [The Impact of Late Tang Hebei on the Development of Early Song Elite Culture], *Tang yanjiu* 19 (2013): 251–281.

— *The Destruction of the Medieval Chinese Aristocracy* (Cambridge: Harvard Asian Center, 2014).

Tan, Qixiang, ed. *Huangheshi luncong* [Studies on the Yellow River History]. Shanghai: Fudan daxue chubanshe, 1986.

— *Zhongguo lishi ditu ji* [Chinese Historical Maps], vol. 6. Beijing: Zhongguo ditu chubanshe, 1992.

Tao, Jinsheng. *Two Sons of Heaven: Studies in Sung-Liao Relations*. Tucson, AZ: University of Arizona Press, 1988.

Topping, David J. et al., "Colorado River Sediment Transport: 1, Natural Sediment Supply Limitation and the Influence of Glen Canyon Dam." *Water Resources Research* 36(2) (2000): 515–542.

Twitchett, Denis. "Provincial Autonomy and Central Finance in Late T'ang." *Asia Major* 11(2) (1965): 211–232.

"Varied Patterns of Provincial Autonomy in the T'ang Dynasty." In *Essays on T'ang Society*, edited by John Curtis Perry and Bardwell L. Smith. Leiden: E.J. Brill, 1976.

Twitchett, Denis and Paul Jakov Smith, eds. *The Cambridge History of China, Vol. 5, Part One: The Sung Dynasty and Its Precursors, 907–1279*. Cambridge and New York: Cambridge University Press, 2009.

U.S. Geological Survey. "Table 1. Discharge of suspended sediment to the coastal zone by 10 major river of the United States, about 1980," online data, accessed on April 13, 2014.

von Glahn, Richard. *The Country of Streams and Grottoes: Expansion, Settlement, and the Civilizing of the Sichuan Frontier in Song Times*. Cambridge, MA: Council on East Asian Studies, 1987.

Fountain of Fortune: Money and Monetary Policy in China, 1000–1700. Berkely, Los Angeles, CA, and London: University of California Press, 1996.

Wallerstein, Immanuel. *World-Systems Analysis: An Introduction*. Durham and London: Duke University Press, 2004.

Wang, Gungwu. *The Structure of Power in North China during the Five Dynasties*. Stanford, CA: Stanford University Press, 1967.

Wang, Lihua. "Wenhua yu huanjing hudong zuoyongxia de zhonggu jingji yu dili bianqian" [Economic and geographic transition under the impact of interactions between culture and environment during middle-period China]. *Lishi kexue yanjiu* 5 (1995): 14–17.

Zhonggu Huabei yinshi wenhua de bianqian [The Transition of North China's Culinary Culture during the Middle Period]. Beijing: Zhongguo shehui kexue chubanshe, 2000.

Wang, Lingling. *Songdai guangtieshi yanjiu* [History of Iron and Steel during the Song]. Baoding: Hebei daxue chubanshe, 2005.

Wang, Shengduo. *Liangsong caizhengshi* [Financial and Fiscal History of the Song]. Beijing: Zhonghua shuju, 1995.

Wang, Shumin. "Yongqing de Liaodai didao" [Tunnels of the Liao Dynasty in Yongqing County]. In *Liao Jin shi lunji*, vol. 5, edited by Chen Shu, 332–334. Beijing: Beijing wenji chubanshe, 1991.

Wang, Yuanlin. *Jing Luo liuyu ziran huanjing bianqian yanjiu* [Transition of Natural Environment in the Jing-Luo Valley]. Beijing: Zhonghua shuju, 2005.

Wang, Zengyu. *Songdai bingzhi chutan* [Tentative Studies on the Song's Military System]. Beijing: Zhonghua shuju, 1983.

Wang, Zijin. *Qin Han shiqi shengtai huanjing yanjiu* [Ecological and Environmental Studies for the Qing-Han Period]. Beijing: Beijing daxue chubanshe, 2007.

Weber, Edward P., ed. *Bringing Society Back In: Grassroots Ecosystem Management, Accountability, and Sustainable Communities*. Cambridge, MA: MIT University Press, 2003.

White, Adam, ed. *The Everyday Life of the State: A State-in-Society Approach*. Seattle, WA: University of Washington Press, 2013.

White, Gilbert. *Human Adjustment to Floods.* University of Chicago Department of Geography Research Paper, 29. Chicago, IL: University of Chicago Department of Geography, 1945.

White, Richard. *"It's Your Misfortune and None of My Own:" A New History of the American West.* Norman, OK: University of Oklahoma Press, 1991.

Will, Pierre-Etienne. "Un cycle hydraulic en Chine: la province du Hubei du XVI au XIX siècle." *Bulletin de l'ecole François d'Extrême-Orient.* 68 (1980): 261–287.

"State Intervention in the Administration of a Hydraulic Infrastructure: The Example of Hubei Province in Late Imperial Times." In *The Scope of State Power in China,* edited by Stuart Schram. London and Hong Kong: SOAS and Chinese University of Hong Kong, 1985. 295–347.

Bureaucracy and Famine in Eighteen-Century China. Translated by Elborg Forster. Standford, CA: Stanford University Press, 1990.

"Clear Waters vs. Muddy Waters: The Zheng-Bai Irrigation System of Shaanxi Province in the Late-Imperial Period," in Mark Elvin and Liu Ts'ui-jung, eds., *Sediments of Time: Environment and Society in Chinese History.* Cambridge: Cambridge University Press, 1998. 283–343.

Will, Pierre-Etienne and R. Bin Wong, with James Lee. *Nourishing the People: The State Civilian Granary System in China, 1650–1850.* Ann Arbor, MI: Center for Chinese Studies, 1991.

Wittfogel, Karl A. *Oriental Despotism: A Comparative Study of Total Power.* New Haven, CT: Yale University Press, 1957.

Worster, Donald. *Rivers of Empire: Water, Aridity, and the Growth of the American West.* New York and Oxford: Oxford University Press, 1985.

Wu, Bochang. "Beisong chunian de beifang wenshi yu haoxia: Yi Liu Kai de shigong ji zuofeng xingxiang wei zhongxin" [Northern scholars and heros in the early years of the Northern Song]. *Qinghua xuebao,* 36(2) (2006): 295–344.

Wu, Chen et al. "Huanghe xiayou kedao bianqian de gu hedao zhengju ji hedao zhengzhi yanjiu" [Ancient River Courses from Course Changes of the Yellow River's Lower Reaches and River Course Management]. *Lishi dili* 17 (2001): 1–28.

Wu, Songdi. *Zhongguo renkou shi* [Chinese History of Population], volume on the Liao, Song, Jin, and Yuan. Shanghai: Fudan daxue chubanshe, 2000.

Xu, Hailiang. "Huanghe gudao Hua Chan duan de chubu kaocha yu fenxi'" [Investigation and analysis of the Hua-Chan section of the ancient course of the Yellow River]. *Lishi dili* 6 (1988): 21–32.

"Lishi shang Huanghe shuisha bianhua de yixie wenti" [Historical changes to water and silt of the Yellow River]. *Lishi dili* 12 (1995): 32–40.

Xu, Jinzhi. "Woguo lishi qihouxue gaishu" [Chinese historical climatology]. *Zhongguo lishi dili luncong* 1 (1981): 176–195.

Xu, Jiongxin. "Renlei huodong yingxiang xie de Huanghe xiayou hedao nishayüji hongguanqushi yanjiu" [The macro-trend of sedimentation in the lower reaches of the Yellow River under the impact of human activities]. *Shuilixuebao* 2 (2004).

Yancheva, Gergana et al. "Influence of the intertropical convergence zone on the East Asian monsoon." *Nature* 445 (2007 Jan): 74–77.

Yang, Rui. *Xixia diliyanjiu: Bianjiang lishi dilixue de tansuo* [Studies of Geography in the Xixia: Historical Geography of the Frontier]. Beijing: Renmin chubanshe, 2008).

Yao, Hanyuan. *Zhongguo shuilishi gangyao* [Essential Outline of Chinese Hydraulic History]. Beijing: Shuili dianli chubanshe, 1987.

Huanghe shuilishi yanjiu [Studies on the Yellow River Hydraulics]. Zhengzhou: Huanghe shuili chubanshe, 2003.

Yoneda, Kenjirō. "Seimin yōjutsu to ninen sammōsaku" [Qimin yaosu and the cropping pattern of three crops in two years]. *Tōyōshi kenkyū*, 4 (1959): 1–24.

Yoshioka, Yoshinobu. *Sōdai Kōgashi kenkyū*; [The Yellow River History during the Song]. Tōkyō: Ochanomizu shobō, 1978.

Zhang, De'er. "Lishi shiqi 'yutu' xianxiang pouxi" [The phenomena of "earth storms" in historical times]. *Kexue tongbao*, 27(5) (1982).

"Synoptic-cimatic studies of dust fall in China since the historic times." *Scientia Sinica* 27(8) (1984): 825–836.

Zhongguo sanqiannian qixiang jilu zongji [Collection of climate records in China's past three thousand years]. Nanjing: Fenghuang chubanshe, 2004.

Zhang, De'er and Sun Xia. "Woguo lishi shiqi jiangchen jilu nanjie de biandong jiqi dui beifang ganhan qihou de tuiduan" [Changes to the southern border of sand-dust storms in historical China and speculation on climatic aridity in north China]. *Disiji yanjiu* 21(1) (2001): 1–7.

Zhang, Jiayan. *Coping with Calamity: Environmental Change and Peasant Response in Rural China, 1736–1949.* Honolulu, HI: University of Hawai'i Press, 2015.

Zhang, Ling. "Changing with the Yellow River: An Environmental History of Hebei, 1048–1128." *Harvard Journal of Asiatic Studies* 69(1) (2009): 1–36.

"Ponds, Paddies, and Frontier Defence: Environmental and Economic Changes in Northern Hebei in Northern Song China (960–1127)." *The Medieval History Journal* 14(1) (2011): 21–43.

"Manipulating the Yellow River and the State Building of the Northern Song Dynasty." In *Nature, the Environment and Climate Change in East Asia*, Kulturwissenschaftliches Institut, edited by Carmen Meinhert, 137–162. Leiden: Brill, 2013.

Zhang, Xiaohua et al., "Huanghe zhongyou ganliu nisha zucheng guilü" [Compositional patterns of silt in the mainstream of the Yellow River's middle reaches]. *Nisha yanjiu* 4 (1999).

Zhang, Xiugui. "Haihe liuyu pingyuan shuixi yanbian de lishi guocheng" [Historical evolution of the Huai River system]. *Lishi dili* 11 (1993).

Zhongguo lishi dimao yu guditu yanjiu [Chinese Historical Geomorphology and Ancient Maps]. Beijing: Shehui kexue chubanshe, 2006.

Zhao, Wenlin. *Huanghe nisha* [Silt of the Yellow River]. Zhengzhou: Huanghe shuili chubanshe, 1996.

Zhao, Xitao. *Zhongguo haian yanbian yanjiu* [Evolution of Chinese Coastlines]. Fuzhou: Fujian kexue jishu chubanshe, 1984.

Zheng, Sizhong and Zheng Jingyun. "Zhongguo lishi shiqi de qihou bianhua jiqi yingxiang" [Chinese historical climate changes and their influences]. In *Zhongguo de qihou bianhua yu qihou yingxiang yanjiu*, edited by Ding Yihui, 166–169. Beijing: Qixiang chubanshe, 1997.

Zhongguo nongye baike quanshu bianji weiyuanhui (comp.). *Zhongguo nongye baike quanshu* [Encyclopaedia of Chinese Agriculture]. Beijing: Nongye chubanshe, 1991.

Zhou, Baozhu. *Songdai Dongjing yanjiu* [Studies on the Eastern Capital of the Song]. Kaifeng: Hebei daxue chubanshe, 1992.

Zou, Yilin. "Lishi shiqi huanghe liuyu shuidao shengchan de diyu fenbu he huanjing zhiyue" [Geographical distribution of rice production and its environmental constraints in historical Yellow River valley]. *Fudan xuebao* 3 (1985).

"Huanghe xiayou hedao bianqian jiqi yingxiang gaishu" [Changes to the lower reaches of the Yellow River and their influences]. In *Huangheshi luncong*, edited by Tan Qixiang, 221–242. Shanghai: Fudan daxue chubanshe, 1986.

"Songdai Huanghe xiayou Henglong beiliu zhudao kao" [An examination of the Yellow River's northern flow of Henglong during the Song] In *Huangheshi luncong*, 1986, 131–145.

"Lishishiqi Huabei dapingyuan huzhao bianqian shulue" [Historical evolution of lakes and ponds in the North China Plain]. *Lishi dili* 5 (1987): 25–39.

Huang Huai Hai pingyuan lishi dili [Historical Geography of the Huang-Huai-Huai Plain]. Hefei: Anhui jiaoyu chubanshe, 1993.

"Woguo shuiziyuan bianqian de lishi huigu – yi Huangheliuyu weili" [Historical review of the evolution of Chinese water resources: The case of the Yellow River valley]. *Fudan xuebao* 3 (2005): 47–56.

Index

Page numbers followed by 'n' refer to footnotes.
Page numbers in *italic* followed by 'illus' refer to illustrations.
Page numbers in *italic* followed by 't' refer to tables.

309

increased consumption of, 230–231
millet compared with, 224, 225,
226t4
Wittfogel, Karl, hydraulic mode of
production theory
hydraulic leader of, 114, 135,
178–179n79
hydraulic mode of consumption
compared with, 12n20, 12, 13, 177,
186–187
and the rise of despotic states, 12n20,
178–179n79
and the Yellow River–Hebei
environmental complex, 135, 142
"world" as a concept. *See* environmental
world
Worster, Donald, xv, 141–142
Wu Anchi, 153–154, 175
Wu Chuhou, 236

Xin Dynasty, 35
Xiongzhou, 61, 69, 70, 167–168, 220,
236–237
Xixia empire, 56, 84, 101
Xue Xiang, 236, 238, 243

Yang Huaimin, 163
Yangzi valley
agricultural productivity, 94–95
early-ripening rice cultivation, 85, 87,
238–239
buds of capitalism in, 283
developmental trajectory advocated by
Tang-Song transition theory, 242
earthquakes in, 101–102
Yellow River
anliu period of tranquility, 31, 36
course of lower reaches
after 1128, 282*illus*14, 284
before 1048, 36*illus*4, 128–132
shifts in the course of, 26*illus*2, 25–26,
284
course of middle reaches of, 29*illus*3,
27–29, 33, 265n58, 277–278
courses 1048–1128, 147*illus*11, 197
courses 1048–1128 in Hebei, 2*illus*1,
1–2, 5, 8–9, 25–26, 160–161,
194–195, 249–256
flooding in 1048, 1–5, 27, 107–110,
132, 143–145
land "north of the river", 36

and sandification, 262–267
course shift encouraged in 972 by
Emperor Taizu, 119, 158, 208
course shift in Mingzhou Prefecture,
208
deforestation and soil erosion in upper
and middle reaches of, 27–33,
265n58, 268–279
discharge
into the Bohai Gulf, 284
rate of, 30, 34
flooding before 1048, 34–35, 111t2,
125–126, 128
flooding between 1099 and 1102, 198
flooding from 1048 to 1067, 199
flooding of Hebei in 1048, 1–4, 23–24,
27–33, 107–110, 143–145
Great Bend, 29, 31, 32, 277n102
Henan as a land "south of the river", 36,
113, 115–117
hydrological dynamics
as a means to transform the landscape,
205
and its muddy nature, 30
and its tendency to flood, 27
legendary Nine Rivers of, 118–119, 152,
158–159
"return the river" of Emperor Shenzong,
154
siltation. *See* silt, Yellow River siltation
See also dykes; frontier ponds in Hebei;
sand; silt; trialectics among a river, a
plain, and a state; Yellow
River–Hebei environmental
complex
Yellow River Conservancy, 27n5
Yellow River–Hebei environmental
complex
creation of, 4–5, 8–9, 23–24, 27–33,
172–174, 177–178
as an "environmental world", 5–9,
16n26, 19, 24–25, 40–41
and the hydraulic mode of consumption,
6, 11–13, 141–143, 177–180,
244–247, 285–286, 287–288,
289–290
political pressure imposed on the state by
the river, 142–143, 186, 215
See also Song dynasty, the state as an
environmental force reshaping the
land of Hebei

Lightning Source UK Ltd.
Milton Keynes UK
UKHW010123220319
339642UK00001B/70/P